D1554788

Childhood

School for Advanced Research
Advanced Seminar Series

Michael F. Brown
General Editor

Since 1970 the School for Advanced Research
(formerly the School of American Research)
and SAR Press have published over one
hundred volumes in the Advanced Seminar
Series. These volumes arise from seminars held
on SAR's Santa Fe campus that bring together
small groups of experts to explore a single
issue. Participants assess recent innovations
in theory and methods, appraise ongoing
research, and share data relevant to problems
of significance in anthropology and related
disciplines. The resulting volumes reflect SAR's
commitment to the development of new ideas
and to scholarship of the highest caliber. The
complete Advanced Seminar Series can be
found at www.sarweb.org.

Childhood

ORIGINS, EVOLUTION, AND IMPLICATIONS

Edited by Courtney L. Meehan and Alyssa N. Crittenden

SCHOOL FOR ADVANCED RESEARCH PRESS • SANTA FE

UNIVERSITY OF NEW MEXICO PRESS • ALBUQUERQUE

Printed in the United States of America
21 20 19 18 17 16   1 2 3 4 5 6

Library of Congress
Cataloging-in-Publication Data

Names: Meehan, Courtney L., editor. |
Crittenden, Alyssa N., editor.
Title: Childhood : origins, evolution, and
implications / edited by Courtney L. Meehan
and Alyssa N. Crittenden.
Description: Santa Fe : School for Advanced
Research Press; Albuquerque : University of
New Mexico Press, 2016. | Series: School for
Advanced Research Advanced Seminar Series
| Published in association with School for
Advanced Research Press. | Includes bibli-
ographical references and index.
Identifiers: LCCN 2015042407 (print) | LCCN
2016003287 (ebook) | ISBN 9780826357007
(paperback) | ISBN 9780826357014 (electronic)
Subjects: LCSH: Children—Evolution. |
Human evolution—Social aspects. | Social
evolution. | BISAC: SOCIAL SCIENCE /
Anthropology / General. | SOCIAL SCIENCE /
Anthropology / Physical.
Classification: LCC GN482 .C54 2016 (print) |
LCC GN482 (ebook) | DDC 305.23—dc23
LC record available at http://lccn.loc.
gov/2015042407

Cover photograph by Alyssa N. Crittenden

For Alden and Josie

CHILDHOOD IN CONTEXT: CONTEMPORARY
IMPLICATIONS OF EVOLUTIONARY APPROACHES

FIGURES

TABLES

CHAPTER ONE

Multiple Perspectives on the Evolution of Childhood

ALYSSA N. CRITTENDEN AND COURTNEY L. MEEHAN

Human life history differs from that of our great ape counterparts in that we have a comparatively long stage of dependence, yet begin to reproduce earlier. Explanations for this protracted period of dependency are associated with our ability to both wean our offspring and resume ovulation earlier when compared to other apes (Bogin 1999b; Bogin and Smith 1996). In addition, extended dependency is considered a necessary developmental stage allowing young to learn key skills necessary for adulthood (i.e., the "embodied capital" of skills and knowledge necessary for reproduction) (Kaplan et al. 2000, but see Bogin 1999b for a history of the notion that childhood is a period of learning). Alternative proposals suggest that slow growth is an adaptive response to ecological risk (Janson and Van Schaik 1993), or argue that a lengthened period of juvenility maps onto a longer life span in general (Charnov 1993). Regardless of which theoretical paradigm one adheres to, the significance of integrating childhood into models of human life history and evolution cannot be overstated. Furthering our understanding of the evolution of dependency has significant implications for interpreting the evolutionary underpinnings of family formation (Crittenden and Marlowe 2013; Lancaster and Lancaster 1983b), social organization (Hrdy 2009), cultural transmission (Hewlett et al. 2011), cognition (Bjorklund, Causey, and Periss 2010; Leigh 2004), ontogeny (Bogin 1999b), and the physical and socioemotional needs of children (Meehan, Helfrecht, and Quinlan 2014; Narváez et al. 2012). Moreover, the significance of studying the evolution of childhood has begun to extend beyond academic theoretical modeling into real world applications for maternal-child health and well-being in contemporary populations around the world (Sellen 2007, chapter 10, this volume).

Within anthropology there has been a relatively recent trend toward incorporating children into evolutionary models of human behavior (see Konner 2010), and, as Hrdy (chapter 2, this volume) notes, evolutionary anthropologists are increasingly focusing on the child as integral to reconstructions of the family life of early hominins. Despite this gradual shift, much of the discussion of the evolution of childhood remains tethered to anthropology subfields, with strikingly little overlap. Thus, the scope of inquiry into the evolution of childhood has historically remained limited due to a lack of discourse between the fields. In order to address this lacuna, we brought together a group of scholars from various anthropological subdisciplines to answer critical questions related to the evolution of human childhood. This book is the outcome of that gathering, a week of fruitful discussion at a School for Advanced Research (SAR) advanced seminar held in Santa Fe, New Mexico. It is the first edited volume specifically aimed at our current understanding of the evolutionary underpinnings of human childhood and, as such, is timely for academic discourse in anthropology, psychology, cognitive science, and multiple domains of public health.

The Seminar

The School for Advanced Research (SAR) sponsored an advanced seminar, co-organized by the editors, entitled "Multiple Perspectives on the Evolution of Childhood," held November 4–8, 2012. In attendance were Robin Bernstein, Barry Bogin, Alyssa Crittenden, Sarah Hrdy, Melvin Konner, David Lancy, Courtney Meehan, Sanae Okamoto-Barth, Daniel Sellen, and Jennifer Thompson. This group is composed of international scholars whose research spans ontogenetic, life-history, developmental, behavioral, psychological, paleoarchaeological, cross-cultural, and applied public health perspectives on childhood. We organized the seminar around the following broad goals: (1) defining "childhood" across subdisciplines; (2) integrating cross-species data and the paleoarchaeological record with current developmental, biological, and ethnographic approaches to studying childhood(s); (3) evaluating how the emergence of cooperation and social cognition are linked to the evolution of human childhood; and (4) identifying the ways in which anthropological research can meaningfully contribute to the burgeoning discourse on contemporary infant and childcare practices.

A Note on Terminology

As evidenced by our first goal, remarkable as it may be, there is little consensus regarding the definitions of the terms *infant*, *child* (including children and childhood), *juvenile*, or *adolescent*. In biological and evolutionary anthropology these terms represent broadly agreed upon stages of human development—stages that are marked by both physical and behavioral attributes. But even within these subdisciplines, as is evident in the volume, there is some variation in the use of these terms regarding the relative importance of specific biological and/or behavioral markers used to delineate stages (e.g., the use of weaning to mark the end of infancy). Additionally, there are considerable conceptual differences in how anthropological subfields, other academic disciplines, and even the lay public conceive of and use these terms. For instance, following Bogin (1999b), the median age range is birth to approximately 30–36 months for *infancy*, 3–6/7 years for *childhood*, 6/7 years to puberty for *juvenility*, and 5–8 years following puberty for *adolescence* (see also Bogin, Bragg, Kuzawa, chapter 3, this volume; Thompson and Nelson, chapter 4, this volume). Cultural anthropologists, alternatively, often note that there is variation in the roles, responsibilities, and behaviors of youth cross-culturally that blur the behavioral markers of these life stages (Lancy 2008) and tend to use the terms more broadly or take a relativistic position (see Bogin, Bragg, and Kuzawa, chapter 3, this volume for a discussion on the antibiological stance taken by some cultural anthropologists). Moreover, colloquial uses of the terms further obscure clarity of meaning. The period of *infancy* is often casually used to refer to the first year of life and the terms *child* and *juvenile* are broadened to encompass all non-adult individuals. The situation is further complicated by the fact that there are few other succinct and accessible options to describe the entirety of the period between birth to adulthood besides the term *childhood*.

The title of the volume is a case in point. Although the term "childhood" is used in the title, the chapters herein focus on multiple stages of human immaturity. Commencing with Sarah Hrdy's chapter focused primarily on infancy, it becomes evident that each stage of human immaturity is intimately linked with the previous one. It is neither possible to discuss human childhood (the 3–6/7-year-old developmental span) without examining infancy, nor is it possible to understand the implications of the developmental life span of childhood without discussing the juvenile and adolescent stages. With clarity in mind, however, contributors note when they refer to the general period of "childhood" (immaturity) and when they refer to a specific developmental stage, clearly defining the lower and upper markers of the stages in question.

Volume Organization

The volume is broadly based on the main themes of the seminar and is organized into four sections: (1) Social and Cognitive Correlates of Childhood and Human Life History; (2) Growth and Development: Defining Childhood; (3) Ethnographic Approaches to Studying Childhood and Social Learning; and (4) Childhood in Context: Contemporary Implications of Evolutionary Approaches. In the first section, contributors introduce the ways in which key differences in reproduction and life history between humans and other primates lead to differences in altriciality, cognition, and social structure. In chapter 2 Sarah Hrdy lays the theoretical groundwork for the volume by introducing the Cooperative Breeding Hypothesis and arguing that apes with life-history characteristics of *Homo sapiens* would only have evolved in a system where parents *and* alloparents invested in the provisioning and care of young. She explores the psychological implications of this type of multiple caregiver social system for developing infants and suggests that selection pressure would favor *Homo* infants who were better at monitoring the intentions and mental states of others. These cooperative and "other regarding" infants, although still highly altricial, would not only read emotional cues more proficiently than their earlier counterparts, but would therefore also be better equipped to solicit care from multiple caregivers. With the conclusion that "emotionally modern" infants were "preadapted for subsequent evolution of coordinated social enterprises," Hrdy introduces the next chapter of the first section.

In chapter 3, Barry Bogin, Jared Bragg, and Christopher Kuzawa outline the four biologically defined stages of human life history between birth and maturity and offer a biocultural definition of childhood that takes into account intergenerational effects and the "material, organic, physiological, social, technological, and ideological interactions" that influence this particular life-history stage. Offering an alternative to Hrdy's use of "cooperative breeding," the authors introduce the term "biocultural reproduction" to refer to the human specific pattern of cooperation in the production, provisioning, and care of young. They posit that this term represents a more accurate categorization of the human system due to "novel cultural traits such as marriage, nongenetic kinship, and symbolic language." This chapter concludes that bio-cultural reproduction, which results in a reduction of lifetime reproductive effort (LRE), allowed for higher quality offspring, increased rates of reproduc-tion, and improved survival, and that the evolution of childhood contributed to the life-history trade-offs that help to characterize our species.

In section 2, "Growth and Development: Defining Childhood," the contrib-utors explore the biomarkers for the biologically defined period of development that we typically refer to as childhood. In chapter 4 Jennifer Thompson and Andrew Nelson compare the human pattern of growth and development with that of nonhuman primates and fossil hominins. Building upon Bogin's (1997, 1999b; Bogin and Smith 1996) stages, they argue that other extant primates pass through infancy, juvenility, and adolescence, while humans pass through all of these stages and add an additional stage of "childhood." They then turn to comparisons with fossil evidence from *Homo erectus, Homo neanderthalen-sis,* and *Homo sapiens* in an attempt to determine when the "modern" human pattern of growth and development evolved. Thompson and Nelson suggest that childhood begins when all deciduous teeth have erupted and children are able to provision themselves to a certain degree, while still relying upon tran-sitional supplemental foods from adult provisioning. This phase of childhood ends when children have obtained enough ecological knowledge and physical maturity to actively participate in adult activities. Using these boundaries, the authors conclude that the distinct modern human pattern of growth, when compared to other hominins, is characterized by notable differences in the stages of infancy, childhood, and adolescence.

Chapter 5, by Robin Bernstein, extends the discussion of growth and devel-opment and assesses whether human childhood is a novel stage of growth using comparative hormone concentrations and gene expression across devel-opment. She focuses on the evolution of adrenarche and suggests that while aspects of development such as dental eruption, brain growth, and body mass growth might differ, the overall patterns among humans and nonhuman pri-mates are similar. These growth periods are somewhat flexible, and thus, sub-ject to changes in timing of adrenal gland zonation and maturation—allowing them to either be extended or compressed. She concludes that the human stage of childhood, although maintaining unique cognitive and behavioral traits, is not a *novel* stage of development. Bernstein argues that while human development varies from nonhuman primates, the difference is one of degree, rather than kind.

In section 3, "Ethnographic Approaches to Studying Childhood and Social Learning," the contributors explore the ethnographic record to address the anthropology of childhood(s) in contemporary, small-scale societies and how these data might inform our understanding of the evolution of this human life-history stage. In chapter 6 Melvin Konner revisits his Hunter-Gatherer Childhood (HGC) model (Konner 2005, 2010) and presents key features of hunter-gatherer childhoods that are often assumed to be characteristics of the ancestral condition. Using ethnographic data from the !Kung and other hunting and gathering populations, he expands his discussion of the HGC model to address challenges proposed by, what he calls, the Childhood as Facultative Adaptation (CFA) model, which is based largely on the notion that childhood follows a flexible pattern that fluctuates and adapts to changes in ecological conditions. Konner summarizes features of !Kung infancy and childhood and then explores the data available for other foraging groups, outlining the traits of the HGC model of childhood, including close physical contact with infants, frequent (or on-demand) breastfeeding, maternal/infant co-sleeping, comparatively late age at weaning and long interbirth intervals (when compared with the general catarrhine pattern), complex social networks, participation in mixed age and mixed sex playgroups, emphasis on play throughout stages of development, and relatively low levels of assigned work. After in-depth cross-cultural examination and a discussion of the comparison between the HGC model and the catarrhine pattern, Konner concludes that the HGC model is supported. Additionally, he argues that our understanding of the evolution of human childhood is enhanced using the framework of hunter-gatherer infant and childcare patterns.

Building upon the framework provided by Konner, Alyssa Crittenden explores juvenile foraging and play among the Hadza hunter-gatherers of Tanzania in chapter 7. She argues that play is typically discussed as critical to psychosocial development or economic productivity, with little emphasis on the dual nature of play among foraging populations. She tests the embodied capital hypothesis and argues that, via foraging, children are simultaneously providing for themselves and their family as well as engaging in developmentally significant play. She concludes that juvenile self-provisioning may have been a "key component of the derived *Homo* complex" and argues that understanding "work play" allows us to better integrate children's foraging into models of the evolution of human childhood.

In chapter 8 David Lancy uses case studies in the ethnographic record to explore the role of children as active "self-starting" learners of culture. The anthropological literature currently juxtaposes the concept of learning as a component of pedagogy or teaching (Csibra and Gergely 2011; Hewlett et al. 2011) or as largely self-initiated (Lancy 2010). Lancy's position emphasizes the latter and highlights the drive that children have to acquire culture on their own, focusing on the myriad of examples of such child-initiated learning in the ethnographic record. Providing a thorough cross-cultural review, he outlines the ways in which children acquire knowledge of their culture and are active learners in play, social interaction, family dynamics, and the "chore curriculum," which is the interaction between the household economy and the developing child's acquisition of motor, cognitive, and social skills. Lancy concludes by summarizing recent trends in the research on infant cognition to argue that children begin to acquire their culture largely on their own initiative and early in development.

In section 4, "Childhood in Context: Contemporary Implications of Evolutionary Approaches," the contributors examine the consequences of our evolved childhood and its associated traits in the contemporary world. In chapter 9 Courtney Meehan, Courtney Helfrecht, and Courtney Malcom build upon contributions by Hrdy (chapter 2) and Bogin, Bragg, and Kuzawa (chapter 3). They examine the implications of the social nature of infant, child, and juvenile development on physical and socioemotional development in contemporary populations. Using available data on the role of allomothers, peers, and the broader social network, the authors review the cross-cultural role of caregivers and their effects on child nutritional status, survivorship, and socioemotional development. Additionally, they highlight that dependency on others is not limited to childhood, as mothers remain dependent upon the solicitude of others to support them throughout their reproductive life spans. The authors explore how the roles of others affect maternal nutritional status, psychosocial health, and investment patterns. They argue that the social worlds of both children and mothers should to be brought to the foreground of investigations, as doing so will enable us to tease apart the multiplicity of influences that contribute to supporting our lengthy dependency and fast pace of reproduction.

In chapter 10 Daniel Sellen argues that understanding childhood in evolutionary perspective enables us to identify a suite of needs of infants and young children. This evolved human care package includes "ancient caregiving behaviors" (such as exclusive breastfeeding for the first six months) that should be retained as "core tools for child survival and well-being in contemporary and future communities." Sellen concludes that this care package, already significantly enhanced by powerful biomedical interventions, can also be bolstered using everyday techno-social innovations, such as mobile health, to deliver much-needed interpersonal support to current and future caregivers that effectively enhances health outcomes during infancy and early childhood.

Combined, the chapters contained in this volume highlight that the life-history stage of childhood is culturally variable, yet biologically based, and was critical to the evolutionary success of our species. While the anthropology of childhood is presently a growing and dynamic subfield, academic discourse that integrates multiple research domains is still in its infancy. Thus, it is our hope that this volume spurs further interest in the field and underscores the significance of incorporating multiple perspectives in such an inherently interdisciplinary investigation.

Social and Cognitive Correlates of
Childhood and Human Life History

Development Plus Social Selection in the Emergence of "Emotionally Modern" Humans

SARAH B. HRDY

Introduction: A More Other-Regarding Ape

It was an inspired guess when Charles Darwin proposed that humans evolved in Africa from now-extinct predecessors resembling today's gorillas and chimpanzees (1974). On the basis of fossil and genetic evidence analyzed since then, we now estimate that apes in the line leading to the genus *Homo* split from that leading to gorillas between ten and seventeen million years ago, and split from that leading to today's chimpanzees and bonobos between six and eleven million years ago (Langergraber et al. 2012). Common descent explains overlap in genomes as well as capacities such as producing and using tools in multiple ways (Roffman et al. 2012). It also helps explain why developmental profiles of a baby chimpanzee can be evaluated using the same Brazelton Neonatal Behavioral Assessment Scale that pediatricians applied to my own infants.

With each passing year, it becomes harder to draw absolute distinctions between the innate capacities of young humans and those of their ape relations. This blurring of boundaries pertains in almost every cognitive realm except those accomplishments requiring language or the kind of sophisticated teaching along with cumulative culture that language facilitates (L. Dean et al. 2012; Matsuzawa, Tomonaga, and Tanaga 2006; Whiten and Van Schaik 2007). Even in tasks such as watching and learning from someone else's demonstration or tasks requiring mentalizing about what someone else is likely to know ("Theory of Mind"), where humans typically test better, considerable overlap exists between the scores of orangutans and chimpanzees and those of two-and-a-half-year-old humans (Herrmann et al. 2007: fig. 2.2; see also L. Dean et al. 2012). In terms of working memory, young chimpanzees can actually outperform human adults. Some specially trained chimpanzees remember ordered symbols briefly flashed onto a computer screen as well as or better than humans do (Matsuzawa 2012:101).

Within minutes of birth, humans are attracted to face-like patterns. By two months of age they recognize their mother's face. But so do other ape newborns. They too occasionally gaze into their mother's face (Bard 2005; Okamoto-Barth et al. 2007), scan expressions of whoever is holding them, even seek to engage this caretaker by imitating what they see there—sticking out their own tongues or opening their mouths (Bard 2007; Myowa 1996; Myowa-Yamakoshi et al. 2004). Whether their face-to-face partner is another chimp or a human caretaker, little chimpanzees respond in kind to all sorts of emotionally charged expressions, suggesting that underlying subjective emotions are being shared. But there are also key differences.

Even though other apes occasionally share food, the possessor is rarely eager to do so (Silk et al. 2005) and typically does so only after being begged (Yamamoto, Humle, and Tanaka 2009). In the wild, an alpha male chimpanzee may tear off a bit of meat from captured prey to proffer to a strategic ally, but only after persistent solicitation (D. Watts and Mitani 2000). A mother chimp or bonobo may allow her infant to take food from her mouth but rarely volunteers it. Bonobos, generally less competitive over food than common chimpanzees (Hare et al. 2007; Hare and Kwetuenda 2010), have been known to open a cage door so that another bonobo can share in a feeding bonanza (Hare 2012). But in no wild ape is voluntary sharing the routine part of life that it is in every human society ever studied.

Clearly, socialization influences willingness to share. But we are left to explain why the social sharing of food that is universal in human societies is rare in other apes. "Mealtime" simply does not mean the same thing among other apes that it does among humans. In the bonobo case, allomaternal provisioning entails little more than an adult not bothering to object when a youngster removes food from her mouth (Kano 1992). By contrast, among humans, parents and alloparents alike routinely proffer food to children, and to each other. Even very young humans spontaneously offer food (figure 2.1) and by eighteen months may select just the item they have reason to believe that another will prefer—even if it differs from their own preference (Repacholi and Gopnik 1997).

Such ingratiating impulses go beyond food sharing. More than two centuries ago in *The Theory of Moral Sentiments* (1750), Adam Smith spelled out how

Figure 2.1. From an early age, humans will select and proffer an item that they have reason to believe someone else will enjoy, even if it differs from their own preferences. Photo: S. Hrdy.

vitally interested people are in the subjective feelings, underlying motivations, and values people use to judge others. Humans also exhibit powerful desires for others to receive information about their own thoughts and feelings and, moreover, to approve of them. From an early age children are eager to learn appropriate "rules," techniques, and social customs, and as David Lancy describes in chapter 8, to fit in. *What I focus on here is the recent realization of just how early in development such ingratiating tendencies combined with mentalizing and questing for intersubjective engagement emerge, and to explore why they would have been crucial for the survival of entirely dependent (but not quite entirely helpless) immatures.*

My starting point is the proposal by Michael Tomasello and Malinda Carpenter that such "intersubjective sharing" (defined by them as two humans "experiencing the same thing at the same time and *knowing together that they are doing this*") is the key sociocognitive difference between humans and other apes. As they put it, following Trevarthen (2005), creating "a shared space of common psychological ground" lays the foundation for a broad range of collaborative activities with shared goals as well as human-style cooperative communication (Tomasello and Carpenter 2007:121–122, emphasis in original, following Trevarthen 2005).

There is an emotional component to this questing for intersubjective engagement that goes beyond "Theory of Mind," or being able to attribute mental states or beliefs to others. By one year of age, even before human babies talk, they respond with pride to praise, and with shame when they sense someone else's disappointment (Darwin 1877; Reddy 2003; Trevarthen 2005). Alone among animals, by age two humans respond to others' assessments by blushing, that peculiarly manifest signal of self-consciousness that led Darwin to wonder why "the thought that others are thinking about us" could "alter our capillary circulation" (1998:335). By age four such coy "aspirations-to-appeal" develop into full-fledged perspective-taking, escalating into outright (not infrequently deceptive) flattery (Fu and Lee 2007), while the underlying concern for what others think emerges even earlier (Reddy 2003). From around age three, most humans are motivated to reveal their "inner selves" to someone else, especially when expressing motivations (e.g., behaving generously) likely to elicit admiration from others (Leimgruber et al. 2012). The same neural regions activated by anticipation of tasty food (the mesolimbic dopamine system and the ventral tegmental area) light up when people talk about themselves (Tamir and Mitchell 2012).

Rather than viewing language as a unique faculty that evolved so that people could coordinate with others in collaborative endeavors, I prefer to assume that questing for intersubjective engagement came first, prompting apes already adept at declarative signaling to become apes capable of producing infinitely recursive symbol-rich vocalizations. On this, I follow psychiatrist Peter Hobson, who argued that "before language, there [had to be] something else . . . that could evolve in tiny steps. . . . That something else was *social engagement with each other.* The links that can join one person's mind with the mind of someone else, especially, to begin with, emotional links" (2004:2, emphasis in original). Colwyn Trevarthen makes a similar point when he suggests the "cooperative awareness" or "secondary intersubjectivity" that permits one-year-old infants to communicate experiences, feelings, and intentions provides the foundation on which language is built (2005:70). Givón similarly argues that grammar emerged so as to communicate information in a way that takes into account someone else's knowledge and current state (2005).

If emotional transformations rendering hominins eager to read, influence, and appeal to mental and subjective states of others preceded the evolution of uniquely human language, it should not be surprising that human toddlers do not just call out for help, utter commands, or announce what they want. They also express feelings, commenting on what seems to them "good" or "bad." By the time a child can talk, perhaps one-third of his or her speech informs others about subjective evaluations, as when Darwin's twenty-seven-month-old son exclaimed, "Oh kind Doddy, kind Doddy" on observing his father give the last piece of gingerbread to the toddler's younger sister (1877). Youngsters may be especially prepared to express inner assessments of others if they are surrounded by encouraging and indulgent others, as is typical among hunter-gatherers (Hewlett and Lamb 2005).

No question, the evolution of language produced potent downstream consequences in terms of cooperation and cultural transmission (Gergely and Gergely 2011; Tomasello and Carpenter 2007). But what I emphasize here is that the apes who first felt a need for forms of communication that went beyond imperative use of communicative signals were already more other-regarding. They were not only cognitively but also *emotionally very different from our last common ancestor with other extant apes.*

How to Explain the Origins of Other-Regarding Impulses?

Efforts to explain humankind's planet-populating, world-dominating "success story" emphasize the cognitive and social processes that facilitate acquisition and transmission of cultural information (Tennie, Call, and Tomasello 2009; Tomasello 1999; Whiten and Van Schaik 2007). Three prerequisites seem especially relevant: closer attention to others, including imitation and observational learning; intentional teaching (including verbal instruction) (L. Dean et al. 2012); and mutual tolerance and other-regarding, helpful impulses (e.g., Burkart, Hrdy, and Van Schaik 2009; Whiten and Van Schaik 2007). But whence such attributes?

Comparative psychologists have done a brilliant job of demonstrating that human social learners focus more on others' actions than do other apes (e.g., Horner and Whitten 2005). They have shown that "uniquely human forms of cooperation" can thus be built up through teaching and transmission of conformity to norms, resulting in a "cultural ratchet" (Tennie, Call, and Tomasello 2009:2413 as cited in L. Dean et al. 2012:1117). It is because our language-using ancestors benefited from new forms of social learning and teaching that, by

100,000 years ago, anatomically modern humans had evolved into fully enculturated ones capable of higher levels of social coordination. But this sequence
begs the question: How did the emotional scaffolding facilitating mutual tolerance, interest in the mental states and thoughts of others, and eagerness to
please and share with them emerge in the hominin line in the first place? It
also fails to explain why these hyper-social impulses evolved in humans but
not other apes. Why do they appear so early and in both sexes?

It is increasingly apparent that other extant apes possess neural prerequisites
to process what someone else does or does not know, read their intentions, and
even figure out how to help them accomplish specific goals (discussed below).
But ingratiating themselves by running over to help another or spontaneously
offering food is not something other apes do. Such behaviors are, however,
observed in some other primates. Humans have not shared a common ancestor
with marmosets and tamarins for over thirty-five million years, yet these
distantly related, tiny-brained monkeys behave in extraordinarily helpful

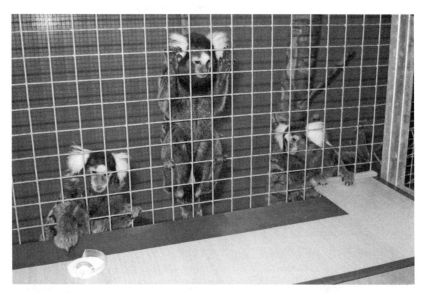

Figure 2.2. The marmoset (*Callithrix jacchus*) on the right has run over to pull in a
tray that will deliver a mealworm to a marmoset on the other side of the cage. This
photograph was taken with the assistance of Judith Burkart, illustrating methods she
devised to compare levels of spontaneous prosociality across species (Burkart and
van Schaik 2012). Photo: S. Hrdy.

Table 2.1. Human-Callitrichid Parallels

Thirty-five million years have elapsed since large-brained human foragers last shared a common ancestor with tiny-brained New World monkeys in the subfamily Callitrichidae (marmosets and tamarins), yet there are remarkable convergences in these otherwise distant taxa that both rely on extensive alloparental as well as parental care and provisioning to rear costly young, including:

1. Extensive alloparental care + provisioning
2. Prolonged post-weaning dependence
3. Reliance on hunting + gathering with learning-intensive extractive foraging
4. Adapted to colonizing new habitats
5. Unusually conditional maternal commitment with high rates of abandonment in situations lacking allomaternal support
6. High levels of foraging cooperation
7. Provisioning by multiple males encouraged by polyandrous mating accompanied by either real chimerism as in marmosets or fictitious beliefs about it as in the human case
8. Nonadvertised ovulation + mating throughout cycle
9. Weakly developed dominance hierarchies where food concerned
10. Variable group compositions + adults of both sexes moving between groups
11. Other-regarding impulses manifested in food sharing + information transfer
12. Endocrinological parallels such as elevated prolactin and reduced testosterone levels in males caring for infants

ways in both the wild (Garber 1997; Bales, French, and Dietz 2002) and in well-replicated captive experiments, as depicted in figure 2.2 (Burkart et al. 2007; Cronin, Schroeder, and Snowdon 2010; Hauser et al. 2003). Striking parallels between humans and this phylogenetically distant subfamily of New World monkeys (among whom, as in humans, mothers also rely on allomaternal care and provisioning to rear surviving young as humans also do) are listed in table 2.1. As discussed elsewhere, this convergent evolution cannot be understood without taking cooperative breeding into account (Burkart, Hrdy, and Van Schaik 2009; Hrdy 2009; Burkart and Van Schaik 2012).

Interestingly, marmosets readily follow others' gazes and eagerly assist them, but they do not appear to take the "mental" perspective of another into account the way humans do (Burkart and Heschl 2007). Other apes are better at doing so, just not as interested in helping. Nor, apart from mutual grooming, do nonhuman apes go out of their way to please others the way marmosets (in their more automatic, "less thoughtful" way) or humans do. In the human case, reward centers in the brain are stimulated just by giving something to someone else (Rilling et al. 2002), but whether such "charitable acts" have comparable effects in any other primate remains unknown. Based purely on behavioral observation, however, other apes do not appear particularly interested in ingratiating behaviors or eager to satisfy another's personal preference. Possessors have to be actively solicited before resources are shared. Apparently other apes do not find it as inherently pleasurable to please others as humans do.

So far, explanations for humankind's peculiarly prosocial impulses have mostly focused on obligate cooperative foraging, especially collaborative hunting and with it the need for equitable sharing (Bullinger et al. 2011; Tomasello et al. 2012) or on the "parochial altruism" needed by a "band of brothers" competing against neighboring bands (Choi and Bowles 2007). Bowles vividly showcases his proposal that "generosity and solidarity toward one's own [group] may have emerged only in combination with hostility toward outsiders" (2008a:326) by asking whether humans "engage in mutual aid because evolution is red in tooth and claw" (2008b). Yet *Pan troglodytes* is also meat-loving and probably even more competitive and dominance-striving than humans are, not to mention xenophobic to the point of reflexively attacking outsiders (Wrangham and Peterson 1996). Hunting and intergroup conflict are integral to chimpanzee life as well. So why didn't their ancestors also spend the past six million years evolving more other-regarding impulses so as to reap manifest benefits of "parochial altruism"? Nor do warfare or hunting models explain why other-regarding impulses characterize both sexes (and indeed may even be more expressed in females, de Waal 2013:51). Nor do they explain why prosocial impulses emerge so early in development. Surely vulnerable immatures would do better to remain self-servingly focused on staying safe, fed, and growing bigger, as earlier generations of behaviorists assumed babies naturally did (e.g., Watson 1928).

Other-regarding impulses lay the groundwork for cooperative potentials that unquestionably have served humans well—as evidenced by all the enterprises, institutions, factories, and gravity-defying machines that coordination with others facilitate. But Mother Nature (my metaphor for Darwinian natural selection) had no way of foreseeing such eventual payoffs. It seems circular to argue that humans evolved other-regarding, culture-acquiring attributes in order to become other-regarding, culture-bearing animals. Rather, we need to ask under what circumstances does an ape benefit from responding to the mental states, desires, and needs of others? From seeking to appeal to and please them? And why should such impulses emerge so early? Rather than viewing prehuman ancestors as already "exceptional," I prefer to view them as creatures subject to the same evolutionary processes that pertain across the animal world.

Such challenges drew my attention to the unusual way that apes in the line leading to the genus *Homo* must have reared their young (Hrdy 1999a). While shared care is typical of human foragers and widespread across primates, it is not found among our closest great ape relations; it was almost certainly absent among the last common ancestor humans shared with them. Why then, and when, did such extremely un-apelike modes of childcare emerge in the hominin line? And what were the ramifications?

Shared Care, Provisioning Immatures, and the Evolution of More Generalized Food Sharing

There is an ongoing paradigm shift in how evolutionary anthropologists reconstruct family life among hominins struggling to stay fed and rear offspring in the unpredictably fluctuating climates of Pleistocene Africa. As has long been recognized, all apes are born relatively helpless, maturing slowly through a prolonged infancy, followed by a juvenile period and adolescence. Debate persists over just how similar or different these growth stages are in humans and other apes (Thompson, chapter 4, this volume). Indisputably though, humans remain nutritionally dependent longer. Nonhuman apes tend to be weaned later, but thereafter provision themselves. By contrast, humans continue to be subsidized as late as early adulthood. No one knows how far back in time such dependency extends. But the emergence of *Homo erectus*, with an adult brain more than twice the size of either the brain of australopithecines or that of today's chimpanzees, presumably meant that the diets of immatures, and perhaps their mothers as well, were subsidized at least by the beginning of the Pleistocene, 1.8 million years ago (O'Connell et al. 2002; Cofran and DeSilva 2013).

Based on data from twentieth-century foraging peoples, it takes ten to thirteen million calories beyond what a child provides for himself to grow from birth to age eighteen, more than a foraging mother could ordinarily provide by herself (Kaplan 1994). Furthermore, shorter interbirth intervals meant another dependent born before older offspring were independent. Even with a father on hand and willing to help, the success rate of a Plio-Pleistocene hunter-scavenger would not have come close to meeting the requirements of a *H. erectus* juvenile needing to be fed several times each day (O'Connell et al. 2002). Alloparental in addition to parental provisioning and processing was essential to ensure that growing children had sufficient palatable foods.

Survival of young required multiple providers. Indeed, fluctuating rainfall together with unpredictable resources (Potts 1996; Wells 2012), specifically in east Africa during the period between 1.8 and 2 million years ago when *Homo erectus* was emerging (Magill, Ashley, and Freeman 2013), produced conditions that, in other animals, tend to be associated with the evolution of cooperative breeding (Jetz and Rubenstein 2011), and with it, prolonged dependence (Hrdy 2005b; Langen 2000). In the early hominin case, opportunistic inputs from multiple scavenger/hunters must have been backed up by more reliable gatherers and processors of plant foods. Other apes exhibit some division of labor (e.g., chimpanzee females fish for termites and crack nuts whereas males do almost all hunting) but the fruits of such gender-specific endeavors are rarely shared, and meat is largely consumed by adult males. So, given notably self-serving, often competitive apes, how does food sharing get underway?

Across primates, voluntary provisioning is uncommon. Humans excepted, it is virtually absent among apes. Shared care is a different matter. Infants are universally attractive to at least some other group members, and are protected and even carried by them. Some form of shared infant care is reported for the majority of species in the Primate order (Hrdy 2009, 2010). Apart from humans and one lesser ape, however (siamang fathers carry older infants [Lappan 2009]), hominoid mothers do not permit access to new infants. Yet so deeply entrenched is responsiveness to infant cues among primates that, even among great apes who do not regularly share care, normally aloof males sometimes respond to signals of need as when chimpanzee males adopt an orphaned youngster (Boesch et al. 2010). Some primate mothers also occasionally allow another female's infant to suckle or to take food. Nevertheless, with the exception of humans, extensive alloparental provisioning is confined to the subfamily Callitrichidae.

Occasionally, sharing food with another's infant does not mean that adults share food, but provisioning young—whether by parents or alloparents—may act as a gateway to sharing among adults. Compiling evidence for sixty-eight species of primates, Jaeggi and Van Schaik (2011) found that adult-to-adult food sharing was disproportionately likely to evolve in taxonomic groups where adult-to-offspring provisioning was already established. This is consistent with the observation that, as with cooperative breeding itself, allomaternal provisioning is more likely to evolve when foods utilized require strength or extractive skills that immatures do not yet possess.

Hamilton's Rule predicts that helping should evolve whenever benefits to the recipient exceed costs to the helper weighted by degree of relatedness. Thus, even a distantly related group member who has already had his fill of a resource may provide some to immatures unable to access it themselves. Exact costs and benefits vary but, across the natural world in species with biparental and/or alloparental care, in thousands of species of birds as well as quite a few mammals, adults transport food back to a nest, den, or other site where immatures are creched. Social carnivores such as African wild dogs and wolves provide classic examples. Adults return from a kill with predigested meat in their bellies, regurgitating it into the mouths of begging pups waiting at a den or central place. In the case of the genus *Homo*, adult provisioning of immatures would have set the stage for more generalized food sharing and, in time, cooking as well (Wrangham and Carmody 2010).

By 800,000 years ago, perhaps earlier, routine cooking would release further energy from "pooled" resources (Kramer and Ellison 2010; Reiches et al. 2009) in a self-reinforcing feedback loop, while adult-to-infant transfers facilitated guided transmission of knowledge about appropriate foods and how to obtain them. As it happens, the best-documented nonhuman instances of "tutoring" come from species where alloparents take the initiative in providing age-appropriate foods to immatures (e.g., Rapaport 2011; Rapaport and Brown 2008; Thornton and McAuliffe 2006). Going beyond merely tolerating a youngster taking food or responding to a beggar (e.g., Jaeggi, Van Noordwijk, and Van Schaik 2008; Jaeggi, Burkart, and Van Schaik 2010; Kano 1992; Silk 1978), callitrichid providers proactively deliver food to infants around weaning age (e.g., Burkart et al. 2007). Allomothers also emit special vocalizations signaling novel foods and actively intervene to prevent youngsters from ingesting inappropriate or toxic items (Byrne and Rapaport 2011; Rapaport and Ruiz-Miranda 2002). Such mentoring helps explain why foragers growing up in groups with many helpers may be more adept at harvesting (e.g., Langen and Vehrencamp 1999:138 for cooperatively breeding magpie jays).

Provisioning of immatures almost certainly preceded the emergence of more generalized adult-to-adult food sharing. This sequence is consistent with accumulating evidence that Pleistocene humans could not have reared young without allomaternal provisioning. Among virtually all Africans still living as hunter-gatherers when first studied, mothers relied on assistance from a fluctuating array of group members of both sexes from as young as ten to over sixty (Blurton Jones, Hawkes, and O'Connell 1997; O'Connell, Hawkes, and Blurton Jones 1999; Burkart, Hrdy, and Van Schaik 2009; Crittenden, chapter 7, this volume; Crittenden, Zes, and Marlowe 2010; Hawkes, O'Connell, and Blurton Jones 1989, 1998; Hewlett and Lamb 2005; Hill and Hurtado 2009; Ivey 2000; Konner, chapter 6, this volume; Meehan, Helfrecht, and Malcom, chapter 9, this volume). According to this Cooperative Breeding Hypothesis, human life histories evolved as byproducts of alloparental supplementation of parental provisioning (Hawkes and Paine 2006; Hrdy 1999a, 2005b; Konner 2010: chap. 16; K. Kramer 2005a; Newson and Richerson 2013). In particular, inclusive fitness benefits accruing to foragers who remained productive and willing to provision younger kin provide the most plausible explanation to date for why human females go on living for decades after menopause (Hawkes et al. 1998; Kim, Coxworth, and Hawkes 2012).

Enhanced buffering of young against food shortages reduces costs of slow maturation and prolonged post-weaning dependence. Even in the face of fluctuating rainfall and unpredictable resources (Potts 1996; Newson and Richerson 2013) hominins could afford to grow up slowly. They could also accommodate steep learning curves and other challenges stemming from migrating into novel habitats (Hrdy 2005b). Meanwhile, stacking offspring improved the capacity of populations to bounce back after crashes (Hawks et al. 2000; Hawkes and Paine 2006).

Augmentation of energy available to mothers and infants probably also played a role in encephalization (Isler and Van Schaik 2012; Navarrete, Van Schaik, and Isler 2011). Isler and Van Schaik (2012) propose that provisioning during periods of rapid brain growth at the end of gestation and during lactation stabilized resource availability. They view this as the "first step" in the threefold increase in brain size characterizing anatomically modern humans. Again, sequence matters. Rather than needing 1,350 cc brains to orchestrate cooperative care, shared nurturing was essential for the evolution of such big brains (Hrdy 1999a:287, 2009).

Changing Our Minds: Psychological Corollaries of Cooperative Breeding

Modern developmental psychology is currently construed as the study of how children's minds grow within the context of their relationships with family. Revising our ideas about exactly who constituted "family" in humankind's Environment of Evolutionary Adaptedness (EEA) means rethinking neural development. Thus, new modes of child-rearing mean changing our minds— literally. This ongoing paradigm shift within evolutionary anthropology requires reassessing assumptions about the ubiquity of exclusive maternal care during humankind's EEA (e.g., Bowlby 1971:228–229), even as new findings from social neuroscience confirm Bowlbian Attachment Theory's central premise regarding the importance of early social experiences (Carter et al. 2005). If infants first develop a sense of self and "internal working models" about their world through responding to others' responses to them, and if, as psychiatrist Daniel Siegel puts it, interaction with "the mind of another seems to catalyze the development of self-awareness" (2012:43), then early social interactions affect both the formation of neural connections and regulation of gene expression.

As in all primates, maternal nurture was critical for hominin infants' survival. Frequent breastfeeding along with co-sleeping continued to guarantee this very special relationship (Konner, chapter 6, this volume). But as new circumstances made allomaternal as well as maternal care and provisioning increasingly essential, the hominin infant's own mother ceased to be the sole source of security, warmth, mobility, and nutrition. Nor could infants rely on their mother to obsessively maintain contact with them day and night for the first six months of their lives as is typical of other extant apes, mothers who thereafter continue to suckle them and remain reliably within eye- or earshot for four or more years. Hominin infants' need for care and feeling secure remained unchanged (Bowlby 1971), but they could no longer count on nearly single-minded dedication from a mother who prioritized their well-being above that of all other current and future offspring.

Prior to conception, all through gestation, lactation, early and late childhood, and beyond, this hominin mother's nutritional status depended on how much social support she had. Her lifetime reproductive success depended on how strategically she allocated maternal investment between costly, closely spaced offspring. In the hours and days immediately after birth, a postpartum mother's perception of social support influenced how primed she would be to pick up and hold close the little stranger who had just emerged from her body, how likely that infant would be to successfully latch onto nipples and, through initiating lactation, promote continued contact and, over time, the formation of a profoundly close social bond. With the exception of very young or inexperienced first-time mothers or unusually dire circumstances (Hrdy 1999a:181–183), most primate mothers are remarkably undiscriminating, displaying nearly unconditional dedication (e.g., Matsuzawa 2012; Turner et al. 2012). The main exceptions fall among marmosets, tamarins, and humans who, unlike other primates, discriminate on the basis of both infant attributes and availability of allomaternal support. They may abandon, actively reject, or kill specific newborns (Bardi, Petto, and Lee-Parritz 2001; Culot et al. 2011; Tirado Herrera, Knogge, and Heymann 2000 for callitrichids; Hrdy 1999a:288–317, 351–380 for review of human evidence).

Increased reliance on allomaternal assistance must have been accompanied by both increased maternal sensitivity to cues of social support and selection on infants favoring aptitudes for eliciting it. At the same time, shorter interbirth intervals combined with prolonged juvenile dependence (and perhaps also a greater need for group consensus regarding a specific infant's viability?), intensified pressure on mothers to evaluate attributes and prospects of each newborn in relation to prospects for older but still dependent siblings, as well as prospects for any future sibling, the arrival of whom might be delayed or accelerated by the fate of this one. Over generations, a mother's reproductive success and that of close relatives would depend upon how well she negotiated cost/benefit trade-offs implicit in Hamilton's Rule. Thus was a newly conditional maternal commitment overlain upon the single-minded dedication typical of most primate mothers, helping to explain the curious ambivalence documented for human mothers (Hrdy 1999a: chap. 20; Parker 1995).

And what of fathers? As in many primates, paternal commitment would be influenced by both paternity probabilities and alternative mating options. But among cooperatively breeding hominins, fathers also needed to take into account availability of alternative nurturers (Meehan 2005a; Meehan, Helfrecht, and Malcom, chapter, 9, this volume). When feasible, hunters preferentially channel meat to their own offspring (Marlowe 2010), but genetic progenitors were not the only hunters bringing back meat to share (R. Lee 1979; Kaplan et al. 2000; Hill and Hurtado 2009). Furthermore, taking advantage of occasional protein and fat bonanzas was only practical if people could count on more reliably provided plant foods gathered by women to tide them over when hunters returned empty-handed (R. Lee 1979; Marlowe 2010: fig. 3.11). As reported by Hawkes and colleagues (1989) and subsequently confirmed by Marlowe (2010: fig. 3.11), postreproductive women without infants of their own forage more diligently and bring in more calories than do mothers of childbearing age, with patrilineal as well as matrilineal grandmothers making substantial contributions to child well-being (Meehan, Helfrecht, and Malcom, chapter 9, this volume). In some African habitats, children as young as ten also share gathered food with younger siblings and more distant kin (Blurton Jones, Hawkes, and O'Connell 1997; Crittenden, Zes, and Marlowe 2010; Crittenden, chapter 7, this volume). Just who contributed how much varied so that fungibility of nurture as well as residential mobility would have been essential for maintaining fits between local conditions and an appropriate mix of providers.

Like other mobile fission-fusion primates (Schreier and Swedell 2012), human hunter-gatherers gravitate away from adversity and toward opportunities including better access to food, water, and security. Add to such incentives the need for allomaternal assistance and variable impulses among postreproductives to provide it (e.g., Blurton Jones, Hawkes, and O'Connell 2005; Scelza 2011). Fortuitously, our last common ancestors with other apes were probably characterized by more flexible transfer patterns than is usually assumed. Far from typical, extreme male philopatry and xenophobia reported for chimpanzees look more like derived troglodytian outliers than hominoid norms (Koenig and Borries 2012). Even among chimpanzees, females remain in their natal range when benefits of doing so outweigh costs of staying (Pusey, Williams, and Goodall 1997). Over time, long-distance relationships maintained with kin and as-if kin alike would have facilitated flexible group composition among hominin foragers and, with it, more flexible parenting.

Porous social boundaries meant that newcomers with useful services to offer, whether skilled hunters or productive older kinswomen, would have been particularly welcome while groups with adept hunters or healers (often older men) might be especially attractive (Wiessner 2002b). In this way, flexible group compositions essential for cooperative breeding would have also enhanced exposure to novel artifacts and technologies, not only laying the groundwork for the more formalized exchanges that eventually became hallmarks of hunter-gatherer lives (Wiessner 1977, 2002a) but also for more far-flung kin and as-if kin networks (Wiessner 2002b). Concurrently, psychological corollaries of alloparental provisioning, such as enhanced mutual tolerance and dependence along with the tutoring impulses seen in many cooperative breeders, would have further encouraged social transmission of knowledge (Burkart and Van Schaik 2010; Byrne and Rapaport 2011; Rapaport and Ruiz-Miranda 2002).

But what of the implications for infants on the receiving end of all this investment by others? Heightened maternal discrimination would have produced selection pressures on neonates to emerge looking full-term and robust and, after birth, to expeditiously get to the critical task of initiating lactation. Should a mother's commitment falter, infants would do well to catch her attention, vocally reminding her of their vulnerability. Over the course of development, hominin infants and children needed to monitor not only their mother's location and intentions but also those of other potential caretakers. In the process, infants become conditioned by rewards when solicitations succeeded, and disappointed or worse when they misgauged. Such social conditioning affects phenotypic outcomes—what a neuroscientist conceptualizes as the individual's "neural net profile" (Siegel 2012:24; also see Gopnik 2010).

When availability of allomaternal care is correlated with child survival, as has been repeatedly documented for cooperatively breeding monkeys and, to a lesser extent, for humans (e.g., see Bales, French, and Dietz 2002 and Garber 1997 for callitrichids; Ivey 2000; Mace and Sear 2005; Sear and Mace 2008, and Lahdenperä et al. 2004 for humans),[1] it produces directional social selection favoring infant phenotypes better at soliciting nurture.

Social Selection Favoring Other-Regarding Aptitudes

Social selection (sensu West-Eberhard 1979, 1983, 2003) entails competition with conspecifics for access to some resource. "Competition" need not imply individuals directly duking it out over a desirable tidbit or location. Consider the conspicuous natal coats typical of many infant-sharing monkeys. Their flamboyance attracts attention from available allomothers while diverting care from other infants born that season (Hrdy 1976; 2009). The situation for human babies is different. Right after birth, it is mothers, not allomothers, that infants need to appeal to. Lacking flamboyant natal coats, human neonates are much fatter than other apes. These fat deposits fuel thermoregulation and stockpile energy for a fast-developing brain (Kuzawa 1998), but plumpness also makes neonates appear full-term and robust, advertising to their mothers that they merit the prolonged investment that will ensue once she allows the baby to suckle, initiating lactation and with it a concatenation of bonding processes (Hrdy 1999a: chap. 21). Even though no other baby is in sight, this newborn is competing with both older siblings in whom the mother might otherwise continue to invest and an as yet unborn sib the mother might produce were she to resume cycling sooner. As they mature, babies need to appeal to others as well through monitoring their tastes and intentions—a psychological dimension to Lorenzian *Kindschenschema*. Mothers also have a stake in making their babies attractive since they, too, are competing with other mother-offspring dyads for allomaternal assistance (Hrdy 2009:225ff).

Conspicuous natal coats presumably attract the attention of predators as well as caretakers, while fetal fat deposits built up just prior to birth can impede passage through narrow birth canals. Such costs must be offset somehow. As with Darwin's example of the peacock's tail, otherwise disadvantageous traits continue to be favored if they increase chances of being "chosen" by another (Lyons and Montgomerie 2012; West-Eberhard 2010). Anyone who doubts the existence of this infantile equivalent of "sex appeal" should consider how reliably reward centers in the brains of human alloparents as well as parents react when looking at cute babies (Glocker et al. 2009; Kringelbach et al. 2008).

"Runaway social selection" has been invoked in other contexts where humans benefit from appealing to others. For example, psychiatrist Randolph Nesse invokes it to explain why humans depart from rational self-interest by remaining loyal to a person or an ideal, behaving generously or otherwise engaging in selfless conduct exceeding reasonable expectations of return (2007, 2010; see also Flinn and Alexander 2007). People do so, Nesse argues, because selflessly generous or honest behaviors enhance that individual's likelihood of being chosen by an advantageous social partner. Such a partner may in turn benefit from that choice. Such "runaway" social selection is possible when signal and response are genetically or culturally correlated and both coevolving. According to Nesse, people's acute sensitivity to embarrassment and the powerful constraining self-consciousness that we call "conscience" (and with it perhaps blushing) evolved through social selection as part of the internal monitoring system that helps an individual "behave well" so as to compete with others directly or, more often, indirectly, to be chosen by advantageous social partners (see also Boehm 2012).

With such logic in mind, consider how early humans manifest self-conscious emotions. I hypothesize that such sensibilities first emerged as corollaries of cooperative breeding in an ape lineage. That is, our ancestors were emotionally preadapted for self-consciousness because, in the high child mortality environments that presumably prevailed throughout the Plio-Pleistocene, prolonged dependence on caretakers with contingent levels of commitment generated novel selection pressures such that, over generations, dependents neurologically disposed to be more "other-regarding" were better cared for. Darwinian social selection would have favored those who grew up more interested in the thoughts, feelings, and needs of others, an emotionally quite distinctive kind of ape prepared to recognize what expressions, vocalizations, or behaviors would appeal to specific others.

Primate Preadaptations for Cooperative Breeding

Old World monkeys and apes navigate complex, emotionally mediated relationships. They remember who they grew up around (and thus are probably related to), who is currently dominant over whom or likely to soon be so. They recognize special competences and track reciprocal interactions over time so as to differentiate between useful versus unreliable, potentially harmful, associates (Cheney and Seyfarth 2007; Mitani 2006; Schino and Aureli 2009). If death of a high-ranking relative disrupts an advantageous relationship, primates opportunistically seek substitutes, related or not (Seyfarth and Cheney 2012).

Internalized systems for emotionally based "bookkeeping" similar to that found in cercopithecine primates (Schino and Aureli 2009) and modern humans (Hrdy 1999a:171) surely characterized early hominins as well. Add to this the neurophysiological scaffolding for registering the whereabouts and current condition of tiny individuals outside themselves that first evolved in mammalian mothers some two hundred million years ago (Carter et al. 2005). Elaborations on these ancient bauplans help mothers decide whether or not to allow allomaternal access to vulnerable newborns. Although all primate infants are attractive to at least some would-be allomothers, voluntary shared care only occurs when mothers feel sufficiently confident of their infants' safe return to permit another to hold them. I suspect this is why shared care is only observed in primates where would-be allomothers can be trusted, as in the case of close matrilineal kin or probable progenitors (Hrdy 2009a, 2010).

Most allomaternal care in nonhuman primates involves pre-reproductive females or else likely progenitors. Less attention has been paid to females nearing the end of their reproductive careers even though selfless impulses often increase as reproductive value declines, as in the case of old female langurs who opt out of competition for food yet risk mortal injury defending younger relatives against infanticidal males. This obvious preadaptation for cooperative breeding did not lead to longer postmenopausal life spans in other primates, as Hawkes hypothesizes it did in humans. Without food sharing, opportunities for postreproductives to enhance the fitness of kin would have been more sporadic than chronic (Hrdy 1999a, 2009).

Meanwhile, over millions of years, as maternal horizons expanded to include caring relationships with others besides their own infants, so did cortical capacities for mediating between complex social experiences, long-term bonds, and emotions (Carter et al. 2005). Given this legacy, it is unsurprising that social experiences early in life continue to shape both brain development and subsequent social relationships across primates, especially in humans (reviewed in Siegel 2012, esp. p. 22ff.). But how can we test the proposition that prehuman apes who relied on multiple caretakers develop different cognitive and emotional aptitudes than apes reared exclusively by their mothers?

Virtual and Real "Tests" of Assumptions Integral to the Mothers-Plus-Others Model

None of us has a machine to go back in time to observe how hominin infants responded to mothers and allomothers. What we do have are observations from collateral lines of extant Great Apes (mostly *Pan troglodytes*) and from modern descendants of those early hominins. They allow us to study how hominoid infants respond to different caretaking regimens. In addition, new findings from neuroscience are beginning to enable us to compare brain development in chimpanzees and humans.

Elsewhere (Hrdy 2009), I reviewed such limited evidence as I could then find that infants with several attachment figures grow up better able to integrate multiple mental perspectives (e.g., Van IJzendoorn, Sagi, and Lambermon 1992). Allomaternal support, whether from a grandmother in the same household or just transient visits by "as-if" supportive kin, accelerates and enhances social awareness and an infant's sense of security. This holds both for infants born to young, inexperienced, or unmarried mothers who might otherwise be at risk of insecure attachments (Hrdy 2009:124–141; Olds, Sadler, and Kitzman 2007; Spieker and Bensley 1994), and for infants among Aka foragers securely attached to their own mothers plus four to six familiar, trusted others (Meehan and Hawks, 2013). Such findings are consistent with my assumption that shared care and provisioning among already highly social, clever, tool-using, bipedal apes produced phenotypes increasingly attuned to others. Then, assume also that in each generation infants a little better at reading the mental states of others and motivated to appeal to them would be better cared for and better fed. Over evolutionary time, immatures would be subjected to directional social selection favoring other-regarding aptitudes (figure 2.3). Although scarcely conclusive, indirect evidence from comparative infant development and comparative neuroscience helps us evaluate the plausibility of these underlying assumptions and also helps to generate new predictions or tests. Let's begin.

DOES ALLOMATERNAL INVOLVEMENT AFFECT DEVELOPING APE PHENOTYPES? IF SO, HOW?

As Bowlby noted long ago, all higher primates are born with innate capacities for emotional engagement and become attached to their most reliable care-taker—usually the mother. Chimpanzee infants cling tightly to this caretaker and calm when held close by her (Bard 2012:228). At night, infant chimpanzees held by their mothers cry even less than co-sleeping human infants do (Matsuzawa 2012:295). By one month of age, both human and chimpanzee infants recognize and preferentially respond to their mother's face. Human infants, however, continue to distinguish between their mother's face and the faces of other individuals long after the stage at which infant chimpanzees cease to do so. By the age of two months or so, infant chimpanzees no longer discriminate between a photo of their own mother's face and that of a composite digitally generated by averaging chimp faces (Tomonaga et al. 2004:229).

The frequency of mutual gazing between chimpanzee infants and their mothers is inversely correlated with how much physical contact they have. Between birth and two months, as the chimpanzee mother cradles her infant less, the incidence of mutual gazing rises (Bard 2005). Experimental psychologists and cross-cultural anthropologists report a similarly inverse correlation for humans. A baby being held by his mother will look into her face less than if securely propped up on a couch nearby (Lavelli and Fogel 2002). Thus, it

MOTHERS-PLUS-OTHERS THOUGHT EXPERIMENT

Start with an intelligent, bipedal primate with the cognitive and manipulative potentials and rudimentary theory of mind found in all great apes.

Lore Ruttan

Rear this ape in a novel developmental context where maternal care is contingent on social support and where offspring survival depends on nurture elicited from multiple caretakers.

Lore Ruttan

This results in a novel ape phenotype in turn subjected to directional social selection such that over generations, those youngsters better at ingratiating themselves with others will be better cared and fed, and hence most likely to survive. The predicted evolutionary outcome is apes more interested in and adept at intersubjective engagement.

Figure 2.3. The Mother-Plus-Others hypothesis attempts to explain the initial emergence of "emotionally modern humans" through development's role in the production of selectable variation as in this graphically presented three-step thought experiment. Art by L. M. Ruttan.

is not surprising that in traditional societies that are characterized by more direct tactile contact between infants and their mothers, babies gaze into their eyes less than do babies who spend more time off their mothers (Keller 2007; reviewed in Bard 2012).

Like chimpanzee infants, human infants out of direct contact with their mother (but still in non-anxiety-provoking situations) feel a need to "stay in touch without touch," monitoring their mothers' expressions more and frequently "checking back" (cf. Falk 2004a, b). Being off the mother alters behavioral phenotypes, increasing how often infants attend to faces and the motivations of those nearby. Apparently, at some point in the past, human infants also became more discriminating about the identity of caretakers. Both observations are consistent with a legacy of multiple caretakers and with it more conditional maternal commitment.

Social referencing like pointing rarely occurs among wild chimpanzees or among captive-born ones with limited human exposure. But even though nothing like the eager questing for intersubjective engagement characteristic of humans has been reported, human-reared chimpanzees do communicate intentions to others and even refer someone else to look at something they are interested in (Bard 2012; Leavens, Hopkins, and Bard 1996; Menzel 1999).

Clearly, rearing conditions, including extent of allomaternal experience (albeit with allomothers of a different species), alter ape phenotypes. Chimpanzees reared in human families (some being trained to use sign language) prove better than their wild counterparts at communicating likes and dislikes through gestures, following with their eyes what someone else is pointing to, and even pointing themselves at what they want. Human-reared chimpanzees are also better at reading human intentions and emotional states, and are more inclined to coordinate activities with others (e.g., R. Fouts 1997; James Marsh's 2011 documentary *Project Nim*). Life stories of human-reared chimpanzees are problematic on both ethical and scientific grounds. However, we are beginning to have more thoughtful, carefully controlled, and also hopefully more humane case studies confirming that chimpanzees possess the basic neurological equipment to register someone else's goals. Exposure to helpful human caretakers really does seem to enhance apes' capacity to understand what another needs. In innovative recent experiments, Shinya Yamamoto, Humle, and Tanaka (2012) demonstrated that some chimpanzees (all had experienced relationships with trusted human caretakers in addition to their own mothers) could correctly identify the intended goal of another chimpanzee in an adjacent cage and sought to help with the task.

Five of these mother-reared/experimenter-trusting, human-socialized chimpanzees were caged beside five other chimpanzees who were either close kin or as-if kin. In one set of experiments, a window in the partition separating the cages permitted the tool-provider to see which tool (from an array of seven) was needed to access a sweet juice reward. In a second set of experiments, the provider was prevented from seeing what the other chimp was trying to do. With vision obscured, tool selection was random. But when the provider could see what the other chimp was trying to do, he almost always selected the correct tool (a brush or a straw), qualifying the assistance as "targeted help" that takes into account the intentions of the recipient. Such findings are consistent with characterizations of chimpanzees and bonobos as possessing capacities for rudimentary empathy and concern for others, as has long been advocated by Frans de Waal (for updates see de Waal 2006, 2012; de Waal and Ferrari 2012; Warneken et al. 2007).

Of Yamamoto's five subjects, a chimp named Ayumu stood out as the most "other-regarding." Like the other chimpanzees in the experiment, Ayumu was cared for by his own mother (Ai) while also repeatedly exposed to the same trusted tester. The chimps in these studies are described as having a "strong bond" with these testers (e.g., Hayashi and Matsuzawa 2003:226). But in Ayumu's case, allomaternal exposure went further. Right from birth, Ayumu had interacted face-to-face with a particularly responsive experimenter in the person of Tetsoro Matsuzawa, who had spent years patiently interacting with Ai and cultivating her confidence. When Ayumu was born, Matsuzawa became the first scientist ever voluntarily granted access to a newborn by a mother chimpanzee. As a consequence, Ayumu was reared as few chimpanzees ever have been. Was it a coincidence then that when paired with his own mother in the experimental condition where the tool provider was prevented from seeing what the other chimp needed, Ayumu was the only one of the five subjects motivated to clamber up the wall and peek over the barrier before handing his mother exactly the tool she needed?

It is not clear whether Ayumu was just innately more resourceful or curious, or whether prolonged and intimate exposure to a human allomother conditioned him to be more interested in what someone else might need. There are few reports of helping behaviors from the wild (e.g., Snare 2012). Nevertheless, even if such capacities usually remain latent, I think we can say that other apes, certainly chimpanzees, possess the basic neural wiring for targeted helping under some conditions. From the wild, the best-documented exceptions in which chimpanzees appear to cooperate involve monkey-hunting by adult males at Taï Forest. As they pursue their prey, one may post himself below a tree where dinner is likely to descend. Depending on the actual intention behind this mutually beneficial act (whether self-serving, other-regarding, or both), it might count as targeted helping (see Boesch and Boesch-Achermann 1990; Boesch, Boesch, and Vigilant 2006; Tomasello et al. 2012). Nevertheless, compared with humans, wild chimpanzees simply do not engage in targeted helping or cooperation as much or as readily as humans do. So, does rearing by multiple responsive caretakers enhance the requisite perspective-taking?

The closest thing to the relevant experiment we have derives from a long-running project that Kim Bard and coworkers set up while seeking ways to improve psychological well-being in captive-born chimpanzees. To this end, Bard monitored outcomes for chimpanzees under three rearing conditions. Infants were either reared by their own mothers or, when maternal care proved inadequate (as is all too often the case in captivity), removed and reared in communal nurseries under one of two conditions, either in "Standard" communal nurseries where their physical needs were met by a series of human caretakers or else in special "Responsive Care" communal nurseries. In the Responsive Care situation, familiar, specially trained human caregivers, essentially allomothers-of-another-species, interacted with and stimulated infants for several extra hours five days a week (Bard 2005, 2012). In what follows, I summarize Bard's findings as if they represented results from a "natural" experiment exploring how "proxies" for humankind's last common ancestors with other apes might have responded to socioenvironmental conditions requiring shared care.

The Responsive Care infants who interacted with multiple (albeit human) allomothers engaged in more frequent and more sustained mutual eye gazing than either wild chimpanzees or captive infants cared for exclusively by their mothers (Bard 2005). By three months of age, they also exhibited more frequent social smiles. Tested at nine months using the Bayley Scale for Infant Development (no language required), chimpanzees receiving extra attention from responsive allomothers exhibited more advanced cognitive development than nursery-reared chimpanzees who had not received extra attention. Bard refers to this "responsivity to social interaction" found in both human and chimpanzee infants during face-to-face gazing as "primary intersubjectivity" (different from Trevarthen's "secondary intersubjectivity").

Under suboptimal captive conditions, emotionally deprived chimpanzee infants exhibit similar behavioral disturbances to those observed among institutionalized human children. Infants receiving inadequate personal attention may be unable to mount any organized response to attachment figures—freezing, for example, instead of running to them for comfort. Bard collaborated with Dutch developmental psychologists who had been comparing attachment styles in children from intact nuclear families versus those reared in understaffed orphanages. Their collaboration (Van IJzendoorn et al. 2009) was the first to document "disorganized attachment" in another species of primate. It was also the first "prospective" intervention study to evaluate how care differing in quality and quantity of interactions affects cognitive development and emotional security in nonhuman apes.

For obvious reasons, infant-care regimens were quite different for colony-reared chimpanzees and children. Twenty-nine infant chimpanzees were placed in Standard Care after being removed from mothers deemed inadequate. They were placed in nurseries with a small group of other infants attended by one of four staff members who provided minimal human contact, feeding them and changing their diapers several times a day. Another seventeen received Responsive Care, spending some four hours, five days a week with one of five caretakers, all familiar and trained to sensitively engage chimpanzee infants (Van IJzendoorn et al. 2009). When tested at nine months using various measures, including the first-ever application of Ainsworth's Strange Situation procedure to nonhuman apes, chimpanzee infants reared with Standard Care exhibited attachment disorders similar to those in institutionalized human children. However, infants from the Responsive Care program tended to be emotionally more secure and also tested significantly better on cognitive development than Standard Care chimpanzees.

Clearly, interpersonal experiences in the months after birth had a profound impact on resulting phenotypes. None of these captive infants were reared under species-typical conditions, but those exposed to multiple responsive others developed to be more other-regarding than their exclusively mother-reared counterparts. Presumably, infants in Bard's Responsive Care nurseries were expressing cognitive and emotional capacities that otherwise remain latent among chimpanzees in continuous one-on-one contact with mothers in natural settings. Nevertheless, "other-regarding" does not mean the same thing in a year-old chimpanzee as in a human.

Among the more striking differences is the relative eagerness with which an infant accustomed to responsive care seeks to share experiences with someone else by calling their attention to some object in a triadic interaction. By nine months of age a human infant will hold out an object to a caretaker while eagerly monitoring their reaction to it (Tomasello 1999), as if inquiring, "What do you think of this? And, what should my response be?" By that age, however, young chimpanzees (even though interested earlier) are losing interest in that game (Tomonaga et al. 2004). It is not that infant chimpanzees never exhibit such joint attention. Outside the lab, young chimps have been observed interacting with other chimpanzees, cueing off one another's responses to an object. The differences seem to lie in frequency and enthusiasm for mutual engagement during shared attention or, as Kim Bard puts it (pers. comm., 2012), the amount of "positive affect" surrounding joint attention.

Like Tomasello (1999), researchers at the Primate Research Institute in Kyoto considered "object-showing" and "object-giving" indicative of "referential communication in a triadic relationship." They specifically set out to learn whether a "nine month revolution" comparable to that in humans occurs in chimpanzees. Given similarities in terms of mutual gazing, smiling, and so on, up until that point, it seems odd that apes endowed with mirror neurons and capable of monitoring and imitating the expressions of others would not develop the same level of interest in sharing another's experience of an outside object that nine-month-old humans do. But they do not, nor do they develop it later on (Tomonaga et al. 2004:232–233; Tomonaga 2006; see also Matsuzawa 2007).

Humans' interest in what others think about something else starts to emerge before language. Six to nine months is also when humans start noting sounds others use to identify specific things and first learn to recognize common nouns (Bergelson and Swingley 2012). This convergence prompts us to ask if the human infant's enthusiasm for triadic interaction might be due to the need to get ready to acquire language. Or, did language evolve among our ancestors because early hominin infants were already interested in monitoring the mental states of others, already prone to "babble?"

Humans start to emit recognizable strings of phonemes around five to seven months of age. I agree with anthropologist Dean Falk (2004a, b) and others (Locke and Bogin 2006) that such babbling probably first emerged as a by-product of infants seeking to attract attention. We differ, however, in our reconstructions of the conditions under which babies did so. In line with this proposed "attention-getting" function, pygmy marmosets as well begin emitting similarly nonsensical but highly appealing vocal streams at just the age when infants in this cooperatively breeding species need to attract allomaternal attentions (cf. Elowson, Snowdon, and Lazaro-Perea 1998). As in marmosets, human "babbling" coincides with the developmental stage at which interactions with allomothers begins to be most relevant (Hrdy 2009:81ff.). In humans this is about six months when the milk teeth come in; infants are fed premasticated or soft foods via kiss-feeding and, among the Aka at least, there is a marked increase in "attachment behaviors" with allomothers (Meehan and Hawks 2013). Thus, I hypothesize that the babbling that eventually provided practice for language first emerged as a solution to a challenge other apes rarely confronted—the need to stay in touch without touch. Elicitation of attention and even, occasionally, tasty rewards would have provided contingent reinforcement (the most powerful kind) for continued elaboration and refinement of vocalizations (Goldstein, King, and West 2003).

Beyond maintaining contact and learning through such conditioning how best to appeal to others, infants relying on multiple caretakers would also benefit from being able to assess intentions. In this respect, humans are notably precocious. When Yale University cognitive psychologists showed six-month-old babies cartoons of a red ball struggling to roll up a hill, either helped by a yellow triangle nudging the ball upward or hindered by a blue square shoving it back down, babies subsequently looked longer and were more likely to reach out to the helpful symbol (Hamlin, Wynn, and Bloom 2007). As early as three months and certainly by six—still before language—infants preferred looking at the helpful character (Hamlin, Wynn, and Bloom 2010; Hamlin et al. 2011). They were, it seems, discerning who is potentially helpful and who is not.

By eight months of age, not only are babies making fairly sophisticated social judgments, but they begin to assign "reputations." By two, toddlers preferentially provide treats to third parties who behaved positively toward someone else who behaved prosocially, withholding treats from obstructive individuals (Hamlin et al. 2011). By ages three to five, children's own experiences of being shared with influence their decisions about how much to share with another depending on that individual's past contributions or "merit" (Kanngiesser and Warneken 2012).

In other words, as Henry Wellman and colleagues put it, "social cognition develops in infancy, revolving around understanding of human agents as intentional goal-directed beings and this understanding develops into preschool understanding of persons as mental beings" (2008:622). Those attending to intentional behavior early in development (at fourteen months) also test better at Theory of Mind tasks as preschoolers. Furthermore, as reported earlier, infants with more older sibs and caretakers manifest Theory of Mind at younger ages (Perner, Ruffman, and Leekam 1994; Ruffman et al. 1998).

Adult chimpanzees can also assess competence and, in laboratory tests, prefer reliable partners (Melis, Hare, and Tomasello 2006). They too respond more positively to "cooperative" versus obstructive others (Hamann, Warneken, and Tomasello 2011). But, to my knowledge, no one has tested infant chimpanzees or bonobos using the sort of experimental protocols Hamlin and colleagues used. Thus, we do not yet know at what age or under what circumstances chimpanzees develop these assessment capacities. Do chimpanzees register social reputations of others as early as human infants do? And do they do so in the wild, or only when socialized in human settings? Nor do we know if social selection operated on earlier humans so as to enhance such discriminative capacities. However, preliminary evidence from the Primate Research Institute in Japan suggests that the neural capacity to make such judgments may indeed develop earlier in humans than it did in our last common ancestor with other apes.

WAS THERE SELECTION FOR EARLIER DEVELOPMENT OF
OTHER-REGARDING CAPACITIES IN HOMININ INFANTS? EVIDENCE
FROM COMPARATIVE NEUROSCIENCE

No mammal takes longer than humans to grow up (Bogin 1997) as reflected in slower brain maturation and later eruption of deciduous (or "milk") teeth and molars (see Bernstein, chapter 5, this volume; Bogin, Bragg, and Kuzawa, chapter 3, this volume). Indeed, the human brain's metabolic demands do not actually peak until around age four or five, after a hunter-gatherer youngster would ordinarily be weaned (Kuzawa et al. 2014), further highlighting the importance of allomaternal provisioning for synapse formation. Whereas the larger part of adult-like myelination in chimpanzees occurs before birth, in humans neocortical myelination takes place throughout childhood, with prolonged neocortical maturation, and synaptic pruning in the prefrontal cortex still ongoing in the thirties (Miller et al. 2012:16482). These are early days in the comparative study of anthropoid brain development, a field outside of my own expertise. Yet it strikes me as noteworthy that, given this general scheme of prolonged development, parts of the brain devoted to interpersonal judgments develop earlier in humans than in chimpanzees.

I rely here on a single study still awaiting replication. Using magnetic resonance imaging, Sakai et al. (2010, 2011) compared trajectories of development for prefrontal white matter in twenty-eight human children between the ages of one month and 10.5 years, three mother-reared chimpanzees between six months and six years, and thirty-seven rhesus macaques between ten months and 5.3 years. Not surprisingly, absolute brain sizes were larger in humans than chimpanzees, and much larger than in macaques. Both human and nonhuman apes exhibit delayed maturation of the prefrontal cortex, the brain region mediating working memory, motivation, temporal awareness, decision making, self-awareness, and, in humans at least, language (Sakai et al. 2010). The right prefrontal cortex also seems peculiarly implicated in inequity aversion and in how subjects respond to "fair" versus "unfair" offers in experimental ultimatum games. When functioning of the right prefrontal cortex was temporarily disrupted, people tended to respond in a self-serving way regardless of whether the offer made to them was equitable or extremely inequitable (Knoch et al. 2006). Presumably this brain region also played a role when infants in Kiley Hamlin's experiments (described above) distinguished "helpful" from "obstructive" cartoon characters.

In the case of unusually clever and Machiavellian, tool-using apes—be they human or chimpanzee—extension of formative periods is assumed to be correlated with neuronal plasticity and enhanced mental flexibility owing to extra opportunities for exploration early in life (e.g., Gopnik 2012). According to this view, prolonged neural plasticity allows for learning through both trial-and-error and observation. Anthropologists have long believed that such extended periods of neuronal plasticity were essential for the evolution of characteristically human higher cognitive functions (e.g., Montagu 1955). Indeed a need for flexibility is often invoked to explain why human brains are so immature at birth and, in this respect "secondarily altricial" (e.g., Portmann 1962). Hence, Sakai and colleagues propose that "brain connection development, particularly in the prefrontal portion, may have been under intense selection pressure to remain immature, producing a brain that is more susceptible to acquiring chimpanzee- and human-specific social and technical skills based on early postnatal experience" (Sakai et al. 2011:5). But Sakai and colleagues also reported something else. When controlled for absolute size, white matter development in the frontal cortex develops more rapidly in humans than in chimpanzees. This faster growth trajectory seems paradoxical since humans absorb more cumulative culture than chimpanzees do. Following Montagu's logic they presumably would benefit from more prolonged neural plasticity and slower development in this respect.

The rapid trajectory of growth in the human prefrontal cortex begins around the second half of the first year of life (a phase marked by increased allomaternal interactions and provisioning among hunter-gatherers), then continues and levels off around age three (Sakai et al. 2011: fig. 3). This faster rate of prefrontal cortical development contrasts with development in other neural systems—for example, those controlling physical coordination and mobility. In contrast to those ungulates with highly precocial infants off and running within minutes of birth, all apes enter the world dependent on someone else for locomotion. Humans are born most helpless of all (see Konner, chapter 6, this volume). With even less muscle tone or coordination than a newborn chimpanzee, human neonates also do not have the option of catching hold of maternal body hair. Unless held up by their mother, the only way a human neonate could reach her nipples would be to inch along caterpillar-like, but only if she was horizontal.

By three to five months of age, chimpanzee infants grasp and mouth objects more competently than human babies can. Chimpanzees will be weaned later, but develop chewing capacities earlier with deciduous teeth erupting at least a year earlier than in children (Bernstein, chapter 5, this volume). Yet by one year of age, chimpanzees still do not perform as well as human infants at collaborative tasks, pointing out objects, turn-taking, or completing puzzles (e.g., Bard 2012:236). This is so even though humans and chimpanzees seem equivalently precocious in terms of manipulating objects, exhibiting great competence in object-object combinations and inserting a stick into a hole by one year of age.

In terms of overall motor maturation, nonhuman ape infants develop faster than their human counterparts, a difference apparent to anyone who has watched infant chimpanzees or bonobos crawl, climb, scamper, or swing circles around humans of comparable ages. In predator-free, captive environments where less-restrictive chimpanzee mothers allow baby chimpanzees to more fully demonstrate innate abilities, youngsters crawl by four months and walk bipedally by nine. By contrast, human babies are only beginning to crawl at that age and do not walk until the end of the first year. These different rates of development are reversed however when assessing or discriminating between others is required. The white matter in the human prefrontal cortex develops faster in humans than in chimpanzees.[2] Apparently, the brains of human infants are *only selectively altricial*. In respect to assessing others and distinguishing intentions, human infants appear surprisingly precocious. Why?

Apes in the line leading to *Homo sapiens* were walking bipedally by four million years ago, so perhaps the brain-body coordination needed for walking required earlier development in the prefrontal cortex. But it takes many months before the irregular stepping motions of a baby become anything like balanced upright walking. Recent analyses reveal that the neural components at work this early are little different from those in other mammals. What distinguishes human bipedality are extra components emerging later in the course of development (Dominici et al. 2011; Grilner 2011)—perhaps only emerging "as needed" when needed.

This speculation brings me to the explanation I favor, that being able to make interpersonal assessments emerges so early because such capacities helped hominin infants judiciously and effectively elicit maternal and allo-maternal care. They developed earlier in hominins than physical coordination or other, arguably useful, abilities because precociality in this interpersonal realm was advantageous. This hypothesis is not mutually exclusive with more conventional "head start" explanations by which infants begin early to build the neural scaffolding and infrastructure for later cognitive development (Leigh 2004:162, cited in Falk et al. 2012) or begin to accumulate experiences acquired through observation, social trial and error, or play that will eventually be useful for negotiating the social and technical complexities of a successful human life (Gopnik 2012).

Various counterarguments involve metabolic costs inherent in building neural connections as well as the many specialized capacities that do not develop until needed (and that might even be disadvantageous if they emerged too early). But glossing over these and taking the "early start" logic at face value, rapid development of prefrontal connections during infancy might facilitate complex social interactions, providing opportunities for such interactions to continue shaping neuronal connectivity as experience-dependent knowledge and skills build up over time (as in Sakai et al. 2011; see also Luby et al. 2012). An early start might build necessary scaffolding essential for language acquisition or other social competencies that evolved later for reasons outside of my scope here. What I want to emphasize here is the sequence. Neither "early start" explanations nor common assumptions about the need for prolonged childhoods in order for humans to fill unusually large, anatomically modern 1,350 cc brains with "social capital" needed for a successful life (Kaplan et al. 2000) are mutually exclusive with the proposal that infants with multiple providers took longer to grow up. All three may have played roles in shaping modern humans. What I hypothesize here, though, is that alloparental care, food sharing, and, with it, youngsters beginning to take longer to grow up, characterized our ancestors prior to the emergence of anatomically modern humans.

Rather than long childhoods evolving to accommodate growing big brains, prolonged dependence emerged as a corollary of cooperative breeding. But with alloparental care came more rapid postnatal development of the frontal cortex and areas of the brain that help infants monitor and assess commitment levels and intentions of others as well as adjust their facial expressions, vocalizations, hand movements, and other actions in ways that engaged and appealed to them. These little apes were already emotionally more similar to modern humans. Shared provisioning permitted the evolution of anatomically modern brains in response to selection pressures favoring them, while "emotional modernity" preadapted these apes to eventually evolve (through processes and feedback loops described elsewhere by Boehm, Flinn and Alexander, Bowles, Tomasello, Knight, and many others) such behaviorally modern human capacities as language, cumulative culture, or consciences peculiarly attuned to the evaluation of others.

My working assumption is that the duration of childhood in *Homo erectus* by 1.8 million years ago fell someplace in between the prolonged childhoods typical of modern humans and the much shorter ones typical of both the genus *Pan* and their anatomically similar australopithecine cousins. There are fascinating hints in the fossil record that larger babies (e.g., DeSilva 2011) and more rapid postnatal expansion of the prefrontal cortex (e.g., Falk et al. 2012; Tague 2012) might go back in the hominin lineage even further than I conservatively postulated in *Mothers and Others*. Either way, it seems unlikely that mothers would have been selected to produce such costly, slow-maturing young without reasonable prospects of assistance. The big question relevant to the evolution of childhood, just when hominins began to be characterized by prolonged nutritional dependence and longer postreproductive life spans, continues to be debated (summarized by Voland, Chasiotis, and Schiefenhövel 2005a: table 1.1).

Evolving "Emotionally Modern" Underpinnings for Cooperation: Recap and Conclusions

As a branch of tool-using, bipedal apes equipped with "Machiavellian" social intelligence traversed the ecologically unstable savanna-woodlands of Plio-Pleistocene Africa, selection favored those with broader diets (including meat and tubers) provided by an array of provisioners. Cooperative breeding is especially likely to evolve in animals living in habitats with unpredictable rainfall and abrupt swings in available resources. Meanwhile, food delivered to immatures produced situations conducive to more generalized (adult-to-adult) food sharing. Such sharing increased chances of survival in famine times while permitting shorter intervals between births when conditions improved, enabling at least some populations to bounce back after crashes.

Cooperative breeding was accompanied by changes in the life history and psychology of all parties concerned: mothers, fathers, alloparents, and especially immatures upon whom selection impacted most immediately and heavily. I hypothesize that, to survive, infants became connoisseurs not only of mothers but of others as well. This transformation was mediated via development's role in the production of selectable variation (West-Eberhard 2003). Over generations, immatures buffered from acquiring and processing their own food could afford to delay costly adult size and dentition as well as bigger brains (see Bogin, Bragg, and Kuzawa, chapter 3, this volume; Bernstein, chapter 5, this volume). But the need to solicit care required speeding up and refining development of other capacities important for perspective-taking, understanding how to appeal to others and assess their intentions—critical preadaptations for the role reputations would increasingly play in human social organization.

In the absence of direct evidence, I attempted to "test" underlying assumptions of this mothers-plus-others model (figure 2.3) by reviewing evidence for how the best available proxies we have for humankind's last common ancestor with other apes (chimpanzees and modern human infants) respond to different rearing conditions. Findings from these "as if" experiments reveal that infants spending time off mothers, interacting with and attended to by multiple caretakers, develop in the predicted directions. They pay more attention to faces and expressions of potential caretakers, strive to attract their attention and to appeal to them, attend better to their communicative cues and goals, and are more likely to engage in targeted helping. Differences between human and chimpanzee infants in brain development during the first years of life appear consistent with the mosaic pattern of physically altricial/emotionally precocial development hypothesized here.

I am not proposing that humans are cooperative because their ancestors were "cooperative breeders." Rather I believe that more other-regarding (and in this sense "emotionally modern") youngsters were predictable corollaries of this mode of child-rearing and as a byproduct of it, preadapted apes in the hominin line for greater social coordination. At the same time, food sharing would have magnified opportunities for already highly social apes to interact with the same individuals over time, benefiting from exchanges and providing fertile ground for selection to specifically favor cooperative responses (e.g., Axelrod and Hamilton 1981; Fehr and Fischbacher 2003; Rand, Greene, and Nowak 2012).

Of course, many other factors and processes were simultaneously at work. My point is that no foresight on Mother Nature's part would have been required to favor the evolution of cooperative breeding in a highly social species struggling to rear altricial young in the face of difficult-to-extract and unpredictable resources. Thus, there is no need to invoke "exceptional" processes to account for the evolution of other-regarding capacities that initially emerged as predictable corollaries of immatures relying on mothers-plus-others. It was because predictable developmental and evolutionary processes impacted what was already a cognitively sophisticated, relatively large-brained ape that foundations were laid for the eventual emergence of such uniquely human attributes as language, conscience-based moral systems, and multifaceted collaborations.

Acknowledgments

This chapter benefited from discussions over many years with Kristen Hawkes, Steve Emlen, Mel Konner, J. Anderson Thomson, and Polly Wiessner, from comments and corrections provided by Kim Bard, Judith Burkart, and Mary Jane West-Eberhard, and from the talented assistance of Lore M. Ruttan and June-el Piper. Additional thanks are due to participants at both the 2012 SAR workshop on the Evolution of Childhood and the 2010 University of California, San Diego Center for Academic Research and Training in Anthropogeny (CARTA) Symposium on the Evolution of Altruism.

Notes

1. Note that, depending on ecological and customary circumstances (usually having to do with inheritance of property), child survival can also be inversely correlated with the presence of allomothers, including grandmothers (e.g., Voland and Beise 2005; Sear 2008 for the Malawi; Strassmann and Garrard 2011). However, such exceptions have never been reported among band-level hunter-gatherers and thus fall outside of the scope of this chapter.

2. Sakai's sample size was small, but it is tantalizing that Ayumu, the chimpanzee co-reared by his mother and human others, was also the chimpanzee exhibiting both unusually well-developed capacities for perspective-taking in targeted help experiments (described above) and the fastest trajectory of prefrontal white-matter development of the three chimpanzees scanned (Sakai 2011: fig. 2.2).

CHAPTER THREE

Childhood, Biocultural Reproduction, and Human Lifetime Reproductive Effort

BARRY BOGIN, JARED BRAGG, AND CHRISTOPHER KUZAWA

Introduction

Life-history theory is a branch of evolutionary biology that studies the evolution of life cycles, which are a product of the organism's lifetime expenditures on growth, reproduction, and survivorship. A species' life-history strategy is a set of biological and behavioral traits that include features such as body size, growth rate, number of offspring, intensity of investment in each offspring, and the pace of senescence. These traits are not conscious strategies, but instead may be understood as evolutionarily derived adaptations; evolved through natural selection because they increase reproductive fitness. Life-history traits are recognized as evolving via a series of trade-offs in which expenditures on one trait are matched by reduced expenditures elsewhere. The central question of this chapter is: How has human childhood contributed to the trade-offs that help define the human species, and how does this help us understand other features of our life history, including our unique pattern of reproduction and unusually long life span?

Does Childhood Exist?

We see "children" everywhere. We speak, read, and write about "the child" relentlessly, or as Lancy (2008) phrases it, "our society is a neontocracy where kids rule" (373). We are so preoccupied with children and their safekeeping that we are often too generous in our conceptualizations and definitions of what we mean by "the child," or more precisely what we mean by "childhood." Listed in table 3.1 are some designations found in an Internet search for "definitions of childhood." Some are based on chronological age ranges varying from birth to twenty-one years, birth to eighteen years, or birth to twelve years. Another definition brackets childhood between birth and puberty. This last definition seems to indicate the importance of biological time, as the age at puberty depends on the pace of physiological maturation more than chronological time. Finally, the definition from a sociology textbook divorces the definition of childhood from both chronology and biology, describing childhood as "attitudes, beliefs, and values of particular societies," which themselves may vary between past, present, and future epochs.

The view that childhood is no more than a set of beliefs and values is normative in much scholarship on children from sociology, social anthropology, history, and related fields in the humanities. The origins of this position may be traced to the historian Philippe Ariès who wrote in his book *Centuries of Childhood*, "In Medieval society the idea of childhood did not exist" (1962:125). By "childhood" Ariès meant a period of life during which youngsters were considered to be different from adults in their basic social, emotional, and psychological characteristics. Ariès proposed that prior to the nineteenth century in Europe, young people were not accorded any special status of this type. In support of his position Ariès claimed that in medieval Europe, by seven years of age youngsters were accorded great freedom by being forced to enter the work and social world of adults.

Ariès infused social and historical research with the attitude that "the child" is a social construct and without any biological characteristics relevant for study. This attitude may be seen in the work of media and social critic Neil Postman. Twenty years after Ariès's *Centuries of Childhood*, Postman wrote, "Children are the living messages we send to a time we will not see" (1982:1). This sentence, which opens Postman's book *The Disappearance of Childhood*, seems to be a poetic and sentimental encapsulation of the biological and cultural nature of childhood. Yet two sentences later, Postman writes this Ariès-inspired sentence: "But it is quite possible for a culture to exist without a social idea of children. Unlike infancy, childhood is a social artifact, not a biological category. Our genes contain no clear instruction about who is and who is not a child . . . [and] . . . there is ample evidence that children have existed for less than four hundred years" (1982:1).

Some twenty-six years later, social anthropologist Heather Montgomery reiterated a biologically agnostic view of children when she wrote:

Biology is not particularly helpful either, although there are obvious

Table 3.1. Definitions of Childhood

Definition	Source
Childhood is the time for children to be in school and at play, to grow strong and confident with the love and encouragement of their family and an extended community of caring adults. It is a precious time in which children should live free from fear, safe from violence, and protected from abuse and exploitation. As such, childhood means much more than just the space between birth and the attainment of adulthood. It refers to the state and condition of a child's life, to the quality of those years.	UNICEF (2005) Childhood Defined, http://www.unicef.org/sowc05/english/childhooddefined.html
The term "child" means an unmarried person under twenty-one years of age.	United States Code, 2006, https://www.law.cornell.edu/uscode/text/8/1101
Biologically, a child (plural: children) is generally a human between the stages of birth and puberty. Some vernacular definitions of a child include the fetus, as being an unborn child. The legal definition of "child" generally refers to a minor, otherwise known as a person younger than the age of majority. "Child" may also describe a relationship with a parent (such as sons and daughters of any age) or, metaphorically, an authority figure, or signify group membership in a clan, tribe, or religion; it can also signify being strongly affected by a specific time, place, or circumstance, as in "a child of nature" or "a child of the Sixties."	Wikipedia, Child, http://en.wikipedia.org/wiki/Child
England, Wales, Northern Ireland and Scotland each have their own guidance setting out the duties and responsibilities of organizations to keep children safe, but they agree that *a child is anyone who has not yet reached their 18th birthday.*	National Society for the Prevention of Cruelty to Children, http://www.nspcc.org.uk/Inform/research/questions/definition_of_a_child_wda59396.html

Table 3.1 (*continued*)

Childhood is not simply a biological stage of development. Rather it is a social category that emerges from the attitudes, beliefs, and values of particular societies at particular points in time, subject to changing definitions and expectations.	David Newman, Sociology: Exploring the Architecture of Everyday Life, Fourth Edition, http://www.sagepub.com/newman4study/resources/childhood.htm
Usually the period between birth and 12 years of age.	Children Webmag, http://www.childrenwebmag.com/articles/child-care-articles/what-is-childhood-and-who-created-it
The time during which one is a child, from between infancy and puberty.	Childhood, http://en.wiktionary.org/wiki/childhood

Note: All definitions are quoted verbatim from the source.

markers such as conception, birth or first menstruation. As an anthropologist, however, I am less interested in chronological or biological markers than in the social significance given to them. . . . One of the most important conclusions for any anthropologist studying childhood is that there is no universal child and that the concept of the child is one that must be defined internally and in its own context. [2008:2–3]

As anthropologists, the authors of this chapter appreciate and are sympathetic to the notion that categories such as age classes and the names that we ascribe to these categories are often fluid across place and time, and are constituted out of an array of varying local economic, social, and historical factors. As evolutionary biologists, however, we do find some analytical value in bracketing "childhood" as a distinct stage of the human life cycle with its own biological, behavioral, and cognitive characteristics.

We are hardly the first scholars to question the value of a purely sociological view of childhood. Zuckerman, for example, critiques Ariès's notion that childhood was invented by writing that Ariès "conjured a world in which, until the 16th century, children were 'little adults'. . . . They heard the same jokes, played the same games, wore the same clothes, and, so far as they were physically able, did the same work as their parents" (2009:60). "Conjured" is the operant word, as the bulk of serious scholarship by historians, anthropologists, and medical/public health researchers since publication of *Centuries of Childhood* rejects Ariès's central idea. Montgomery (2008), quoted above as diminishing biology, similarly dismisses Ariès's main point. In her careful review of the ethnographic, social, and psychological literature relating to children, Montgomery finds definitions of "the child" or childhood in all human cultures, both historical and contemporary. For Montgomery, these definitions are socially based and completely labile to symbolic meaning within a given human culture.

Anthropologists Robert LeVine (2009) and David Lancy (2008; chapter 8, this volume; Lancy and Grove 2011) also found obvious and well-characterized definitions of "the child" and childhood in all of the human cultures they surveyed including both historical and contemporary cultures. This was especially so in medieval Europe where "detailed historical research into Ariès' claim in France, England, and Germany . . . has shown that it does not stand up to close examination" (LeVine 2009:139).

This scholarship from historians and cultural anthropologists was focused on the social history of childhood as a stage of human development and was largely limited to written records. Archaeological and paleontological research finds that children and childhood have a deeper history than the 5,000 or so years of writing (Bogin 1999b; J. Thompson and Nelson 2011, chapter 4, this volume). Childhood is part of human biology, and is at least as old as the origin of the species *Homo sapiens* (T. Smith et al. 2007a). There is evidence that the childhood stage may predate the evolution of *Homo sapiens*, perhaps being present in fossils assigned to *H. antecessor* dated between 800,000 and 960,000 years ago (Bermúdez de Castro et al. 2010), and perhaps as early as two million years ago in fossils assigned to *H. habilis* (reviewed in Bogin and Smith 2012; but also see T. Smith et al. 2007a).

Childhood: A Biocultural Definition

Postman was correct about children traveling "to a time we will not see." Our children are biocultural packages of simultaneously interacting genetic, epigenetic, metabolic, socioeconomic, political, emotional, and ideological material that we and previous generations influence, but whose futures we ultimately do not control. The present authors view children, and all other people, as biocultural creatures. Humans are simultaneously and inextricably the product of material, organic, physiological, social, technological, and ideological interactions. As biological anthropologists, we have an abiding interest in the growth, development, nutritional status, health, and well-being of young people including children. Each of the present authors conducts research with living children, juveniles, and adolescents. We base our research on the realization that understanding contemporary young people requires an appreciation of intergenerational effects. These effects include not only the degree of health and well-being of their parents and grandparents, but also the more deeply rooted evolutionary foundations of humanity. Several books, chapters, and refereed articles present our definitions of human life-history stages (Bogin 1997, 1999a, 1999b, 2011; Kuzawa and Bragg 2012). Here, we provide the essence of these definitions and outline some of the reasons that have been proposed to explain the evolution of human childhood.

Human ontogeny is characterized by changes in both the distance (amount) and the velocity (rate) of physical growth and other discernible developmental changes in the biological and behavioral capacities of individuals (figure 3.1; readers may refer to this figure for all references to rates of growth elsewhere in this chapter.) A list of the major stages of human life history is given in table 3.2. The age brackets for these life-history stages are approximate and correspond with changes in rate of growth as shown in figure 3.1 and other biological developments listed in table 3.2. The biological changes listed in table 3.2 for growth rates, dental development, brain growth, and reproductive development reflect age-specific changes in the allocation of limited resources to growth (increase in cell number or size/mass), maintenance (e.g., fighting infection, DNA/cellular repair, increasing life span), physical activity (work/play), or reproduction (gonadal maturation, gametogenesis, prenatal and postnatal feeding and care). The study of life-history evolution attempts to understand the relationship between various life cycle patterns and their consequences for reproductive success. There are many definitions of reproductive success. The one we use here is the number of offspring an individual has that survive to adulthood and reproduce.

From the perspective of life-history theory, which seeks to characterize changes in vital rates (growth, reproduction, and mortality) over the life course, it is possible to identify four biologically defined stages of human life

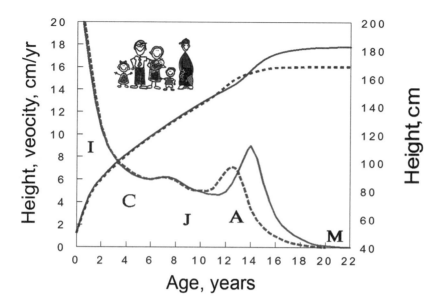

Figure 3.1. Distance and velocity curves of growth for healthy, well-nourished human beings. Boys, solid line; girls, dashed line. These are modal curves based on height data for Western Europe and North America populations. The stages of postnatal growth are abbreviated as follows: I, infancy; C, childhood; J, juvenile; A, adolescence; M, mature adult. Weaning, the cessation of breastfeeding, takes place at a median age between 30–36 months in traditional human societies, at approximately the age of the infant-to-childhood transition. The distance curve (right Y-axis) indicates the amount of height achieved at a given age. The velocity curve (left Y-axis) indicates the rate of growth at a given age. Growth velocity during infancy is rapid with a steep deceleration. Childhood growth is relatively constant at about 6 cm per year. Growth rate slows during the juvenile stage and then accelerates during the first phase of adolescence—the adolescent growth spurt. Growth rates decline during the second phase until all growth in height stops at the onset of the adult stage. The image of the "family" is not meant to promote any particular type of family as desirable or normal, rather the cartoon figures illustrate the stages of human life history between birth and adulthood (original figure, modified from Bogin, 1999a).

Table 3.2. Stages in the Human Life Cycle

Stage	Duration or Age at Onset	Events
First trimester of pregnancy	Fertilization to week 12	Embryogenesis
Second trimester of pregnancy	Months 4 to 6	Rapid growth in length
Third trimester of pregnancy	Month 7 to birth	Rapid growth in weight and organ maturation
Neonatal period	Birth to 28 days	Extrauterine adaptation, most rapid rate of postnatal growth and maturation
Infancy	Month 2 to end of lactation (usually by 36 months)	Rapid growth velocity with steep deceleration in velocity with time, feeding by lactation, deciduous tooth eruption, many developmental milestones in physiology, behavior and cognition
Childhood	3 to 6.9 years	Moderate growth rate, dependency for feeding, mid-growth spurt, eruption of first permanent molar and incisor, cessation of brain growth by end of stage
Juvenile	7 to 10 (girls) or 12 (boys) years	Slower growth rate, capable of self-feeding, cognitive transition leading to learning of economic and social skills
Puberty	Brain: onset between 9 to 10 years; Body, onset: girls, 10 years, boys 12 years	In the brain, puberty is an event of short duration (days or a few weeks) that reactivates the hypothalamic GnRH pulse generator leading to a massive increase in sex hormone secretion; on the body, puberty is noted by a darkening and increased-density pubic hair

Stage	Duration or Age at Onset	Events
Adolescence	The 5 to 8 years following onset of puberty	Adolescent growth spurt in height and weight, permanent tooth eruption virtually complete, development of secondary sexual characteristics; sociosexual maturation, intensification of interest and practice in adult social, economic, and sexual activities
Prime and transition	18–20 years for women to 45 years (end of childbearing) and from age 21–25 years for men to about age 50 years	Commences with completion of skeletal growth; homeostasis in physiology, behavior, and cognition; menopause for women by age 50
Post-reproductive or "Grandmotherhood"	10 to 20 years following menopause	Culturally defined stage of women's life often characterized by investments of time and energy in caring for grandchildren
Old age and senescence	From end of childbearing years to death	Decline in the function and repair ability of many body tissues or systems
Death		

Source: Modified from Bogin 1999a.

history between birth and maturity. These stages have been referred to as *infancy, childhood, juvenile,* and *adolescence*. Growth rate during infancy is rapid, as is the rate at which growth decelerates (figure 3.1). Infancy in humans is comparable in many respects to infancy in other mammalian species because all infant mammals are fed by maternal lactation. For most mammals, including primates, infancy is also the life-history stage during which deciduous teeth erupt; infancy and lactation tend to end with eruption of the first permanent teeth, usually the molars. In humans, by contrast, there is an interval of about three years between weaning (cessation of nursing), which takes place at a median age of thirty to thirty-six months in preindustrial societies, and eruption of the first permanent molars at about six years of age. This interval is the childhood stage of life history. The biological constraints of childhood—including an immature dentition, small digestive system, and a calorie-demanding brain that is both relatively large and growing rapidly—necessitate care and feeding from older individuals. We discuss the biocultural nature of this care and feeding in more detail below.

The rate of body growth during childhood proceeds at a steady rate of five to six centimeters per year for healthy, well-nourished children. The pattern of velocity growth from birth to adulthood is similar in all human populations, but growth rates and total height gain vary in relation to health and nutritional status. Some studies find that up to two-thirds of children experience a transient and small acceleration, or spurt, in growth rate as they transition into the juvenile stage. The cause of this so-called mid-childhood growth spurt is not known (B. Campbell 2011b; Bernstein, chapter 5, this volume). It has recently been shown that brain metabolism and the rate of body weight gain from infancy until puberty are strongly inversely related in humans, supporting the idea that the unusually slow pace of human childhood growth reflects an energetic trade-off with costly brain development (Kuzawa et al. 2014).

Juvenile mammals are sexually immature but, unlike human children, are physically and mentally capable of providing for much of their own care. In many human societies, juveniles perform important work, including food production (see Crittenden, chapter 7, this volume) and childcare (i.e., "babysitting"). Juvenile growth rates decline until puberty, an important transitional event in life-history development. From a biological perspective, puberty is a short-term physiological event, taking place over a few weeks, whereby the central nervous system reinitiates positive feedback within the hypothalamic-pituitary-gonadal axis, increasing the levels of sex steroid hormones in the circulatory system, which is suppressed by negative feedback from about age two years. Puberty reestablishes positive feedback, promoting reproductive maturation. In humans, puberty normally occurs during the transition from the juvenile to the adolescent stage of the life cycle (approximately age nine to ten years). Some of the sex hormones responsible for sexual maturation, such as estradiol and testosterone, also cause the adolescent growth spurt in stature and other skeletal dimensions. Sufficient levels of sex hormones may also assist with the eruption of the second permanent molar at about twelve years of age. Adolescence ends with the completion of skeletal growth, at about eighteen to nineteen years for girls and twenty to twenty-two years for boys, and the eruption of the third permanent molar, if it is present. After these events, adulthood—the reproductive stage of life history—begins. In addition to changes in the rate of skeletal growth and tooth eruption, significant changes in motor control, cognitive function, and emotions are also associated with infancy, childhood, juvenile, and adolescent development (Bogin 1999b; Konner 2010, chapter 6, this volume).

The Origins of Childhood

The biological origins of human childhood have fascinated scholars from many disciplines, but there is contention regarding childhood's evolutionary emergence. Some argue that evolutionary evidence and the ontogenetic characteristics of human life history favor the hypothesis that childhood evolved as a novel developmental stage in the life history of the hominins, perhaps as early as two million years ago during the time of *Homo habilis* (Bogin 1999a, b; Bogin and Smith 2012; Thompson and Nelson, chapter 4, this volume). Others have suggested that childhood is merely an extension of life-history stages found in other primates (e.g., Bernstein, chapter 5, this volume; B. Campbell 2011b). An analogy in support of childhood as a novel and emergent feature of the human life history is the evolution of the elephant's trunk. The trunk evolved from the mammalian nose and upper lip, but at some point in its history became far more than just these. The elephant trunk has tactile, feeding, grooming, and social functions (see video clip at http://www.bbc.co.uk/education/clips/zf7w2hv). In a similar vein, human childhood evolved by altering the timing of the transition from infancy to the juvenile stage. This entailed changes in feeding (especially earlier weaning), motor and cognitive abilities, emotional aptitudes, and social relationships (see in this volume Crittenden, chapter 7; Hrdy, chapter 2; Konner, chapter 6; Meehan, Helfrecht, and Malcom, chapter 9; Sellen, chapter 10). The childhood stage likely emerged in a mosaic fashion as each of these changes occurred. Although it is unknown when all of these changes were in place, current dental evidence indicates that key features of childhood were likely in place by about 160,000 BP in *Homo sapiens* (T. Smith et al. 2007a).

Childhood and Reproductive Fitness

One argument in favor of the idea that childhood comprises a novel life-history stage stems from the commonly invoked principle that Darwinian processes of natural selection will only tend to favor the evolution of complex novelties that increase genetic fitness via reproductive success, such as increases in adult fertility or the survivorship of offspring prior to their own reproductive age. Following from this principle, many researchers now accept that the characteristics of human childhood show evidence of having been shaped as a reproductive adaptation. Childhood may be viewed as critical to a human reproductive strategy that increases genetic fitness by enabling women to give birth to new offspring while allowing existing dependent offspring to receive care and feeding from close kin and other members of the social group.

Human women living in a range of subsistence ecologies tend to provide the majority of care to infants for at least three years, but many other individuals are also involved in the care, provisioning, and social life of infants. Indeed, by the stage and age at which human mothers tend to wean their infants (the onset of "childhood," about age three), a greater percentage of the care of offspring tends to be provided by other family members including fathers, older siblings, aunts, and grandmothers (Gettler et al. 2011; Hawkes et al. 1998; Hrdy 1999a; Hurtado et al. 1992; K. Kramer 2005a; Meehan, Helfrecht, and Malcom, chapter 9, this volume). Nonfamily members may also provide care and food to children. Indeed, all human social groups include a variety of childcare and feeding arrangements that make use of both biological kin and socially defined relationships such as in-laws by marriage, fictive kin, servants, friends, or employees paid in cash or kind. With these sources of childcare assistance, human women may reproduce every two to three years without sacrificing their own health or the health of their current offspring.

COOPERATIVE BREEDING AND HUMAN BIOCULTURAL REPRODUCTION

The type of highly social childcare practiced in human social groups has been equated with cooperative breeding (Burkhart, Hrdy, and Van Schaik 2009; Emlen 1995; Hill and Hurtado, 2009; Hill, Barton, and Hurtado, 2009; Hrdy 1999a, 2009, chapter 2, this volume; Meehan, Helfrecht, and Malcom, chapter 9, this volume). To be "cooperative" in breeding is often defined to mean that individuals of a species live in groups and that members of the group help to feed, care for, or protect offspring that they did not bear. Individuals providing these services are called alloparents. Another commonly cited criterion is that the provisioning, care, and protection that alloparents provide must come at some cost to the alloparents. That cost may be measured in terms of assisting others to gain access to food or in terms of reducing the alloparents' opportunities to reproduce (Hurtado et al. 1992). The chapter by Hrdy in this volume provides examples of these costs for marmosets and tamarins, the only species of cooperative breeding nonhuman primates. Meehan, Helfrecht, and Malcom's chapter in this volume provides some costs of alloparenting for the Aka, a Central African foraging society. Meehan, Quinlan, and Malcom (2013) found that when Aka grandmothers help with infant care, the energy expenditure of the mother decreases. In contrast, when the infant's father or older sibling helps with care, the mother's energy expenditure increases. Without accounting for such costs, behaviors that might appear alloparental may instead be selfish or aggressive, increasing the risks of injury or death for the offspring or others (Digby, Ferrari, and Saltzman 2007; Enstam, Isbell, and de Maar 2002; Maestripieri and Carroll 2000; MacKinnon 2007).

Cooperative breeding and alloparenting take place within social groups that are often called families. Emlen established the "evolutionary framework for viewing the formation, the stability, the organizational structure, and the social dynamics of biological families" (1995:8092). Emlen restricted his analysis to only animal "biological families," which he defined as "those cases where offspring also continue to interact regularly, into adulthood, with their parents" (8092–8093). Emlen included humans in his analysis and defined human families as "kin groups through which descent lines are traced and which consist, at a minimum, of parent(s) and unmarried offspring" (8092). By the words "kin," "parent," and "offspring," Emlen was defining genetically related individuals. We show later in this chapter that a genetic definition of this type for human families is incomplete as it does not take into account the many nongenetically based kinship and social relationships that typify human biocultural families. First, we set the stage for this discussion by reviewing recent research in nonhuman animal cooperative breeding.

In principle, cooperative breeding behavior has fitness value, because the alloparental care and provisioning provided by others allows mothers to breed at a faster pace without sacrificing the survival of current offspring. Despite these benefits, cooperative breeding is relatively rare (Hrdy 2009; Clutton-Brock 2002). In their systematic review[1] of the literature on breeding systems in mammals, Lukas and Clutton-Brock (2012) make a distinction between cooperative breeders, communal breeders, and social breeders. The new definitions proposed by Lukas and Clutton-Brock supersede those employed by Emlen (1995) and, generally, by most authors writing about human cooperation in reproduction. As defined by Lukas and Clutton-Brock (2012), cooperatively breeding species are those in which most of the females do not breed regularly and instead provide alloparental care to the offspring of breeding females. In contrast, communal breeders are species in which "most adult females breed regularly and share care such as allonursing or feeding offspring" (2151). Finally, social breeders are species in which the females live in groups and virtually all breed, but rarely, if ever provide allomaternal care to others. Lukas and Clutton-Brock conclude that only 1.8 percent of mammal species, or thirty-four of the 1,874 species listed in *Walker's Mammals of the World* (Nowak 1999), meet their proposed conservative definition of cooperative breeding.

Lukas and Clutton-Brock (2012) further define key attributes of a cooperatively breeding species and interested readers may consult that article. By their criteria, the nonbreeding helpers in cooperative breeding social groups are close genetic relatives of the mother or the father. By assisting the mother in caring for her offspring, the helpers increase their own inclusive fitness, meaning that they help to ensure that their genetic kin survive to reproductive age. Most analyses of cooperative breeding emphasize that this type of social system can only evolve if it increases the inclusive fitness of the participants; otherwise, there is no advantage to the nonbreeders. Inclusive fitness is usually measured by Hamilton's Rule (W. Hamilton 1964), which may be expressed as $C < rB$, where C is the cost in fitness to the actor, r is the genetic relatedness between the actor and the recipient, and B is the fitness benefit to the recipient. While most studies focus on r, Lukas and Clutton-Brock suggest that it may be equally important to focus on C and B. Reproduction in unpredictable environments or in environments with scarce resources increases the benefits of cooperation or reduces the costs, perhaps enough to reduce the need for high r (Faulkes and Bennett 2007; Hamilton et al. 2009; Jetz and Rubenstein 2011; Rubenstein and Lovette 2007).

According to Lukas and Clutton-Brock's definition, nine species of non-human primates, all New World Callitrichidae (marmosets and tamarins) meet the criteria for cooperative breeding. They identified four species of primates as communal breeders: Goeldi's monkey (*Callimico goeldii)*, the Weeper capuchin (*Cebus olivaceus*), the lesser mouse lemur (*Microcebus murinus*), and the black-and-white ruffed lemur (*Varecia variegata*). The majority of the other nonhuman primate species such as ring-tailed lemurs, rhesus monkeys, spider monkeys, baboons, chimpanzees, gorillas, and bonobos are classified as social breeders.

Human Reproduction Compared to Cooperative Breeding

In light of these considerations, how might the breeding system of humans best be described? The authors of other chapters in this volume describe humans as cooperative breeders (Hrdy, chapter 2; Konner, chapter 6; Meehan, Helfrecht, and Malcom, chapter 9; Sellen, chapter 10). Do humans cooperate in the same way as other mammals, birds, and insects? Human reproduction arguably meets many of the criteria of Lukas and Clutton-Brock's (2012) definition of communal breeding, as most adult women breed regularly and also alloparent by feeding, carrying, and protecting others' offspring. However, Lukas and Clutton-Brock do not define *Homo sapiens* as a cooperative or communal breeder in their data lists (2012: supplementary table 2), citing three reasons for their rationale. First, they define near-exclusive monogamy as a requirement for both the evolution of cooperative breeding and its stability over many generations. This definition is based on the hypothesis that exclusive, lifetime monogamy and mating fidelity assure high genetic relatedness between the offspring of the mating pair and both of their parents. High genetic relatedness promotes allomaternal care via "inclusive fitness" (see Nonacs 2011 for an alternative hypotheses). Living humans certainly do not conform to near-exclusive monogamy and several lines of evidence (e.g., sexual dimorphism in height, testis size) indicate that human ancestors were not monogamous (Kramer and Russell 2014). Second, cooperative breeding tends to be restricted to lineages with multiple births (litters). Twins and triplets are the norm for cooperative breeding nonhuman primates (the marmosets and tamarins), but singleton births are the rule for the human species. Third, cooperative breeders tend to give birth to altricial infants. Human infants are altricial insofar as they need to be fed by others and are incapable of effective locomotion. Other human infant traits, however, are precocial, such as their relatively large brains, visual acuity, ability to smile at about six weeks after birth, and ability to engage in social relationships with older individuals (Hrdy 2009, chapter 2, this volume). Overall, based upon their systematic review, Lukas and Clutton-Brock conclude that humans do not meet their conservative definition of cooperative breeding.

Based on the definitions and discussion of Lukas and Clutton-Brock we may consider ways in which humans differ from most communal breeders. Communal breeding mammal species commonly evolve from polygynous ancestors (one male mates with several females) or polygynandrous ancestors (two or more males mate with two or more females). The majority of human societies practice polygynandrous mating, in which men and women may have multiple mating relationships, either sequentially or simultaneously. Polygynandrous mating is the norm for chimpanzees and bonobos and, as such, it is possible that it was also the mating system practiced by the last common ancestor (LCA) to African apes and humans. According to the definitions of Lukas and Clutton-Brock, the living African apes are social breeders, but none is a cooperative or communal breeder. It is vitally important to note here that human mating takes place within and outside of marriage, which we discuss in greater detail below. If we accept the definitions of Lukas and Clutton-Brock, then human behaviors that conform to cooperative or communal breeding are, like marriage, also derived traits since the LCA. Lukas and Clutton-Brock (2012) propose that the human similarities to cooperative and communal breeding evolved along a different pathway than did cooperative breeding in nonhuman species. The pathway for the nonhuman species evolved as cooperation in breeding based on genetic relatedness and inclusive fitness. The pathway for human ancestors began with the evolution of larger brains and greater cognitive abilities, including advanced social behaviors and more complex forms of communication. These allowed for greater prosocial behavior in human groups, including the shared care of each other's offspring. In the present chapter, we amass evidence that the human alloparental shared care of offspring may take place between genetically close or distantly related individuals, as well as genetically unrelated people. Our point is that the human pathway toward biocultural reproduction was not dependent on inclusive fitness.

While humans may not correspond closely to examples of cooperative breeding in other mammals and primates, it has been argued that they do share important similarities with the breeding systems in some insect societies. In a recent review, Crespi (2014) points to broad parallels between human cooperation and that of some insect societies, and goes so far as to characterize humans as "Insectan Apes." He notes that, like humans, social insects band into groups, pool resources such as food, and exhibit extensive allomaternal care in raising young. At the same time, Crespi also notes a fundamental difference between human cooperative care and that present in social insects: unlike insect societies with cooperative care, in which individuals commit to a particular reproductive or nonreproductive caste for life, few humans have no opportunities to reproduce. Humans divide labor not only by gender, but also by age class, and as such an individual's role as a net producer or dependent (and thus the relative costs and benefits of cooperation) shifts with age and life stage. He also notes that the flexibility of the human system far exceeds that of any given insect society leading to "tremendous diversity among human groups with regard to ecological and social traits that impact upon local forms of extramaternal care" (2014:20). Because of this flexibility, he argues, the logic of the human system may not be generalized across the species as a whole, but instead "implies that understanding human extramaternal care systems requires linking of ecology, demography, and sociality with female reproductive behavior strictly on a population-by-population basis" (2014:21). This extreme human capacity for facultative adjustment in the social structuring of resource flows, shaped by both local ecological realities and cultural norms, is integral to what we see as unique about the inherently biocultural nature of the human breeding system.

Human Biocultural Reproduction

The above considerations lead us to conclude that the human strategy of offspring care—biocultural reproduction—is distinct from that of other mammals, including our closest genetic cousins, the African apes. Although the childhood life-history stage likely played a pivotal role in the evolution of human biocultural reproduction, childhood alone was not sufficient. Human biocultural reproduction also required other unique human characteristics, such as marriage and kinship. The characteristics of primate biology and psychology that foster intimacy between mother and offspring are necessary foundations for biocultural reproduction (see in this volume Hrdy, chapter 2; Konner, chapter 6). It is reasonable to speculate that some early hominin ancestor, after the divergence from the LCA with the ape lineage, evolved communal or cooperative breeding. To evolve from communal or cooperative breeding to the human practice of biocultural reproduction would have required new cognitive-emotional capacities. Goldschmidt, for instance, emphasized the importance of "affect hunger," which he defined as "the urge to get expressions of affection from others" (2006:47). For the human species this means affection from many others. Konner (chapter 6, this volume) provides several examples of the importance of affection in human development, especially affection between children with their alloparents, and also between children and their teachers of essential survival skills.

Hrdy focuses on the ways in which intense alloparenting by human ancestors "changed our minds" (chapter 2, this volume); in other words, infant attachment was spread across many alloparents rather than just the mother. She provides evidence that having a broader range of alloparents and attachments changes mental phenotypes and promotes Theory of Mind, the ability and desire to adopt the mental perspective of others. She also proposes that the new emotional capacities of hominin ancestors promoted those human cognitive accomplishments that distinguish our species from other extant apes.

The conclusion from these studies of the special nature of human emotion and cognition is that people are different from other mammals, even the apes, in terms of social interactions and the quality and richness of our emotional attachments to others. Our ability to form strong social bonds, not only with mothers but also with others through social institutions such as marriage and kinship, are critical to understanding how biocultural reproduction operates.

Marriage, Kinship, and Culture in Human Reproduction

Marriage is a uniquely human practice with strong ties to human systems of social, economic, and political organization, as well as moral codes, religious behavior, and other forms of ideology (see Keesing 1975; Fox 1984). As noted above, human mating is not confined to marriage and in some societies there is little correlation between the two. However, all human societies practice marriage and, along with systems of kinship, these cultural behaviors are the central organizing principles for alloparental care in traditional human societies. By "traditional societies" we refer to foragers, horticulturalists, pastoralists, and preindustrial agriculturalists, which collectively describe human social organization for more than 99 percent of the evolutionary history of *Homo sapiens*. It was within traditional societies that the biology of childhood and the cultural power of marriage and kinship fostered the emergence of human biocultural reproduction.

Based on a survey of 563 human societies, Murdock (1981) found that about 18 percent of human cultures prescribe monogamous marriages, about 80 percent permit polygynous marriage, and the remaining 2 percent permit polyandrous marriage. In practice, the most common form of marriage is one man with one woman, on account of the often high material resource costs of marriage to multiple partners. Marital dissolution due to death, divorce (legal or de facto), and abandonment is known in all human cultures and remarriage is also common. This leads to "serial monogamy" and polygynandrous mating, with both men and women having multiple marriages or mating partners.

Human marriage is one basis for kinship determination, although there are others. Human societies define kinship relations on the basis of familial and social ties. Humans are the only species to use language and the cultural institution of marriage to define kinship categories. The application of nonbiological criteria results in what is sometimes called "fictive kinship," the application of kinship names to people unrelated by marriage or genetic descent. Fictive kinship can at times be a tie between people as strong, or stronger, than biological kinship. Because the social nature of human kinship often overrides biological descent, some anthropologists avoid the dialectical constraints between the biological and the social by eschewing any distinction (Schneider 1984; Carsten 2000). Here, we use the distinction to emphasize the integrated biocultural nature of human reproduction and alloparental care.

Within the context of human biocultural reproduction, fictive kinship serves to enhance social relations including affection, concern, obligation, and responsibility toward each other's offspring. An example is calling the close friend of one's mother by the name Aunt Maria instead of Mrs. Smith. "Aunt Maria" may provide food, supervision, protection, gifts, and other types of parental investment to her "niece," and the "niece" is expected to behave in accordance with the rules of interaction between family members. Some cross-cultural examples where fictive kinship is an essential feature of social organization include: 1) *compadrazgo* in Latin America where friends become "co-parents" of each other's offspring; 2) adoption and foster care in most human cultures, by which biologically unrelated infants and children are treated as biological kin; 3) cultures practicing Hawaiian kinship terminology where, for example, all women of one's mother's generation are referred to with the kinship name of "mother"; 4) the military of many nations where soldiers call each other "brother" and in some cases where new recruits are "twinned" with an older soldier; and 5) "milk kinship" where the allomother who breastfeeds a mother's infant becomes part of the mother's kin group (Hewlett and Russell 2014). It is also common for anthropologists conducting fieldwork to be given a kinship name by their hosts. Doing so defines, justifies, and facilitates social relationships. Well-known ethnographic examples are provided by Richard Lee (1979), who lived with the !Kung, now called the Ju/'hoansi, and by Napoleon Chagnon (1992) who lived with Yanomamö. Similar fictive kinship designations were given to the present authors during fieldwork in Guatemala and the Philippines. Bogin was adopted as the "son" of a middle-class family in Guatemala City, while Kuzawa is treated as a "son" by someone from the neighborhood in Cebu City where he has lived in the Philippines. These fictive kin designations came with much of the affection and the responsibilities of biological kinship.

Human reproduction is organized by these types of social kinship, as well as by genetic kinship. Indeed, people will marry and reproduce according to the rules of kinship, no matter their degree of genetic relationship. Lee (1979) found that !Kung regard people with the same name as equal in kinship. A man will regard all women with the same name as his sister as a sister. Marrying a sister is forbidden, so all women a man calls sister are unmarriageable. More recently, Hill and colleagues (2011) surveyed thirty-two present-day foraging societies, including the !Kung (Ju/'hoansi), and reported that human hunter-gatherer societies have a social structure that is unique among all primates. They found that, on average, about 75 percent of individuals in residential groups were genetically unrelated, or at least not genetically related by descent from common parents or grandparents. The latter category makes up an average of only 7 percent of the people living in a social group in their sample. Social group members related by up to 5 meiotic links make up only about 25 percent of all people in the social group. The practice by both men and women of dispersing from their natal group acts to dilute genetic kinship. Because of these migrations to new groups, social kinship designations are required to structure relationships between people.

Chagnon (1992) reports that the Yanomamö practice a type of kinship classification by which a man calls his mother's sisters and some other women by the kinship name "mother." The daughters of these "mothers" are not eligible for marriage. A shortage of eligible women is often a problem for Yanomamö men. Chagnon describes the social mechanisms by which a man can change the kinship name of his mother's sister from "mother" to "mother-in-law" and thereby make her daughters eligible for marriage.

These examples, and hundreds of others described in the literature on cross-cultural kinship research, show that human biocultural reproduction has an impact beyond that of other mammalian cooperative or communal breeding systems. Human kinship and marriage systems cast new light on Hamilton's Rule ($C < rB$). Unlike in other species, the genetic relatedness between the actor and the recipient (r) is often of reduced importance in human social systems. The cost in fitness to the actor (C) becomes quite difficult to measure, as the actor is part of kinship networks and families created by marriage, which structure the flow of energy and other resources in ways that do not always map onto genetic relatedness. Equally important, the obligations and prohibitions entailed by kinship categories result in emotional costs and benefits that may offset any material or biological costs. The fitness benefit to the recipient (B) also becomes more complicated to measure. This is because biocultural reproduction requires novel cognitive, emotional, and attachment capacities. These human capacities allow a shift from the genetically based prosocial behavior of the apes to hyper-cooperation based on nongenetic marriage and kinship relationships. In addition to the metrics of survival, growth and development, and future reproduction used for nonhuman animals, human reproduction entails nonbiological contributions to the members of the social group such as emotional affection and the teaching of culturally acquired skills. In these ways, biocultural reproduction differs from other mammalian examples of cooperative or communal breeding, because it not only contributes to the inclusive fitness of parents and genetically related helpers, but it also serves to continually reproduce and recreate the social, economic, political, and moral cohesion of social group members.

Human Childhood and Lifetime Reproductive Effort

In this final section we tie together our discussion of the biocultural nature of human childhood and human reproduction by analyzing their consequences for lifetime reproductive effort (LRE) and the broader implications of these ideas for understanding the evolution of the human life history. LRE may be defined as the metabolic energy devoted to reproduction, relative to maintenance costs, over the average adult life span. To explain this definition of LRE we first provide background on reproductive effort (RE). Reproductive effort is typically defined to include expenditures of energy and time in: 1) mating, that is, searching for, finding/attracting, and keeping a mate(s); 2) offspring production, including gametogenesis, siring, and gestating offspring along with (in mammals) milk transfers during infancy; and 3) parental investment (PI), which is all expenditures of the parents' time, energy, and future reproductive effort on one offspring. All of these expenditures are viewed as coming at a cost to parental abilities to invest in their own somas, in other current—or future—offspring, and to enhance their own fitness (W. Hamilton 1964, 1966).

Human reproductive effort is highest between the ages of eighteen and fifty in most societies. After typically initiating reproductive careers in the early twenties, female biological capacity to conceive (fecundity) begins to decline slowly from about the age of thirty-five until menopause, which entails cessation of monthly menstrual cycling and the absence of menses in adult women. Menopause is usually reached by about fifty years of age, although there is some evidence that it may occur earlier when women have been subjected to poor-quality environments in terms of nutrition, infection, or heavy workloads (Murphy et al. 2013). In societies in which there is no parity-specific limitation on the number of children and hormonal contraception is not used, completed fertility rates may exceed fifteen per woman; in modern high-income settings with wide use of birth control, fertility typically falls below two per woman (Larke and Crews 2006). Men's reproductive success follows closely that of women in the same population, although in many traditional settings a larger variance in men's total fitness is observed due to inter-male competition for access to mates via aggression and/or cultural rules that channel women to older, wealthier, or more socially dominant men (Alexander and Noonan 1979; Chagnon 1979; Crews 2007; Marlowe 2000).

Extensive, high-quality PI is a hallmark of human reproductive effort, and it sets humans apart from all other mammals and other large-bodied apes (Lancaster and Lancaster 1983a). The intensive PI that characterizes human biocultural reproduction is made possible by intergenerational transfers, and the kinship and marriage rules noted above that organize patterns of investment by alloparents in mothers and their offspring. This style of alloparental care allows human societies to maintain extremely high PI, while also allowing human women to achieve the highest fertility and shortest interbirth intervals of all the apes (Bogin 2001; Bogin and Smith 2012; Hrdy 1999a; Kramer and Ellison 2010; Short 1976). Perhaps the most extreme manifestation of this strategy is seen in the Hutterites, a Christian religious sect of North America, traditionally rural farmers, who prize high fertility and do not practice contraception. Between the years 1920 and 1950, the Hutterites achieved the highest recorded average fertility per woman of all human societies. Between 1936 and 1940 Hutterite women had a rate of 466 births per 1,000 women aged twenty-five to twenty-nine years old (Eaton and Mayer 1953). Median number of live offspring was 10.4 per family. Hutterites are not typical of many subsistence level societies in that the Hutterites were well nourished and had access to Western biomedicine. These conditions, along with their religious promotion of large family size, no doubt allowed the Hutterites to achieve exceptionally high fertility and keep their offspring alive. Even so, the Hutterites underscore the extreme potential of human biocultural reproduction to produce many high-quality offspring.

Lifetime Reproductive Effort

Early historical "seeds" of the modern notion of reproductive effort (RE) were planted by Ronald A. Fisher (1930) who formulated the concept of "reproductive value," which he explained as the direct reproductive contribution that an individual of a given age, on average, will make to future generations. Fisher wrote that this is "of some interest, since the direct action of Natural Selection must be proportional to this contribution" (1930:27). Lack (1947) extended this concept when he analyzed egg clutch size in birds and reported a trade-off between the number versus the size of offspring, concluding that "the parental feeding rate tends to increase if the brood is larger, but not proportionately, so that each nestling gets a smaller share of the food in a large than a small brood" (1947:331). Lack's observations of these trade-offs in reproductive rates and success have been cited by subsequent theorists as part of the early development of life-history thinking (Ricklefs 2000). Building on Fisher, Lack, and others, George Williams (1966) proposed an elegant way to express the propagative part of these basic trade-offs. He called this "Reproductive Effort" and defined it as that portion of adult body mass devoted to reproduction per unit time (G. Williams 1966). Much life-history literature was then devoted to further discussion of RE and how best to measure it (e.g., Gadgil and Bossert 1970; Hirshfield and Tinkle 1975; C. Smith and Fretwell 1974), but Williams's definition remains the most commonly used method to calculate RE.

Charnov, Warne, and Moses (2007) further extended the RE concept by devising a method for estimating a species' average lifetime reproductive effort (LRE) by taking the RE of an average reproductive bout multiplied by the average number of bouts across the reproductive life span of a member of that species. It is important to distinguish LRE from a related measure called life-time reproductive success (LRS). The LRS of a female equals the total number of surviving offspring that she produces in her lifetime (Robbins et al. 2011). It is well-known that the human species has the highest LRS of all primates and many mammals (Bogin 2001, 2006; R. Walker et al. 2008). In contrast, LRE encapsulates the metabolic burden of reproduction over a female animal's life course, and thus is a way of expressing the relative "overall" amount of energy a typical member of a species allocates to reproduction, on average, over the life course.

Specifically, Charnov, Warne, and Moses (2007:E131) express LRE as

(litters/clutches per year) × (litter/clutch size) × (average reproductive life span) × (offspring mass at independence/adult mass at first reproduction)

Calculating LRE for fifty-four lizard species, Charnov, Warne, and Moses (2007) find a mean LRE of 1.43 (1.3–1.5, 95 percent confidence interval [CI]) and, for forty mammal species, a mean LRE of 1.41 (1.2–1.6, 95 percent CI). These results indicate that across this range of animal species, with varying growth and production rates, the average female in a typical mammal or lizard will generate a mass of offspring approximately 1.4 times her own body weight. Based upon this finding, LRE has been interpreted as an approximate life-history invariant trade-off: the average value of RE per unit time—operationalized analytically as the mass-adjusted investment per offspring raised to nutritional independence—tends to decrease as adult life span increases, thus maintaining a relatively constant ratio (Charnov, Warne, and Moses 2007). Charnov and colleagues explain that LRE is of theoretical importance because it "is a key component of fitness . . . and it encompasses the central core of 40 years of life history thought—reproductive allocation, size at maturity, and adult life span. This places it central to the study of life histories" (2007:E135).

Following the approach developed by Charnov, Warne, and Moses (2007), Burger, Walker, and Hamilton (2010) calculated the average LRE of human women using data from seventeen small-scale societies. By multiplying the average fertility rate, offspring size relative to maternal body mass, and reproductive life span of women within these populations, they calculate an average LRE of 1.45 (± 0.12, 95 percent CI). This value is statistically indistinguishable from the predicted average LRE value calculated by Charnov, Warne, and Moses (2007) for other mammals.

While an important initial step, the assumptions employed by Burger and colleagues do not fully account for the energetic and reproductive benefits accrued to human mothers through the processes of biocultural reproduction discussed above. Burger and colleagues' analysis relies on the assumption—central to the estimation of LRE in nonhuman mammalian species by Charnov, Warne, and Moses (2007)—that maternal per-offspring RE is reflected in the size of an offspring at nutritional independence from maternal metabolism. Independence for a reptile is when the egg is laid or the viviparous offspring are birthed. For most mammals, independence is achieved at weaning (end of lactation). These definitions of nutritional independence do not apply to a species like our own, in which there are extensive nutritional transfers in support of infant and child growth long before the age of weaning. In their estimation of human LRE, Burger, Walker, and Hamilton treat humans as they do all mammals in the sample, and assume that the age of independence in humans occurs at the age of complete weaning, which they define as three years after birth. They then use values for average offspring weight at that age as the variable for "litter size" (in grams) in the empirical estimation of LRE.

Elsewhere we have examined these assumptions, and explored strategies for calculating LRE that account for more of the features of our unique strategy of biocultural reproduction (Bragg, Bogin, and Kuzawa 2012). Across all placental mammals, the phases of maternal investment in reproduction can be conceived of as comprising three distinct phases: direct metabolic transfers during gestation, a period of exclusive breastfeeding when all of the infant's nutritional needs are met via breast milk, and in many mammals, a period of "mixed" feeding during which infant nutritional requirements are met by a mix of infant self-provisioning and breast milk (Langer 2008). The nature of this transitional feeding phase is greatly modified in humans compared to all other great apes and noncooperatively breeding primates. Rather than shifting from milk to a combination of milk and self-provisioning, humans shift from milk to "complementary feeding" wherein still-dependent and nursing offspring are fed nutritionally rich, specially prepared foods (Bogin 1999b; Knott 2001; Lancaster and Lancaster 1983a; P. Lee 1996; Sellen 2006, chapter 10, this volume). Complementary feeding of infants generally begins around six months of age and often earlier, which means that, for the majority of the period of lactation, infants receive both their mother's milk and foods supplied from outside the mother's body. These complementary foods should *not* be included in the calculation of LRE that, according to Charnov, Warne, and Moses (2007), is reserved for the amount of energy that mothers provide as *direct metabolic transfers* to offspring.

The highest energetic output that an average human woman achieves during lactation is about 2.7 MJ/d^2 (Prentice et al. 1996; Sellen 2007), which is already outstripped by infant energy requirements at six months of age (Butte et al. 2000). Because energy needs continue to increase with age, the proportion of infant needs met by breastfeeding will tend to progressively decline following peak lactation (P. Lee 1996; Sellen 2007). All of this theoretical discussion is consistent with empirical observations from ethnographic research of human societies on the role of mothers and alloparents in providing a variety of foods to still breastfeeding infants (Hurtado et al. 1992; in this volume Hrdy, chapter 2; Konner, chapter 6; Meehan, Helfrecht, and Malcom, chapter 9; Sellen, chapter 10), which can even include breast milk from wet nurses (e.g., Hrdy 1999a for historical sources and Tronick, Morelli, and Winn 1987; Hewlett and Winn 2014 for a contemporary example). Taking such factors into consideration, Sellen (2006, 2007) has estimated that supplementary feeding could account for 1.8 MJ/d of infant needs during the first year, which is over half (67 percent) of the energetic cost of peak lactation.

Using the same dataset as Burger, Walker, and Hamilton we re-estimated human LRE by modifying the equation for LRE to reflect these unique, species-defining characteristics of the human life history (Bragg, Bogin, and Kuzawa 2012). We recalculated LRE by "adjusting" offspring size at weaning to more accurately reflect the proportion of offspring weight gained from conception through size at weaning (size at age three years as was assumed by Burger and colleagues) actually "paid for" by maternal metabolism as well the portion paid for by complementary feeding. We calculated both "high" and "low" estimates of the energy savings afforded by complementary feeding from the data on infant energetic requirements and maternal breast milk production.

In short, we found that the LRE of human women is probably more on the order of 1.02–1.23, assuming high (67 percent) to low (33 percent) proportions of the energetic needs of weanlings older than six months being met by complementary foods in lieu of breast milk (Bragg, Bogin, and Kuzawa 2012).

Our estimates of human LRE are 14 to 29 percent lower than that calculated by Burger and colleagues. This difference represents a significant savings of energy expended on reproduction in both statistical terms and also in biological function. Statistically, the difference between a mean LRE of 1.44 (sd 0.22) and 1.23 (sd 0.20) based on a sample of fifteen societies results in a $t = 2.65$ with $p<0.01$. Biologically, the human LRE values ranging from 1.02–1.23 result in a substantial energy savings that may be invested in other functions or needs, including maintenance of the mother's body, defense against infection, and perhaps also an increase in the maintenance expenditures that allowed the evolution of a human life span longer by several decades than our closest great ape kin (Bogin 2009; Bragg, Bogin and Kuzawa 2012; Kuzawa and Bragg 2012). In this way, the features of human biocultural reproduction, which coevolved with the unique stage of human dependence known as childhood, may be directly linked with the evolution of our unusually long life span.

Conclusions

Childhood does indeed exist as a fluid, culturally defined category that varies across societies and generations, as many have emphasized. But we have argued that it is also a defining feature of human biology and the human life history and one that was critical to the geographic and demographic success of our species. In this chapter we have defined the biological and behavioral characteristics of human childhood, which is a stage of human life history that was added between the infancy and juvenile stages of species ancestral to the modern human lineage. The evolution of the childhood life-history stage in the human lineage made possible new opportunities for reproductive success, in particular by allowing infants to be weaned earlier and shortening interbirth intervals. This strategy would only be favored by natural selection if this increased rate of offspring production were not followed by a decline in survival to adulthood. Perhaps in service of this need, the evolution of human childhood was accompanied by a shift from the typical mammalian pattern of a unique attachment dependence between the infant and her biological mother to the human pattern, in which attachment is expanded outward to other members of the social group. Contrary to some recent work, we estimate that the human strategy of biocultural reproduction results in a sizeable reduction in lifetime reproductive effort in humans. The excess internal energy freed up through this strategy may have played an important role in the demographic success of humans over that of other ape species. In particular, lower human LRE may have contributed the "fuel" necessary to slow the pace of aging and extend life span, thereby expanding the pool of allocaregivers that are critical to the human strategy.

Acknowledgments

We thank Courtney Meehan and Alyssa Crittenden for organizing the School for Advanced Research advanced seminar that was the basis for this chapter and this book. We thank all of the participants at the advanced seminar for their discussions, especially Sarah Hrdy and Mel Konner, which have improved our chapter. We thank Kim Hill for his comments on previous versions of our text. Some sections of this chapter appeared in the article by Barry Bogin, Jared Bragg, and Christopher Kuzawa (2014): Humans Are Not Cooperative Breeders but Practice Biocultural Reproduction, Annals of Human Biology 41(4):368–380. Finally, we thank the staff of the School of American Research for their hospitality and many kindnesses during our research seminar.

Notes

1. The review by Lukas and Clutton-Brock was systematic in that the authors included all known mammalian species. To our knowledge, no previous research on cooperative breeding was as comprehensive. Systematic reviews are designed to replace traditional narrative reviews and "expert" commentaries. Narrative reviews and commentaries may reflect the biases of the authors toward one, or a few, ways of searching for research evidence and interpreting that evidence. "Systematic reviews attempt to bring the same level of rigour to reviewing research evidence as should be used in producing that research evidence in the first place" (http://www.medicine.ox.ac.uk/bandolier/painres/download/whatis/syst-review.pdf).

2. MJ/d = megajoules per day. A megajoule equals 239.005736 kilocalories (kcal). 2.7 MJ/d equals about 645 kcal and a six-month-old infant of median body weight requires about 3.055 MJ or 730 kcal per day.

Growth and Development
Defining Childhood

CHAPTER FOUR

Childhood and Patterns of Growth
in the Genus Homo

JENNIFER L. THOMPSON AND ANDREW J. NELSON

Introduction

The pattern of growth and development we see today in modern humans did not appear suddenly in its present form but instead evolved over millions of years. In the process, it became differentiated from the pattern expressed by living apes in several important ways (Bogin 1988, 1997, 2006; Bogin and Smith 1996; Robson, Van Schaik, and Hawkes 2006; Schultz 1960; E. Watts 1986). Apes and other nonhuman primates pass through three stages of growth on their way to adulthood: infancy, juvenility, and a short adolescence. From birth to adulthood, growth takes place over approximately twelve years. In contrast, modern humans have an additional period of growth, childhood (see Bogin, Bragg, and Kuzawa, chapter 3, this volume), and have a greatly elongated adolescence extending the duration of growth about six years beyond that seen in apes. These differences are not, however, simply a matter of humans growing over a longer period of time. For example, the nature of the adolescent period has also changed, with different skeletal elements maturing at different rates and times (J. Thompson and Nelson 2011). The result is significantly delayed sexual and somatic maturation until adolescence, with important social, behavioral, and psychological consequences (Bogin 1999b).

Childhood has been defined by Bogin (1999b) as a period of dependency starting after weaning and ending with the eruption of the first permanent molars, when the brain has reached approximately 90 percent of adult weight, and when a shift in cognitive abilities allows for greater independence. During the childhood stage, youngsters receive most daily caloric needs from adults/others; food must be specially prepared due to their immature dentition and digestive tract at a time when their brain is growing rapidly. Children do not walk quickly and do not achieve an adult gait until toward the end of this life stage. They are protected—to a greater or lesser extent—by older individuals, including siblings. They are small, not forward thinking, and easily lost. The picture we get of this stage is of a fairly dependent, costly individual, so one might wonder when and how childhood evolved in the first place. In harsh environments such as the glacial periods of Pleistocene Europe, and when foraging as our ancestors and close relatives did for millennia, some mitigating factor would logically need to outweigh the cost of childhood and instead select for this stage. Chimpanzees, for instance, pass from infancy directly into an independent juvenile phase. They grow quickly (relatively speaking) and reach adulthood by approximately twelve years of age. So why change from this pattern to elongate the growth period and add a somewhat costly extra stage of growth? And when would this have taken place? One key element in this discussion, of course, is the fossil record and what it might reveal concerning these questions.

Studies of Plio-Pleistocene hominins (the Australopithecines and habilines) have demonstrated that early hominins followed a rate and pattern of growth and development similar to that of apes. In particular, specimens allocated to *H. habilis* and *H. rudolfensis* exhibit body proportions (Ruff 2009; Skinner and Wood 2006; Wood and Collard 1999) and dental development (Anemone, Mooney, and Siegel 1996; Beynon and Dean 1988, 1991; Bromage and Dean 1985; M. Dean 1989; M. Dean et al. 2001; Moggi-Cecchi 2001; B. H. Smith 1986, 1989, 1991, 1992) so similar to the Australopithecines that some have suggested that they be excluded from the genus *Homo*. Thus, none of these early hominins were likely to have experienced a childhood stage. For these reasons, this chapter will focus on fossil evidence from *Homo erectus* and more recent members of the genus *Homo* (*neanderthalensis, sapiens*) to assess when the modern human pattern of growth and development evolved and, in particular, the evidence for childhood.

Life-History Stages

While other chapters in this volume will cover life-history stages in more detail (see Bogin, Bragg, and Kuzawa, chapter 3; Bernstein, chapter 5), a brief review of what constitutes the modern pattern of growth and development is warranted prior to assessing when the unique aspects of our pattern evolved. We find it useful to start with the four stages of growth as defined by Bogin (infancy, childhood, juvenility, and adolescence) because "each stage encompasses a set of biological and behavioral traits that define" (2006:205) when they start and when they end. (Note that the juvenile period is sometimes referred to as "middle childhood"; see J. Thompson and Nelson 2011; S. White 1996.) Although results are not always as precise as we would like, these stages give us skeletal and dental markers of maturity that provide us with a way to organize and assess the immature fossil record (see also J. Thompson, Krovitz, and Nelson 2003).

As noted by Bogin (2009), in most mammals sexual development takes place at the end of the infancy period so that there is no significant change in growth rate between infancy and adulthood. Thus, most mammals go through one life-history stage, infancy, prior to adulthood. Nonhuman primates experience three stages of growth before adulthood: infancy, juvenility, and adolescence. Old World monkeys and apes share with modern humans the feature of delaying sexual development for some time after infancy. Growth and sexual maturation are therefore delayed relative to other mammals.

The juvenile stage begins in humans after the eruption of the first permanent molars (M1s) and when brain growth reaches 90 percent of adult size, which occurs by about five years of age (mature brain weight is complete at about six-and-a-half to seven years). This stage ends with puberty several years thereafter (Robson and Wood 2008). The juvenile stage in humans and apes, although sharing certain developmental and biological similarities, also exhibits important differences (see J. Thompson and Nelson 2011 for further discussion). For example, at the beginning of the juvenile stage (five to seven years of age), human offspring (but not apes) experience a psychological milestone, a "cognitive shift" sometimes described as "entry into the age of reasoning" (S. White 1996:17). This shift involves changes in cognitive abilities and includes "the emergence of increasing capabilities for strategic and controlled self-regulation, skills at inhibition, the ability to maintain attention and to focus on a complex problem, and planfullness and reflection" (Weisner 1996a:295). This shift has only been documented in humans (see Bogin 1999b for further discussion).

The modern human pattern of growth and development differs from that of apes due to the presence of a childhood stage, between the infant and juvenile stages. As defined by Bogin (1997) and Bogin, Bragg, and Kuzawa, chapter 3, this volume (see above), a "child" has been weaned but remains dependent upon adults for food and protection. This stage ends when 90 percent of adult brain weight has been achieved and M1s have erupted (i.e., childhood ends and the juvenile stage begins). The addition of the childhood stage in humans leads to further delay in sexual development beyond what is seen in apes and other primates. The result is a need for more parental care for offspring dependent for a longer time, in absolute terms, than any other primate, making the modern human pattern of growth unique (Bogin 1999b). In addition, humans experience an extended and elaborated adolescent stage (including a growth spurt), and they delay reproduction to the end of the growth period, the duration of which is longer than in apes.

Rethinking Childhood

Past studies have tied the beginning of childhood to weaning. For example, Bogin states that "childhood is the period following infancy, when the youngster is weaned from nursing" (1997:63). As part of the SAR workshop that produced this volume, participants (including Bogin) discussed the logic behind using weaning as a biological marker for the beginning of this stage because the timing of this event is highly variable in humans (e.g., Kachel, Premo, and Hublin 2011). Furthermore, Sellen (2006) has demonstrated that weaning is not an event but a long-duration process during which offspring transition from acquiring all of their nutrients from the mother to obtaining all of their food independently. Moreover, recent work by T. Smith and colleagues (2013) highlights some problems with the traditional use of M1 eruption as a signal of weaning in apes because some wild chimpanzees continue to suckle after M1 eruption, up to 4.4 years in one individual. Thus, the timing of the end of infancy in apes is also less fixed than previously thought. At the SAR workshop, although we came to no conclusion about how to redefine childhood's beginning, we did begin to shift away from using weaning as the primary marker of this transition. What follows is our independent analysis of the transition from infancy to childhood.

INFANCY/CHILDHOOD TRANSITION

The first twenty-eight days after birth in humans is sometimes distinguished as a separate neonate stage but in both this and the infancy stage that follows, the subadult individual is totally dependent on adults, usually the mother, for nourishment and care (Bogin 1999b). During the first year of life, brain growth proceeds at the same rapid rate as in utero, presumably to allow smaller-brained infants to be born "prematurely" in order to accommodate to the size of the mother's pelvis, as well as to allow our brains to achieve such a large volume for a primate of our size.

Summarized similarities and differences in development between humans and apes can be seen in table 4.1. Both humans and chimpanzees appear to go through two phases of so-called infancy, with the key difference being what happens at the end of the infancy stage. We propose that these infancy phases be clearly delineated from each other to emphasize the differences between human and ape development. The first stage, which we refer to as infancy I (or "nursing phase"), lasts from birth to six months in both species during which all nutrition is provided by the mother's breast milk, at least in human societies where breastfeeding is the norm. The second stage, infancy II (or "suckling phase"), lasts from six months to three years. However, during the suckling phase of infancy, important contrasts emerge between apes and humans. Human offspring from six months to three years are provisioned while chimpanzee offspring are not. Provisioning (called complementary feeding by Sellen 2006) is needed to fuel the fast velocity of both brain and somatic growth in human offspring (Bogin 1999b:67). From six months to three years human offspring's deciduous teeth erupt, they receive supplementary foods to augment nutrition received from breast milk, and they must be carried (or cached). They become "toddlers" or independent walkers in their second year (Konner 2010), making it easier to walk, but not for long distances as they tire easily (Bird and Bliege Bird 2005:291). Infant chimpanzees start to supplement milk with solid foods by about six months (mostly fruit up to the end of the first year) and begin to sample most items that make up an adult diet by three years (T. Smith et al. 2013:2789). Some may continue to suckle, especially if the mother has not resumed ovulation and become pregnant again, but can feed themselves if the mother is not there. T. Smith and colleagues suggest that "M1 emergence in eastern chimpanzees may relate to a key dietary transition around age three, before which infants are fundamentally dependent on their mothers for support, as they develop the *requisite anatomy and ecological knowledge to survive on their own, if necessary*" (2013:2789; emphasis added). Notably, the chimpanzee mother does not provide food; instead, offspring learn how to feed and what to eat by observing the mother, so technically provision themselves. This would seem to indicate that this dietary transition, *not weaning* (as was previously assumed), is what is tied to M1 eruption in chimpanzees. By three years of age, chimpanzees are not only eating an adult diet but are *able* to provide all of their own food so that if they are orphaned, their probability of survival is much higher than a younger animal (T. Smith et al. 2013). At this turning point, chimpanzees enter the juvenile stage. Thus, weaning is no longer relevant as a biological marker of the end of infancy, dietary independence is.

When did this change in the suckling phase evolve? We know that, in modern humans, endocranial volume nearly doubles in the first year of life alone (Coqueugniot and Hublin 2007). At some time in our evolution, adult brain size increased to a point at which post-fetal brain growth was a necessity (Martin 1983). This rapid growth after birth would necessitate, from six months of age onward, complementary food to supplement the mother's breast milk. At this time the suckling phase changed for our ancestors in that adults (others) must provide foods since, at least for modern humans, sucklings cannot obtain food for themselves as do chimpanzees of similar age.

Between three years to about five to seven years, modern humans have an additional stage (or phase) not seen in primates: childhood. All immature dentition is in place but, as deciduous teeth have thinner enamel and shallower roots than permanent teeth, children still cannot process all components of an adult diet. As a result, "transitional foods" (Sellen 2006) are provided by older individuals (Leonard and Robertson 1994, 1997; Bogin 2006). During childhood, the brain develops faster than any other part of the body, much faster than the digestive system that is needed to nourish it. The digestive system is small and immature, yet the brain is growing rapidly, demanding a diet that is low in total volume, but is full of energy, fats, and proteins (Bogin 1999b:75) and children lack the motor and cognitive skills to prepare such a diet by themselves. As noted by Leonard and Robertson (1994: 191), 40–80 percent of resting metabolism is used to maintain the brain of a child less than five years of age, while in adults this drops to 16–25 percent. These large caloric needs of the developing brain mandate a prolonged period where adults/others must supplement a child's diet.

After three years of age a child can walk upright, but without the characteristic gait of an adult and with a greater energetic cost since motor control has not yet matured. This age is often when children are carried less and forced to walk more to save the mother's energy (P. Kramer 1998) despite the fact that the energy costs of walking are higher in these individuals (DeJaeger, Willems, and Heglund 2001). Human offspring experience delayed somatic growth so

Table 4.1. Human and Chimpanzee Comparisons

Stage	Age	Chimpanzee	Age	Human
Infancy I/ Nursing	0–6 months	Breast milk from mother	0–6 months	Breast milk from mother
Infancy II/ Suckling	6 months– 3 years	• Between 0.5 and 1.0 years of age, when infants feed on solid food, they primarily consume ripe fruit • Infants begin eating same percentage of fibrous foods as adults early in second year of life, well before emergence of any permanent teeth but still nurse • By 3 they have sampled all adult foods and could survive on own • No provisioning of young	6 months– 3 years	• Complementary, soft food introduced after 6 months • All deciduous teeth in place by 3 years • Provisioning of young
Infancy III/ Childhood		• No childhood, enter directly into juvenile stage	3–6 years	• Transitional food introduced, but includes specially prepared adult foods (child-sized portions) • Some self-provisioning possible (see Crittenden, chapter 7, this volume) • Continued provisioning by others

that while more mobile at age three, they lack the motor skills and coordination and cognitive skills to forage independently of others until reaching the juvenile stage. (See Crittenden, chapter 7, this volume, for a discussion of the extent of participation of children in food collection.) Not until the end of childhood do children approach adults in terms of locomotor efficiency and gait, at about seven to eight years of age (P. Kramer 1998; Nakano and Kimura 1992). This increase in locomotor efficiency ties in with increasing independence as children approach the juvenile stage.

Finally, a child's developmental and psychological immaturity makes them vulnerable to dehydration (B. Bird and Bliege Bird 2005) and they are more prone to getting lost. Children are also at risk of predation, accidents (Henry, Morelli and Tronick 2005), and disease, and so require protection from others. Bogin (1999b:75) has made the astute point that there is no society where children can survive if care from older individuals is not provided.

Based on this evidence we argue that, for humans, childhood begins at about age three when human offspring can *begin* to provision some of their daily energy requirements themselves (e.g., Crittenden, chapter 7, this volume; Crittenden et al. 2009, 2013; Tucker and Young 2005). We suggest that childhood evolved as a further elaboration of infancy—a transitional feeding stage allowing for rapid brain growth while maturation of gait, skeleton, and gut proceeds more slowly (see figure 4.1). In fact, childhood might be conceptualized as having evolved as a third phase of infancy. It is not a sudden insertion, rather it evolved out of, and perhaps as a result of, an extension and elaboration of the suckling phase of infancy we discussed above. As during the suckling phase, provisioning and protection continues. But in contrast, to allow for more brain and somatic growth, the transition into the juvenile stage is delayed for several years. When this evolved may be revealed by the fossil evidence. We discuss this further below.

CHILDHOOD/JUVENILE TRANSITION

As during infancy, brain growth continues at a rapid rate during childhood, while somatic growth is slow. Higher rates of brain growth and a longer time to 90 percent maturity (four years in apes, five to six years in humans) contribute to the adult outcome of a large relative brain size. Childhood in humans is thought to end at about five years of age (Robson and Wood 2008) when 90 percent of adult brain size has been achieved, or at seven years of age as

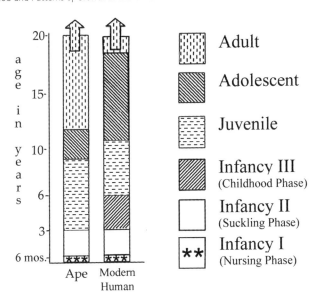

Figure 4.1. Life-history stages in apes and humans compared. Figure modified from Bogin 2003 and J. Thompson and Nelson 2011.

argued by Bogin (2003) when 90 percent of brain weight has been achieved, and the first permanent molar erupts (about 4.7 to seven years of age). Given this range, we have argued elsewhere (J. Thompson and Nelson 2011) that an age of six years is a reasonable compromise estimate to mark the end of the childhood stage in modern humans. At the end of childhood (beginning of the juvenile stage), human children experience a "cognitive shift" and have the mental acuity necessary to become more independent of adults; before this time they are less likely to survive without adult help and protection (Bogin 1999b). Thus, childhood involves a period during which offspring are dependent on adults for some food, protection, and guidance because human children, like immature chimpanzee offspring (see above), do not yet have, to quote Smith et al., the *requisite anatomy and ecological knowledge to survive on their own*" (T. Smith et al. 2013:2789; emphasis added).

JUVENILE

The juvenile stage, also referred to as "middle childhood" by developmental psychologists (J. Thompson and Nelson 2011; S. White 1996), is seen in modern human and nonhuman primates and represents a delay in sexual maturation and growth (Bogin 1999b). The work of T. Smith and colleagues (2013) suggests that, in chimpanzees, this stage begins around age three when the transition to adult foods is largely complete. In modern humans, the juvenile stage begins after childhood, at around six years of age (as argued above). Apes and modern humans, unlike other mammals, have a long juvenile period. This longer stage of juvenility likely evolved to allow more time for brain development and social learning (B. Campbell 2006, 2011; but see Blurton Jones 2006; Kaplan et al. 2000; Kaplan, Lancaster, and Robson 2003; Kaplan and Robson 2002; Pagel and Harvey 1993; Bogin 2006). It is during the juvenile stage when individuals begin behaving more independently (Bogin and Smith 1996; Hochberg 2008; Leigh 2004; Pereira and Altmann 1985). In African apes, the juvenile stage lasts for three to seven years and ends with sexual maturation at about seven to eleven years of age (see also Bernstein, chapter 5, this volume). In humans it lasts about five to six years and ends at about eleven to twelve years of age (Leigh 1996; Strier 2007). To identify this stage in the fossil record, dentition must be present and indicate eruption of the first molar (M1), marking the beginning of this stage. Brain growth should have achieved 90 percent adult volume threshold and growth now slows. There should be no evidence from the skeleton that the adolescent growth spurt has begun. There also may be some demonstration of semi-independence such as traumatic or pathological lesions or evidence of stress that might leave traces on the bones and teeth.

ADOLESCENCE

Adolescence begins at puberty and ends at adulthood. During this phase individuals reach full sexual maturity, develop secondary sexual characteristics, undergo a growth spurt, and adopt adult behaviors (Bogin 2003; Bogin and Smith 1996; Tanner 1990; E. Watts 1985). In African apes, puberty begins at seven to ten years of age and lasts for about two years. Menarche begins for females, testes growth accelerates for males, and sexual characteristics appear in both sexes (Leigh and Shea 1996). Some debate exists whether apes experience an adolescent stage as they do not experience a pervasive, accelerated growth spurt resembling a human adolescent growth spurt (e.g., Bogin 2003). However, given the delay between menarche and adulthood, as well as the presence of growth spurts in body mass, other researchers recognize this stage (e.g., Leigh 1996; Pereira and Altmann 1985; E. Watts 1985). Certainly the nature of adolescence exhibits unique characteristics in humans, including a "long absolute delay in the initiation of the human growth spurt" (Leigh 1996:455), the size of the spurt affecting all parts of the skeleton, and its longer duration. Puberty in modern industrial populations is somewhat variable in its timing but on average begins at about age ten in girls and two years later in boys (Robson and Wood 2008; Rosenfeld and Nicodemus 2003). Pubertal timing in small-scale, natural fertility populations is more variable (e.g., R. Walker et al. 2006). Puberty marks the beginning of adolescence, which lasts for about six to eight years and ends with adulthood.

The magnitude of the human growth spurt makes it identifiable on the skeleton. One means of identification is plotting long bone growth on dental age for fossil individuals (e.g., Nelson and Thompson 2005). Another way to identify this stage is to use the correlation between epiphyseal fusion and bone size and/or the proportional relationships between various bones of the skeleton (B. H. Smith 1993; Anton and Leigh 2003).

ADULTHOOD

Adulthood is achieved when the body ceases to grow and full sexual maturity is attained, and ends with death. Somatic growth ceases around age ten to twelve years in African apes and their maximum life span in the wild is fifty to fifty-four years. In contrast, humans finish the majority of their growth much later, by eighteen to twenty years, and have a maximum life span of eighty-five years—at least in nonindustrialized countries (Robson and Wood 2008). On the skeleton, adulthood is marked by epiphyseal fusion in the major long bones and eruption and full occlusion of the third molars (M3s) (Buikstra and Ubelaker 1994).

Childhood in the Fossil Record

When assessing the juvenile hominin record, establishing a fossil's age at death is key to analyzing when the human growth pattern emerged. Published age standards have been established for both humans and apes, but care must be taken in applying these to fossils without considering rates of development.

For instance, new advances in age determination techniques have revealed important contrasts between various species of hominins that must be accounted for (see below in sections on fossil evidence).

To address the question of when childhood evolved, we first have to determine when our modern growth pattern evolved. At some point in our evolutionary history, selective pressures led to changes in the developmental pattern of early members of the genus *Homo*. We begin to see significant changes in body and brain size that would have been impacted by new patterns of growth and development (see Ruff, Trinkaus, and Holliday 1997). With increases in brain size and continued growth of the brain outside the womb during the first year of life (at the same rate as in utero), special, supplementary foods would need to be provisioned after six months of age. Therefore, the infancy II, or suckling phase of infancy, would have changed compared with that of apes (see table 4.1). This may not involve a significant change in growth duration, but could mean that perhaps the juvenile stage was somewhat foreshortened (with a longer infancy stage). The evolution of childhood, however, would require further extension of the growth period and delay of sexual maturation. Once the duration of growth extends beyond that seen in apes, significant cost/benefit trade-offs occur (Bock and Sellen 2002; Brumbach, Figueredo, and Ellis 2009; Hawkes and Paine 2006; Leigh 2001) affecting nutritional requirements (Gurven and Walker 2006), offsetting a larger brain and body as well as changing dietary needs. A longer duration of growth may have allowed more time to learn complex survival skills (Bogin 2003; Kaplan, Lancaster, and Robson 2003). It would also allow more time to grow a larger brain, perhaps reallocating metabolic energy to that end with the resulting delay in somatic growth that characterizes childhood in modern humans. With the lengthening of infancy (nursing and suckling) to include an additional phase, childhood, resulting in an increase in the number of vulnerable individuals, mortality rates would also likely have been affected (Migliano, Vinicius, and Lahr 2007; Stearns and Koella 1986; R. Walker et al. 2006). The following is a review of the fossil record and discussion of what it reveals about the changing and evolving pattern of growth over the span of the genus *Homo*.

H. ERECTUS

We begin our review of the fossil record with *Homo erectus*, who some argue was the first obligate biped, able to endure travel over long distances compared with facultative bipeds. We see a dramatic increase in body and brain size over previous and coexisting hominins and limb proportions that are similar to those of modern humans (Kappelman 1996; McHenry 1991; A. Walker and Leakey 1993). Subadult *Homo erectus* individuals are found at a variety of sites including Zhoukoudian in China, Ngandong and Modjokerto in Indonesia, and several sites in Africa. However, there are only two partial skeletons, one calvarium, few postcranial elements, and many cranial fragments and isolated teeth. Here, we focus on the most complete and best-described specimens.

The *H. erectus* Mojokerto infant provides some evidence for assessing the nature of infancy in this taxon. Dating to circa 1.8 million years ago, this one-year-old had a cranial capacity 72–84 percent of that of an adult of that species (Coqueugniot et al. 2004; see also Leigh 2006), similar to that of apes at the same age, suggesting a relative brain growth pattern more in line with apes (see Leigh 2004; Robson, Van Schaik, and Hawkes 2006 for discussion). Zollikofer and Ponce de León (2010) argue that endocranial volume of the Mojokerto infant falls within the lower end of the modern human range, suggesting that early brain growth in *H. erectus* was more rapid than in earlier hominins but was not sustained for as long as in modern humans, resulting in adult endocranial volume values lower than modern adults. Based on this latter finding, we would argue that, with increases in average brain size seen in fossils from this species (e.g., Aiello and Dean 1990), special, complementary foods during the suckling phase of infancy (after six months) may have been necessary. With this species we see a greater variety of stone tools and more significant meat consumption than in earlier hominins. Hunting and/or scavenging would have provided access to energy-dense foods like bone marrow or honey (cf., Crittenden 2011) to help fuel rapid early brain growth. How long such foods were provisioned is unknown but likely for less time than seen in modern humans.

Did *H. erectus* experience childhood? Bogin argues (2006) that they and earlier members of the genus *Homo* did. We do not entirely agree and have argued elsewhere (2011) that it is certainly unlikely that any of the habiline species experienced childhood, given their Australopithecine-like rates of dental growth mentioned previously. In *H. erectus*, a childhood stage (or phase) would have likely required an extension of the duration of growth or a significant foreshortening of the juvenile stage (which we think unlikely, see below).

Was the duration of growth longer in *H. erectus* than in previous hominins?

M. Christopher Dean and colleagues (2001:629) demonstrate that dental development in *H. erectus* was faster than in our species. They consequently presented a new age estimate for the Nariokotome boy of about eight years at age at death and they have recently (Dean and Smith 2009) refined this age estimate to 8.2 years with a range of 7.6 to 8.8 years, throwing into question earlier estimates of twelve and fifteen years. With this information and the state of maturation of the proximal femur in hand, we can estimate the duration of the *H. erectus* growth period. Tardieu (1998) states that the distal femoral epiphysis takes about three years to fuse. In modern humans, this process ends at sixteen to eighteen years of age; in chimpanzees, eleven to twelve years of age (Tanner 1990; E. Watts 1985). The distal epiphysis of this eight-year-old *H. erectus* boy had not yet fused, and it is reasonable to estimate that it would have done so by age eleven to twelve at the same age as living apes, meaning that the duration of growth was not extended. Moreover, in a previous study (J. Thompson and Nelson 2000), we calculated femoral age by expressing length as a percentage of average adult length for a number of juvenile hominins including the Nariokotome boy. We plotted this "proportional femur length" against dental age and included data from modern humans and an extant ape for comparison. We concluded that both dental and postcranial growth patterns were more apelike in *H. erectus* (con. Dean and Smith 2009). We also noted that his femoral length falls within the adult range for *H. erectus*. We assert that the dental age estimate and proportional growth data also demonstrate that the duration of growth in *H. erectus* was similar to that seen in extant apes.

Did *H. erectus* experience a modern, humanlike adolescence? Holly Smith (1993), based on the advanced maturation state of the skeleton of Nariokotome boy, argues against an adolescence like ours. Tardieu (1998) also argues against the presence of a pervasive growth spurt. Her examination of the distal femoral epiphysis of this specimen led her to claim that the *Homo erectus* growth spurt was probably less pronounced, and shorter, than in modern humans. However, Anton (2002) and Anton and Leigh (2003) argued that some growth spurt in the facial bones of the Nariokotome boy was still probable. According to Begun and Walker's (1993) estimate of cranial capacity, this boy had reached about 97 percent adult brain size, at which time a modern human boy would be entering adolescence. However, while some growth spurts in some parts of the skeleton of this individual are possible, such as those documented by Leigh (2004) in extant primates, we argue that these spurts were not delayed as in modern humans.

Another adolescent fossil hominin, known from approximately the same time period as the Nariokotome boy, is the Dmanisi 2700 individual from the Republic of Georgia. The Dmanisi hominins have been identified as early *Homo* (Lordkipanidze et al. 2007), *Homo ergaster* (Gabunia et al. 2000) and *Homo erectus* (Vekua et al. 2002), so its taxonomic relation to Nariokotome and other *Homo erectus* individuals is not entirely clear. This individual is not as complete as Nariokotome but is represented by a cranium, a complete humerus, and several other skeletal elements (Lordkipanidze et al. 2007). The age derived for this individual—eleven to thirteen years—was based on modern human criteria. Following the example of WT 15000, this estimate is likely to fall in light of further analysis of dental developmental rates (see above). However, even with that age range, based on humeral length (in comparison to the adult humerus from Dmanisi), this individual had achieved 95.7 percent of its height (bone length data from Lordkipanidze et al. 2007:307) at an age at which modern humans are just entering their growth spurt. Geographic differences between these groups as well as the uncertainty of their taxonomic affiliation must make any comparison tentative. However, it is telling that this second early Pleistocene hominin adolescent had also achieved a very high proportion of adult body size by an early age. Therefore, we find it reasonable to assume that the modern version of adolescence had not yet evolved in *Homo erectus*.

Given the likely apelike pattern and growth duration for these hominins, including a lack of a near-global skeletal growth spurt as experienced by modern humans, if childhood was something experienced by *Homo erectus* it must have been very short, requiring shortening of infancy (either nursing or suckling phases) and/or the juvenile stage. If *H. erectus* did experience childhood, it is difficult to say what it entailed as M1 eruption was not delayed (as in modern human children) and we cannot tell whether the digestive tract was immature (thus requiring special, transitional foods). Overall, the rate of somatic growth in this species was likely fairly rapid, as in apes. Thus, instead of experiencing childhood, we think a more elaborate suckling phase of infancy would have evolved that may have involved provisioning of complementary foods to fuel rapid, early brain growth. Once this had been achieved, the *H. erectus* infant would have entered the juvenile phase as is seen in apes.

EARLY ARCHAIC *HOMO*

Archaic *H. sapiens* include fossils assigned to *H. antecessor* and *H. heidelbergensis* (Bermúdez de Castro et al. 1997; Schoetensack 1908). *H.*

antecessor specimens come from a site in Spain called Gran Dolina and date to more than 780,000 years ago (Arsuaga et al. 1999; Bermúdez de Castro et al. 1997; Falguéres et al. 1999). Specimens attributed to *H. heidelbergensis* have been found throughout Europe, but those with dentition available for study are also from Spain, from a site called Sima de los Huesos, dating to about 300,000 years ago (Arsuaga et al. 1997; Arsuaga, Bermúdez de Castro, and Carbonell 1997).

Studies of *H. antecessor*'s and *H. heidelbergensis*'s patterns of dental development match those of modern humans (Bermúdez de Castro et al. 1997, 1999; Bermúdez de Castro and Rosas 2001), but patterns of dental development are not the same as rates of dental growth (M. Dean et al. 2001). Bermúdez de Castro and colleagues (2003) examined dental microstructures (perikymata) on the anterior teeth of *H. antecessor* specimens and found some teeth formed at a rate within the modern human range. In contrast, Ramirez Rozzi and Bermúdez de Castro (2004) asserted that both Archaic *sapiens* enjoyed shorter periods of dental growth than seen today. Given these contrasting findings, and the fact that we cannot assess the presence of skeletal growth spurts, more data is needed to assess the nature of growth patterns in these species (note the contrasts in maturation rates in anterior versus posterior teeth in Neanderthals discussed below). We would not be surprised, however, if based on further increases in adult brain size over what was seen in *H. erectus*, the suckling phase of infancy was more elaborate in these archaic hominins than in apes and may have included provisioning of young.

NEANDERTHALS AND EARLY MODERN HUMANS

We follow other scholars, including Hublin, in accepting Neanderthals as an "operative paleontological species, distinct from *H. sapiens*" (Hublin 2009:16023). While there is some genetic evidence (Green et al. 2010) to suggest the possibility of limited interbreeding between *H. neanderthalensis* and early modern humans, we choose to assess dental and skeletal fossil evidence for these two groups separately given their potential to tell us when the modern human pattern of growth and development evolved. Furthermore, the complex gorilla genome (Scally et al. 2012) shows that speciation does not preclude limited gene exchange around the time of lineage separation (see also Sankararaman et al. 2014 for a discussion of negative selection on Neanderthal alleles).

Before addressing the stages of growth in Neanderthals and the earliest modern humans, we need to address rates of growth. Over the past decade, several studies of Neanderthal dental formation and eruption have been undertaken (e.g., Guatelli-Steinberg 2009, Ramirez Rozzi and Bermúdez de Castro 2004, T. Smith et al. 2011). Guatelli-Steinberg and colleagues (2005, 2007) have argued that the rate of development of Neanderthal anterior teeth falls within the modern human range of variation. Reid, Guatelli-Steinberg, and Walton's (2008) study of posterior teeth (premolars and molars) also found that the rate of formation of premolars in Neanderthals fell within the modern human range. Studies of molar teeth reveal a different story. Work by several different research teams (e.g., Bayle et al. 2009a; Macchiarelli et al. 2006; T. Smith et al. 2007b) found that first and second molars formed faster in Neanderthals than in modern human samples. Macchiarelli and colleagues (2006) found more rapid lower canine formation as well. Furthermore, they estimated that M2 eruption occurred before eight years of age; this occurs around age ten to thirteen years in modern humans (Liversidge 2003). A study by T. Smith and colleagues (2009) found that the M3 of Neanderthals also developed quickly. Bayle and colleagues (2009b) studied the early modern human juvenile from La Madeleine and found its dental development within the modern human range. The enamel and root formation of an immature individual from Jebel Irhoud, Morocco, who died about 180,000 years ago, was examined, and estimated age was found to be eight years old thus following a modern human rate of dental growth (T. Smith et al. 2007b).

In sum, there is convincing evidence from dentition that at least the second and third molars (and perhaps the first molar; Bayle et al. 2009a) formed at a faster rate in Neanderthals than in extant humans. We take away from these studies that, if we apply modern human standards of crown and root formation to estimate age at death of juvenile Neanderthals, we will systematically overestimate ages of individuals with second and third molars, while age estimates of younger individuals, with developing anterior teeth, will yield reliable results. In fact, the similarity in rates of anterior permanent dental growth support the proposition that childhood was a stage experienced by Neanderthals. Overall, though, Neanderthals developed molar teeth faster than even the earliest modern humans.

That Neanderthals and the earliest modern humans achieved average adult cranial capacities much larger than those seen today makes it reasonable to surmise that the infancy stage of growth for these two paleontological species was similar to that of modern humans and involved an elaborated suckling phase. In fact, a recent study by Austin and colleagues (2013) of barium distributions in the teeth of the Scladina Neanderthal indicate that this individual was exclusively breastfed for seven months, followed by seven months of complementary feeding, after which the infant was abruptly weaned. We cannot know whether supplementary food was provided by adults/others or obtained by the individual. However, endocranial volumes (Gunz et al. 2011) and estimated ratios of and adult to newborn brain weight (Rosenberg 1992; B. H. Smith and Tompkins 1995) suggest that Neanderthals were secondarily altricial, supporting the suggestion of complementary food provisioning.

Early weaning also warrants some discussion. Work by Bocherens and colleagues (2001), using isotopic analysis and estimates based on maternal body size (J. Thompson 1998), suggest that Neanderthals, like many modern humans (Dettwyler 1995), weaned their offspring at about three to four years of age. This hypothesis is also documented by the timing of enamel defects in Neanderthal teeth (e.g., Bilsborough and Thompson 2005). Perhaps the Scladina individual was unusual in being weaned so early. Alternatively, it could be that the mother could no longer breastfeed for some unknown reason. Kachel and colleagues point out that "life-history theory predicts that selection will favor females who concentrate their reproductive potential earlier in their reproductive period when adult mortality is high" (2011:481 citing Kirkwood 1987). As we discuss below, Neanderthals suffered high rates of mortality and so perhaps early weaning was an adaptive strategy followed by some female Neanderthals to increase their reproductive success.

The adult skulls of modern humans are globe-shaped, or rounded, while those of Neanderthals are more elongated. At birth, modern human braincases are elongated like those of Neanderthals. However, in the first year after birth, modern humans go through a "globularization phase" of brain growth causing the braincase to become more rounded while those of Neanderthal infants remain elongated (Gunz et al. 2011). This phase appears unique to modern humans and in this way the infancy stage of growth between these two species is differentiated. Martín-González and colleagues (2012) found that while Neanderthals and modern human statural growth was similar at birth, from the age of about five to six months (end of infancy I/nursing phase in humans), Neanderthals gained height more slowly. This confirms our earlier (Nelson and Thompson 2002) work where we found that lower limb proportions in adult Neanderthals and modern humans appear to be the product of an ontogenetic trajectory set very early in life.

Did Neanderthals experience childhood? Mann, Lampl, and Monge (1996) have argued that Neanderthals experienced childhood because they exhibited a period of stasis between the eruption of lateral incisors and second molars. Apes do not undergo this stasis in dental/gnathic growth, and so it seems that the Neanderthal growth period was extended relative to earlier hominins. Childhood was present, but was it of the same length as in modern humans?

The length of childhood in Neanderthals can be estimated based on brain growth. Neanderthal adults had a very large mean brain volume compared to recent humans. Bogin (2003) has argued that the growth of such a large brain supports the existence of childhood in Neanderthals; that is, a larger adult brain size required a higher growth rate during infancy and childhood. At birth, Neanderthal neonates possessed endocranial volumes similar to those of modern humans (Gunz et al. 2011). Yet on the basis of cranial growth, at about six years Neanderthals still had some brain growth left to achieve but, by eight years, adult brain volume was completed (Coqueugniot and Hublin 2007). This evidence supports Bogin's hypothesis. We (J. Thompson and Nelson 2001), along with Coqueugniot and Hublin (2007) and Ponce de León and colleagues (2008), have analyzed proportional growth in linear and volumetric measurements of the cranial vault. We suggest that, since the end point—adult cranial vault size—was greater than in recent modern humans, absolute vault dimensions of Neanderthals were actually advanced relative to modern humans throughout postnatal growth (J. Thompson and Nelson 2001), supporting the conclusions of Coqueugniot, and Hublin (2007). Thus, Neanderthals had a higher rate of brain growth than modern humans during their infancy and early childhood growth. This conclusion is also supported by T. Smith and Alemseged, who note that, at the age of three years, the Engis 2 individual "had a remarkably high" endocranial volume of 1400 cubic centimeters (2013:2).

Turning to juvenility, if this stage began in Neanderthals at about six to eight years of age then it began about the same time as it does in extant humans. Since the Le Moustier 1 Neanderthal youth (mentioned in more detail below) was approximately eleven when he died and had not yet entered his growth spurt, the juvenile stage lasted at least as long in Neanderthals as in modern humans. We owe our understanding of adolescent growth in Neanderthals to two relatively complete pre-adolescent specimens: Le

Moustier 1 from France dating to circa 40,000 years ago (J. Thompson 2005; J. Thompson and Bilsborough 1997, 2005; Weinert 1925) and Teshik-Tash 1 from Uzbekistan dating to circa 70,000 years ago (Johanson and Edgar 1996). We have used these specimens and compared their relative postcranial growth to that of recent modern humans, early modern humans, gorillas, and other Neanderthal nonadults (Nelson and Thompson 1999, 2002, 2005; J. Thompson and Nelson 2000, 2005a, 2005b, 2011; J. Thompson, Nelson, and Illerhaus 2003). Recently, T. Smith and colleagues (2010) have used synchrotron technology to estimate the age of Le Moustier 1 yielding an age of 11.6–12.1 years. Given that Neanderthals likely grew their second and third molars faster than us, and based on data from a histomorphometric analysis (Ramsay, Weaver, and Seidler 2005), we arrive at a consensus age of eleven for Le Moustier 1 (see J. Thompson and Nelson 2011 for further discussion). Given more rapid molar growth, we estimate the dental age of Teshik Tash 1 to be about eight years (see Coqueugniot and Hublin 2007; Ullrich 1955). Other, younger Neanderthal ages were estimated using modern human standards given that these early erupting teeth developed at the same rate as ours do today. We (J. Thompson and Nelson 2011) plotted dental age against relative postcranial age for these Neanderthal nonadults as well as early modern humans, recent modern humans, the *H. erectus* youth, and an ape species. The results suggest that Neanderthal proportional femoral growth was like that of recent and early modern humans (con. J. Thompson and Nelson 2000).

While the pattern of growth, but not its magnitude, in Neanderthals and early moderns is similar, we have argued that the duration of growth was different (J. Thompson and Nelson 2011). As stated previously, dental and skeletal growth in apes and humans stops at about the same time (Anemone, Mooney, and Siegel 1996; Kuykendall and Conroy 1996; Leigh and Shea 1996; Simpson, Russell, and Lovejoy 1996; Tanner 1990). We assume that this is also true for Neanderthals and early modern humans. Le Moustier 1 died at about eleven years of age with only one quarter of his third molar root completed. While we do not yet know the rate of development of the third molar root in Neanderthals, a conservative estimate of two to three years, as in recent modern humans, seems reasonable. This would mean that the Le Moustier boy would have stopped growing at about thirteen to fourteen years of age. We argue that the duration of growth in Neanderthals, while longer than that in *H. erectus*, still fell short of the eighteen to twenty years seen in modern humans (Robson and Wood 2008).

Neanderthal adolescence was likely much shorter than is seen in recent humans, but we can still assess whether a growth spurt was present or not. We have previously examined this question (Nelson and Thompson 2002) using comparative data from modern populations. Our work assessed whether an accelerated growth spurt was expressed in Neanderthals and early modern humans, or whether growth was more constant. We plotted femoral midshaft area (proxy for body size) and length (proxy for stature). This analysis revealed that there is a nonlinear relationship between body size and stature. We used regressions (one for juveniles and another for adults) to reveal sample differences. Our comparative samples (Khoisan and Inuit) and Neanderthals employ a two-step process for robusticity—a long shallow slope before adolescence, after which the line flexes sharply upward in adults. Femoral bone robusticity may, then, increase more rapidly at the adolescent growth spurt when the bone stops growing in length but continues to increase in breadth. Similar results were found for the tibia (see J. Thompson and Nelson 2011 for more detailed discussion). Our results support the idea that both Neanderthals and early modern humans experienced growth spurts in adolescence. However, the Neanderthal adolescence and growth spurt must have occurred in a shorter time, given that they finished growing at thirteen to fourteen years of age.

Discussion

What would *H. erectus*'s early life have been like? We posit that they did not experience childhood, but instead a more elaborate second phase of infancy, what we call the suckling phase (from six months to three years, to distinguish it from the nursing stage during which all nourishment is received from breast milk alone, from birth to about six months). We suggest that early, rapid brain growth required mothers (and perhaps others) to introduce supplementary foods (Aiello and Key 2002; see also Hrdy, chapter 2, this volume). Cooperative hunting in *H. erectus* may also have included cooperative feeding. We argue that the duration of growth in this species is too short for it to have experienced childhood. There is also no evidence of M1 delay, one of the hallmarks of childhood in modern humans. Skeletal growth appears to follow a more rapid, apelike pattern with no pervasive growth spurt. Instead, *H. erectus* infants would reach the juvenile stage by about three years, as in apes. Judging from the hypoplastic lesions on the teeth of the Nariokotome boy (Dean and Smith

2009), estimated to have occurred between 3.3 to 4.2 years of age (different aging methods were used) the transition was likely stressful. While *Homo erectus* juveniles would have undoubtedly been taking on adult roles, they would likely have needed nutritional supplementation to sustain the growth rate allowing them to attain adult size by eight to ten years of age. This would place further stress on the group as a whole to support subadult individuals.

Archaic *H. sapiens*, like *H. erectus*, probably also provided nutrients to their young after about six months to complement those received in breast milk. A short childhood is possible, but confirmation requires more fossils with both dental and skeletal elements preserved. Gurven and Walker (2006) argue that the childhood stage required help from other group members and would therefore incur higher energetic costs for the group as a whole (Hawkes 2003; Lancaster and Lancaster 1983a; Mace 2000). A childhood stage in these hominins would have important energetic consequences for the mother and the group, including older juveniles and adolescents who might be pressed into helping with food acquisition and/or care for these dependent individuals.

Given the longer duration of growth in Neanderthals than in earlier hominins, a childhood stage (or phase, if this is merely an extension of the Infancy stage) lasting from about three to six years of age is probable, but its nature differed by including more rapid cranial growth during this phase than seen in modern humans. Neanderthals were large-game hunter-gatherers with meat and other animal byproducts making up most of their diet (Mellars 1996; Speth 2010; but see Henry, Brooks, and Piperno 2011 and El Zaatari et al. 2011 for a discussion of dietary variability). Archaeological evidence indicates that adult males and females, and most probably all subadults, were involved directly or indirectly in hunting (Kuhn and Stiner 2006). We know from work of behavioral ecologists and cultural anthropologists (Crittenden, chapter 7, this volume; Lancy, chapter 8, this volume) that from childhood (ca. three years of age) onward modern human individuals make contributions to their own diet but are usually not involved in risky hunting activities. This was not the case for Neanderthals, at least from the juvenile stage onward (see J. Thompson and Nelson 2011 for case study). Sorensen and Leonard (2001) argue that the Neanderthal's body size and proportions would have taken a lot of energy to maintain even as adults. We know that younger Neanderthals had high activity levels compared with modern humans of similar ages which, in turn, would affect their dietary/energy needs (Ruff et al. 1993; Ruff, Walker, and Trinkaus 1994; Trinkaus 1997). Leonard and colleagues (2003) maintained that fast brain growth during infancy and childhood would demand that these individuals be given high-energy foods. The impact of putting females and subadults (infants, children, juveniles, and adolescents) in harm's way during the hunt would have also had significant demographic consequences, resulting in low population numbers (e.g., Caspari and Lee 2004; Mellars and French 2011; Trinkaus 1995). Furthermore, Kuhn and Stiner state that the unpredictable nature of hunting would "place greater periodic nutritional stress on juveniles during development, again limiting reproductive potential" (2006:959). Such a harsh and unpredictable environment would favor a fast life-history strategy (Brumbach, Figueredo, and Ellis 2009; Ellis 2004) and fits with a shorter duration of growth in Neanderthals. Gurven and Walker (2006) studied the energetic consequences of several offspring on modern human parents, generating growth trajectories comparing fast/ape versus slow/human patterns. Their work led us to conclude that, for Neanderthals, neither of the above growth trajectories would have been feasible given their high-energy needs during growth. Since adult Neanderthals needed 3,000 to 5,500 kcal/day to maintain their own metabolic needs (Sorensen and Leonard 2001), dependent offspring who grew extremely rapidly and required energy to fuel that fast growth would have placed a very costly burden on adults. Delaying growth and extending the growth period so that subadults could grow more slowly does not make sense either, as this would also place a high energetic cost on older subadults and adults. Instead, a more constant rate of somatic skeletal growth during childhood and the juvenile stage is likely. It also seems reasonable, based on the archaeological and fossil data (Kuhn and Stiner 2006; J. Thompson and Nelson 2011), that juveniles contributed more to their group either earlier, or in greater quantities, than we see in their modern human counterparts. This, in turn, could affect life-history patterns (Migliano, Vinicius, and Lahr 2007; Stearns and Koella 1986; Van Schaik et al. 2006; R. Walker et al. 2006). Population numbers would have been small due to high mortality rates in juveniles (and perhaps younger individuals), adolescents, and adults.

Modern humans possess several life-history traits distinguishing them from apes including a more elaborate suckling phase of infancy where nutrition from breast milk is augmented by the provisioning of complementary foods after six months of age to about age three, childhood, evolving as a result of further extension and elaboration of infancy where individuals begin their transition to an adult diet, lasting from about three to six years (recognized as a separate life-history stage), a longer duration of the subadult period, delayed reproduction, a longer life span and, for females, a long postreproductive phase. Various explanations of these characteristics include the grandmother hypothesis (Hawkes 2006 a, b) and the embodied capital hypothesis (e.g., Kaplan, Lancaster, and Robson 2003). The former emphasizes the role of women of postreproductive age in providing food for their daughter's children, resulting in a shorter interbirth interval for the mother and increasing her potential reproductive success. The embodied capital hypothesis links increases in brain size, longer duration of growth, and longer life span to changes in diet to include high-quality, difficult to obtain, nutrient-rich foods, thus emphasizing learning and surplus production posited to have begun from the time of *H. erectus* onward (e.g., Kaplan, Lancaster, and Robson 2003). Both hypotheses assume relatively low adult and nonadult (particularly juvenile) mortality rates (e.g., Blurton Jones 2006; Paine and Boldsen 2006; Sellen 2006). In Neanderthals, this was not the case. Neanderthals did not lack the potential to live longer, but their lifestyle and environment made doing so unlikely. Living in an ice-age climate with higher metabolic needs than modern-day foragers, plus their dependency on large-bodied game, likely demanded that all individuals capable of helping in the hunt be involved including women, juveniles, and perhaps children. The median age at death of Neanderthals was likely lower than in living forager populations. While they had the potential to live long lives (based on the relationship between brain and body weight; Sacher 1959, 1975) and some did, such as Shanidar I (Trinkaus 1983), the chances of living longer were low. Instead, longer-lived individuals were more common in populations of early modern humans when female adults and younger nonadults could avoid high-risk hunting activities. The demographic profile of early modern humans would have changed with increased population numbers, allowing for the expansion of modern humans throughout Africa and beyond (see Mellars and French 2011). We have suggested that a shift to a more broad-based foraging economy would have allowed this to unfold by removing the strong selective pressures experienced by Neanderthals. Only then could the modern life-history pattern fully emerge.

Conclusions

Reviewing the fossil record to assess when and how the modern pattern of growth and development evolved, we conclude that the modern pattern of growth and development is just that—modern. It evolved in a mosaic fashion from the time of *H. erectus* onward. The first step involved an elaboration of infancy in which, from about six months of age onward, breast milk was augmented by foods provided by the mother and/or others (suckling phase). We hypothesize that this began with *H. erectus* when larger adult brain sizes required rapid postnatal brain growth. Given the short, apelike duration of growth and lack of biological markers for childhood (delay in M1 eruption, for example), *H. erectus* was unlikely to have experienced this life-history stage. Over time, with increases in adult brain sizes, infancy's suckling phase became more elaborate and entrenched, allowing for very rapid brain growth especially up to age three, after which at least *H. erectus* offspring would have entered the juvenile stage. At some point, selective pressures required more time for both brain and somatic growth and this resulted in further elongation and elaboration of infancy beyond three years of age resulting in what is now recognized as the childhood stage. By the time of the Neanderthals, a short childhood, beginning after about three years, was likely present. However, its nature differed from that experienced in modern humans by including more rapid cranial growth, with high energetic consequences for the child and group. Those high energetic demands would have placed extreme adaptive pressures on these hunters to provide food for their children. During the juvenile stage, linear growth may have been more constant, ending with a fast skeletal growth spurt in bone robusticity (see Nelson and Thompson 2002) during a short adolescence. The role growth spurts played is unclear, but Neanderthals experienced them at the end of the nonadult period after about eleven years of age with growth terminating at about thirteen or fourteen years. The shorter duration of growth allowed Neanderthals to reach adulthood/full reproductive maturity in less time in order to maximize their reproductive success (Charnov and Berrigan 1993). It will be interesting to see how the Denisova hominins and *Homo floresiensis* fit into this picture when subadult dental and skeletal material for these species becomes available. Early modern human teeth seem to grow at the same rate as do those of recent modern humans (not more rapidly as in Neanderthals), with the implication that at least dental growth ended later than in Neanderthals. Long bone growth follows a recent modern human pattern, including the presence of growth spurts in all long bones.

With regard to how the modern pattern of growth and development evolved, we note that Bernstein (chapter 5, this volume) argues that "the underpinning physiology of this growth period [childhood] does not reveal any evidence of it having evolved as a novel insertion to the human growth trajectory" (119). However, elsewhere, she argues that evolution proceeds by "tinkering" with existing parts and processes (e.g., 103). The model presented here suggests that the full expression of childhood as a life-history stage is indeed unique in modern humans, but also that it did evolve by tinkering with the basic process that existed in the last common ancestor with the apes. The tinkering involved modifications in timing, growth rates, and the beginning and end of this period, with changes accumulating bit by bit over several million years. Thus, Bernstein's conclusions and ours are entirely consistent. We see the evolution of the human growth pattern as including several "phases": nursing (exclusively breastfed; zero to six months); suckling (breast milk augmented by complementary foods; six months to three years); and childhood (a transition to eating adult foods involving provisioning and nurturing until somatic and cognitive development allows the individual to self-provision, independent of others, if necessary; three years to about six years). We realize that the concept of childhood is entrenched in the literature as a "separate" growth stage and may well be one in modern humans. However, in discussion of the evolution of this phenomenon, we find it useful to conceptualize it as having evolved after, and perhaps as a result of, the changes to the suckling phase. Once provisioning of sucklings became entrenched, it likely had consequences including allowing a delay in somatic growth and, over time, allowed an additional stage to evolve: what we and others call childhood.

In conclusion, it is unclear when childhood first evolved, but we provide a new definition of when it begins in modern humans—at age three when all of the deciduous teeth are erupted and the child is able to provision him/herself to a certain extent, but needs special transitional foods (smaller portions, special types of food due to immature gut size, rapidly growing brain)—and when it ends, with the beginning of the juvenile stage at about six years of age (for biological markers, see above) when human offspring have the *requisite anatomy and ecological knowledge*" to actively participate in adult activities (cf. Smith et al 2013:2789; emphasis added). We redefine infancy to include the two phases, nursing and suckling. The nursing phase lasts from birth to about six months of age and the suckling stage lasts from six months to about three years. The suckling phase is very different in apes and humans (see table 4.1). The suckling phase of infancy likely evolved as an adaptive strategy in *H. erectus* to fuel brain growth when breast milk alone did not provide sufficient nutrients and when the offspring was not yet able to provision itself. As brain growth continued to expand in subsequent species of *Homo*, this suckling phase likely lengthened to include a childhood phase, which can be envisioned as a third phase of infancy (infancy III). At some point—possibly by the time of Neanderthals—somatic growth became somewhat delayed, resulting in a short childhood during which brain growth continued at a pace more rapid than in modern humans, requiring transitional foods. Childhood likely evolved as an adaptive strategy, not just for mothers (e.g. Bogin 2006), but also for the individual. It allowed more time for offspring to achieve 90 percent of their adult brain growth and extended the time for social learning while in close contact with the mother. Consequently, somatic growth slowed so that, at least at the start of this phase, children had not yet achieved an adult gait and certainly still needed protection from and provisioning by older individuals in their group. By the time of the Neanderthals, all of the life stages seen in modern humans were present, but their length and nature were not yet fully modern. The elaboration of infancy II (suckling phase), the delayed somatic and rapid brain growth of childhood (a separate life-history stage or infancy III), and the elongated adolescent stage with its pervasive growth spurts are, collectively, the hallmarks of the modern human pattern of growth and development, differentiating us from all hominins that came before us. That pattern may, in fact, define the emergence of our species.

CHAPTER FIVE

Hormones and the Evolution of Childhood in Humans and Nonhuman Primates

ROBIN M. BERNSTEIN

Introduction

The developmental path that humans traverse is different from that of our closest living relatives, but is the difference of degree or kind? Given the specific nature of human growth and development, characterized by a prolonged period between birth and sexual maturity, much focus has been placed on the earliest stages of human development as ones that set us apart from nonhuman primates and some of our fossil ancestors. Other social mammals pass through stages of infancy and juvenility, but it has been suggested that humans alone have a childhood (Bogin 1997). From this perspective, childhood represents a new phase of life history, inserted between infancy and the juvenile stage. Its emergence dates back to early members of the genus *Homo* (Bogin, Bragg, and Kuzawa, chapter 3, this volume; but see also Thompson and Nelson, chapter 5, this volume), attributable both to expanding brain size and to the benefits provided by an extended period of postnatal developmental plasticity (Bogin 1999a). Several aspects of behavioral and cognitive development have been proposed to take place during childhood such that this phase of development is part of an overall growth strategy associated with the evolution of our sociality and the growth of our brain (B. Campbell 2011b). It is worth asking which of the following processes has characterized the evolution of childhood, as outlined by Gould (1977): is it the result of something novel being introduced to the developmental sequence of an ancestor, or is it the result of changes in developmental timing of something that already exists?

The idea that evolution proceeds by "tinkering" with existing parts (e.g., genes, developmental processes, structures) rather than building from scratch to produce novel traits (Jacob 1977) suggests that we take a broadly comparative and deeply mechanistic approach to understanding the evolution of human development. Including investigations of nonhuman primate development to contextualize what we know (or think we know) about humans is critical in this respect. While the fossil record might offer us glimpses into the developmental course of our ancestors, these glimpses remain only snapshots, and cannot provide the depth of information that detailed studies of nonhuman primate growth can. As our closest living relatives, nonhuman primates provide the best possible perspective for assessing novel aspects of the human life course. Since closely related organisms can use similar genes, processes, or structures in different ways (Shubin 2002), a developmental approach can also reveal the layers of homology or homoplasy underlying shared traits (Lockwood and Fleagle 1999). Identifying truly "novel" traits, as well as defining what constitutes a "novelty" from an evolutionary perspective, is challenging. According to several different perspectives, a true novelty is defined by one or all of the following: it functions to open a new adaptive zone for a species (Mayr 1963), it must be based on a distinct developmental variant (West-Eberhard 2003), it must be an apomorphy (Arthur 2000), it cannot be homologous to any ancestral structure or function (Muller and Wagner 1991). While it is difficult to collapse these into a definition of novelty that can be operationalized, it is clear that, at the very least, identifying something as novel requires a consideration of its evolution, its ontogeny, and its role as a functional variant on what came before (Pigliucci 2008).

Defining Childhood: Traditional Markers and Measures in Comparative Perspective

How can the novelty of human childhood, or any developmental stage for that matter, then be evaluated? First, a clear definition of the stage must exist with easily identifiable markers that can be assessed comparatively across other taxa. Childhood begins at the end of infancy (generally around three years) and ends at the beginning of the juvenile stage of development (around seven years). A set of morphological and behavioral characteristics has been proposed to define human life-history stages in general and childhood in particular (Bogin 1999b). The end of infancy is usually described as being coincident with weaning, defined as complete cessation of nursing, rather than the introduction of complementary weaning foods (see Thompson and Nelson, chapter 4, this volume, for an expanded discussion of the use of weaning as a marker of childhood). While there is considerable variation in age at weaning across modern human populations, two and a half to three years encompasses the time at which many agricultural, pastoral, and forager populations cease breastfeeding (Sellen and Smay 2001). Around this time the eruption of deciduous dentition is also completed. The juvenile phase represents the maturation of the dependent child into an independent individual capable of sustaining his or her own needs (but see Hrdy, chapter 2, and Meehan, Helfrecht, and Malcom, chapter 9, this volume for discussion of extended nutritional dependence in humans). The onset of this phase is associated with the completion or near completion of absolute brain size growth and emergence of the permanent dentition (the first molar) and usually takes place around seven years of age. The intervening time period, childhood, is a time when human offspring are weaned yet still provided cooperative care by other members of their social group (Bogin 2009; Bogin, Bragg, and Kuzawa, chapter 3 this volume).

In order to proceed with a traditional comparative analysis on the presence and length of childhood based on the definitions provided above, the following information is usually compared among humans and nonhuman primates (usually the great apes): approximate weaning age, approximate age of eruption of complete deciduous dentition and emergence of first molar, and approximate ages at which brain growth is complete. Such investigations have been performed and results have been reported in detail elsewhere (e.g., B. H. Smith, Crummett, and Brandt 1994; Bogin and Smith 1996). These comparisons suggest that, first, humans wean their offspring at relatively early ages compared to other great apes (around three years, compared to around four years for gorillas, five to six for chimpanzees, and seven to eight for orangutans). Deciduous dentition is fully erupted in humans by 2.33 years, chimpanzees by 1.12 years, gorillas by 0.99 years, and orangutans by 1.05 years (B. H. Smith, Crummett, and Brandt 1994). First molar emergence at approximately six years of age in humans is relatively delayed compared to great apes (between three and four years of age). Humans, therefore, live for about three and a half years with their full complement of deciduous dentition before their adult teeth begin to erupt, whereas great apes on average wait only two and a half years.

The correlation between dental eruption and brain growth is often included in discussions of the linkage of several traits proceeding along a slower trajectory in humans compared with other primates. Specifically, the linkage

between brain growth and the eruption of the first adult molar and the timing
of first molar emergence relative to other developmental events is valued as an
informative life-history marker (B. H. Smith 1992). The correlation between
first molar emergence and brain weight is strongly positive across primates
in general (e.g., B. H. Smith 1989), although recent work with wild populations underscores the need for caution when extending the timing of dental
emergence to important life-history traits such as weaning (T. Smith et al.
2013). One early report provides information on the relationship between dental eruption status and brain weights for all great ape taxa (Keith 1895). Based
on the reported measures, great apes in the process of cutting their first permanent molar have attained between 80 percent (orangutans) and 95 percent
(gorillas, chimpanzees) of their adult brain weight, similar to humans. Even
values reported for macaques suggest that the eruption of their first molar
coincides with the growth of approximately 90 percent of their adult brain
size. While growth in human brain size may continue for one to two years
after absolute brain size growth ceases in chimpanzees (ending at five to six
years and four to five years, respectively), the most marked difference in the
rate of brain growth between humans and chimpanzees is seen in the first year
of postnatal life with nonsignificant rate differences after eighteen months of
life (Leigh 2004). Given that the human pre-adult growth period continues
well past the age at which the majority of brain growth is completed, this suggests that the brain or brain growth itself cannot be seen as a direct pacesetter
of prolonged duration of human growth generally, or differences in patterns
of dental eruption specifically.

Another difference between human and nonhuman primate growth is that
humans have subadult growth spurts in linear dimensions (e.g., leg length,
overall height), while nonhuman primates do not (but see Tanner, Wilson, and
Rudman 1990). Despite this difference, the nature of human and nonhuman
primate growth patterns can still be considered to be overall quite similar.
Growth spurts in height are much less pronounced and sometimes seemingly
absent in some human populations where the overall period of growth occurs
over a longer period of time and at a lower rate than others. This suggests
that the timing and nature of the subadult human growth spurt is responsive
to nutritional and health status (e.g., Eideh, Jonsson, and Hochberg 2012). In
addition, many nonhuman primate species do have very clear growth spurts
in body mass, and some have growth spurts in facial dimensions (Leigh 1992).
Analyses of growth patterns in several nonhuman primate taxa show that,

while the timing of the human subadult spurt is relatively delayed according to size-based predictions derived from other anthropoid species—thus creating a period during which growth continues at a slow rate—there are several other species with similarly delayed timing, suggesting that the prolongation of human growth is a matter of degree (Leigh 2001). Therefore, a broadly comparative perspective on growth patterns weakens the argument for the insertion of a phase of development as a new element in human life history and lends support to the idea that any additional prolongation seen in human ontogeny is the result of "tinkering" with a preexisting pattern.

Taken together, the comparative information on weaning age, dental maturation, and brain growth suggest that human "childhood" seems to be defined by a shift to an earlier weaning age coupled with a slight delay in eruption of deciduous dentition, a later absolute age for first molar emergence, and a later absolute age for completion of brain size growth (although the coordination of first molar eruption and brain growth remains constant among all primates, including humans). Comparative studies of growth also support the idea that the pattern of human ontogeny is not unique and that other species, while not delayed absolutely as long as humans, also have prolonged subadult periods of growth. While these studies can suggest how patterns of development appear similar or different among species and can be used to generate hypotheses concerning the evolution of such patterns, the analysis of behavioral or morphological traits does not necessarily get at the underlying physiological mechanisms regulating the pace of development. Why is it important to look at such regulators of development in addition to the more easily measurable manifestations of these processes? It is important because it is through modification of these regulators that development evolves.

For example, while it is easy to think of brain size as evolving, since this is what we are able to easily estimate from measurements of cranial capacity in fossilized remains, it is the physiological regulators of brain development (e.g., those genes, and gene products that determine how fast the brain grows, for how long, and how much of the brain is devoted to processes such as synaptogenesis or myelination) that actually drive change in this characteristic over time. Therefore, an investigation of the regulatory mechanisms that underlie life-history stages, their duration and transitions, is likely to reveal how stages are shortened, lengthened, and whether novel additions to a developmental trajectory have occurred. The expectation is that, if there is a truly novel addition to a developmental trajectory, a "signature" of this modification will be apparent in the regulatory mechanisms responsible for the new phase of development.

For the remainder of this chapter, I will review some of the regulatory mechanisms associated with growth during the childhood phase of development and take a comparative perspective toward addressing the question of whether human childhood is unique, or whether it represents a modification of an ancestral developmental pathway. I will focus on hormones as the class of regulatory mechanisms for this comparison for several reasons. If life-history patterns are adaptive, then responses to selection should involve the evolution of mechanisms that allow a degree of flexibility in life histories in order to meet environmental challenges (Ross 1998). Previous research suggests that genetic variation provides a mechanism by which life histories change and are selected and that reproductive traits such as age at first reproduction and menarche have a strong heritable component. Other researchers point out that life-history variation is better explained as the interaction between the genotype and the environment (Stearns 1992).

Hormones are physiological mechanisms that mediate the "crosstalk" between the genotype and the environment. They have long been recognized as important mediators of life-history trade-offs and, consequently, as important for understanding how life histories evolve (e.g., Ketterson and Nolan 1992; Sinervo and Svensson 1998). As Zera and Harshman explain, "life-history traits, which determine age-specific patterns of growth, sexual maturity, and longevity, are precisely those organismal features that are known to be tightly controlled by hormones" (2001:538). According to DeRousseau (1990), studies of life-history traits should first determine the ontogenetic basis of a trait by examining processes at the proximate level, then compare the trait phylogenetically. Since the hormonal regulation of growth is intertwined with other aspects of life history due to the pleiotropic nature of hormone activity, it is essential to consider the species-specific contexts of hormonal patterns in order to begin to understand why they evolved.

The Hormonal Regulation of Childhood Growth

Since growth is a continuous process, it is difficult to compartmentalize the physiological regulation of growth into different phases. A useful way of conceptualizing both growth processes and their underlying endocrine regulation, the infancy-childhood-puberty (ICP) model, was suggested by Karlberg

(1989). While this model does not formally include a juvenile phase of growth, it is based on differences in growth pattern (specifically, growth rate) that occur from birth through adolescence and explicitly seeks to unite these patterns with key hormonal regulators of growth during infancy, childhood, and puberty by breaking down the postnatal curve of linear growth into three additive and slightly overlapping components.

In this model, the infant stage of growth is considered to begin in midgestation and to taper off at two to three years; therefore, early postnatal human growth is really an extension of fetal growth. Growth during this phase is dependent on insulin, the insulin-like growth factors (IGFs, -I and -II), and the IGF binding proteins (IGFBPs). The fetal system is sensitive to maternal nutrition and these factors are largely nutritionally regulated up through approximately six months after birth (Yeung and Smyth 2003). Breast milk, in addition to providing the main source of nutrition for the early months of an infant's life, also contains IGFs, insulin, and a host of other growth factors and cytokines (Donovan and Odle 1994). It is likely that these constituents contribute to growth differences between breast- and formula-fed infants. Formula, higher in protein, has been associated with higher IGF-I concentrations in infants and may relate to an earlier onset of the infancy-childhood transition (see below). Growth hormone (GH), one of the main regulators of somatic growth during postnatal life, peaks at midgestation in humans, levels, then falls in the third trimester and into the early neonatal period (Kaplan, Grumbach, and Shepard 1972).

The transition from the infancy to the childhood stage of growth (infancy-childhood transition, or ICT) is associated with the point at which endogenous GH begins to exert a significant effect on growth in postnatal life, both independently and through its influence on IGF-I secretion (Karlberg and Albertsson-Wikland 1988). This transition can begin as early as six months in affluent countries and is evidenced by an abrupt, transient increase in growth rate during this time. "Normal" ICT is thought to occur between six and twelve months and an ICT occurring later than this is considered delayed (delayed ICT, or DICT). The delay in ICT is important since it has been shown to have a negative impact on growth outcomes, where each month of delay in transition results in a growth deficit at five years of age (Hochberg and Albertsson-Wikland 2008). The longer the delay, the shorter resultant prepubertal stature; in particularly marked cases of DICT, the growth deficit can be quite pronounced, as in Malawian children whose ICT between three and

Table 5.1. Ages of the Infancy-Childhood Transition (ICT) across Different Human Populations

Population	Age at ICT	Reference
Sweden	9 months	Karlberg et al. 1987
Israel	10 months	Zuckerman-Levin and Hochberg 2007
Shanghai	11 months	Liu, Albertsson-Wikland, and Karlberg 2000
Pakistan	15 months; suburban	Liu, Jalil, and Karlberg 1998
	13 months; village	
	10 months; urban	
Malawi	36–48 months	Zverev and Chisi 2004

Source: From references cited in Hochberg 2012.

four years culminates in an estimated pre-pubertal height deficit of 15–20 cm (table 5.1). DICT is not necessarily a negative process for although it leads to smaller body size, in certain circumstances smaller size is advantageous for survival (reviewed in Bernstein 2010). In this way, the flexibility of the ICT in response to prevailing conditions during infancy is thought to provide a mechanism for setting the pace of growth, and eventual size, that provides a "best fit" with the individual's environment (Hochberg 2012).

The timing of ICT is directly related to differences in growth-regulatory hormones. In children with earlier onset of the childhood phase of growth, higher IGF-I levels are found, corresponding to the earlier increases in GH. Children with a GH deficiency, left untreated, do not have an ICT (Karlberg and Albertsson-Wikland 1988). In children born at low birth weight, increases in IGF-I are associated with periods of "catch-up growth" (Leger et al. 1996).

IGF-I levels increase slowly throughout childhood and are positively correlated with many different growth-related parameters (Yanovski et al. 2000). During human childhood, the role of sex steroids in growth processes is apparently of little importance. From clinical studies on children with hypogonadism and ovarian dysfunction (Blum, Albertsson-Wikland, and Rosberg 1993; Veldhuis 1996), it is apparent that these hormones are not important determinants of GH release in the pre-pubertal child. Myriad other factors such as nutrition, body composition, genetic constitution, presence or absence of systemic disorders, and psychosocial well-being exert their influence via the GH-IGF pathway that, itself, is influenced by other hormones.

While growth rates are further slowed during human juvenility, a change in body composition is associated with the juvenile phase. Specifically, the so-called adiposity rebound, which initiates increases in body mass index, typically occurs in affluent populations between four and six years of age (Hochberg 2012). This rebound is defined as an increase in BMI after a decrease during the late infancy and childhood stages of growth in preparation for the high energy costs associated with accelerated adolescent growth (B. Campbell 2006). During this phase of growth, both males and females show continuous increase in adrenal androgens such as dehydroepiandrosterone (DHEA) and its sulphoconjugate (DHEAS), the first significant concentrations of which become measurable in circulation at the end of childhood and are associated with adrenarche. These hormones have been suggested to play important roles in body composition changes during juvenility, in brain development, and in the suppression of skeletal growth during this phase (see below for a detailed discussion of adrenal androgens and adrenarche).

In summary, the IGFs, their binding proteins, and insulin are associated with the infant's growth pattern (which begins prenatally and continues postnatally), and GH begins to exert significant effects on growth, independently and together through its stimulation of IGF-I, with the onset of the childhood phase of growth (Low et al. 2001). During childhood, IGF-I increases slowly and is associated with body growth. At the end of childhood and the onset of juvenility, adrenarche leads to an increase of circulating DHEA and DHEAS. While linear growth slows down during the juvenile phase, an "adiposity rebound" takes place and begins an increase in body mass index that will continue through adolescence. With onset of puberty and adolescence and the rapid increase in circulating steroids (androgens and estrogens), hormones such as testosterone and estrogen assume a major role through their modification of the pulsatile secretion of GH (Veldhuis 1996), thereby contributing to the GH- and IGF-driven adolescent growth spurt.

If these hormones play main roles in the regulation of the human growth pattern, is nonhuman primate growth controlled similarly? Several studies, on a broad range of nonhuman primate taxa, demonstrate that these hormones play the same central regulatory roles during the same phases of growth as they do in humans. During the fetal phase, for example, circulating IGF concentrations increase with advancing gestation and with increasing growth in both humans and nonhuman primates (e.g., Liu et al. 1991). Similarities in physiological regulation of fetal growth are further supported by studies documenting the localization of IGF and IGFBP gene expression, providing more substantial evidence of these proteins' roles in fetal growth. For example, the expression of IGF-II both overlaps and differs across locales in human and rhesus macaque placenta, whereas insulin-like growth factor binding protein-1 (IGFBP-1) is expressed in the same location in both species (Coulter and Han 1996). Furthermore, IGF-II and IGFBP expression in fetal macaque tissues (kidney, lung, liver, brain) during the second and third trimester is similar to that seen in human fetal development.

Postnatal studies of nonhuman primate development also show similar roles for hormones associated with growth and transition between growth stages during postnatal life in humans. Several studies, mostly of Old World monkeys in a laboratory context, have confirmed the central role of IGF-I and IGFBP-3 and their interaction with steroids in postnatal growth and attainment of adult size. Pre-adult rises in IGF-I are significantly correlated with growth velocity in macaques (Styne 1991) and in yellow baboons (Copeland, Kuehl, and Castracane 1982). Subordinate macaques with lower IGF-I levels have retarded skeletal development (Ochoa 1995), a finding repeated in wild olive baboons (Sapolsky and Spencer 1997). Other detailed growth studies of sooty mangabeys, baboons, and other papionin primates show that variation in concentration of components of the GH-IGF axis can be used to predict growth in several different measurements (Bernstein et al. 2007, 2008; Bernstein et al. 2013). These relationships have been borne out in investigations of great apes as well (Bernstein 2005). These studies suggest that the broad similarity in human and nonhuman primate growth patterns seen in comparative studies (e.g., Leigh 2001) is underwritten by similar physiological mechanisms with some variations in timing, duration, or localization of hormone activity. However, one hormonal component of human ontogeny—adrenarche—has been repeatedly singled out as uniquely human or else, perhaps, shared between humans and chimpanzees. Adrenarche has been proposed to be particularly important in investigating the novelty of human childhood. My colleagues and I have undertaken hormonal and genetic investigations to address whether we can find support for this position.

Adrenarche: Uniquely Human?

Given the similarity among hormonally driven growth patterns in humans and nonhuman primates reviewed above, are there any notable differences that may remain to "rescue" the idea that the period of ontogeny that we define as childhood is uniquely derived in humans or, at least, identified as such through a novel proximate mechanism? Adrenarche, suggested to distinguish human development, can be defined by morphological (changes in the morphology of the adrenal gland), biochemical (changes in the activity of the adrenal gland), and hormonal (changes in hormone production) criteria. Adrenarche is most commonly identified by a pre-pubertal increase of circulating adrenal androgens, specifically DHEA and DHEAS. In humans, associated phenotypic changes include the appearance of axillary and pubic hair and evidence of a "midgrowth spurt" in stature around seven years of age in some populations, although adrenarche is likely not the mechanism driving this transient increase in growth rate (e.g., Remer and Manz 2001). Adrenarche occurs independently of actions of the gonads or gonadotropins (Saenger and Dimartino-Nardi 2001), and has been proposed as a mechanism to delay skeletal maturation, permitting a prolonged pre-pubertal growth period (Bogin 1997). The outward effects of adrenarche (e.g., changes in body composition, growth of axillary and pubic hair) noticeably alter an individual's physical appearance. They have, moreover, been suggested as critical to the development of an individual's cognitive function as well as the perception of an individual by others as transitioning from a childhood to a juvenile phase (B. Campbell 2006). It is worth noting that one of the commonly cited correlates of adrenarche—the growth of pubic and axillary hair—is something that clearly will not offer any insight as to the presence or absence of this process in any primate other than humans.

Adrenal androgens are produced by the adrenal gland. Located atop the kidneys, the adrenal glands are comprised of two main parts: the outer medulla and the inner cortex. The adrenal medulla is responsible for production of catecholamines (e.g., epinephrine, norepinephrine). The adrenal cortex consists of differentiated zones, principally responsible for the production of different types of steroids. In adult humans, the zona glomerulosa (ZG) produces mineralocorticoids, the zona fasciculata (ZF) produces glucocorticoids, and the zona reticularis (ZR) is the major source of adrenal androgens. The fetal zone (FZ) is the main site of adrenal androgen production during late gestation in humans and nonhuman primates (e.g., Axelson, Graham, and Sjövall 1984), and regresses shortly before birth or during postnatal life. In humans, the functional ZR develops at the end of the childhood stage of growth, while in some nonhuman primates it appears to develop during the first few months after birth (Rhesus macaques, Conley et al. 2011), and in others it appears to not develop altogether (male marmosets, Pattison et al. 2007). Variation in the presence of a functional ZR and the timing of its appearance has contributed to the debate over whether human adrenarche is a unique derived trait or one shared with other primates.

Studies have indicated that a morphologically distinct human ZR is formed by six to eight years and grows in size during the period of increased adrenal androgen production (Dhom 1973). However, evidence from enzyme activity suggests that human adrenarche may actually be a more gradual process with an onset as early as about three years of age, although circulating concentrations of adrenal androgens are not yet elevated at this point (Palmert et al. 2001). Several enzymes are involved in the production of adrenal androgens (figure 5.1). It has been suggested that due to their temporal- and zone-specific expression, the enzymes CYB5, HSD3B2, and SULT2A1 are particularly important for understanding ZR adrenal androgen production at adrenarche (Rainey and Nakamura 2008).

DHEAS is the most abundant product of the fetal adrenal gland and young adult human adrenal cortex (Mastorakos and Ilias 2003) and can function as a major precursor of testosterone and estradiol in peripheral tissues (Rainey et al. 2001). Circulating DHEAS concentrations are very high at birth, show a steep postnatal decline through infancy and childhood with the involution of the FZ, and begin to rise again around six years of age. In humans, DHEAS concentrations continue to increase throughout early adulthood, peak around twenty-five to thirty years, and then slowly decline to low levels in old age. DHEAS has several physiological functions including promotion of neuronal and glial survival and differentiation, positive influence on memory and learning, and neuroprotective effects advantageous for prolonged development of the human prefrontal cortex (B. Campbell 2011b). The decrease in DHEAS with aging is associated with a fall in the formation of androgens and estrogens in peripheral tissues; this has been linked with insulin resistance, obesity, and breast and prostate cancer (Labrie et al. 1998).

There are few studies documenting DHEA and DHEAS levels in early postnatal through adult life in nonhuman primates. Those that have been conducted on rhesus macaques, baboons, and chimpanzees suggest that chimpanzees most closely approximate human DHEA and DHEAS levels and secretory patterns (e.g., Copeland et al. 1985). However, no evidence currently exists to describe the nature of this similarity in pattern; in other words, it remains unclear whether the postnatal rise in chimpanzee DHEA and DHEAS comes as a result of the same ZR maturation seen in human adrenarche. It has been suggested that differences in patterns of adrenal androgen secretion among primates may be due to differences in the relative timing of the regression of the FZ and development of the ZR region of the adrenal gland. Specifically, these two events may occur in closer temporal proximity in primates other than chimpanzees, such as baboons, whose DHEAS levels peak shortly after birth and decline steadily thereafter (Castracane, Cutler, and Loriaux 1981).

Baboon and macaque DHEA and DHEAS levels decline at older ages, similar to the pattern seen in humans and potentially also chimpanzees (Sapolsky et al. 1993; Conley, Pattison, and Bird 2004). However, few studies have examined the structure and function of the senescing nonhuman primate adrenal gland. Some studies, using a test of adrenal responsiveness to a stimulus, have provided insight into the age-related decline in production function (baboons, Goncharova and Lapin 2000). Nevertheless, samples from senescent nonhuman primate individuals are too few to draw any firm conclusions about similarities or differences with aging human adrenals or adrenal androgens.

Adrenarche has been posited to be a derived characteristic in humans, and perhaps other great apes, because no conclusive evidence for adrenarche has been documented in other primate species. The lack of an identifiable prepubertal rise in adrenal androgens is the sole evidence cited to support the position that most nonhuman primates, like the rhesus macaque and baboon, do not experience adrenarche (Cutler et al. 1978). However, expectations of when we should expect to see this increase are based on what has been documented in humans, that is, with what has already been established as a prolonged developmental period. Given the shorter duration of ontogeny and relatively compressed stages of growth seen in other primates, it should be predicted that such an increase would be seen earlier and with shorter duration.

Recent work examining functional changes in the adrenal gland in the early postnatal life of rhesus macaques suggests that a reexamination of various nonhuman primate taxa is warranted (Nguyen and Conley 2008). Specifically, there is now good evidence—morphological, biochemical, and hormonal—that adrenarche occurs in rhesus macaques in a restricted time window very early in postnatal life (Conley et al. 2011). Convincing evidence is presented that the early high levels of adrenal androgens seen in *Macaca* are actually products of a much earlier-timed adrenarche resulting from a near-coincident development of the ZR and regression of the FZ (Conley et al. 2011). This intriguing finding points to the possibility that adrenarche is not a uniquely derived aspect of development in *Pan* and *Homo* but, rather, that it has deeper evolutionary roots and may instead be delayed in onset and prolonged in hominins.

To broaden the comparative approach to the question of the uniqueness of adrenarche, we measured circulating adrenal androgens in a large, taxonomically diverse sample of nonhuman primates (N = 698, from ten primate genera). We concurrently investigated whether there is evidence for adaptive evolution in genes coding for enzymes involved in DHEA/DHEAS synthesis and in their promoters (Bernstein, Sterner, and Wildman 2012). While a previous study of gene sequence divergence and activity of one enzyme (CYP17) in humans, chimpanzees, macaques, and baboons found no differences between humans and chimpanzees (Arlt et al. 2002), this study compared the sequence of genes that code for five enzymes involved in the synthesis of DHEA and DHEAS (*CYB5A, CYP17A1, HSD3B, POR,* and *SULT2A1*), as well as the promoters of *CYP17A1* and *SULT2A1*. These enzymes serve as potentially potent mediators of evolutionary change in the timing of adrenarche and for patterns of adrenal androgen secretion throughout life.

Our results support previous research suggesting that *Pan* most closely approximates human postnatal adrenal androgen levels and patterns of secretion (Cutler et al. 1978; Smail et al. 1982), as well as more recent work showing increased DHEAS output in bonobos older than five years of age (Behringer et al. 2012). These results are perhaps not surprising given the close phylogenetic affinity of *Homo* and *Pan* as well as the similarity between the two genera in having a relatively prolonged developmental trajectory. Our results

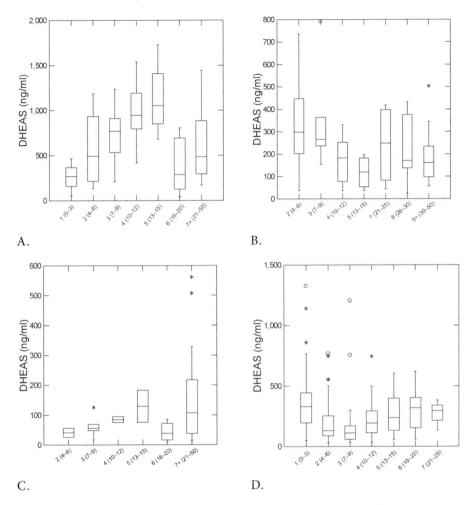

Figure 5.1. DHEAS (ng/ml) across age categories (range in years indicated in parentheses, after Orentreich et al. 1984) in (a) chimpanzees and bonobos (*Pan*), (b) gorillas (*Gorilla*), (c) orangutans (*Pongo*), and (d) baboons (*Papio*).

also suggested that gorillas experience a transient increase in DHEA/DHEAS levels prior to sexual maturation, a pattern not previously appreciated. The increase in DHEAS seen in *Gorilla* is modest compared to that seen in *Pan* and peak levels in *Pan* are two times as high as peak levels in *Gorilla* (figures 5.1a, b). The overall pattern of DHEAS in *Gorilla*, however, is not similar to that seen in *Pan*; concentrations are highest at four to six years and then decline until the second decade of life (figure 5.1b). The potential for an earlier adrenarche in gorillas is in line with what is generally known about patterns of growth and development in these taxa: *Gorilla* grows faster and reaches sexual maturation earlier than *Pan* (Leigh and Shea 1996). Since adrenarche is an endocrine event normally occurring prior to the onset of gonadarche, it should be seen earlier in *Gorilla* than in *Pan*. Surprisingly, while the overall concentrations are some of the lowest measured in all of the taxa studied, the pattern of DHEAS in orangutans coincides more closely with that seen in chimpanzees (figure 5.1c). The gorilla pattern overall is more similar to that shown for the baboon (figure 5.1d). It may be that more extensive sampling of very young individuals of both taxa would reveal the same increase seen in *Pan* and *Pongo*, but on a more compressed time scale.

Although the specific mechanisms underlying initiation of adrenal androgen production during adrenarche are unclear, changes in human adrenal tissue morphology and gene expression levels associated with an increase in adrenal androgen (namely DHEA and DHEAS) production have been described (Nakamura et al. 2009). Human or primate-specific changes in adrenal androgen output may suggest that enzymes involved in the biosynthesis of these hormones have evolved adaptively in certain taxa. We found that *CYB5A, POR, HSD3B* (1 and 2) and *CYP17A1* protein-coding sequences are conserved across primates and show no evidence of purifying selection. While some substitutions vary, the amino acid replacements are mostly conservative and thus probably do not greatly affect protein structure. We did not find any evidence to suggest that humans and chimpanzees share exceptionally divergent protein-coding sequences. Overall, then, our results lend further support to the recently described evidence of adrenarche in macaques (Conley et al. 2011). In other words, adrenarche is probably not unique to chimpanzees and/ or humans (Conley, Bernstein, and Nguyen 2012). What might be unique, or at least uniquely shared among humans and *Pan*, is the extended delay in the timing of adrenarche.

Conclusions

Growth patterns in humans and nonhuman primates are broadly similar. Different aspects of development, such as dental eruption, brain growth, and body mass growth, proceed along slightly different courses. Intense growth in linear dimensions seems to be the single most differentiating aspect of human growth, although this too shows significant variation among populations and is influenced by nutrition and disease. However, while linear growth in humans during infancy, childhood, and juvenility has been demonstrated to covary with patterns of GH, IGFs, IGFBPs, and DHEA/S, nonhuman primate growth in mass also covaries with the same hormones in similar ways. A detailed genetic and hormonal investigation into the presence and evolution of adrenarche suggests the possibility that, instead of modification through the insertion of evolutionarily novel phases, early growth periods can be truncated or extended through alterations in the timing of adrenal gland zonation and maturation. Human childhood, therefore, may very well represent a phase of development where uniquely human cognitive and behavioral traits are shaped, but the underpinning physiology of this growth period does not reveal any evidence of it having evolved as a novel insertion to the human growth trajectory. Instead, a comparison of the hormones involved in regulating the timing and rate of bodily growth suggests that phases of growth can be compressed or extended, even among human populations. The flexibility of these pathways affords great potential for evolutionary modification. Further detailed examination into their action in the early life of great apes, in particular, will likely offer further insight into the degree to which we can consider our developmental trajectory unique.

Ethnographic Approaches to Studying
Childhood and Social Learning

CHAPTER SIX

Hunter-Gatherer Infancy and Childhood
in the Context of Human Evolution

MELVIN KONNER

Introduction

From initial research among the !Kung San (Ju/'hoansi), then hunter-gatherers of northwestern Botswana, and reviews of older ethnographic literature using the Human Relations Area Files (HRAF) and other sources, some generalizations about hunter-gatherer childhood have been suggested (Konner 1977, 1981; Konner and Worthman 1980). Features of !Kung infancy and childhood were representative of hunter-gatherers as described by classic ethnographers, which I have called the Hunter-Gatherer Childhood (HGC) model (Konner 2005, 2010). Viewed in the range of the infant and juvenile care of higher primates, the hypothesized HGC model was a species-specific derivation of a characteristic catarrhine (Old World monkey and ape) pattern. Early research on hunter-gatherer childhoods also addressed specific developmental theories. For example, the intensity of the hunter-gatherer mother-infant bond was viewed as supporting John Bowlby's theory of attachment in ontogeny and phylogeny.

At the time, it was common to use Bowlby's phrase "the environment of evolutionary adaptedness" (EEA) (Bowlby 1971) to refer to both what could be learned from extant or recent hunter-gatherers, and what could be reconstructed from archeological and paleontological data. Today, the known variability among hunter-gatherer adaptations (Bird and Bliege Bird 1997; Kelly 1995; Kent 1996; Lee and Daly 1999) requires us to recognize environments of evolutionary adaptedness (EEAs). However, it is still possible to make generalizations about hunter-gatherer subsistence ecology and social organization (Marlowe 2005a, 2010).

The HGC model proposed generalizations about infancy and early childhood; hereafter referred to simply as childhood. But subsequent systematic research on infants and children among the Agta, Efe, Hadza, Aka, Ache, and other hunter-gatherer groups challenged some of these claims (Konner 2005, 2010). At least as much as the !Kung research and unlike classic ethnography, these studies were methodologically sophisticated and focused on infancy and childhood. Meanwhile, theory in life-history evolution strongly suggested that hunter-gatherer childhood should not follow a single pattern but should adjust itself to widely varying ecological conditions (Belsky 1997; Chisholm 1993, 1999; Hrdy 1997, 1999a); hunter-gatherer patterns of infant and child development and care should be facultative adaptations. I call this the Childhood as Facultative Adaptation (CFA) model (Konner 2005). Questioning whether hunter-gatherer childhood is in any meaningful sense a general adaptation, CFA challenges the HGC model and the claim that hunter-gatherer infancy and childhood support specific theories of behavioral ontogeny.

This chapter includes a partial summary, major update, and complete revision, motivated by and contextualized in a different theoretical context, of a previous review (Konner 2005). It considers what was actually said about HGC in the 1970s and 1980s based on !Kung research and classic ethnography, against the higher primate comparative background, and makes additional reference to more recent analyses of !Kung data. It goes on to consider newer challenges to the HGC model and asks whether the model has any further value. The elements of the model were as follows:

Prolonged close physical intimacy with the mother
Exceptionally indulgent response to infant needs and demands
Highly frequent breastfeeding (four times an hour) during the
    waking hours
Sleeping immediately beside the mother, with night nursing on demand
Weaning around age three, with four-year interbirth intervals **
Marked protest against separation and strangers into toddlerhood *
Dense social context that relieves stress on mother
Much less nonmaternal than maternal care during the first year **
Much less father than mother involvement, yet more than in most
    cultures

Gradual shift to a mixed-sex, multi-aged playgroup
Little childhood responsibility for subsistence or infant care **
Few restrictions on childhood or adolescent sexuality

These generalizations were presented as hypotheses, in the hope that others would do serious research on hunter-gatherer childhood. This hope was realized (Hewlett and Lamb 2005). Features in the list above with two asterisks signify items for which important challenges have come from new research. Separation and stranger protest has one asterisk to signify that there is too little information in other studies to generalize. The results of those studies are considered below.

!Kung Infancy and Childhood

Classic ethnographers described !Kung infants as physically extremely close with their mothers and highly indulged. They suggested that !Kung childhood, and even adolescence, were largely carefree and emphasized the playgroup as a socializing context. Physical punishment was said to be rare. Later quantitative observations supported these descriptive accounts.

BREASTFEEDING

!Kung infants were breastfed whenever they cried as well as other times. Dawn-to-dusk observations showed breastfeeding a few minutes at a time, several times an hour (Konner and Worthman 1980). This was later confirmed in forty-five infants observed with a higher-resolution procedure (fifteen-minute sessions made up of five-second time blocks). Although observations had not begun during breastfeeding, the proportion of fifteen-minute periods without breastfeeding was less than 25 percent for children up to age eighty weeks old. Separately, seventeen mother-infant pairs (infants aged twelve to 139 weeks, mean = 63.9, s.e. = 9.9) were observed for six hours in three two-hour sessions on different days, with breastfeeding bout lengths noted to the nearest thirty seconds (Konner and Worthman 1980). Resulting measures were: bouts per hour, mean = 4.06; total nursing per hour, mean = 7.83 minutes; bout length, mean = 1.92 minutes; average time between bouts, mean = 13.9 minutes; and longest time between bouts, mean = 55.16 minutes. The child's age strongly predicted the interval between bouts (r = .71, two-tail p < .005) but not total breastfeeding time or bout length.

WEANING AND BIRTH SPACING

Modal weaning age in traditional !Kung bands was three to four years (Konner 1977). Weaning was gradual, typically during the next pregnancy, and completed well before the birth of the subsequent child. Absent a pregnancy, children could breastfeed past age five. Supplementing with varied foods, initially premasticated, began around six months. Weaning did not typically include punishment, but weaning conflict could be marked (Shostak 1981). Still, some children were weaned with little difficulty.

SLEEPING DISTANCE AND NIGHT FEEDING

Direct observations were not made at night, but interviews revealed that it was universal for !Kung infants to sleep with their mothers at least until weaning. Of twenty-one mothers nursing infants up to age three years, twenty reported waking to breastfeed at least once each night. All said that their infants also breastfed without waking them up, from two to "many" times or "all night." Highly frequent daytime nursing supplemented by night nursing produces hormonal changes that help prolong birth spacing (Konner and Worthman 1980; Stern et al. 1986).

PHYSICAL CONTACT

The !Kung had very high levels of skin-to-skin contact in infancy, mainly with the mother: "[!Kung] newborns . . . are carried in a sling which keeps them upright and pressed against the mother's side. No clothing separates the infant's skin from his mother's" (Konner 1972:290). Quantitative data based on spot observations "indicate a gradual decline in passive physical contact from a high of about 70 percent in the first months to about 30 percent in the middle of the second year" (Konner 1976a:224). Passive physical contact with anyone peaked at about 90 percent between age ten and twenty weeks, and declined to about 42 percent by around eighteen months.

NONPHYSICAL INTERACTIONS

Traditional societies with more physical contact and breastfeeding could, in theory, have low levels of nonphysical communication, while Western cultures compensate with vocal and visual communication. Guatemalan and Boston US data (Klein et al. 1977) were compared with data on interaction among the !Kung collected with a very similar method. In the data collected in the US from Boston, Massachusetts, professional-class infants had more verbal interaction than working-class infants (Tulkin 1973; Tulkin and Konner 1973), but Guatemalan infants had much less verbal stimulation than did even the Boston working class: 4 percent versus 10 percent of five-second blocks. !Kung levels of infant vocalization, caregiver vocalization, and reciprocal vocalization resembled those of the Boston working class (Konner 1977).

OVERALL INDULGENCE

In wide cross-cultural comparisons, the !Kung ranked extremely high in indulgence, with punishment, especially physical punishment, rare in infancy and early childhood and uncommon in later childhood. There was a prompt and reliable response to crying !Kung infants (Konner 1972), with a 78 percent rate of response between eight and twelve months old (Konner 1977). !Kung infants displayed the cross-culturally common "normal crying curve" with a peak in the first three months and had the same number of crying bouts as Dutch infants. Bouts were shorter and total crying duration about half that in the Dutch sample (Barr et al. 1991). The difference in cry/fret duration appeared to be due to differences in caregiving, including physical contact and responsiveness to crying.

NONMATERNAL CARE (EXCLUDING RELATIONS WITH THE FATHER AND WITH OTHER CHILDREN)

An early publication noted that other caregivers frequently engaged with infants (Konner 1972); 20–25 percent of physical contact was with individuals other than the mother (Konner 1975). Nonmaternal caregivers respond to approximately half of infant crying bouts, although many of these responses occur in tandem with mothers (Kruger and Konner 2010). Despite investment from nonmaternal caregivers, !Kung mothers accounted for 75–80 percent of all physical contact that infants received (Konner 1975) and were primary responders to infant crying bouts (Kruger and Konner 2010). However, strong maternal dependency did not persist into childhood (Blurton Jones and Konner 1973). Between ages two and five years old, !Kung children roamed a greater distance from their mothers than did London children and received less nurturing.

Nancy Howell's recent reanalysis of life history and anthropometric data on the !Kung from the 1960s (N. Howell 2010) clearly shows that nonmaternal care is vital to child survival. Nuclear families with two or more children run an energy deficit and must be provisioned by others, not necessarily relatives, and indicate no special role for grandmothers. Howell concludes that !Kung adults operate with a rule of thumb approximated by "feed the thinnest child."

FATHER CARE AND INVOLVEMENT

An early paper stated that !Kung fathers "account for a greater proportion of vocalizations to infants during the first three months (10 percent) than do American fathers" (Konner 1976b:114). The point of comparison was a study in Boston, Massachusetts, (Rebelsky and Hanks 1971) that measured fathers' vocalizations to three-month-olds at thirty-seven seconds per twenty-four hours. We emphasized both !Kung fathers' lesser involvement compared with mothers, and their greater involvement compared with Western fathers of that era: "Since [!Kung] fathers . . . are often available . . . their potential contact with infants and children is high. They often hold and fondle even the youngest infants, though they return them to the mother whenever they cry and for all forms of routine care. Young children frequently go to them, touch them, talk to them, and request food from them, and such approaches are almost never rebuffed" (Katz and Konner 1981; West and Konner 1976:167); further, "The !Kung are classified as 'high' on closeness of fathers to infants and young children in a sample of eighty independent nonindustrial societies (Barry and Paxson 1971)—they represent the upper end of the range of direct male care . . . seen in the ethnographic record."

!Kung father participation (father score divided by combined parental score) was 2.3 percent for younger infants and 6.3 percent for older infants. However, considering only the observations in which the father was present, the corresponding figures for physical contact are 26 percent for younger infants and 35 percent for older infants, and for face-to-face contact they are 45 percent and 28 percent. In the study of two- to six-year-olds, the father was present in 30 percent of observations of !Kung children, versus 19 percent in London (Blurton Jones and Konner 1973).

RELATIONS WITH CHILDREN

During the second year of a child's life, toddlers began actively to play with other, mainly older, children (Konner 1975). Given hunter-gatherer band size, peer groups—children the same age and sex—were demographically unlikely and were not observed. Playgroups consisted of both sexes and a range of ages. Possible adaptive functions of mixed-age playgroups were suggested, including facilitating relationships in two- to five-year-olds (bypassing the oft-noted Western developmental "stage" of parallel play), socializing younger children, providing practice-caregiving to older children, and diffusing a mother's childcare burden.

"CAREFREE" CHILDHOOD

Extensive studies of older children by Draper and others (Draper 1972, 1976; Marshall 1976) showed that children were neither assigned tasks of economic importance, nor were they expected to feed themselves by foraging, although they sometimes did. Draper showed that the assignment of responsibility to children depends on subsistence ecology: children in more settled !Kung groups were given more tasks, while traditional !Kung children were almost responsibility-free. Still, although "the principal concern of the group is always play . . . this may and typically does include . . . play at subsistence," which "may produce food. . . . It invariably includes also, though incidentally, protection and care and teaching of infants and children by older children" (Konner 1975:111).

Hunter-Gatherer Childhood: Recent Scientific Studies

This section considers recent quantitative and qualitative studies of hunter-gatherer infancy and childhood, offering information on most or all claims in the HGC model. This includes the Hadza, Efe, Aka, Ache, and Agta, and (less comprehensively) the Bofi, Martu, and Toba.

HADZA

The Hadza inhabit the rocky hills near Lake Eyasi in northern Tanzania and were about 95 percent hunting and gathering when studied (Blurton Jones 1993; Kaare and Woodburn 1999; Marlowe 2010; Woodburn 1968a). The environment is climatically milder and produces more game and plant foods than that of the !Kung environment. Nutrition is adequate and the population continues to grow slowly. Hadza infancy and childhood have been well described (Blurton Jones 1989, 1993; Blurton Jones et al. 1989; Marlowe 2005b, 2010), and in some ways conform to the HGC model. According to the descriptions, during the first year of life, Hadza mothers were primary caregivers. The infant was carried the majority of the time in a sling and breastfed frequently. Hadza infants routinely interacted with other caregivers of all ages (Blurton Jones 1993; Crittenden and Marlowe 2008; Marlowe 2005b).

Mothers, by far, accounted for most interactions with infants during their first year and predominately through their third year. During thirty-minute focal follow observations of infants, mothers interacted with them 78 percent of the time (43 percent over the first four years). Fathers and older sisters each interacted with infants 18 (17) percent of the time, older brothers 8 (9) percent, maternal grandmothers 9 (10) percent, and others 29 (41) percent (Marlowe 2005b). As in the recent analysis of !Kung response to infant crying (Kruger and Konner 2010), several people often responded to a crying bout, but the mother predominated: "about 30 percent of all holding of children ($\leq$ four years old) is by someone other than mother" (Marlowe 2005b:185). Later research confirmed maternal predominance (69 percent of holding), as well as important roles for fathers (7.1 percent) and maternal grandmothers (3.7 percent). It also showed that the strongest predictor of nonmaternal care is relatedness, confirming the kin selection hypothesis (Crittenden and Marlowe 2008). Thus, the Hadza show maternal primacy in the context of multiple caregiving.

Given the theoretical emphasis on grandmothers (e.g., Hawkes et al. 1998; see also Meehan, Helfrecht, and Malcom, chapter 9, this volume), it is surprising to find fathers interacting with infants substantially more (or at least equally, controlling for residency in camp) (Crittenden and Marlowe 2008). Fathers did more when they were genetically related rather than stepfathers, a common role due to the divorce rate (Marlowe 2005b, 2010). Absent a genetic father, the maternal grandmother's role grew, and grandmothers played an important role in food provisioning (Hawkes, O'Connell, and Blurton Jones 1997). Fathers communicated with, played with, and nurtured genetic children more than stepchildren, and paternal care was inversely correlated with a father's mating opportunities as measured by the number of single, younger women in the camp (Marlowe 1999).

Weaning time for the Hadza was earlier than for the !Kung and occurred around age 2.5 years (Blurton Jones 1993). The fertility rate was higher than for the !Kung, but this was mainly because of a more extended reproductive period for women (Blurton Jones et al. 1992). Once weaned, Hadza children stayed in camp in mixed-age and mixed-sex playgroups, typically under the supervision of one adolescent or adult camp member or unsupervised. Unlike the !Kung, they often did chores for the household, such as water collection, sending messages back and forth between adults, and childcare, in addition to foraging for themselves and other children left in their care (Blurton Jones 1993; Crittenden, chapter 7, this volume; Crittenden et al. 2013; Marlowe 2010). Hadza children ages three to seventeen successfully foraged mainly for fruit (64 percent of their yield), but also birds (16 percent), tubers (9 percent), small mammals (3 percent), and drupes and legumes (1 percent). Girls made more trips and brought back more calories than boys (who ate more of the proceeds along the way), and yield increased with age (Crittenden et al. 2013). Of thirty-four children who foraged at least once, a slight majority collected less than 25 percent of their daily caloric needs, but seven met 25–50 percent of their daily needs, five met 51–75 percent, and four met or exceeded their daily requirements. Two of the girls produced large surpluses that helped feed their disabled parents. Alyssa Crittenden and her colleagues rightly call attention to the fact that children may be contributors as well as dependents, giving rise to the concept of children as "embodied capital" (Crittenden et al. 2013:303).

Finally, the Hadza were seen as "strikingly different" from the !Kung in the amount of punitive, prohibitive, and directive parenting: "We see Hadza parents use physical punishment, and we see and hear them shout prohibitions and commands at children" (Blurton Jones 1993:317). Alyssa Crittenden endorses this view (pers. comm., 2012). Despite this, Hadza children are cherished and parents often speak very fondly of their children (Blurton Jones 1993). Mothers and fathers were described as sensitive to fussing and crying, although mothers were more effective: "children received considerable affection and were rarely punished" (Marlowe 2005b:179).

EFE

The Efe are small-stature hunter-gatherers of the Ituri tropical rain forest in northeastern Democratic Republic of the Congo, formerly Zaire (Bailey 1991; Peacock 1991). They spend a great deal of time in the forest, but "the majority of their caloric intake comes from cultivated foods acquired from the Balese" (Tronick, Morelli, and Winn 1987:97), for which they trade hunted game. They are seminomadic, living in small camps of six to fifty people made up of several extended families.

Sophisticated research on Efe infancy began in the 1980s. An initial paper proposed a contrast between the Efe and !Kung, challenging what the authors called the Continuous Care and Contact (CCC) model, as opposed to the Caretaker-Child Strategy (CCS) model (Tronick, Morelli, and Winn 1987; Tronick, Morelli, and Ivey 1992). The contrast between the !Kung and Efe was striking and began with birth. Ideally, the birth of a child is a solitary event among the !Kung, but a group affair for the Efe. Among the Efe, other women typically breastfed the infant until the mother's milk came in, but mothers also nursed the infants during this period. Mother-infant contact began within hours after birth, with the infant remaining in nearly constant close contact with the mother or another person. This nearly constant close contact continued through toddlerhood until the age of three years. When the mother resumed work postpartum, the infant either accompanied her or was left in camp with an allomother.

Multiple care, which is highly indulgent, is common for the Efe, with individuals other than the mother accounting for 39 percent of physical contact with three week old infants and 60 percent at eighteen weeks old. Infants were cared for by five to twenty-four different people (mean = 14.2). Multiple caregiving, although high, is quite variable; the proportion of time an infant spends with someone other than the mother ranges from none to about 65 percent at three weeks old and about 20–80 percent later. The authors conclude, "the developmental course of the Efe infants' and toddlers' social relationships does not conform to the patterning of relationships predicted by CCC models" (Tronick, Morelli, and Ivey 1992:573). Later, Ivey (2000) confirmed the major role played by nonmaternal caregivers, referring to the Efe as "the most extreme example of alloparenting in a foraging population" (Ivey 2000:857–858) and showed that women strongly predominate. Children between ages four and twelve spend about 4 percent of their time caring for infants, increasing after age twelve to about 8–10 percent, although they are in proximity to infants much more than that (Ivey, Morelli, and Tronick 2005). Also, "the ubiquitous mixed-age and -sex play group of children among foragers" (Ivey Henry, Morelli, and Tronick 2005:210) is the context in which much care occurs. As with the Hadza, genetic relatedness strongly predicts nonmaternal care (Ivey 2000).

Fathers contributed much less than the sum of other adults or children, but more than the *average* other adult at most ages. This may mean that the father is the second most important caregiver after the mother (although not a close second). In another study on Efe children at ages one, two, and three years, Morelli and Tronick (1992) compared the father with other men and boys, but not with all other adults and children. The time that a child spent with an average other man was more than half of that spent with the father. The time spent with an average boy was greater than the time spent with the father at one year, after which the disparity increased markedly. Thus, "the role Efe fathers played in the lives of their children relative to other males did not appear to be particularly special or unique" (Morelli and Tronick 1992:49).

Infants' social contact with other children tripled over the first three years, reaching 29 percent at five months and 62 percent at three years, whereas contact with adults did not change (Tronick, Morelli, and Ivey 1992). At the earlier age, contact with the *average* child was about 9 percent, declining to 5 percent at eight months and then rising to 18 percent at three years. Contact with the *average* child at three years was twice that with the father and almost equal to that with the mother. In an average hour, five-month-olds encountered from none to four children, three-year-olds from one to six.

AKA

The Aka are small-stature hunter-gatherers of the tropical forest in southwestern Central African Republic and northern People's Republic of the Congo (Bahuchet 1999). Their tropical rain forest environment is varied and rich. At the time of Hewlett's (1991b) study, they were predominantly foraging for a living, spending 56 percent of their time hunting, 27 percent gathering, and 17 percent working for nearby agriculturalists. Their diet, however, was mainly farm produce for which they traded hunted game. Infertility was infrequent and total completed fertility was 5.5, with an interbirth interval

(IBI) of 3.6 years. Infant mortality was approximately 20 percent in the first year. Camps consisted of twenty to thirty-five people (half younger than fifteen) in one to fifteen nuclear families. People moved, aggregated, and dispersed depending on food availability. According to Hewlett's classic monograph, Aka infancy is indulgent and "lacks negation and violence. . . . Seldom does one hear a parent tell an infant not to touch this or that or not to do something" (Hewlett 1991b:35). Either parent hitting an infant is said to be grounds for divorce. Furthermore, infants are held "almost constantly, they have skin-to-skin contact most of the day . . . and they are nursed on demand and attended to immediately if they fuss or cry. Aka parents interact with and stimulate their infants throughout the day. They talk to, play with, show affection to, and transmit subsistence skills to their infants. . . . Unlike their village neighbors, Aka infants are carried in a sling on the side rather than on the back, which allows for more face-to-face interaction with the caregiver" (Hewlett 1991b:32–33).

Allomaternal care among the Aka is also important and has been carefully studied (Hewlett 1991b; Meehan 2005a, 2009; Meehan, Helfrecht, and Malcom, chapter 9, this volume). Hewlett (1991b) found that "while in the camp setting" (i.e., not during transport), "Aka one-to-four-month-olds are held by their mothers less than 40 percent of the time, are transferred to other caregivers an average of 7.3 times per hour, and have seven different caregivers" on an average day (Hewlett 1991b:34). Outside the camp, however, the mother holds the infant nearly 90 percent of the time.

Provisioning of food to the young supplements breastfeeding, eventually enabling weaning, and here too Aka nonmaternal care is critical. Aka weaning usually takes place around three or four when the mother becomes pregnant again (Hewlett 1991b:36–37), although supplementation of food and water begins before weaning (Meehan and Roulette 2013). A study of Aka in the Republic of Congo followed twenty-two children between ages two and four, finding that "even though mothers were the single highest contributor to child feeding, combined allomaternal contributions (i.e., contributions by fathers, grandmothers, aunts, siblings, and cousins) to child feeding was higher than that of mothers" (Jung and Fouts 2011:285). Elderly female relatives provided not much less food than mothers did, and they provided more than fathers, as did adult female relatives (under age forty-five) and juvenile relatives (Fouts and Brookshire 2009). Furthermore, adult female relatives increased the amount of food they gave to a child with an infant sibling, confirming the importance of cooperative breeding in the wake of weaning in the human species (Kaplan et al. 2000).

Additionally, Aka infants display attachment behaviors to an average of five to six caregivers (including mothers) (Meehan and Hawks 2013). Infants are unlikely to fuss or cry when their mothers leave them with an allomother or upon her return, and fussing is negatively related to allomaternal sensitivity. However, these separations average about three per day, with 80 percent lasting less than ten minutes, 55 percent less than five minutes, and only 11 percent over an hour. Mothers hold infants about three times as much as the allomaternal total in the first six months, five times as much in the key period of 6.5 to eleven months, and three times as much from twelve to thirty-two months. Regarding the child's attachment behaviors as classically defined, mothers receive almost 75 percent of attachment behaviors from 6.5 to eleven months, and more than 60 percent thereafter. Given that an average of five allomothers are in the attachment-related category for each infant, no one allomother nor all of them together rivals the mother in time spent with the infant, time holding, or receiving attachment behaviors.

Most distinctive about Aka infancy is the intimacy of fathers (Hewlett 1988, 1991b), as "Aka fathers do more infant caregiving than fathers in any other known society" (Hewlett 1991b:169). However, the highest number reported for Aka father involvement is 22 percent—the percentage of all infant holding done by the father during the first four months, while the mother accounted for 51 percent, and others, 27 percent (Hewlett 1991b:79, table 15). The mother remained the overwhelmingly important caregiver during infancy, accounting for 87–96 percent of holding during net hunts. When in the forest camps while not hunting, mothers accounted for 51 percent of the holding in the first four months, 87.5 percent in the eight to twelve month period, and 57.3 percent between thirteen and eighteen months. Fathers received 15.5 percent of attachment behaviors, others (totaled) 22.2 percent, and mothers 58.8 percent. Fathers, then, received about a fourth as many attachment behaviors as mothers at this age, rising to 58.4 percent of the mother's tally in the second year (see also Meehan and Hawks 2013). Over the whole age range the behavior "fuss for" was coded for mothers almost eight times as often as for fathers, even though fewer than one in five instances of fussing for mother ended in nursing (Hewlett 1991b).

Fathers' contributions among the Aka, however, are not always easy to interpret. A detailed analysis of nonmaternal care for a small sample of infants and toddlers showed that mothers' working energy expenditure (EE) was decreased by 28 percent due to nonmaternal care (Meehan, Quinlan, and Malcom 2013), which roughly corresponds to the estimate that a fourth of care is done by nonmothers (Meehan 2005a). However, the EE reduction is not due to fathers, who actually increase mothers' EE (as do juveniles). Instead, the mothers' EE reduction can mainly be attributed to grandmothers, who were likely to be involved since the sample consisted of *young* mothers. In direct care, as measured by physical contact, grandmothers provide more care and substitute for mothers in a roughly equal exchange. By contrast, the frequency of fathers' direct care reduced mothers' physical contact, yielding a net reduction for the child.

Unlike the !Kung or Hadza, the Aka multi-age playgroup could be same-sex. When they could keep up, children followed their parents on net hunts. They might or might not help in the hunt. From around age eleven or twelve the sexes segregated, as in most cultures (Schlegel and Barry 1991). Girls collected water, nuts, or fruit together, while boys hunted small game. As in all hunter-gatherer groups, children inevitably experienced loss of loved ones through untimely death, and they were deeply affected (Hewlett 2005, 2013). Adolescents may sleep and eat with their parents but often traveled to visit relatives and explore the region. Initiation included circumcision for boys and filing the incisor teeth to a point in both sexes. There is not much ritual attached to these events, but they are painful, require courage and fortitude, and give the initiate a sense of having left childhood behind.

ACHE

The Ache (Guayaki) of eastern Paraguay traditionally foraged in a dense, subtropical, broadleaf, evergreen forest (Hill and Hurtado 1996, 1999). Although settled on a Catholic mission, they had been full-time hunters until the 1970s, and in the 1980s were studied with a focus on demography, subsistence ecology, life history, and child development. At that time, they obtained 20–25 percent of their food from foraging, and their patterns of life before settlement were reconstructed: "Women spend very little time in direct food acquisition and in activities incompatible with childcare. Instead, they focus their attention on child supervision when not walking from one campsite to another. . . . Children younger than three years of age rarely venture more than a meter from their mother and spend some 80–100 percent of the time in tactile contact with them" (Kaplan and Dove 1987).

The Ache were traditionally nomadic; men provided 87 percent of subsistence (by energy intake) and spent twice as much time as women in the food quest. The women deferred subsistence work for childcare, which is not true of most hunter-gatherers. As for indulgence, "Ache children of less than four years of age are spoiled by American standards (they are almost never chastised and win most conflicts with parents simply by crying and whining)" (Kaplan and Dove 1987:197). However, they were helpful and obedient when older.

Quantitative research confirmed these accounts (Hill and Hurtado 1996): Ache infants, much like the !Kung, spent the first year of life in almost constant contact with their mothers—even sleeping in their laps at night. Infants under one year of age spent over 90 percent of daylight hours in direct physical contact with their mother or father (Hill and Hurtado 1996). This contact seems needed to keep infants alive in a hostile environment characterized by predator pressure, and "high-quality childcare overrides other competing needs" (Hill and Hurtado 1996:220). Mothers collect less food than other women, despite having more mouths to feed.

The pattern of breastfeeding partly conforms to the HGC model in nursing frequency, but not in weaning age or birth spacing. Ache infants nurse on demand until their mother is pregnant with the subsequent child. The mean interval between nursing bouts was about thirty minutes, with the mean nursing bout length declining from more than ten minutes to about two minutes over the infants' first eighteen months. This pattern, which may have emerged after reservation settlement, could have led to shorter birth spacing. However, within the small sample studied there was no relationship between nursing measures and birth interval. Furthermore, birth spacing even in the precontact period was shorter than that of the !Kung. The investigators believe that Ache demographic history was characterized by rapid growth followed by sudden declines, in contrast to the very slow, steady growth of the !Kung population. Median age at weaning was twenty-five months. Weaning was described as an "extremely unpleasant experience for mothers (and apparently for their children), with children screaming, hitting, and throwing tantrums for several weeks" (Hill and Hurtado 1996:220–221).

Extensive provisioning of food occurred among the Ache, mainly in the form of hunted meat provided by men. The father played a major role, but a couple with children required supplementation by others, mainly men other than the father (Hill and Hurtado 2009). Grandmothers contributed little to supplementation in the Ache, unlike the Hadza and the Aka where both grandmothers and fathers contribute in various ways. The Ache pattern may reflect the high degree of dependency on meat in a setting where women did little or no hunting.

After infancy, younger children tended to stay in camp playing with objects, pets, and each other, and seeking maternal attention. Transportation in the forest depended on a sling that kept infants in contact with their mothers, their heads resting on her chest. At around eighteen months they began to ride on top of the mother's carrying basket, clinging to her head and ducking to avoid branches and vines. Between three and five years they might ride "piggyback" on their fathers, grandparents, or other adults. After age five they were weaned from the back and encouraged or forced to walk on forest trips, a crisis in their lives just as it is for !Kung children.

Subsistence learning also began by age five, intensifying in middle childhood. Children learned about edible fruits, stinging plants and animals, and vines with thorns. As they spent time following women, boys and girls became skilled foragers for fruit, insect larvae, and small animals. By age eight they had learned the crucial, difficult, and subtle art of tracking adults in the forest. "There is no segregation of play or foraging parties by sex, and children spend most of their time within fifty meters of the adult women in mixed age-sex groups" (Hill and Hurtado 1996:223).

At around ten years of age boys and girls began to be independent, sometimes sleeping at a relative's fire or traveling with another band for a time. Godparent-like relationships became important. Boys carried bows and arrows (but did not learn to make them), and girls babysat, ran errands, and drew water. Girls might produce as much food as adult women by age twelve, but did not carry a burden-basket until they were married. Boys exceeded girls in food production by sixteen, but did not reach adult male levels until their mid-twenties, by which time they were producing a surplus to help support couples with children.

AGTA

The Agta occupy habitats in the rugged Sierra Madre mountain range on the main island of the northern Philippines (Griffin and Estioko-Griffin 1985); a semi-seasonal tropical rain forest crossed by many streams, rivers, and waterfalls. Like the Aka and Efe, they depended on neighboring agricultural people for the bulk of their plant foods and other consumer goods, which they got in trade for hunted game. They were seminomadic and widely distributed in small camp groups. Agta men were full-time hunters and fishermen, but women hunted to a degree unknown in any other human group, killing up to half of the hunted game (Estioko-Griffin 1985; Estioko-Griffin and Griffin 1981). Since hunting is often viewed as incompatible with infant and childcare, the Agta are a key test of the HGC model.

Their population was found to be declining due to a high death rate, especially in infancy and childhood (Headland 1989). Crude birth rate was slightly higher than that of the !Kung; Agta birth spacing, which was determined retrospectively for women over forty-five, was slightly over three years when the last child lived until the birth of the next sibling (Goodman et al. 1985). Infants remained in almost constant contact with their mothers for the first few weeks, yet also routinely interacted with fathers, grandmothers, and other kin. Infants were carried by their mothers in a sling for the first year and nursed on demand. During this time, women were "engaged in collection of forest materials, and some sporadically hunt[ed] and kill[ed] game while transporting the baby" (Griffin and Griffin 1992:301). This account highlights the fact that mothers did some of their hunting without interrupting continuous physical contact.

Weaning was gradual, but weaning age can be roughly estimated from the following: "Sometime when the child is roughly between age twenty to twenty-eight months, it nurses less and less. . . . This gradual decrease in nursing seems to run about three to six months" (Thomas Headland 2004, pers. comm.). Since the criterion for the !Kung was complete weaning, we can estimate the earliest completed weaning age for Agta at twenty-three months. Also, "small children are almost never nursed after twenty-eight to thirty months." From this, a reasonable estimate of weaning age would be midway between twenty-three and twenty-nine months, or twenty-six months, but this is a slightly earlier age than stated in a previously published estimate of Agta weaning age: "With the appearance of the child's molar at about two and a quarter years, the nursing often continues but with less intensity" (Early and Headland 1998:92–93).

Quantitative data, based on spot observations of children under age eight, were quite consistent with maternal primacy. Within the residential cluster, mothers of children from birth to eight years are caregivers slightly more than 50 percent of the time. Care from grandmothers and elder sisters come in at a modest 7.5 percent and 10.4 percent respectively, and fathers follow with only

4.4 percent (Early and Headland 1998:303). However, multiple caregiving, as observed by descriptive ethnographers, was substantial: "The infant is eagerly passed from person to person until all in attendance have had an opportunity to snuggle, nuzzle, sniff, and admire the newborn. . . . A child's first experience, then, involves a community of relatives and friends. Thereafter he enjoys constant cuddling, carrying, loving, sniffing, and affectionate genital stimulation" (Peterson 1978:16, cited by Hewlett 1991a:13).

Fathers "are most often seen carrying toddlers and older children on subsistence trips and on residential moves" (Early and Headland 1998:306); they were "never observed" in pacification play with a fussing or crying baby (Early and Headland 1998:307). There is considerable individual variation, however. Of seven fathers of infants under age two, the ratio of observations of paternal ("babysitting") to maternal caregiving was two-thirds in one case, more than half in another, and zero in two others. However, all four with infants under age one had father-to-mother ratios between about one-sixth and zero. Overall, "the Agta fathers are not particularly active with children when compared with the !Kung, the Aka, and even the Ache" (Early and Headland 1998:317). Fathers' limited role is more remarkable given Agta women's time spent hunting.

"Play groups are not age or gender segregated, but made up of most children in [the] local group. . . . Teen-aged girls bring toddlers on their hips to observe or join play" (Early and Headland 1998:302). As with the !Kung, this play included care of younger children by older ones, but Agta children also contributed to subsistence. All Agta fished beginning in early childhood and were adept at it by adolescence. Both sexes began hunting after puberty (Estioko-Griffin and Griffin 1981).

BOFI

Bofi foragers live in the southwest Central African Republic, part of the Congo Basin rainforest (H. Fouts 2004; Fouts, Hewlett, and Lamb 2001; Fouts and Lamb 2005). Although sometimes considered part of the same cultural group as the Aka, they speak a distinct language, that of the nearby Bofi farmers. Bofi forager subsistence consists mainly of gathering and net hunting, in which all take part. The foragers have gender and age egalitarianism, sharing within and among families. The IBI was three to five years and completed fertility was 5.5 births per woman. As with other hunter-gatherers, mortality was very high in infancy (20 percent in the first year) and childhood (40 percent before age fifteen) (Fouts and Lamb 2005).

Much like the other groups discussed in this chapter, parenting was characterized by close physical proximity. Parents were permissive and indulgent by Western standards and children were rarely directed or punished. As children grew, but prior to weaning, they might be left in camp from time to time although, if a child protested, he or she would be carried by the parent on the outing (Fouts and Lamb 2005:314).

Weaning occurred at approximately thirty-five months (Fouts, Hewlett, and Lamb 2001, 2005, 2012; Fouts and Lamb 2005). Thus, there were typical hunting and gathering patterns of nursing and very late weaning, but weaning appeared to be more child-directed and less stressful than among some other hunter-gatherers (Fouts and Lamb 2005).

Father involvement was studied in both Bofi foragers and Aka living in Congo (not the Central African Republic Aka described originally by Hewlett) (H. Fouts 2008). It was comparable in both groups (slightly more than in the !Kung) but much less than in Hewlett's study. For the Bofi, there was significantly less father involvement when a postmenopausal female relative was in the camp. Bofi children's touch interactions with toddlers resemble play, not physical care (Jung and Fouts 2011). A study of cultural and social learning in foragers (Bofi and Aka) and farmers in children four to twelve years old showed that play took up 31 percent of their day (as measured by focal follows), and idleness ("laying around") took up another 38 percent. "Forager play is relatively equally divided between solitary play, social play, and work play (children imitating/emulating adult tasks)" (Hewlett et al. 2011:1173), and is considered an important learning context, although it appears that more is learned from parents when children are at younger ages.

MARTU

The Martu (Mardu) live in the northwest part of Australia's Western Desert. After an exile in the mid-twentieth century, many returned to their traditional lands to live in small outstations where they continued to forage regularly (Bliege Bird and Bird 2008; Scelza 2009). Infants and young children were seen as the "center of attention" in the family and frequently given affection by parents, siblings, and other kin (Tonkinson 1991:83). Infants did not cry for extended periods without being consoled, were breastfed on demand,

and weaned themselves because mothers could "see no point in deliberately or traumatically ending the practice" (Tonkinson 1991:83). Because the traditional system was often polygynous, "if an older wife no longer has young children of her own, she shares fully in the rearing of her co-wife's children and is as much a mother to them. . . . Most children grow up with at least two 'real' mothers to whom they have emotional ties, as well as many other 'mothers' toward whom they feel varying degrees of attachment" (Tonkinson 1991:99). Generally, Australian aboriginal infants rarely or never slept alone (A. Hamilton 1981).

Despite considerable assimilation, Martu infants are "held 23.7 percent of the time; for the youngest age set (zero to six months) this number rises to 74.3 percent. Martu babies are not held as often as those among more traditional hunter-gatherers, due at least in part to the introduction of strollers and cribs (although the latter are still rarely used). Still, there is a much higher level of physical contact directed toward Martu babies than has been reported for American babies" (Tulkin and Kagan 1972). Babies become more active and more independent as they grow, and begin playing and walking around. There is little crying after the first six months. However, "Mothers spend more time caring for their children than any other caretaker. Grandmothers also spend a great deal of time caring, more than fathers, siblings, or grandfathers" (Scelza 2009:451).

Fathers did not stand out in this data set, but half of the infants did not have fathers present in the community. Also, "one reason for the conspicuous lack of paternal care might be the age restrictions of this study. Although no scans were done on children over the age of three, it was very common to see fathers with children between the ages of three and six" (Scelza 2009:452–453). Siblings' care was "focused mainly on holding, watching, and playing with babies," rather than more intensive care. "The small effect of siblings overall in these analyses may be partly circumstantial, as 40 percent of the babies in the sample were first-borns and another 30 percent did not have a sibling over the age of five" (Scelza 2009:453).

Regarding the development of participation in the food quest, "children above the age of five often search for and pursue game animals. But they focus their efforts in different resource patches than adults" (Bird and Bliege Bird 2005:132). Children were expected to help collect plant foods and grubs, but did not really fend for themselves, and were not encouraged to accompany adults on hunting trips until their mid-teens (Scelza 2010). Among the Martu and also the Meriam aborigines, women tend to hunt small game such as lizards, fish, and shellfish, reliable and low-risk efforts that help ensure steady offspring provisioning, while men's strategies vary between low- and high-risk hunting depending on ecological conditions and available alloparental support (Codding, Bliege Bird, and Bird 2011).

TOBA

The Toba (Valeggia 2009; Valeggia and Ellison 2004, 2009) are former hunter-gatherers of the Gran Chaco region of Argentina, traditionally seminomadic, equestrian, and warlike, practicing occasional horticulture. Women's gathering was and is important, as were the men's activities of hunting, fishing, and honey collecting. They were organized in bands (groups of extended families). Monogamy was the most prevalent mating pattern. Until the 1930s, they relied on foraging, but disruptions to their lifestyle and habitat destruction forced settlement. The Toba were studied in two settings: first, a remote, rural area of the Western Chaco 500 kilometers west of the city of Formosa; and second, the peri-urban village of Naqom, located eleven kilometers northwest of Formosa.

In the rural setting (Valeggia 2009), many Toba did substantial foraging, obtaining 25–50 percent of subsistence from gathered foods and hunted game, with fishing and honey collecting prominent. During the lush months of October through February, wild food is abundant so some families moved to temporary camps near the wetlands where they fished. Very few men, but about half of nulliparous and postreproductive women reported engaging in childcare. In a study of twenty-four families with at least one infant, all-day spot observations noted who was caring for the infant at fifteen-minute intervals. Adult men (including fathers) held infants less than 2 percent of the time, while the mother was the main caregiver in 60 percent of the observations. Older sisters and maternal grandmothers contributed most to alloparental care, followed by aunts and female cousins. However, *ad lib* observations suggested that young, related girls did most of the nonmaternal care. "During the fruit-gathering season, mothers usually take their nursing infants with them, but they also take along older daughters, young sisters, or nieces that carry the baby when they are actively gathering fruits in the forest. Weaned children (approximately two to four years old) usually join older children's groups and roam around the community with them, only going to their mothers when they are sleepy or hungry" (Valeggia 2009:106). Total fertility was 6.7 births per woman (Valeggia and

Ellison 2004) and the median IBI in this population was 28.5 months (mean 33.2). "Toba women still practice on demand, exclusive breastfeeding for an extended period of time" (Lanza, Burke, and Valeggia 2008:32).

The peri-urban center's 2,300 inhabitants relied mainly on men's wage labor for subsistence (Valeggia and Ellison 2004). Women cared for children and did household chores and basket weaving. Fewer than 5 percent of women had paid jobs, but some went to the city once a week to sell their weavings or wild herbs and attend government sponsored pre- and postnatal care programs. Mothers spent 34 percent of their waking time caring for infants and were the primary caregiver 77 percent of the time.

Infants were breastfed for two to three years, or until the second trimester of the next pregnancy. Co-sleeping and nighttime nursing were universal. Exclusive breastfeeding lasted 5.7 months, with 10 percent of mothers introducing cow's milk (from powder) at or before age three months. At four to six months some soft solid foods were introduced. For the first eighteen months, infants were nursed an average of 2.9 times per hour for about two minutes each time. Mean interbout interval was five to nine minutes, with no significant change predicted by infant age. Mothers spent an average of 49 percent of the day in infant and childcare, 19 percent chatting with relatives and friends, and the remainder in household work, mainly washing and cooking.

Nonmaternal care averaged 22 percent (increasing from 17 percent in the first three months to 42 percent after eighteen months) and was almost exclusively provided by kin (Valeggia 2009). In contrast to the rural Toba, fathers were the main nonmaternal caregivers, increasingly so as infants aged. Grandmothers and aunts provided additional care at all infant ages, with girls helping after around fifteen months. However, "it is possible that weaned children receive more allomothering care than nursing infants. In fact, the most frequent sight in Toba villages is the multi-age sets of children playing in common areas (streets, plazas) and going from household to household. . . . These multi-age sets include toddlers usually carried by older siblings" (Valeggia 2009:110).

Summary of the Newer Evidence

New quantitative studies have focused on infancy and childhood in at least eight hunter-gatherer cultures: Hadza, Efe, Aka, Ache, Agta, Bofi, Martu, and Toba. Each of these groups has been described as departing from the HGC

Table 6.1. The Hunter-Gatherer Childhood Model in Nine Cultures

	Frequent nursing	Weaning age/interbirth interval, mos.	Sleeping with mother	Physical contact, all	Overall indulgence	Nonmaternal care	Father involvement	Maternal primacy	Multi-age child group	Assigned chores	Self-provisioning
!Kung	+++	42/48	+++	+++	+++	++	++	+++	+++	-	+
Hadza	+++	30/38	+++	+++	+	++	++	++	+++	++	+++
Efe	+++	30/38	++	+++	+++	+++	+	++	++	+	+
Aka	+++	42/48	+++	+++	+++	+++	+++	++	+++	+	+
Ache	+++	25/37	+++	+++	++	+	+	+++	+++	-	+
Agta	+++	27/36	+++	+++	+++	++	+	+++	+++	++	?
Bofi	+++	35/48	++	+++	+++	++	++	+++	+++	-	+
Martu	++	"several years"	++	++	+++	+++	+	+++	++	?	+++
Toba	+++	30/36	+++	+++	++	++	++	+++	+++	+	+++

Note: *The !Kung are compared with eight other recently studied hunter-gatherers on eleven aspects of infant and childcare included in the HGC model.*

model as it was originally presented based on studies of the !Kung and reviews of older literature on other hunter-gatherers.

Table 6.1 shows the findings of recent studies regarding key features of the HGC model. They suggest a high level of support for most of the original generalizations. Hunter-gatherers exhibit frequent nursing, mother-infant co-sleeping, high physical contact, high overall indulgence (questionable only for the Hadza), substantial to high nonmaternal care and father involvement, maternal primacy, transition to a multi-age child group, and a childhood *relatively* free of assigned chores (questionable for the Hadza and Martu). Only the Aka match the !Kung in weaning age and IBI, but all have weaning ages over two years and IBI over thirty-three months. All are in the upper half of the range for nonindustrial cultures (Sellen 2001).

Meeting the Challenges

Divergences from the HCG model have been observed in four main areas: weaning and birth spacing, maternal primacy, overall indulgence, and responsibility in childhood.

WEANING AND BIRTH SPACING

One strong challenge comes from age of weaning and IBI (see table 6.1). These are, respectively (in months): Hadza thirty and thirty-eight (Blurton Jones 1993; Frank Marlowe, pers. comm. 2004); Efe thirty and thirty-eight; Aka forty-two and forty-eight; Ache twenty-five and thirty-seven; Agta twenty-seven and thirty-six; and Bofi thirty-five and forty-eight. Mean IBI is thirty-three months for rural and thirty-six for peri-urban Toba (data are insufficient to estimate these measures for Martu). Among the Aka, the process closely resembles that of the !Kung, with about forty-two months of nursing and forty-eight months between births. For the Bofi, the estimates are thirty-five and forty-eight months. The Hadza and Efe, and even more so the Ache and Agta, clearly have younger weaning ages and shorter IBI.

However, prospective measures of Ache weaning were made during the reservation period, and the possibility that weaning was later and IBI longer in the forest period is acknowledged (Hill and Hurtado 1996). Given the forest period birth spacing of just over three years, and the fact that "Ache children generally continue nursing on demand until their mother is pregnant with her next child" (Hill and Hurtado 1996:221), it is likely that traditional Ache weaning age was around thirty months. Indeed, the observation that Ache mothers, "if the interbirth interval was too short (i.e., less than two years), would simply kill the newborn child and continue nursing the first" (Hill and Hurtado 1996:220–221), strongly suggests a traditional desired weaning age of more than two years. The Hadza have a weaning age of thirty months in a setting far closer to their traditional way of life. The Efe IBI of thirty-eight months occurs against a background of exceptionally high infertility in the population. This could explain shorter IBIs in the fertile women, achieved in part through multiple caregiving, including nursing.

Overall, however, these seven populations have a lower limit of weaning age that is high by developing-world standards and extremely high by Western standards. Even if most hunter-gatherers were more like the Hadza, the Efe, the Ache, and the Agta rather than the !Kung and the Aka, Paleolithic weaning would likely have been late and IBI long. Against the background of ape patterns, however, this would represent a significant evolutionary shortening, a departure from the catarrhine mother-infant complex. A key difference between human parenting and parenting in other primates is the fact that only humans substantially provision young with food after weaning (Lancaster and Lancaster 1983a). Provisioning evidently shortened nursing and birth spacing, but less so in the EEAs than in subsequent human adaptations.

MATERNAL PRIMACY

One of the most contested claims of the HGC model has been that hunter-gatherer maternal care supports the Bowlby approach to the development of attachment, which includes a hypothesis of monotropy—attachment behaviors focused on a single caregiver (Belsky 1999; Bowlby 1970, 1980; Bretherton 1992; Sroufe et al. 1991; Sroufe and Waters 1977). Both the Efe and Aka studies have been cited as undermining this claim, but this challenge is easily met. First, the claim of maternal primacy in the !Kung was never as strong as it was made out to be; the importance of multiple caregivers there and among other hunter-gatherers was always clear. Second, to the extent that maternal primacy was emphasized, there is little in later research to undermine it.

The first of these statements is supported above, so we can focus here on the second, with an emphasis on maternal primacy, deferring discussion of attachment monotropy (see also Meehan, Helfrecht, and Malcom, chapter 9, this volume). With the exception of weaning age, the Ache experience is virtually superimposable on that of the !Kung. The Hadza represent more of a departure, since mothers wean earlier and separate more frequently from their children than the !Kung do, but there is nothing in the Hadza literature inconsistent with maternal primacy and quantitative analysis strongly supports it (Crittenden and Marlowe 2008; Marlowe 2005b).

The Aka seem more of a challenge. They have the highest level of father involvement of any culture, and this represents a very important addition to our understanding of social development. Still, even in forest camps where their involvement was highest, fathers held infants less than half as much as mothers held children at all ages, with a decline to 25 percent during the eight- to twelve-month period during which attachment is intensifying. Nonparental involvement in care was very high by hunter-gatherer standards, yet mothers held their infants 87 percent of the time on net hunts and more than half the time in the forest camps, rising to 87 percent during the eight- to twelve-month period (Hewlett 1991b). Because there were numerous nonparental caregivers, the average nonparent did not approach the father's involvement, which was a distant second to the mother's (Hewlett 1991b; see also Meehan, Quinlan, and Malcom 2013). In a detailed study of attachment behaviors, 75 percent were directed toward the mother in the key period of 6.5 to eleven months, and more than 60 percent thereafter. Since the remaining 25–40 percent of attachment behaviors was distributed over an average of five allomothers, none of them was likely to rival the mother as the main attachment figure (Meehan and Hawks 2013).

The Efe studies have been cited as strongly undermining both the !Kung model and the maternal primacy hypothesis. There is extensive multiple caregiving among the Efe—substantially more than among the !Kung—but no evidence that any individual could rival the mother's primacy. Mothers accounted for about half the social contact with infants during the first half year, rising to 63 percent at eight months. There was no time in infancy during which the father, the average nonparent adult, or the average child accounted for more than a fraction of the mother's social contact, even when they collectively accounted for half the care. Furthermore, it was shown that fussier infants had fewer allomaternal caregivers and spent more time with their mothers (Tronick, Morelli, and Winn 1989; Winn, Tronick, and Morelli 1989).

Finally, all the above comparisons rely on daytime observations. Proximity, nursing, and other aspects of parenting during the night have been repeatedly emphasized as important aspects of hunter-gatherer and other traditional childcare (Konner 1976a, 1981, 2010; Konner and Super 1987; McKenna et al. 1993; McKenna, Ball, and Gettler 2007). Ache, Hadza, Aka, and Agta mothers slept with their infants, with ample opportunity for night nursing. Even for the peri-urban Toba, co-sleeping and night nursing were universal. Efe infants are reported to sleep with others at times, but descriptions suggest maternal co-sleeping on the vast majority of nights throughout infancy.

The theoretical question of attachment monotropy is far more difficult. Bowlby's claim was that the infant will tend to focus on one primary caregiver, usually but not necessarily the mother, even in the context of multiple caregiving and beyond what would be predicted by the distribution of contact time (Cassidy 2008). However, many studies show that multiple caregiving does not prevent the development of attachment to the mother or other primary caregiver (Van IJzendoorn and Sagi 2008). For the Nayaka, foragers of south India, Nurit Bird-David has emphasized the embeddedness of the mother-infant or mother-child pair in a dense social world in which feeding and giving imbue all of life (Bird-David 1990, 2005, 2008). This could be said of many hunter-gatherer groups, including the !Kung: "The dense social context, by providing ample alternative stimulation for both mothers and infants, improves the likelihood that mothers will accept the dependent demands of infants" (Konner 1977:318; see also Kruger and Konner 2010). Exclusive maternal care is nonexistent, and was never claimed, but maternal primacy is a general feature of hunter-gatherer childhood. Yet maternal primacy does not mitigate the importance of helpers who may enhance, not dilute, the mother-infant bond. Compared to our ape relatives, human hunter-gatherers have increased offspring productivity due to cooperative breeding. Finally, in a broader cross-cultural context, many aspects of infant and childcare are clearly facultative, departing from the HGC model within the human adaptive spectrum (Lancy 2008; LeVine, Miller, and West 1988; Whiting and Whiting 1975).

RESPONSIBILITY IN CHILDHOOD

Here, the newer studies present their strongest challenge. Hadza and Martu children forage for themselves very extensively, and the contrast between Hadza and !Kung has been explicitly addressed (Blurton Jones, Hawkes, and Draper 1994b). While !Kung children do make a contribution to subsistence, it is very small compared with the Hadza, who live by hunting and gathering in a rich environment that is closer to our EEAs than that of the !Kung. Hadza children's foraging is substantial and increases with age (Crittenden et al. 2013), and an "embodied capital" hypothesis has been proposed to suggest that this success may have enabled the prolongation of immaturity in the human past (Kaplan et al. 2000). Those familiar with both cultures suggest that it is less safe for !Kung children to forage because they can be more frequently out of the line of sight to their parents or the village camp (Blurton Jones, Hawkes, and Draper 1994b). Other recent studies have confirmed the importance of child foraging in some other hunter-gatherers. Both Aka and Bofi children do some foraging for themselves, Agta children of both sexes fish, and Martu children capture small game.

The universal importance of play (see contributions by Crittenden, chapter 7, this volume, and Lancy, chapter 8, this volume) has also been noted. Among the Baka, now-settled former hunter-gatherers of Cameroon, a study of 269 play sessions revealed a child community operating in parallel to adult life, both imitating adult activities and carrying out play versions of them (Kamei 2005), although there were also some more formal, usually noncompetitive games, as among the !Kung (Marshall 1960, 1976; Sbrzesny 1976). Bofi and Aka children also spend most of their time at play or idle, and play is clearly an important mechanism of enculturation (Hewlett et al. 2011). Among the Ache and Hiwi (partly assimilated hunter-gatherers of southwestern Venezuela), children under ten do almost no foraging, except for larvae collected by Ache (especially girls). There is a sharp rise during adolescence, especially in hunting, in both groups. However, there are also increases in gathering, with Ache boys (honey) and Hiwi girls (palm fiber) achieving about half their peak levels. Peak hunting is delayed until the late thirties in both groups, and peak gathering for Hiwi of both sexes much later (Hill and Hurtado 2009).

Among the Mikea of Madagascar and the Meriam of Torres Strait, conditions were even more favorable to children's foraging than for the Hadza. Due to low predator pressure and other factors, child foragers have very high acquisition rates. Mikea children make a contribution to the household food economy and average 536 net kilocalories per hour for girls and 504 net kilocalories per hour for boys when digging tubers (Tucker and Young 2005:150). Tucker and Young suggest that Mikea children are not attempting to forage efficiently, but that "foraging is an extension of play that occurs outside camp" (Tucker and Young 2005:168). Two clam species and one conch species made up 90 percent of the catch of Meriam children, while adults collected quite different species, disdaining the ones children easily catch (Bird and Bliege Bird 2000). Bird and Bliege Bird argue that the common archeological finding of shell piles or middens needs to be rethought in terms of the range of species collected by children and child–adult differences in where and how shells are discarded.

In view of the importance of shellfish collecting in human evolution, going back at least 164,000 years (Marean et al. 2007), the rapid spread of *Homo sapiens* from Africa to Australia (probably largely along coastlines), and the importance of omega-3 fatty acids for brain growth, it is possible that children's shellfish collection played a key role in our species' success.

Thus, the amount of foraging children do for themselves is a facultative adaptation among hunter-gatherers, calorically very significant in a number of groups. But even serious foraging is often playful (see Crittenden, chapter 7, this volume). It is usually not assigned although it may be expected, and play of all kinds, including but not limited to imitations of adult subsistence activities, is universal. Because play typically occurs in multi-age groups, some of the care and even feeding of younger children is effectively distributed to them. Children play a role, often informal but very valuable, in foraging and in cooperative breeding, and these contributions help explain human success (K. Kramer 2005a, 2011).

There is also a difference in the amount of infant care and childcare assigned to older children when comparing !Kung to other cultures. The !Kung multi-aged child group occupies and supervises young children and even toddlers, but there is little or no formal assignment of infant care to older children. The rural Toba do assign infant care to older girls, although the multi-age child group is also important.

Direct Comparisons

The validity of the HGC model is confirmed by direct comparisons, whether between more traditional and more settled hunter-gatherers within the same culture, or between a hunter-gatherer and a farming culture in adjacent ecological settings. Among the !Kung, as hunting and gathering were increasingly replaced by pastoral and horticultural subsistence, children were assigned and did more work, wandered farther from home, interacted more with peers, and showed more male-female differences in behavior (Draper 1976; Draper and Cashdan 1988). Several studies have now compared hunter-gatherer infant and child experience with that of farmers in adjacent ecological settings using the same methods. These consistently find that the hunter-gatherer groups conform more closely to the HGC model than do their farming neighbors. This has been true for the Baka (Hirasawa 2005), Aka (Hewlett et al. 2000a; Hewlett 1998; Hewlett 2013; Meehan 2009), Bofi

(Fouts, Hewlett, and Lamb 2005), and in an extended four-way analysis of the latter two groups and their farming neighbors (Fouts, Hewlett, and Lamb 2012). Such controlled comparisons confirm findings in broader statistical cross-cultural surveys, both old and new, using the HRAF. Hunter-gatherers are more likely to have indulgent care in infancy including intensive, frequent, and prolonged breastfeeding, high levels of physical contact, direct father involvement, a playful childhood *relatively* unburdened by assigned chores and responsibilities, and an adolescence characterized by sexual freedom, autonomy, and exploration in an atmosphere of adult tolerance. All these characteristics are also consistent with the catarrhine higher primate phylogenetic background.

Conclusion

Facultative adaptation is always an option; it certainly applies to infant and childcare in the whole cross-cultural range, and should also apply to infant and childcare in the human EEAs. But natural selection in any species must contend with constraints derived from phylogenetic history. In the case of the HGC model, there are deep homologies with parallel patterns in Old World monkeys and apes, suggesting that the common ancestor had already evolved some of these patterns between thirty and forty million years ago. Excellent recent studies have challenged some aspects of the HGC model. The Ache keep their infants and toddlers off the forest floor and wean them at age two, but otherwise bear a strong resemblance to the !Kung in their patterns of care. The Aka and the Efe have more multiple caregiving and the Aka have more paternal care, but when compared to the !Kung, the differences are less than have been suggested. Multiple caregiving and father involvement are greater in the !Kung than in many, perhaps most cultures, and both were part of the original HGC model. Moreover, maternal primacy is high in both the Efe and the Aka.

The Hadza not only exhibit earlier weaning than the !Kung (as do the Ache), but were reported to have significantly lower indulgence in infancy. Recently, however, more detailed studies of parent-infant interaction have suggested that this difference may have been overemphasized (Marlowe 2005b, 2010). The data on task assignment and foraging in childhood show a marked contrast to the !Kung. Although !Kung children forage, including hunting small game, it is not strongly expected of them and their productivity is much lower; it is clear that child foraging is a facultative adaptation. It is also likely that weaning age is partly facultative, varying between two and 3.5 years of age, probably in response to the quality and predictability of the foraging environment, the availability of suitable weaning foods, and the presence of infertile women who aid in infant care. Although of poorer quality, the descriptive data in older ethnographies should not be discounted. There is no reason to believe that classical ethnographers who studied hunter-gatherers had a bias that would lead them to the HGC model, yet their accounts support most aspects of it.

But even without the older data, high-quality recent studies allow some generalizations. Hunter-gatherer childhood was characterized by close physical contact, maternal primacy in a dense social context, indulgent and responsive infant care, frequent nursing, weaning between two and 3.5 years of age, high overall indulgence, multi-aged child playgroups, paternal care that is variable but higher than the cross-cultural average, and variable responsibility in childhood. These appear to be durable features of the model, and core features are similar to the general catarrhine pattern.

Nevertheless, crucial departures from the great ape background were made during our evolution, notably provisioning of the pregnant mother, the mother-infant pair, and weaning by a variety of helpers, as well as many other aspects of allomaternal care, including paternal, grandmaternal, other adult, and sibling care. Given the importance of these derived human traits, together with the well-known facultative changes in infant and childcare *after* the hunting-gathering era, it is tempting to conclude that hunter-gatherer infant and childcare is also strongly facultative. It clearly is in some ways. But the robustness of the Hunter-Gatherer Childhood (HGC) model suggests that a core of ancestral traits shared with other catarrhines has persisted during the transformations of hominin evolution. This includes close physical contact throughout infancy, co-sleeping with mothers, highly frequent nursing, a dense social context, late weaning (compared to other humans) and long IBI, a transition to a mixed-age playgroup, opportunities for social (including sexual) play throughout development, and a low burden of assigned work compared with other kinds of cultures. To this we can add the ancestral trait of self-feeding by foraging in childhood, but with the provisos that (1) in humans the techniques of extraction and the variety of foods have expanded the learned repertoire of children's and adults' subsistence activities, and (2) the extent of children's contributions to subsistence is variable in hunter-gatherers.

Two more derived traits of hunter-gatherer childhood must be mentioned. First, we added a new, neurologically based, universal, developmental stage—language acquisition—between age one and three—which maps on to time at weaning in hunter-gatherer populations. Language acquisition facilitated development of a wider circle of social relations and helped recruit postweaning allomaternal care. Second, the period from weaning to sexual maturity is much longer in humans than in great apes (Bogin 1999b, 2006; Gurven and Walker 2006), even after accounting for life-span differences; this serves enculturation. Cultural learning is unique to humans and involves teaching and collaborative learning (Kruger 2010; Kruger and Tomasello 1996; Tomasello, Kruger, and Rattner 1993) among hunter-gatherers as well as among other human groups (Hewlett et al. 2011). Pedagogy is part of the function of strong adolescent initiation rites. In any case, the unique shape of human childhood can best be understood against the background of hunter-gatherer infant and childcare patterns, both ancestral and derived (Konner 2010).

CHAPTER SEVEN

Children's Foraging and Play among the Hadza
The Evolutionary Significance of "Work Play"

ALYSSA N. CRITTENDEN

Introduction: The Nature of Children's Foraging—Work or Play?

The nature of children's play is regularly described in juxtaposition to economic contribution or, conversely, play is touted as the "work" of children (Gaskins, Haight, and Lancy 2007; Isaacs 1929; Montessori 1964). It has been proposed that children "work where and when they can be of economic value and play when and where they cannot" (Chick 2010:136). Play is largely discussed in the context of psychosocial development or economic productivity, with little regard to the dual nature of work and play in most small-scale societies. The construction of this dichotomy, although common in the literature, obscures not only the value of the experiential learning of play but also the discussion of the costs and benefits of foraging and play (see Bock and Johnson 2004 for a discussion of trade-offs and opportunity costs). Hunter-gatherer children provide a unique opportunity to study this duality, as their economic contribution is often described as "an extension of play" (Tucker and Young 2005:168). Despite the inherent value of this type of analysis, the majority of data on the relationship between food collection and play among children of foraging populations remain anecdotal (Gosso et al. 2005).

In this chapter, I analyze children's foraging among the Hadza hunter-gatherers of Tanzania and determine the degree to which children's foraging has direct implications for self-provisioning. I then situate children's foraging in the larger context of play and argue that foraging represents a type of "work play," dually functioning as economic contribution and developmentally significant play. This chapter, which provides the first forager data set that explicitly highlights the dual nature of children's foraging, stresses the need to understand the functional significance of work play in the context of the evolution of childhood.

Children's Foraging as Embodied Capital

The extent to which children collect their own food is dependent upon the type of foods available and the collection and processing constraints associated with participation in food-collection tasks. Existing quantified data on food collection among foraging children and juveniles suggest that they may spend a considerable amount of time collecting food when environments are both safe (e.g., have low predator pressure and are located close to water) and contain foods that are easy to locate and collect close to camp (D. Bird and R. Bird 2005; R. Bird and D. Bird 2002; Blurton Jones, Hawkes, and O'Connell 1989, 1994; Bock and Johnson 2004; Tucker and Young 2005).

 The bulk of research exploring children's foraging in small-scale societies is largely economic, focusing on the age at which children become net producers and the ways in which this may affect reproductive success (Gurven and Kaplan 2006; Kaplan et al. 2000; K. Kramer 2011). The "embodied capital model" argues that natural selection favors prolonged investment in growth and delayed reproduction. Proponents reason that potential reduction in fertility (due to a late age at first birth) is superseded by the benefits of a long training period in which to learn difficult foraging tasks that may reduce adult mortality (Gurven and Kaplan 2006; Kaplan et al. 2000). This model emphasizes the role of learning subsistence skills. It asserts that adult-level foraging competence is limited by body size and accumulation of "brain based capital" skills and knowledge (Gurven and Kaplan 2006). Food-collection tasks are seen as training for the adult versions of the same foraging behaviors.

Hadza child productivity has been noted for some time (Bleek 1931; Blurton Jones, Hawkes, and O'Connell 1989; Blurton Jones, Hawkes, and Draper 1994a; Jelliffe et al. 1962; Woodburn 1968b), yet strikingly little quantified naturalistic foraging data have been presented. In this chapter, I build upon previous analyses (Crittenden et al. 2013) and revisit data used to test the embodied capital hypothesis using naturalistic juvenile foraging data collected among the Hadza. The Hadza are an ideal population in which to study foraging behavior using an evolutionary framework because they live in an area of East Africa commonly referred to as the "crucible of human evolution" and practice a foraging lifestyle that has characterized the majority of human evolution. Data collected among young foragers is critical to understanding the evolutionary significance of child productivity. Here, I use detailed foraging and consumption data to determine if foraging efficiency increases with age. Additionally, I report the extent to which Hadza children are able to collect enough calories to meet or closely approach their daily energetic requirements. This chapter provides a bridge between life-history theory and developmental psychology, highlighting how Hadza children's foraging provides economic benefit and also fits into the larger play complex.

Hadza Childhood

The Hadza live in a savanna-woodland habitat in northern Tanzania. Approximately 250 out of a total population of 1,000 still practice hunting and gathering, the way of life that has characterized the majority of human evolution. Camps, which are typically composed of an average of thirty individuals, move roughly every two to three months in response to the seasonal availability of resources (Marlowe 2010). The Hadza practice a strict sexual division of foraging labor (Crittenden 2014a). Women forage in groups and focus collection efforts on plant material, primarily fruits (baobab fruit, palm fruit, drupes, figs, and berries), tubers (starchy underground storage organs), and nuts (mainly the marula nut). Men forage alone or in pairs and focus their subsistence efforts on hunting (ranging from birds and small game to large game animals), honey collection (including the liquid honey and bee larvae of stinging and stingless bees), and baobab fruit (typically targeted if they have been unsuccessful on a hunt and/or if they happen upon a baobab tree with ripe fruit).

Nursing infants, who are breastfed on demand, accompany their mothers on daily foraging trips until they are too heavy to carry long distances. At this point, when they are two to three years old, they are left in camp and have already begun the weaning process. Infants are first introduced to supplemental foods around six months of age, although parents and alloparents might provide small tastes of soft or liquid foods before then. For younger children, parents or older siblings may engage in what Hrdy calls "kiss feeding," which is provisioning with premasticated food (Hrdy 2009:81). Weaning foods include ground baobab powder mixed with berry juice, animal fat and/or broth, premasticated or shredded meat, and honey. Once weaned, toddlers begin to spend the entirety of their days in camp with other children. Children are often left in camp without adult supervision but generally remain under the charge of an older juvenile caregiver or elderly camp member. The Hadza participate in cooperative childcare, where a large constellation of allomothers, both related and unrelated, provide high-quality care to Hadza infants and children (Crittenden and Marlowe 2008, 2013). Hadza childhood has often been categorized as relatively carefree (see Konner, chapter 7, this volume). Young children are raised in a communal setting and spend the majority of their time in camp in large mixed-age and mixed-sex playgroups.

The most well-known attribute of Hadza childhood is the astounding productivity of young foragers (see figure 7.1). Children and juveniles most often forage on their own, unaccompanied by adults, in large parties of their peers. They may also accompany their mothers on foraging excursions, depending on the distances traveled. Early anecdotal reports of foraging by Hadza children suggested high productivity (Bleek 1931; Jelliffe et al. 1962; Woodburn 1968b). More recently, Blurton Jones, Hawkes, and O'Connell have provided estimations of collection rates per hour for three types of food: baobab, tubers, and berries. Their data show that by the end of middle childhood, children may collect up to half of their daily energy requirements, depending on the season and availability of certain resources (Blurton Jones, Hawkes, and O'Connell 1989, 1994).

Hadza children have been shown to exhibit a marked sexual division of foraging behavior, even at young ages. Young boys tend to limit their hunting play to the confines of camp where they practice shooting small game, such as mice and birds, with miniature bows and arrows. As they mature, the size and precision of their bows and arrows also mature and they begin to target larger prey, such as hyrax or galagos. While boys begin to hone their hunting skills, girls hone their skills at fruit and tuber collection. Tuber digging can be an arduous process, often involving the retrieval of tubers that are located several feet below the ground's surface in hard-packed soil. The digging returns of young female foragers increase through adolescence and by the time that they are eighteen or nineteen years old, they are fully proficient at locating and extracting all species of tubers (Blurton Jones, Hawkes, and O'Connell 1997).

Foraging Productivity among Hadza Children

This chapter expands upon data originally presented by Crittenden and colleagues (2013). Below, I analyze collection rates of the full complement of Hadza children's food collection to determine whether Hadza juvenile foraging data support the embodied capital hypothesis. Foraging data were collected in two Hadza camps over four months during 2005. Data were

Figure 7.1. Young Hadza foragers returning to camp with their collection of baobab fruit. Photo: A. Crittenden.

collected in the first camp, located in the Tli'ika region, during the late wet season from April through May and in the second camp, located in the Yaeda Valley, during the late dry season from October through November. Resource availability and rainfall patterning during these months map onto the greater resource availability throughout the wet and dry seasons of 2005 (Crittenden 2009) as well as general seasonal trends in this region of Lake Eyasi over the past two decades (Marlowe 2010). The data collected in these camps, although representing a relatively small sample size of foraging days, is therefore representative of the general seasonal pattern of foraging and consumption among Hadza children.

Foraging returns were recorded for sixty-five out of a total of seventy days of residence in the Hadza camps. All food brought back to camp was measured using a hanging spring scale. Focal follows were conducted during fourteen out-of-camp food-collection trips. Recorded information included time out of camp, time spent foraging, distance traveled, and amount of food collected and consumed. The energy values used for the calculation of kilocalories back to camp are based on previous publications that used standard nutrient analysis methods for wild foods (Conklin-Brittain, Knott, and Wrangham 2006; Crittenden 2009). The energy values for birds and small game meat were determined based on published values (Clum, Fitzpatrick, and Dierenfeld 1996; Prange, Anderson, and Rahn 1979; USDA 2008).

A total of forty-three individuals (eighteen males, twenty-five females) ranging from one to seventeen years of age resided in the camps during the study period. Of the total camp population, thirty-four individuals (fourteen males, twenty females) ranging from three to seventeen years of age foraged out of camp at least once. Individuals aged two to twelve years are referred to here as "children," including the developmental stages of early childhood and middle childhood/juvenility. Individuals aged thirteen to seventeen years are referred to here as adolescents. Seventeen is the cut off, as most Hadza are considered to be adults by the biological age of eighteen years.

Foraging trips ranged from forty minutes to five hours and distance traveled ranged from three hundred meters to approximately seven kilometers. Of the total kilocalories young foragers brought back to camp, the majority (64 percent) was composed of fruit (baobab, figs, and berries), followed by birds (19 percent), tubers (9 percent), and honey (7 percent). The lowest contributions came from small game meat (3 percent) and drupes and legumes (1 percent).

Age influences the types of food that young Hadza foragers target (Pearson's X-squared = 146.36, df = 24, p < .001, n = 480 food returns). Children tend to focus almost exclusively on easy-to-collect foods like baobab fruit, berries, and figs. Adolescents, while also focusing on these foods, incorporate more difficult to acquire foods (such as birds, honey, tubers, drupes, and legumes) into their repertoire. Age was not a significant predictor of distance traveled (r = 0.26, p = 0.37, by permutation test) or how much food they brought back to camp to share (p = .872, df = 33, $R2$ = −.030, n = 34 individuals). Age was, however, a significant predictor in terms of the total amount of food collected, with adolescents collecting significantly more kilocalories (Pearson's r = .74, p = .001, n = 13 focal follows).

Individual food-return profiles can be used to estimate the extent to which young foragers self-provision. Estimates of the age- and sex-specific daily energy requirements for each forager were calculated, using the known age and weight of each individual, and then compared to published values of energy requirements (Institute of Medicine of the National Academies 2002). If the lower range of daily energy requirements is used as the estimate (approximately 1,300 kcal per day), the average daily collections of seven individuals in the sample met 25–50 percent of their daily needs on the days foraged. The average collections of five individuals in the sample met 51–75 percent of their daily needs, and the average daily collection of four of the individuals in the sample met, or very closely approached, the lower range of their daily energy requirements.

The daily return rates fluctuate both *between* foragers and *within* the daily foraging profiles. This wide variation suggests that in addition to differences in yield based on age or sex, other mitigating factors, such as individual motivation to forage or differences in skill, may influence foraging success. These results are consistent with published values on variation in return rates among children of other foraging populations, such as the Meriam of Eastern Torres Strait (R. Bird and D. Bird 2002), the Martu of Australia (D. Bird and R. Bird 2005), and the Mikea of Madagascar (Tucker and Young 2005). It remains to be determined whether differences in the types of food targeted are based on strength and size (i.e., ability to target particular food items with more success), or whether the correlation between increase in foraging skill and age is a direct result of practice.

The data presented above lends modest support to the embodied capital hypothesis that predicts that an increase in age correlates with an increase in foraging proficiency, yet the data also provide an interesting departure from expected outcomes. First, as noted above, it remains difficult to determine if foraging proficiency evidenced among Hadza children is a byproduct of learning, strength, or individual motivation. Second, a handful of child foragers collected enough food to meet or exceed their daily energy requirements—which appears counterintuitive to the embodied capital model that suggests net production is not reached until very late into the teen years.

The majority of life-history models evaluating child and adolescent contributions measure net economic value. Young foragers, however, are simultaneously collecting, giving, and receiving resources before they become net producers (K. Kramer 2011). Young Hadza foragers are no exception; they are not collecting the entirety of their daily caloric requirements, but they are making substantial contributions by way of self-provisioning. The caloric contributions provided by both children and adolescents underwrite the cost of their care, possibly contributing to a mother's ability to successfully raise multiple dependents (Apicella and Crittenden 2015). This suggests utility of juvenile foraging among the Hadza, as their productivity provides economic contribution (albeit small in some cases). I will argue below that among the Hadza (like other hunting and gathering populations), young foragers not only collect food for economic productivity, but also as a form of play. Addressing this duality of foraging highlights the developmental significance of play, allowing us to further understand how foraging fits into the play complex in the context of the evolution of childhood.

Developmental Significance of Play

Play is often considered to be "a universal activity of childhood" (Göncü and Gaskins 2007:viii). While the adaptive significance of play is regularly identified (Bateson 2005; Bruner, Jolly, and Sylva 1976; Gray 2009, 2013b; Groos 1901; Pellegrini, Dupuis, and Smith 2007; P. Smith 1982), little quantified data exists to support the notion that play may shape both immediate and future development. As is true with most classes of behavior, a myriad of definitions of "play" exist. It is most typically used as a broad term encompassing children's general social behavior among peers and is argued to be self-directed (not coercion based) (Gray 2013a). Play scholars generally agree on four broad types of play: physical/locomotor (i.e., rough-and-tumble), object, fantasy/social, and structured (i.e., rule governed). Play has both immediate and future payoffs. Immediate benefits include physical and social development. Future benefits include socialization and increased efficiency in adult skills, which may lead to increased reproductive success (Pellegrini and Pellegrini 2013). Additionally, play impacts physical, cognitive, language, social, and emotional development.

The development of fine motor skills is fostered by object play (Miquelote et al. 2012; Mori et al. 2013), whereas the development of large motor skills is fostered by physical, locomotor, or rough-and-tumble play. Physical play includes activities such as running, chasing, wrestling, jumping, and dancing; activities that encourage the training of muscles, strength, and endurance (Pellegrini and Smith 1998). Physical play also enhances neural maturation and synaptic differentiation (Byers and Walker 1995).

Social (or fantasy) play fosters an understanding of cause and effect relationships in "make-believe" social situations (Piaget 1954; Vygotsky 1978). During play, children learn how to communicate and negotiate with others, both in dyads and in larger aggregations, giving them the opportunity to "play" adult roles (Piaget 1962; P. Smith 2005; Vygotsky 1978). During social play, children must understand the intentions of others, encouraging the development of theory of mind (Smith 2007) while also exercising self-regulation (Elias and Berk 2002). Imaginary play also encourages language development (Brown, Rickards, and Bortoli 2001; Iverson 2010) and fosters creativity (Morrissey and Brown 2009).

The developmental significance of play is often analyzed under a functionalist perspective emphasizing socialization (Roberts and Sutton-Smith 1962), as a children's culture model (Kamei 2005), or as a combination of both (Gaskins 2014; Lancy, chapter 8, this volume). The functionalist/socialization models suggest that play is largely the acquisition of culture and represents a particularly significant pathway to learning how to be an adult (Gaskins, Haight, and Lancy 2007; Lancy, chapter 8, this volume; Turnbull 1962). Play is "the way children make a start on learning many things" (Blurton Jones 2005) and functions as a way for children to enact social roles and learn adult responsibilities. The socialization perspective has recently been expanded to suggest that play is the foundation of hunter-gatherer social life and may be integral to the development of egalitarianism (Gray 2009, 2014). The children's culture model argues that children are not simply mimicking adult activities, but may be inventing elements of their own culture. This invention, however, typically falls within the boundaries of the "real world" experienced by children (Gaskins 2014:230) and is likely to encompass components of adult culture. Kroeber was an early supporter of this theoretical perspective, arguing that children have play impulses that lead to cultural innovation with regard to neither technology nor utility (Kroeber 1948). An analysis of the Hadza play complex suggests that Hadza play exhibits characteristics of both models.

Hadza Play

Hadza children, like those of other foraging groups, spend much of their day engaged in activities that can be classified as play, which occurs both in and out of camp. Much of children's play happens in common use areas, such as the central baobab pounding area of camp, in and around homes, on the periphery of camp, and out of camp while foraging or collecting water. Hadza children exhibit play behavior that falls into all of the traditional categories: physical/locomotor, structured, object, and fantasy/social (see table 7.1).

PHYSICAL PLAY

Physical/locomotor play among Hadza children involves running, chasing,

Table 7.1. Hadza Types of Play

Physical/Locomotor

Acting as couriers carrying messages to adults between camps
Bow and arrow target practice (both competitive and noncompetitive)
Catching small animals and birds (for consumption and play)
Chasing games
Climbing trees
Collecting fruit
Dancing
Running
Swimming
Tuber digging
Water collection
Wrestling

Structured

Competitive target practice (typically with age mates)
Gambling game—based on the similar adult game
Hand-clapping game—learned from the neighboring pastoral tribe

Object

Beading necklaces and bracelets
Building small-sized grass huts
Dolls made from baobab fruit and/or mud
Making digging sticks, bows and arrows, and modified slingshots out of reeds
Making and maintaining fire
Preparing food on a small hearth
Slings for carrying dolls and/or infants
Wearing small birds or other animals as jewelry prior to consumption

Fantasy/Social

Building small grass huts and playing "house"
Carrying dolls or infants in a sling
Making and maintaining fire
Mimicking animal sounds and bird calls
Play arguing
Pretending that small animals that they have hunted (e.g., mice) are large game
Singing and storytelling

swimming, climbing trees, and dancing. They also occasionally engage in more rough-and-tumble play, which can involve mock fighting, typically among boys of roughly the same age. Sexual play between opposite-sex and same-sex children has been witnessed as well, but the frequency of this type of play decreases with age (Marlowe 2010).

STRUCTURED PLAY

The majority of Hadza play falls under physical, object, and fantasy, and very little of their play is rule governed. This is consistent with the literature on hunter-gatherer play (Hewlett and Boyette 2013) and is likely because playgroups are typically composed of mixed-age, mixed-sex groups. Children must include all members of the group, regardless of skill level, making rule-governed play difficult to accomplish (Lancy 1984).

I have observed only three cases of structured play among the Hadza: (1) a hand-clapping game introduced by the Datoga, a neighboring pastoral tribe, (2) target practice among peers, and (3) a gambling game that is modified from the adult game that men play with great relish. The hand-clapping game is a dyadic game played exclusively by girls during middle childhood. It involves a rhythmic pattern of clapping between partners at a very fast pace. If one of the girls loses pace and misses one of the beats, she loses the game. This activity was introduced in the last ten years by children from the neighboring Datoga and was not historically a part of the Hadza children's play repertoire. Target practice is most often a carefree and ruleless game among boys, with the only exception occurring among age mates. When young boys hit puberty, they begin to target larger animals and want to increase their accuracy. During this time, they can become playfully competitive and start engaging in more structured competition with their bows and arrows. The gambling game is a modified version of the adult game called *lukuchuko*. It entails throwing discs against a tree and administering points based on the orientation of the discs landing on the ground. Historically, the discs were made out of bark. More recently, however, Hadza men have begun to use coins (Tanzanian shillings) to play the game and use the coins as the gambling currency. This differs from historic versions of the game where Hadza men played for bows, arrows, necklaces, and other trinkets. The juvenile version of this game is similar, although they use bark discs or recycled tops from soda bottles rather than shillings.

OBJECT PLAY

Hadza children engage in a considerable amount of object play. Young children are often given spinning tops made out of plant materials or rattles made out of hollowed-out baobab fruit pods as first toys (Woodburn 1970). Girls often make dolls out of a mixture of mud, clay, and sand, which they decorate with beads and carry in slings on their backs. They also carry around baobab fruits, imagining that they are babies and oftentimes giving them names (Crittenden 2016). Additionally, children decorate themselves with small birds and the nestlings of larger birds by placing them in their headbands or wearing them around their waist tucked into their beaded belts. They only remove the birds when they wish to consume them.

Many of the objects that children play with are smaller versions of the adult item, which appears to be common among hunter-gatherer children (Chick 2010; Lancy, chapter 8, this volume). Children of both sexes use a pounding rock that is smaller in size compared to the adult pounding rocks used to process baobab fruit. Boys are given small bows and arrows, made for them by older boys or men in their family, from the time they begin to walk independently. The size of the bow and complexity of the arrow mature along with the boy who is using them. The first bow is made from a small twig and the accompanying arrows are made out of grass. The grass arrows are tipped with beeswax or plant resin to weight the arrows so that they can successfully be shot from the bow (Crittenden 2016). By the age of eight or ten years, boys are able to produce their own functioning bows and arrows. Girls, alternatively, are given their first digging stick when they are around three years old. It is approximately one to two feet long and is not very sharp. As the girl matures, so does her digging stick; she is able to make her own digging stick by the time she reaches adolescence.

Object play extends to the construction of miniature grass houses (see figure 7.2) and small, but entirely functional, three-stone hearths. The huts do not typically last more than one day of play, as they are not very sturdy; the hearths, however, are often used repeatedly over several days, as children build fires in them to cook the food that they have collected. Much of the above mentioned object play also falls under the domain of fantasy and/or social play.

Figure 7.2. Two young girls constructing a miniature Hadza hut. Photo: A. Crittenden.

FANTASY/SOCIAL PLAY

Fantasy play includes singing, storytelling, mimicking animal sounds, and the use of many of the objects listed above that are coopted for imaginary play. Hadza children "play house" and embody adult roles while playing with their miniature grass huts and toy dolls. Girls also engage in play arguing, which is primarily a female activity. Foraging tools are additionally used in fantasy play. Boys often pretend that the small animals they have targeted with their bows and arrows, such as hyrax and bush mice, represent larger game such as kudu, impala, or zebra.

Hadza Children's Foraging as "Work Play"

Most foraging play falls into multiple domains. For instance, bow and arrow practice can be characterized as physical (practice), structured (competitive bow and arrow practice), object (using bow and arrow, digging stick, fire), and fantasy (pretending that the target is a game animal). The ways in which foraging play occupies multiple domains of play and supports both socialization and children's culture models is exemplified by the seasonal collection of weaver birds.

Weaver birds (*Quelea quelea*) are colonial breeders that commence breeding during the rainy seasons when occupying habitats close to the equator (Dittami 1986). One tree can house approximately one hundred nests located at various branch heights. The hatchlings are exploited on a daily basis by all active foragers in camp for a short period of time, approximately five to eight weeks per year. A long stick is sharpened and then used to pull individual nests down from the branches. In addition to targeting nestlings, young foragers participate in a foraging activity that adults do not engage in. It happens only when children are out of camp on their own during this short period of time each year. This food-collection task involves targeting fledgling birds that have recently left the nest. Children prepare a stick (approximately one to two feet in length) with the sticky pulp of an inedible berry called *rembo*. The rembo is used like a paste and spread on the stick, which is then placed in a small body of water, typically a watering hole. When the young weaver birds fly to the water to drink, several birds land on the stick, get stuck in the paste, and are then captured and consumed by the young foragers waiting at the water's edge. Children will spend several hours, and sometimes an entire afternoon, relaxing near watering holes and catching and roasting the birds. The watering holes are never far from camp, allowing children of all ages to participate.

The utility of this activity cannot be disputed: children are, indeed, feeding themselves and providing substantial caloric investment by way of self-provisioning and food sharing (older children share their catch with younger children who are not yet skilled enough to catch and kill birds on their own). It is clearly also a form of play. During trips to the water's edge to collect their spoils, children run, chase, laugh, shriek, dance, and sing. Once they have collected the birds from the stick, they go back to a collective fire (built and maintained by the cadre of children participating in this event) to roast, distribute, and consume the birds. Children swim and paddle in the water during this activity, while simultaneously ensuring that they remain quiet and stop moving when the birds approach. It is similar to the western game of freeze tag where children stop what they are doing mid-activity to "freeze" in place. Once the birds have landed on the stick, the swimming and jumping and paddling ensues.

This activity is not an adult foraging activity and acts not only as a medium for creativity, but may also lead to cultural transformation, characteristics that support the children's culture model (Huizinga 1955; Kamei 2005). Targeting weaver birds using rembo is an activity enacted exclusively by children. While it is a heavily modified version of the adult activity, it is clearly part of the child's domain. This foraging activity, like all others, mimics adult foraging behavior. It thereby also supports the socialization models that argue play is part of the process by which children become functional adults in their culture. Hadza children are learning as they go, often targeting smaller animals (such as hyrax, bush mice, or galagos), but hunting nonetheless. They collect honey, but do so from small trees that house smaller beehives. Hadza children might sing while they forage or stop amidst the berry bushes for a game of tag or a nap, but they are foraging. They are engaging in work play, which functions as both economic contribution and developmentally significant play.

Conclusion: Broader Implications of Children's Work Play

Children's play is ubiquitous across cultures and takes on a critical role in shaping both immediate and future development. Evolutionary approaches to play theory, while gaining momentum, are largely tethered to the domain of the developmental psychology literature, paying little attention to life-history theory. Alternatively, behavioral ecologists in anthropology have largely analyzed the patterns of children's foraging from economic and life-history perspectives. They regularly ignore the developmental psychological implications of foraging as part of the play complex. Given this dearth of communication between disciplines, the integration of these perspectives is critical to our understanding of how foraging fits into models of the evolution of human childhood. The data presented in this chapter underscore the duality of children's economic contributions, which simultaneously function as both work and play.

This chapter provides the first documentation and analysis of play among the Hadza. Play is critical for physical, cognitive, language, social, and emotional development. Furthermore, play provides children the opportunity to practice necessary skills, both physical and social, before reaching adulthood. Hadza children engage in various types of play, including structured, physical/locomotor, object, and fantasy, all of which contain elements of foraging and/or food collection. Hadza children are free to spend their time as they wish with no adult demands of labor or productivity. This freedom afforded to Hadza children echoes what other ethnographers have documented for hunter-gatherer children worldwide: an independence that characterizes the bulk of their daily activities, including work and play. While Hadza children spend much of their time playing, this is coupled with foraging and economic contribution. Little distinction between work and play exists in Hadza childhood, supporting Lancy's assertion that work in small-scale societies is almost always "leavened by play" (Lancy 2014:270) and Tucker and Young's (2005) claim that foraging is an extension of play among hunters and gatherers.

Much of the analysis on children's foraging has been in service of analyzing various life-history models, such as the embodied capital hypothesis. The data presented here explore juvenile foraging in this context and suggest that Hadza children collect a significant portion of their daily caloric requirements, where an increase in age correlates with an increase in overall foraging productivity. These data lend modest support to the embodied capital hypothesis, suggesting that children do require some sort of training period to acquire adult-level foraging skills. There are children, however, who meet or exceed their caloric needs from a young age. These individuals might be motivated to collect more or target different resources, suggesting that continued research on children's foraging is key to understanding how age-dependent correlation relates to productivity. Despite high rates of individual variation, the caloric contributions provided by children function to underwrite the cost of their care. The economic utility of children's foraging has implications for our understanding of the evolution of cooperation and food sharing among hominins (see also Crittenden and Zes 2015).

Juvenile self-provisioning may have been a key component of the derived *Homo* complex. Food sharing is thought to be one of the key factors that allowed for increased brain growth in hominin evolution. In turn, it improved the survival of both children and adults (see Bogin, Bragg, and Kuzawa, chapter 4, this volume), permitting the evolution of longer life spans. The cooperative breeding system is flexible (Hrdy, chapter 2, this volume; Meehan,

Helfrecht, and Malcolm, chapter 9, this volume). Underscoring the importance of self-provisioning by children, whether it is at the age of net production or as part of learning to forage during work play, allows us to more fully understand how children's foraging impacts models of the evolution of childhood.

Acknowledgments

I would like to extend my gratitude to the Lincy Foundation at the University of Nevada, Las Vegas, for research funding; to Melvin Konner, David Lancy, and Courtney Meehan, for fruitful discussion and helpful comments on an earlier draft of this chapter; to Sarah Hrdy and Nicholas Blurton Jones for inspiration and introduction to ethology; to Frank Marlowe for introducing me to the Hadza; and to the Hadza children and their families who continue to welcome me into their lives and who make this type of work so gratifying.

CHAPTER EIGHT

Ethnographic Perspectives on Culture Acquisition

DAVID F. LANCY

Introduction

The study of cultural transmission has been dominated by the view that it occurs largely through a process by which adults—especially parents—transfer what they know to children (Chipeniuk 1995:494; King 1994:111; Pelissier 1991:82; Rowell 1975:126; Schönpflug and Bilz 2009:213). However, "instructed learning" (Kruger and Tomasello 1996:377) or teaching is, in fact, quite rare in the ethnographic record (Lancy 2010). Rogoff reports of the Highland Maya that "of the 1708 observations of nine-year-olds, native observers could identify only six occasions as teaching situations" (1981:32). Bruner (1966:59), in viewing hundreds of hours of ethnographic film shot among !Kung and Netsilik foraging bands, was struck by the total absence of teaching episodes. In a very recent study of traditional ecological knowledge (TEK) in fishing communities on Buton Island, Vermonden reported that "during two years of participant observation, I rarely observed oral transmission of fishing knowledge or techniques" (2009:205). Similarly, among Yukaghir [Siberian] foragers, their "model of knowledge transferal could be described as 'doing is learning and learning is doing'" (Willerslev 2007:162). Indeed, in numerous cases, direct instruction would be considered an infringement of the child's autonomy and an unwarranted assertion of rank (Gray 2009:507; Hewlett et al. 2011:1172).[1]

Standing in contrast to the conventional view that culture is transmitted via teaching, the ethnographic record is replete with instances of children taking the initiative to learn important aspects of their culture.[2] According to Esther Goody, "culture is learned less because of the pedagogical efforts of the adults than because of the predispositions, agency and intentionality of the children" (2006:11). The goal of this chapter is to review relevant materials illustrative of children's acquisition of their culture and to present those materials in a meaningful way. To that end, children will be viewed as active learners in: play, including make-believe and in game-play; the context of interaction with a peer group that provides supervision as well as play; the family circle or casual interaction in a family setting; and carrying out chores. Based on recent research in infant cognition, it is clear that children begin to acquire their culture quite early.

Infant Studies

Human infants can generally be distinguished from the young of other mammals because while their brains are large and growing rapidly, representing over half of their metabolism, they remain virtually helpless and in an immature state for a very long time. Both folk and scientific theories of infancy failed (until very recently) to wrestle with this paradox. Indeed, most would agree with the !Kung view, expressed by Nisa—the subject of a noted biography: "A child who is nursing has no awareness of things. Milk, that's all she knows. Otherwise, she has no sense. Even when she learns to sit, she still doesn't think about anything because her intelligence hasn't come to her yet. Where could she be taking her thoughts from? The only thought is nursing" (Shostak 1981:113). In the last thirty years, there has been a revolution in research on infants with the invention of very clever paradigms to study what would earlier have been called an oxymoron: infant cognition (Gopnik, Meltzoff, and Kuhl 2000). Studies have established that babies have a range of hardwired capacities that aid them in making sense of the world including basic principles of physics, mathematics, biology, and psychology (Bloch, Solomon, and Carey 2001; Norenzayan and Atran 2004:151). This laundry list of capacities can also be mined for evidence of "core knowledge" systems (Carey and Spelke 1996) that function as "learning devices" (Baillargeon and Carey 2012:58). As an alternative to the empty vessel waiting patiently to be filled, evolutionarily inclined scholars posit the untutored emergence of key concepts and modules that facilitate learning about the world (MacDonald and Hershberger 2005:25).

Infants not only deploy these domain-specific modules that help them make sense of particular aspects of the world, but also reveal more general abilities such as the "Goldilocks Effect," by which seven- to eight-month-olds carefully attune their attention to stimuli that are neither too simple nor too complex "and avoid wasting cognitive resources on overly simple or overly complex events" (Kidd, Piantadosi, and Aslin 2012). Among the infant's suite of capacities for learning culture, "parsing" is attracting increased attention. The most obvious application for parsing is in language acquisition (Saffran, Aslin, and Newport 1996:1927), but the infant's segmentation or parsing capacity has also been extended to the realm of physical objects (Spelke 1990:54). Infants may, moreover, be able to parse the behavior of their companions. The young seem to apply a parsing strategy to "'see below the surface of behavior,' and detect the logical organization that produced it" (Byrne 2006:494). This strategy, according to Byrne, may account for children's evident ability to acquire complex skills via "social learning" (Bandura 1977).

In addition to decoding their physical world, babies must also be busy decoding their social world and learning their native language must be seen as the keystone of this effort (Flinn and Ward 2005:27). Flinn argues that the social world is far more challenging than the physical: "The primary mental chess game was with other intelligent hominid competitors and cooperators, not with fruits, tools, prey, or snow" (2005:74). In short, instead of a "scientist in the crib" (title of the Gopnik et al. 2000 volume), we may have a "Machiavellian in the crib" (Lancy and Grove 2010:97).

Well before language develops, studies document children's early understanding of social relations (Callaghan et al. 2011). By three months infants can distinguish faces and familiar versus unfamiliar individuals, they can detect various facial expressions and, by five months, decode them. At seven months they discriminate between more and less emotional expressions and respond appropriately (LaFreniere 2005:192). At twelve months they attend to and follow their mothers' gaze (Okamoto-Barth et al. 2011), beginning the "education of [the child's] attention" (Ingold 2001:139). At a year they can respond, appropriately, with pride or shame (Trevarthen 2005). By eighteen months infants reliably use others' facial expressions as a guide to their own behavior, reacting appropriately to expressions showing fear, joy, or indifference (Klinnert et al. 1983).[3] Infant cognition studies are generally supportive of the position that children take the initiative in the acquisition of culture. But, at the same time, universal aspects of culture seem designed to facilitate this process.

Learning through Play

An important component of the culturally constructed childcare package is play, especially within an ongoing peer group (Konner 1975:116, chapter 6, this volume). According to the Mandinka view, "with the arrival of the next sibling, infancy (*dénanola*) is over. Now, play begins . . . and membership in a social group of peers is taken to be critical to . . . the forgetting of the breast to which the toddler has had free access for nearly two years or more" (Whittemore 1989:92).

With few exceptions (e.g., Fajans 1997:92), early childhood is a time for play. Parents may vary in how positively they view this activity but, at a minimum, they see its value for keeping kids busy and out of the way. Toddlers are supervised during play by explicitly delegated sib-caretakers, but they may also be confined to playing on the "mother-ground" where they can be more casually supervised by older children (Lancy 1996).

Virtually all ethnographers who have observed children at play in village settings cite a wealth of opportunities for the acquisition of culture (Schwartzman 1978). Many would also agree that play is a "form of buffered learning through which the child can make . . . step-by-step progress toward adult behavior" (Roberts and Sutton-Smith 1962:184). I have argued that learning through play is more efficient than learning from instruction for several reasons, not least because the latter is rather boring to the young while play is arousing, and because the latter "requires an investment by a second party, the teacher" (Lancy 1980a:482).

PLAY WITH OBJECTS

Certain forms of play occur with great regularity: object play, make-believe, and rule-governed play such as games. The object play of toddlers seems to be a continuation of the infant's visual exploration of objects. Now the child can explore the properties of objects with its hands and its mouth, it can throw them, use them as hammers, toss them into puddles, and experiment in other ways. But, more to the point, the child will inevitably lay hands on objects that are tools. These may be rough replicas made by an older sibling (Peters 1998:90), broken or cast-off tools (Ruddle and Chesterfield 1977:34), miniatures or scaled-down versions of the real thing (Hewlett et al. 2011:1174), or adult tools, which may have been "borrowed" (Odden and Rochat 2004:44).

A "tool" may be an outrigger canoe. Ifaty village in southwest Madagascar depends primarily on marine resources and a modest-sized outrigger sailing canoe is the primary means of accessing and marketing such resources. Virtually all adult males use such canoes almost daily. On the beach and in the shallows, I observed (almost simultaneously) a two-year-old splashing alone in a tide pool, learning about water; three boys around age five clambering over a beached canoe, learning an agile dance from thwart to gunwale; two boys about age seven independently preparing and then sailing model canoes, making appropriate adjustments to sail angle and rudder; two eight-year-old boys playing with an abandoned outrigger in the shallows. They climbed on, paddled it, capsized it, and took turns as captain and mate. When two young men began to rig and prepare to launch a full-size outrigger, the two boys paddled over to watch this unfold. Shortly after the men sailed away, a boy of about ten years came *paddling* in to shore in a half-size canoe (Lancy 2012a:26–27). Extrapolating from more thorough studies of children learning to use canoes (Pomponio 1992:72; Wilbert 1976:318), I am confident that these experiences prepare Ifaty boys to become mariners.

As noted by Donald (1991:309) and others (Flinn 2005:78), one attribute of culture facilitating transmission is that human artifacts including tools, houses (Winzeler 2004:70–71), and villages (Strathern 1988)—the "stuff" of culture—serve as a form of "external information storage." This point is obvious when we consider writing, books, computer programs, and the like (J. Goody 1977), but information is also embedded in the simplest artifact (Renfrew 1988). When a Bamana child plays with the characteristic short-handled hoe (Polak 2011:103), there are only so many ways it can be effectively grasped. If he uses it to pierce the soil, as he has observed his siblings doing, the number of possibilities is further reduced. Neither the grasping end of the handle nor the top side of the head makes much impression on the earth compared to the bottom edge. The proposition that human artifacts convey culture was supported by an experiment in which children aged eighteen to thirty-six months were given a range of tools of varying utility to pull a desired object within reach. Nearly all quickly eliminated the unlikely candidates and succeeded in accomplishing the task (Brown 1990:121). Of course, children at play have an almost inexhaustible reservoir of curiosity and energy to apply to the task of decoding the information embedded in objects.

The literature is replete with instances of children transitioning from scaled versions of tools to potent, usable versions as they graduate, seamlessly, from play-working to working (Lancy 2012a; Crittenden, chapter 7, this volume). Perhaps the most persuasive evidence regarding the attitude of adults toward children acquiring culture through play, without the need for adult guidance, comes from widespread reports of parents' indifference to and even encouragement of toddlers playing with machetes and other sharp and dangerous tools (Lepowsky 1987:79; Little 2011:51; Marlowe 2010:198; Ochs and Izquierdo 2009:395; Whiting 1941:25). By indulging children's curiosity about their environment and the things in it, parents ensure that children learn useful information without the necessity of instructing them.

MAKE-BELIEVE PLAY

In "Becoming a Blacksmith in Gbarngasuakwelle," I described Kpelle children's amazingly detailed and faithful replication of the blacksmith's forge in an episode of make-believe (Lancy 1980b). It is impossible to say whether the boy who scripted the play and took the lead will actually become a blacksmith although, in studies of apprenticeship, such evidence of early interest is sometimes cited in accounting for the decision to place a child with a master craftsperson (Lancy 2012b). This level of verisimilitude and the effort invested has been recorded in other societies such as Katz's account of Sudanese boys carefully replicating their farming systems in great detail (C. Katz 1986:47–48).

Ethnographic descriptions of make-believe play are rich and varied. Esther Goody (1992) describes a continuum from make-believe to "for real" food preparation in which older children model for younger ones, real but scaled-down pots may substitute for toy pots, and, if mother is willing, edible ingredients go into the pot rather than grass. Franz Boas describes Baffin Inuit boys "play-hunting" for seal using miniature harpoons fashioned by their parents (1901:111). While the everyday work activities of adults provide a common theme, we also see children mimic the processes involved in carrying out trance-induced shamanism (R. Katz 1981), simulated marriage including copulation (Gorer 1967:310), and religious rituals (Fortes 1970:68).

Parents are generally supportive of children's learning through make-believe as evidenced by the widespread practice of donating appropriate objects and materials as props (Laguna 1965:14; Grindal 1972:29; Hewlett et al. 2011:1175). For example, "[Inuit] girls make dolls out of scraps of skin, and clothe them like real men and women. Their mothers encourage them, for it is in this way that they learn to sew and cut out patterns" (Jenness 1922:219).

The public nature of most adult activity facilitates children's engagement at a safe distance where they cannot interfere (Lancy 2014:180). Anthropologists often note adult awareness and sympathy toward children's mimicry: "When adults are asked about children's mimetic play they reply: 'That is how they learn'" (Fortes 1970:23). "Biyaka parents [say] the primary duty of young children is to play. In fact [if] children do not play, they will fail to learn anything" (Neuwelt-Truntzer 1981:106). This presumption on the part of both anthropologists and parents was supported in a series of empirical tests carried out among several groups in Botswana (Bock 2002, 2004; Bock and Johnson 2004).

The idea that make-believe play may have an important role in children's acquisition of culture—Barber calls it "vocational kindergarten" (1994:85)— has also received theoretical support. The importance of children acquiring useful skills from those older and more expert via imitation is widely acknowledged. "We are such a thorough-going cultural species that it pays children, as a kind of default strategy, to copy willy-nilly much of the behavioral repertoire they see enacted before them" (Hopper, Marshall-Pescini, and Whiten 2012:105). Children's make-believe may closely replicate the scenes of village life but does not do so slavishly. There is invention in the roles assigned, in the props used, in the script followed, and, importantly, children may "twist" the tale. That is, we have a limited number of examples of children behaving like young social critics in their sometimes ribald and irreverent portrayals of adults (Goldman 1998; Gregor 1988:113; Hogbin 1970:138). Fortes notes "the Tale child's play mimesis is never simple and mechanical reproduction; it is always imaginative construction based on the themes of adult life" (1970:475). Crittenden (chapter 7, this volume) records a type of foraging invented by Hadza youth that does not replicate any specific adult practice. She also makes clear that the successful harvest of Weaver bird fledglings, while effectively providing calories for the group, is conducted entirely in a spirit of play.

GAMESMANSHIP

Like make-believe play, games are also ubiquitous cross-culturally and anthropologists have long speculated that core cultural values are transmitted to the young through games (Roberts, Arth, and Bush 1959). Within-culture studies illustrate this link between aspects of play and cultural values. Marquesan (but true broadly in Polynesia) children's awareness of social rank leads them to *avoid* play requiring leaders or lengthy negotiation of rules or roles (Martini 1994:80). In small-scale, band societies, the playgroup—necessarily of mixed ages—must allow all players, no matter how inept, to participate so the playing field is always level, thereby supporting the prevailing egalitarian ethos

(Lancy 1984). Among the Tangu of Papua New Guinea, teams of children play a game called *taketak*. Taketak is designed, in keeping with local values, to end in a tie (Burridge 1957). Aymara boys in the Andes play marbles (girls play jacks) while herding their flocks far from the village. Benjamin Smith's (2010) careful description of these games complements his in-depth analyses of speech and social interaction patterns during play. He illuminates the importance of bad luck (*qhincha*) in marbles. By confronting and enduring qhincha in the game, boys successfully fend off accusations of being feminine or homosexual. By implication, a boy who keeps his cool when something goes wrong (a pebble in the path deflecting his shot, a toddler tramping through the play area) demonstrates "*chacha*-ness" or "toughness"—the essence of masculinity. In the Brazilian rainforest where, until recently, intergroup warfare was endemic, Xavante boys' games/sports extract and ritualize many aspects of fighting (Gosso et al. 2005:232). In contrast, in Semai farming villages in Malaysia, children rarely see aggression.

For example, "two children . . . put their hands on each other's shoulders and wrestle, giggling, but never quite knocking each other over . . . [and] pairs of children in the two- to twelve-year age range flail at each other with sticks, but stop just before hitting each other" (Fry 2005:68).

One prominent perspective on games has been that they provide opportunities to contest one's rank in the dominance hierarchy (Weisfeld 1999:55). For example, "among [Pashtu] nomad boys . . . whenever a new household pitched their tent . . . boy(s) of the new household were invited to wrestle, and very soon, everybody knew the position of the new boy(s) in the rank order of the peer group" (Casimir 2010:50). However, a more general utility of games lies in what I call "gamesmanship" (Lancy 2014:224–228; Lancy and Grove 2011b:491–492). If the growth of the human brain has been driven by the need to adapt and survive within fairly large social groups, successful individuals will be those who act Machiavellian: maintaining social ties to (and benefitting from) the group while also taking advantage of group members to gain disproportionate resources including mating opportunities. "Their manipulations might as easily involve co-operation as conflict, [and] sharing as hoarding" (Byrne 1995:196).

Extrapolating from this argument, if children have social brains that need to be exercised to fully develop, games should be the perfect mental gym. The key elements of the game experience are rule-governed play, flexibility in applying the rules, and an absence of adult umpires. That is, children must be free to construct successful gaming sessions without adult interference (in contrast to contemporary Little League baseball; see Fine 1987). In this way rules can be bent, for example, to lower the threshold for participation by younger or less able players, or renegotiated so that play can continue even if one player wins consistently. A common strategy is to "self-handicap" (Boulton and Smith 1992:436). Plentiful opportunities of this sort will nurture children's gamesmanship or the ability to negotiate the complex social world faced by adults.

Learning in the Peer Group

In the previous section I noted the case of the Mandinka, where mothers strongly encourage toddlers to forget the breast, in essence shooing toddlers away to join the playgroup. This pattern of behavior is so common that it has a name: "toddler rejection" (Weisner and Gallimore 1977:176). It is an obvious complement to weaning in that, when infants are weaned relatively early, their displeasure can lead to an escalating battle where others—grandmothers and older siblings particularly—come to the mother's aid (Leavitt 1989:147; Gallimore, Howard, and Jordan 1969:393; Meehan, Helfrecht, and Malcom, chapter 9, this volume). Across the Primate order, juvenile females show great interest in infants (Hrdy 1999b:157, chapter 2, this volume) and it is not hard to sustain an argument that their supervised interaction with younger siblings prepares children for the task of parenthood (Fairbanks 1990; Riesman 1992:111). The weanling's need for mothering corresponds to the alloparent's need to mother. In the process of becoming initiated into the peer group, the toddler must shape up or suffer the consequences. The toddler must "fit in." Teasing, pranks, and other forms of correction are to be expected (Broch 1990:81) except where parents exercise close oversight (Gaskins, Haight, and Lancy 2007). This is a familiar scene to those studying childhood in small-scale face-to-face communities:

> When [Hadza] children are one to three years of age, they often throw tantrums, during which they may pick up a branch and repeatedly whack people over the head. The parents and other adults merely fend off the blows by covering their heads, laughing all the time. They do not even

take the stick away. When the child hits another child who is a little older, however, that child often grabs the stick and hits the little one back. This is the way young children learn they cannot get their way; older children train them. Thus, it is not necessary for adults to discipline them. [Marlowe 2010:197]

Excepting the Aka and other pygmy groups (Hewlett et al. 2011:1172), children are far more likely to be in the company of peers than parents. Weisner argues that "children care for other children [under a mother's or other adults' management] within *indirect chains of support*" (1996b:308, emphasis added; see also Rogoff 1981:31). Toddlers are managed by slightly older siblings who are, in turn, guided by adolescents. Adults, meanwhile, serve as rather distant "foremen" for activities. This phenomenon is illustrated in Bogin's portrait of a multi-generational gathering of Kaqchikel-speaking Maya women (Bogin 2013:37, chapter 3, this volume).

Children consigned to the company of older siblings and their friends join a cadre of excellent role models: "Mayan toddlers learn primarily by observing and interacting with their sibling caretakers" (Maynard 2002:978). Older siblings supervise and instruct by example whether engaged in foraging (Bird and Bird 2005:135; Rohner and Chaki-Sircar 1988:33), planting (Polak 2003, 2011), or personal grooming (Martini and Kirkpatrick 1992:124). Siblings can be more patient and sympathetic teachers than adults (Maynard and Tovote 2010). A contrasting pair of anecdotes is illustrative. Raum observed a Chaga mother and her little daughter cutting grass to take home to feed the cattle. Tying the stalks into a bundle is difficult but the "mother refuses requests for help by saying: 'Haven't you got hands like me?'" (Raum 1940:199). Now consider a vignette of Pushtun children gathering and bundling shrubs (*buti*) to bring home:

Khodaydad . . . showed and explained to his younger brother Walidad . . . how to put [shrubs] (*buti*) together: He made up a small pile while Walidad squatted next to him and watched. Tying them together, he explained how to do it. Then he untied the bundle and bound it up again to show how it was done. Walidad then wanted to carry it home. His elder brother helped him shoulder it and his sister guided him home, and it was obvious that little Walidad was very proud of being able to accomplish the work. [Casimir 2010:54]

What Motivates Culture Acquisition?

Walidad's pride in his accomplishment is consistent with an early and enduring theory of child development. White proposed that, from birth, humans are motivated to act on the environment in every way open to them in order to develop competence. Humans find such mastery rewarding and experience a "feeling of efficacy" (R. White 1959:329). According to Weisfeld and Linkey, this drive transitions at age three or four into a more general motive to "strive for success" (1985:110). They argue that even the young are able to translate practical accomplishments, such as successful foraging or carrying home some firewood, into social capital. A great deal of what one needs to master can be learned through observing and emulating conspecifics.

Humans share with most primates the ability to learn from others even when the models are not intending to demonstrate or instruct. It is patently less costly for an individual to observe and attempt to replicate the proficient behavior of an expert than to operate in a social vacuum or to "learn individually" (Richerson and Boyd 1992:70). But, aside from offering a pathway to competence, imitation is also the highest form of flattery (Henrich and Gil-White 2001:167). The child who tracks and attempts to replicate the purposeful behavior of others is appreciated by them and by others (Balikci 1970:45; Barlow 2001:86; Fortes 1970:22; Rival 2002:116; Wenger 1989:93). Outright praise for children's work efforts is not common, so children's "rewards" are instead subtle signs of fitting in such as being fed regularly and tolerated in adult company.

Reviewing these various "drives" across a spectrum from psychology to primatology might seem like the proverbial five blind men describing an elephant. To summarize, it seems to me that children learning their culture are demonstrating at least two powerful drives: to acquire the skills to survive and to affiliate securely with a group. It is likely that, in evolutionary terms, the latter drive appeared more recently (Boyd and Richerson 2006:469). Happily for the child, culture is organized into "routines" that facilitate these goals (Lancy 1996:2). We now consider cases in which the twin drives are quite evident as children attempt to "fit in."

Fitting into the Family Circle

In a pattern that must be very old, humans conduct their business in a public setting with multiple participants and onlookers including, especially, children.

Numerous studies of the stone scatter from sites where stone tool production occurred show incomplete tools and debris consistent with a mixture of skill levels, including beginners (Dugstad 2008:70; Pigeot 1990:131). At two sites in France, "highly skilled knappers occupied places closest to the hearth, the less skilled knappers and the novices sat further back from it" (Shennan and Steele 1999:375). Contemporary Iban children observe their parents working in the fields from an early age and "both boys and girls begin to join in tasks which lie within their powers, and soon come to make valuable contributions to the working of the family farm" (Freeman 1970:231–232). Ingold defines the essence of this dynamic as the "education of attention" (2001:139). This idea applies to most primates since juveniles remain in proximity to foraging adults who, unwittingly, draw "the juvenile's attention to a specific object or location in the environment that it otherwise would not have noticed" (Tomasello, Kruger, and Ratner 1993:496). Ingold continues: "In the passage of human generations, each one contributes to the knowledgeability of the next . . . by setting up, through their activities, the environmental contexts within which successors develop their own . . . skills" (2001:142).

Here follows a small sample of cases illustrating the atmosphere of one such environment—the family circle (for other good examples, see Ainsworth 1967:12; Laguna 1965:15; J. Campbell 1964:157; Fortes 1970:37; Philips 1972:385).

[Matsigenka] infants and young children are embedded in the middle of quotidian activities where they are positioned to quietly observe and learn what others are doing. [Ochs and Izquierdo 2009:395]

At the age of three he chooses his own place at the [Wolof] family meal, and here he is encouraged to acquire social norms. [Zempleni-Rabain 1973:222]

[Biyaka] children . . . have almost ubiquitous opportunity for observational learning of adult subsistence behaviors. Furthermore, "watching" . . . was a very high-frequency activity across all age groups. [Neuwelt-Truntzer 1981:109]

As social learners, children require models and most theories of culture transmission accord special status to parents and other family members. Zafmaniry believe that "children come to resemble their parents, in great part, because of the house they grew up in, the environment in which they live, and the people with whom they have interacted" (Bloch, Solomon, and Carey 2001:50; see also Euler, Hoier, and Rohde 2009:85). From the ethnographic record, we learn that girls are far more likely to attach to their mothers as social learners than boys are to their fathers. Among the reasons for this gender bias is that tasks tend to be gender specific. Girls, because of their service as "helpers-at-the-nest" (Crognier, Baail, and Hilali 2001) remain firmly in their mother's orbit as they mature, whereas boys are usually free to roam more widely (Lancy and Grove 2011a:288). Parallel relationships between boys and their fathers are more rare. In pastoral societies, boys herd solo or with other boys. Among hunters, boys are likely to be excluded from their father's hunting forays because of the danger, their slower travel and their inability to remain silent (Reyes-Garcia et al 2013:208). Even in cases in which the father has a skill set that he would like to see transmitted to his son, he will find another male to whom his son can apprentice because he cannot bear to administer the necessary punishment that learning is presumed to require (Ames 1973:153; Lancy 2012b:117). And, as the child grows older and moves out into the community at large, new role models become available (Aunger 2000:471; McElreath and Strimling 2008:307; Tehrani and Collard 2009).

Many societies negatively sanction children who are "forward" and ask questions or offer opinions to adults (Bledsoe 1992:192; Lancy and Grove 2011a:285; Paradise and Rogoff 2009:121), but, on the other hand, children are expected to attend to "subtle, low cost teaching" (Kline, Boyd, and Henrich 2013). For example, León (2012; see also J. Campbell 1964:157; Silva, Correa-Chavéz, and Rogoff 2011) describes the "overhearer" as one of the cornerstones of traditional Zinacantecan child-rearing. Older family members critically discuss the child's behavior when the child is present but not otherwise interacting with them. The child, who is expected at all times to pay attention to those older, is expected to listen to these discussions and reflect upon his or her actions. Less subtle but quite common means of shaping children's behavior (Lancy 2014:193–198) include the use of scare tactics (Gorer 1967:312; Hernandez 1941:130; Leavitt 1989:150; T. Williams 1969:94, 114) and corporal punishment (Borofsky 1987:97; Freeman 1983:206; Musil 1928:256; Shelton 1998:31).

These subtle and not-so-subtle messages to very young children are often designed to socialize the child to broad cultural expectations. For example, Papel infants are given something desirable, such as a snack, then immediately told to pass it on to another, particularly a sibling (Einarsdottir 2004:94). The Kwara'ae also do this and "infants who cry or resist sharing are gently chided, teased, or laughed at, and told to share because 'he or she is your older or younger sibling'" (Watson-Gegeo and Gegeo 1989:61). There is no suggestion that children will not learn the appropriate prosocial behaviors with time (d'Andrade 1984:97; Fehr, Bernhard, and Rockenbach 2008; Rheingold 1982:114; Warneken and Tomasello 2006:1301).[4] After all, the success of the species has rested on *voluntary* compliance with social norms (Boyd and Richerson 2006:469). Characteristically, in societies explicitly promoting prosocial behavior, the child is encouraged to behave "correctly" vis-à-vis the very individuals—older siblings, grandmothers, and other close kin—who are also likely recruits to serve as substitute caretakers (Weisner and Gallimore 1977).

Still within the family circle, the child matures into a "legitimate peripheral participant" (Lave and Wenger 1991) who "pitch[es] in" and helps with ongoing activity such as food preparation, crafts, and housework as soon as he or she can do so without damaging resources or interfering with those who are more productive (Krause 1985:95). Children can expect some attention from family members as long as they are focused on a task (Weisner 1989:78). "[Mazahua] children participate in . . . family . . . activities [and] conversation and questions . . . occur for the sake of sharing necessary information . . . integral to the endeavor at hand" (Paradise and Rogoff 2009:118). Indeed, scholars have advanced the idea that merely by approving or disapproving of children's early attempts, older family members can dramatically improve their efficiency as social learners (Castro and Toro 2004). The general philosophy might be that "an individual does not learn from another but through another" (Schönpflug 2009:466).

One of the better-described elements of childhood is children's work. I think one reason for this is that anthropologists are often shocked by the sight of very young children carrying out vital work for the family. Margaret Mead offered one of the earliest descriptions of a phenomenon often recorded since:

> [On Samoa] the tiniest little staggerer has tasks to perform—to carry water, to borrow fire brands, to fetch leaves to stuff the pig. . . . Learning to run errands tactfully is one of the first lessons of childhood. [1928:633]

In spite of her use of the term "lessons," these undertakings are typically initiated by the child: the "assumption of work and responsibility comes about gradually, and largely on the child's own initiative" (Edel 1966:178). Mayan children "are eager to participate in the economic activities of the household" (Rogoff 1981:31). The "family circle" can be set in motion as family clusters go on foraging expeditions. Among the Cree,

> as soon as a Cree child learned to walk, she was expected to help with and share in the work of the bush camp. The child was not usually given verbal instruction but encouraged to learn skills by playing and by imitating adults through participation in subsistence production activities. . . . [She] was told, "Keep trying, never give up until you get it right." . . . When she did it properly, the teacher praised her saying that is the way (*"ekute"*). [Ohmagari and Berkes 1997:206]

The extraordinary capacity of the very young for social learning is exercised to its fullest extent in the family circle. Children can create a kind of mental Rolodex of the behavior and needs of other family members. They can create a blueprint of activities within the domestic sphere, fitting themselves into the flow of events, and attempting to help out or mimic the actions of those older "as if" they were helping out.

From Making Nice to Making a Contribution

Ideally, children's desire to be helpful and their level of competence, like gear wheels, mesh with the needs of the family. Two areas where this intricate process is readily observed, even among the very young, are in the relationship between a sib-caretaker and her baby sibling and in the task of errand running. As I have discussed elsewhere (Lancy 2012a), one robust feature of the chore curriculum is its "staged" character. That is, realms of work are usually partitioned in a way allowing the child to move smoothly from rudimentary participation to competence.

A survey of the Human Relations Area Files (HRAF) archive found that, in 186 accounts of childcare, 40 percent of infants and 80 percent of toddlers were cared for primarily by someone other than their mother, most commonly older sisters (Weisner and Gallimore 1977:170). A three-year-old will seek to hold her newborn brother and be permitted to do so, usually under supervision, for short periods (Ottenberg 1968:80). As the two grow older, she will become responsible for longer periods of care and meet a wider array of needs including dressing, feeding, delousing, and, above all, entertaining (Rindstedt and Aronsson 2003:8). Failure will be noted and chastised (Schlegel 1973:454). At seven, we might find her caring for several children, out of sight of their mother, perhaps taking them to a pond to bath them and clean off any urine or excrement (Rohner and Chaki-Sircar 1988:70–1). At nine she could be simultaneously tending her charges and foraging for edibles that she will share with them, thereby meeting a significant portion of her own and their caloric needs (Crittenden et al., 2013). Years later, she may be "proudly possessive of the achievements and exploits of younger brothers and sisters who had been [her] special responsibility" (Elmendorf 1976:94).

The first chore for boys will probably be errand running. A barely mobile toddler may be asked to carry a cup from its mother across an evening family circle to its father. The same toddler will tag along as an older sibling makes a longer delivery excursion, in effect serving as an understudy. Later, "between eighteen and thirty months of age . . . the Guara child begins to act independently as a messenger" (Ruddle and Chesterfield 1977:31). "Very young children (age three) may start with one or two sticks of wood, or yams in a carry net, but by age eight they are carrying firewood, water, produce, and messages" (Zeller 1987:544). Errands vary in length and territory (Nerlove et al., 1974:276), can involve either close kin or strangers, can involve loads of varying size and fragility, and can include an exchange of some kind including a market transaction. Adults match their assignments to the child's level of skill and size and each new assignment ratifies (and motivates) the child's growing competence (Lancy 1996:146).

A second case illustrating the graded nature of the chore curriculum comes from Polak's meticulous description and analysis of the education of Bamana bean farmers. Note that at every age level mentioned in the quotation, the "task" is somewhat different. Just as an array of siblings going off to fetch water from the stream are given appropriately sized vessels (Lancy 1996:144), bean farming can be partitioned to match the skill and endurance levels of the worker-learners:

> [At harvest] three-year-old Daole . . . begins to pluck beans from the tendrils. After he has filled the lid with a handful of beans, his interest fades. [He] carelessly leaves the lid with the beans lying on the ground and goes looking for some other occupation. . . . Five-year-old Suméla . . . looks out for a corner not yet harvested and picks as many

beans as will fill his calabash. . . . [He] keeps on doing this for more than one and a half hours. . . . Eleven-year-old Fase has been busy harvesting beans . . . since morning. He works as fast as . . . his father and grown-up brother . . . and only takes a rest when they [do]. . . . Fase . . . even takes on the role of supervising his younger brothers and checks their performance from time to time. [Polak 2003:130–132]

We learn from Polak's (2011:104–105) work that children are given worn hoes to practice with and, while hoeing, that they are gently nudged by older siblings to work an area not already cultivated to avoid damaging the work of others.

We have considerable evidence (Piel 2012) that children are "natural foragers" with a strong tendency to learn about their natural environment "even in the absence of adult instigation or favorable environments" (Chipeniuk 1995:494; see also Barrett 2005:217). Hunting can be more challenging (MacDonald 2007:391) than bean farming but the acquisition process is similar. Older siblings again serve as models. A boy is not typically permitted to accompany adults on the hunt until he is in his teens and fairly proficient (Peters 1998:90–91; Puri 2005:233–234). There is graduated movement (Goodwin and Goodwin 1942:475) from toy to child-scaled to full-size weapons, or from slingshot to spear to blowgun. Boys roam playfully but purposefully through the forest and savannah with peers, gradually learning to read the "signs . . . of bent leaves, twigs, and shrubs that the Ache call a *kuere* . . . [enabling them to undertake] hunting forays without getting lost" (Hill and Hurtado 1996:223). As the nascent hunter becomes more proficient, more serious, and less playful, his catch may range from grasshoppers to birds to rodents to a "real" kill (Turnbull 1965:257) that can be proudly shared with the family. Full proficiency may not occur until the hunter is in his third decade.

In earlier surveys (Lancy 2012a, b, 2014; Lancy and Grove 2010) we have reviewed dozens of cases across the entire spectrum of skills from subsistence to crafts. All incorporate this staged quality, usually with a play stage at the outset (Lancy 2012a). There are, of course, exceptional circumstances when a stage is missing. That is, the step up from one level of skill to the next is too great for the child to manage and an adult will intervene to show the child how to circumvent this roadblock. Bamana boys, for example, master the tasks of farming largely on their own but encounter one distinct challenge in planting millet seeds. They must in one fluid motion open a hole in the soil with their hoe, tilt a gourd filled with seed attached to their wrist just enough to deposit two or three seeds in the hole, and then cover up the hole again. Adults explicitly demonstrate this process for boys who have been unsuccessful (Polak 2011:85).

Underlying Processes in Skill Acquisition

Children take advantage of opportunities to observe and emulate the more competent in order to achieve competence and to be helpful and accepted. They bring innate gifts to this process as discussed earlier. At around four to six years of age[5] children begin to display something called Theory of Mind (TOM) (Wellman, Cross, and Watson 2001). TOM allows an individual to get inside the head of another person. The child can now read others' intentions and can construct the others' trajectory and goals. The terms "intersubjectivity" and "perspective taking" are also applied in discussions of this phenomenon (Tomasello, Kruger, and Ratner 1993). Anthropologists have noted such a concept in a number of parental ethnotheories. The child has reached a point in their development where they start to "get noticed" (Lancy and Grove 2011a) due to their evident intelligence or common sense, referred to among the Kipsigis as *ng'omnotet,* among the Ayoreo as *aiuketaotiguei,* the Sisala as *wijima,* and the Ifaluk Islanders as *repiy,* to name a few examples (Lancy 2012a:34). Many of the qualities attached to folk definitions of sense or intelligence suggest that the child is now much better at perspective taking and can better anticipate another's intentions and desires. The child contributes appropriately without bidding or guidance (Lancy 2014:200).

Isolated studies indicate that humans are capable of extraordinary feats of navigation without instruments. Examples include ocean navigation in the Carolines (Gladwin 1970) and long-distance herding of reindeer in Siberia (Istomin and Dwyer 2009). Studies of child navigators are rare, but Ache (Hill and Hurtado 1996:223), Kpelle (Lancy 1996:156), Tzeltal Maya (Zarger and Stepp 2004), and Zapotec (Hunn 2002:610) children have all demonstrated what to the ethnographer seemed extraordinary talent in navigating a thickly forested environment to forage. The forager's ability to take in and process information from the environment suggests an unlearned capacity for what Gaskins and Paradise call "open attention" (2010:104), which can be deployed to good effect in social settings as well as in the natural environment. Hilger (1957:50) was impressed by Araucanian children's keen eyesight, hearing, and powers of observation. Yukaghir hunters insist that, while you can learn by observing others, to become a really proficient hunter you must hunt on your own: "Only then do you really start noticing the myriad of details around you" (Willerslev 2007:169).

Gaskins and Paradise (2010:99–100) describe open attention as wide-angled and abiding. The first means that the individual is aware of and attends to a great deal of the environment at one time rather than attending to only one stimulus such as the teacher. The second means that attention is sustained rather than episodic or short-term. They cite a study, which found that children and adults from the WEIRD (Western, Educated, Industrialized, Rich and Democratic; see Henrich, Heine, and Norenzayan 2010b) society displayed short, fleeting attention whereas Mayan mothers and children displayed open attention (Chavajay and Rogoff 1999; see also Silva, Correa-Chavéz, and Rogoff 2011). It may well be that open attention is subject to a critical period during which, if it is not exercised (because, for example, WEIRD parents spend so much time focusing the infant's or child's attention on them as a teacher or on educational toys), it will be extinguished.

The Economic Value of Children's Work

Another issue that concerns us is the child's level of productivity as a function of age. As children become older they gain both knowledge and strength. Bock carried out systematic measurements of production as a function of strength and skill in several groups in Botswana. For some tasks, experience is the best predictor of proficiency; for others, strength is critical. Processing baobab fruits requires neither great strength nor skill and can be undertaken by four-year-olds. Mongongo nut processing requires both, and Bock (2002) finds that the most proficient women are twenty-five to fifty-five years old. Researchers have also looked at this question among Tsimanè hunters (Gurven, Kaplan, and Gutierrez 2006).

A related factor is demand. How productive the child is will depend in part on the expectations of family for assistance. Karen Kramer (2005b:135) compared gross levels of productivity as a function of age among Mayan farming children and their counterparts in two South American foraging groups. The Mayan children reached an equilibrium of producing as much as they consumed by thirteen, whereas foraging children took five to ten years longer. The nature of subsistence plays a role. Hewlett and colleagues' (2011) long-term study of the Central African Aka foragers and Ngandu farmers illustrates this well. Ngandu children are expected to contribute to the domestic economy from an early age and they are able to do this, in part, because the skills they will need are readily learned by the onset of adolescence. Ngandu subsistence relies heavily on children's desire to be compliant, less on their desire to achieve. This pattern is very typical in farming and herding communities (Hames and Draper 2004:334). By contrast, the Aka—like the !Kung but unlike another pygmy band, the Biyaka (Neuwelt-Truntzer 1981:138,147)—do not expect children to contribute greatly to the domestic economy. Nevertheless, by age ten, both boys and girls have mastered a large repertoire of sometimes-complex foraging skills: "If need be . . . Aka ten-year-olds have the skills to make a living in the forest" (Hewlett and Cavalli-Sforza 1986:930). Learning to make a living, for Aka children, seems to be less driven by the need to conform to family requirements than by the desire to achieve competence.

This gap between the age at which children achieve adequate levels of competence in the local subsistence system and, separately, the age at which they achieve significant production levels has theoretical significance. Many evolutionary theorists consider the prolonged period of semi-dependency and the long-delayed onset of puberty and mating as providing a sheltered learning environment. They reason that the human adaptive model requires the gradual acquisition of an entire array of increasingly more challenging skills (Kaplan et al. 2000:156). However, there have been a rapidly accumulating series of studies (Lancy 2014:278–280), of child foragers in particular, showing what we might call precocity in learning to forage (Crittenden, chapter 7, this volume). These studies include young Martu children hunting and surviving on goanna lizards (Bird and Bird 2005), Hadza four-year-olds gathering and eating quantities of baobab fruits (Blurton-Jones, Hawkes, and O'Connell 1997), six-year-old reef foragers on Mer Island achieving full proficiency (D. Bird and R. Bird 2002), Zapotec children having a "precocious" command of ethnobotany (Hunn 2002), young Ache female foragers matching adult women's foraging returns by the age of ten to twelve (Hill and Hurtado 1996:223), Samoan ten-year-olds fishing successfully using a variety of methods (Odden and Rochat 2004:45), !Kung boys being considered successful hunters and being feted for bagging their first large mammal at least ten years before they marry (Shostak 1981:84), and Kutenai boys being able at age ten to bring down a bison calf with bow and arrow (Turney-High 1978:117). These studies cast considerable doubt on the necessity of a lengthened childhood to learn subsistence skills (Blurton-Jones and Marlowe 2002:199). We should also take note of the fact that while humans take many years to reach physical maturity, brain growth—critical for learning one's culture—is essentially complete by age seven (Bogin 1999b:130; Bogin, Bragg, and Kuzawa, chapter 3, this volume).

I believe that the solution to this apparent paradox lies in the elastic nature of human ontogeny (Bernstein, Sterner, and Wildman 2012:398; Bernstein, chapter 5, this volume).[6] It is very clear from the literature, as just discussed, that children can acquire subsistence skills quite early. It is also the case that their application of those skills in a significant way to support themselves and close kin may occur early or very late in childhood (Kramer and Greaves 2011:308). Under adverse circumstances, such as the death of a parent (Polak 2011:142; Sugiyama and Chacon 2005:237); a drastic change in the food supply; the loss of males from the community to distant opportunities like trade, warfare, herding, and hunting or fishing; unstable or unsupportive family; or the arrival of a new baby, children "can ratchet up their productivity quickly and execute efficiently those skills they've been perfecting through playful work" (Lancy 2014:280). Kin selection theory might also suggest that the child will increase production in order to aid and maintain his or her family. The family has nurtured the child in the past and may well aid his or her survival and reproductive efforts in the future. Piel (2012) has documented an extraordinary example of this in the behavior of rural and urban Japanese children during and after WWII. They taught themselves and their younger siblings how to forage for foodstuffs (acorns, nuts, aquatic plants, and shellfish) to provision their families and forestall starvation. An alternative to provisioning self and kin may be to accelerate the process of mating and family formation, reproducing early and often (Belsky, Steinberg, and Draper 1991:507; Giudice and Belsky 2011). Lastly, it is likely that Pleistocene foragers enjoyed much better nutrition than contemporary hunter-gatherers. The juvenile period may have been shorter (Blurton-Jones 2006:252), giving children a greater incentive to capitalize on their skill set at an earlier age.

Conclusion

I have endeavored to weave together various strands of evidence to make a case for children learning their culture via informal processes, largely at their own pace and initiative. Children bring a suite of innate tools to the process of culture acquisition. Recent studies of infant cognition have revealed a repertoire of emergent capacities for making sense of and interacting with the physical and social world. Older children reveal additional capacities for learning, including abilities to carefully observe others and the physical environment. These capacities facilitate the "precocious" acquisition of environmental information and subsistence skills.

Even very young children display a willingness to "help out," "fit in," and receive approval (Hrdy, chapter 2, this volume). The child's eagerness to interact with others facilitates language acquisition, which then enables social learning. Another "drive" appears to be the need to emulate the skills of those more expert. This tendency is encouraged by, for example, giving toddlers sharp knives to practice with. Those older and more expert serve as role models, not always willingly. They may adjust their behavior in response to cues provided by the learner (Thornton and Raihani 2008:1826). The child's elders may use subtle hints to shape behavior or more forceful strategies such as threats or punishment. Many societies accelerate the timetable for children to acquire prosocial patterns of behavior and speech. Still, intensive, direct verbal instruction is quite rare and the construction of lessons where the practice is reorganized completely to optimize learning rather than production is almost unheard of.

Important arenas for children's acquisition of culture include several kinds of play including make-believe and games, participating as an observer at family gatherings, helping with household tasks, carrying out chores, and engaging in various activities with peers. Children emulate those slightly older and more expert, generally learn at their own pace, and gradually climb a ladder of mastery from rudimentary elements of the larger task (whether play, work, or social role) to acknowledged expertise and the supervision of younger participants. Children's acquisition of culture may be overlooked because they may be thought of as lacking "sense" and/or because they may not be called on to make significant contributions to the family. However, these latent talents may be called upon in a time of crisis when children can ratchet up their productivity. While we might conventionally think of childhood as a period of dependency on others, that period can be significantly shortened as the need arises.

Acknowledgments

I am extremely grateful to Alyssa Crittenden and Courtney Meehan for creating a setting where each participant had many opportunities to interact with and learn from others. We all were learners and teachers. Their editorial assistance was invaluable as well. Last, I'm grateful to Annette Grove for her careful editing of the final paper.

Notes

1. This pervasive attitude toward children's acquisition of culture has implications for cultural devolution. Village practitioners don't necessarily feel obligated to assume a more active teaching posture when the young fail to take the initiative to learn from them and the skills are lost (Friedl 1997:4; S. Howell 1988:162).

2. Space limitations preclude any consideration of culture acquisition during adolescence but see (Lancy 2012b).

3. Hrdy (2012) suggests that the infant's gaze-following and close attention to facial expressions and moods—along with a plump body and other neotenous features—are designed to send a clear signal to its mother and other caretakers: "Keep me!"

4. Recent laboratory studies underscore that human children exhibit prosocial behavior spontaneously from the age of three or earlier and are more readily prosocial than juvenile chimps (House et al. 2012).

5. Or as early as twelve months in a very recent study of the false belief component (Barrett et al. 2013).

6. Evidence for plasticity and "reserve capacity" is readily noted in primates as "orangutans, gorillas and bonobos use tools with dexterity and sophistication in captivity but rarely use them in the wild" (King 1994:121). Reserve Capacity (RC) is also evident in the human growth pattern where the growing child overshoots the necessary capacity to begin reproducing (Crews 2003). And RC can "be channeled into trade-offs between greater growth, immune function, mating behavior, and/or reproduction and parental investment (Bogin 2013:34)."

Childhood in Context: Contemporary
Implications of Evolutionary Approaches

CHAPTER NINE

Implications of Lengthy Development and Maternal Life History

Allomaternal Investment, Peer Relationships, and Social Networks

COURTNEY L. MEEHAN, COURTNEY HELFRECHT, AND COURTNEY D. MALCOM

Humans, like other cooperative breeding species, require that others invest in their children to ensure successful development (Hrdy 2009, chapter 2, this volume). Yet much of developmental theory still rests on the idea that the mother-child dyad is somehow separate from the social world in which they live. Here, we review evidence that the mother-child dyad is not isolated, but rather is steeped in and affected at both the physical and psychological levels by the broader social world. We argue that not only did prosocial behavior support the evolution of extended dependency, but that sociality and its associated components are so tied to human development and our ability to rear children that it must be central to our investigations. Questions on successful physical, social, and emotional development and well-being must incorporate others, including allomothers, peers, and extended social networks. Such an approach to child development highlights core needs (see Sellen, chapter 10, this volume) and properly situates human childhood and maternal investment in their evolutionary contexts.

In development of this argument, we bring together, review, and expand upon our recent arguments regarding the role of allomothers in infant and child development and reproduction (see Meehan and Hawks 2013, 2014; Meehan, Helfrecht, and Quinlan, 2014; Meehan, Quinlan, and Malcom 2013). We provide a brief summary of life-history theory and cooperative breeding, as human ontogeny, discussed next, cannot be evaluated outside of this context (Hrdy, chapter 2, this volume). We then review the literature on allomaternal care in cross-cultural perspective (see also Meehan 2014) and further examine evidence regarding the essentiality of the social world and the contemporary implications of dependency not just in infancy and childhood but throughout the life span. We pay specific attention to the role of others, including peers, in successful physical and socioemotional development and examine the effects of others on maternal reproductive strategies, physical and socioemotional health, and parental effort. The results indicate that an understanding of child development and maternal care and investment is only possible when it is situated within the lifelong interdependency that characterizes our species. This evolutionary perspective enhances our insight on the implications of human childhood, providing a more comprehensive understanding of child development and caregiving strategies in contemporary populations.

Human Life History

Life-history theory is based on the premise that species-specific characteristics are generated through allocation of energy to somatic (growth, development, survival/system maintenance) and reproductive (mating, parenting) efforts (Stearns 1992). Energy allocated to one of these areas cannot be allocated to another. The resulting trade-offs are influenced by both the physical and social environments (Bogin, Bragg, and Kuzawa, chapter 3, this volume; Charnov 1993; Ellison 2001; Stearns 1992). It should be noted, however, that our biology limits the range of these potential trade-offs; there are upper and lower limits on, for example, height or timing of menarche. Our growth patterns, the length of our development, and decisions concerning investment in current versus future offspring are all characteristics influenced by our environments.

Human life history differs from that of other great apes in part due to the length of our developmental dependency, which spans infancy to early adulthood. Extended dependency is hypothesized to be the result of insertion of an early childhood phase coupled with prolonged juvenility (Bogin 1999b, 2010; Bogin, Bragg, and Kuzawa, chapter 3, this volume). Alternatively, others have suggests that it stems from the extension of existing components of non-human primate development (Bernstein, chapter 5, this volume; Bernstein, Sterner, and Wildman 2012; Conley, Bernstein, and Nguyen 2012) or, even more simply, the extension of the human life span in general (Charnov 1993). Regardless of origin, infant altriciality, extended child development, and short interbirth intervals, compared to other apes (Bogin 1997; Hrdy 2009), result in the cost of child-rearing being more than what a mother alone can provide (see Kaplan 1994). Thus development requires significant energetic contributions from others.

Cooperative Breeding and Prosociality

Cooperative breeding is "an umbrella label that includes a diverse array of mating and social systems" (Ligon and Burt 2004:5) where individuals other than parents invest in offspring through caregiving and provisioning. Unlike Bogin, Bragg, and Kuzawa (chapter 3, this volume), who adopted Lukas and Clutton-Brock's (2012) more restrictive definition of cooperative breeding, we suggest that it is best defined broadly, as a system "where more than two individuals contribute" to offspring survival (Cockburn 2004:81). This definition acknowledges the tremendous ecological and behavioral variation that exists among cooperative breeding species (Stacey and Koenig 1990), yet unites these species through key shared characteristics—comparatively long postnatal dependence and the need for nonmaternal solicitude through care and provisioning to successfully rear offspring (Hrdy 2005b; Langen 2000; Ligon 1999; Ligon and Burt 2004).

Humans clearly display these hallmarks (Hrdy 2005a, 2009). Throughout our evolutionary history, human mothers were not likely to successfully meet the demands of multiple dependents on their own (Hrdy 2005a, 2009; Kramer and Ellison 2010). However, humans have found the means to successfully reproduce in nearly every physical environment and have done so because allomothers, as with other cooperative breeding species (see Koenig and Dickinson 2004; Solomon and French 1997), offset the costs of reproduction. While similar to other cooperative breeding species, human allomaternal investment stands out as remarkable in the frequency, depth, and breadth of investment contributed (e.g., Crittenden and Marlowe 2008; Gottlieb 2004; Hewlett and Winn 2014; Ivey Henry, Morelli, and Tronick 2005; Konner 2005; K. Kramer 2010; Meehan 2005a; Meehan and Roulette 2013; Tronick, Morelli, and Winn 1987). Nonmaternal assistance is generally, although not exclusively (e.g., Sear 2008), linked to improved child outcomes (Beise 2005; Euler and Weitzel 1996; Hawkes, O'Connell, and Blurton Jones 1997; Leonetti et al. 2005; Sear and Mace 2008; Sear, Mace, and McGregor 2000; Sear et al. 2002). Additionally, this investment alters life-history trade-offs, enabling women to produce more costly, more dependent, and more closely spaced offspring than they would be able to sustain on their own (Hrdy 2009; K. Kramer 2005b;

Mace and Sear 2005). Through allomaternal investment of time and energy in children, women are able to simultaneously rear multiple dependent offspring at varied developmental stages, thereby increasing fertility (Crognier, Villena, and Vargas 2002; K. Kramer 2005b; Marlowe 2001; Turke 1988).

Human Ontogeny

Human developmental stages are typically divided into infancy, early childhood, middle childhood (alternatively referred to as juvenility), adolescence, and adulthood (see also Bogin, Bragg, and Kuzawa, chapter 3, this volume). Yet development, within a bounded framework, demonstrates some plasticity. Stages, while useful heuristics, can fail to recognize intra- and inter-cultural variation and the complexities of developmental trajectories (see Thompson and Nelson, chapter 4, this volume). Thus we stress caution in terms of strictly defining developmental stages.

Human infants (birth to weaning), born neurologically and immuno-logically immature, experience rapid postnatal growth and require the most intensive investment of any human developmental phase (Bogin 2002; McDade 2003). The infant is entirely dependent on mothers and others for survival. This phase, however, also represents a lengthy and gradual transition from complete physical dependency to independent mobility, and from solely consuming breast milk to a reliance on a complementary diet, with the stage's ending marked by a child's complete transition to an adult diet. Given extensive variation in age at weaning and the developmental changes that occur from newborns to almost-weaned offspring, it is often difficult to succinctly categorize human infancy in a cross-cultural perspective. However, this general "phase" is when children experience the highest mortality risk and when their care is the most intensive and energetically demanding on those who provide it.

During early childhood, the post-infancy stage, children are fully weaned and have increased (although certainly not complete) physical independence. In natural fertility populations, weaning often marks the forthcoming arrival of a new sibling (e.g., Fouts, Hewlett, and Lamb 2005; Hawkes, O'Connell, and Blurton Jones 1997). Linear growth begins to slow and continues to do so across the next stage of development, which may reduce competition for limited energy resources (Janson and Van Schaik 1993). However, brain growth, a calorically expensive component of childhood development, is not complete until approximately age seven (e.g., Bogin 1997, 2002), leaving children still heavily reliant upon others for their well-being.

Middle childhood commences around five to seven years of age. During this time, the energetic allocation to growth slows even more but has not yet shifted to reproduction (Bogin 1997, 1999b). The role of this phase is often debated, but explanations tend to center on the development of sociocultural skills necessary for survival (e.g., Flinn and Ward 2005; Kaplan, Lancaster, and Robson 2003; Tomasello 1999). Children remain dependent on others but are capable of making small contributions to the household economy (Crittenden, chapter 7, this volume; Crittenden et al. 2013; Lancy and Grove 2011; Rogoff et al. 1975; S. White 1996). As a result, energetic allocation becomes multidirectional—children are able to receive and return investment to and from adults, siblings, and peers (Kramer and Ellison 2010). However, middle childhood is still risky. Children have not yet completed their growth, and poor nutrition can lead to growth faltering and associated increases in childhood morbidity and mortality (Beaton 1992; Chen, Chowdhury, and Huffman 1981; Martorell 1999). In addition, children almost certainly have at least one sibling, and likely more than one, at this point in their development. These siblings are not without costs. When resources are limited, there can be an inherent tension among multiple dependent siblings (Trivers 1972), which can have tangible fitness consequences. For example, older brothers and younger sisters are associated with reduced muscle and fat composition for Tsimane girls in Bolivia (Magvanjav et al. 2013) and the odds of death for Dogon children (up to age ten) in Mali increase by a factor of 1.26 with each additional sibling (Strassmann 2000).

At adolescence, a final allocation of energy to growth occurs before we see a shift to reproductive effort (Bogin 2002). During this transition, sociocultural and sociosexual skills necessary for adult reproductive and social success emerge. Adolescents participate in more adult economic and social activities, undergo various rites of passage necessary to being seen as an adult, and increasingly engage in sexually oriented behaviors (within cultural restrictions) (see Bogin 2010 and Konner 2010). They are not, however, fully independent; they are typically sub-fecund for a few years (e.g., Bogin 1999b) and often reside with their parents. Adolescents continue to require energetic investment by others, even as they are able to meet the majority of their needs on their own after mid-adolescence (Bogin 2010), and are increasingly making significant contributions to the household economy in both forager

(Crittenden et al. 2013; Kaplan, Lancaster, and Hurtado 2000) and farmer (K. Kramer 2002, 2010) societies.

Adulthood reflects the cessation of energy allocation to growth and a significant shift to reproductive effort, be it through mating or parenting. Motherhood, for instance, requires substantial energetic expenditure, particularly throughout pregnancy and lactation (Prentice et al. 1996). In natural fertility populations, where women breastfeed for two to four years and give birth to a subsequent child relatively quickly thereafter (Fouts, Hewlett, and Lamb 2005), women are rarely *not* lactating during their reproductive lives. Lactation can require as much as half of daily energy for calorically deficient women (Valeggia and Ellison 2001). Mothers' energetics are further taxed through time allocation to both work and caregiving (Bove, Valeggia, and Ellison 2002; Hurtado et al. 1992; Meehan 2009; Valeggia and Ellison 2001). These costs remain and increase, albeit unlikely in a one-to-one ratio, throughout a woman's reproductive career due to the stacking of offspring. Thus, human dependency—and interdependency—persists throughout the life span; even in adulthood, humans are reliant on others to support their own and their children's physical and socioemotional needs.

The Breadth and Extent of Allomaternal Caregiving and Provisioning

Some of the best-documented examples of the breadth and extent of children's social worlds come from hunter-gatherer studies (for review, see Konner, chapter 6, this volume; Meehan 2014). Hunter-gatherer infants are in almost constant contact with a caregiver and, while mothers are primary caregivers in all known examples (Konner 2005), the extent of shared care is remarkable. Among the Aka, tropical forest foragers in the Central African Republic (CAR), allomothers are responsible for approximately one-quarter of the care children receive in infancy (Meehan 2005b). Efe, also central African foragers, infants at three and eighteen weeks are in physical contact with allomothers 39 and 60 percent of the time, respectively (Tronick, Morelli, and Winn 1987). In Tanzania, Hadza hunter-gatherer allomothers donate close to a third of child holding (Crittenden and Marlow 2008). Additionally, the Kalahari !Kung, the primary example of the continuous care and contact model, also have significant levels of allomaternal care (Konner 2005; chapter 6, this volume). !Kung allomothers are responsible for one-fifth to one-quarter of all recorded instances of infant physical contact (Konner 1975), half of vocalizations directed to children (Bakeman et al. 1990), and allomothers respond to children's crying bouts 42 percent of the time (inclusive of 14 percent combined responses by mothers and allomothers) (Kruger and Konner 2010).

Perhaps most importantly, this pattern of extensive nonmaternal caregiving is not limited to hunter-gatherer populations. The Ngandu, a horticulturalist population in the CAR, also have a highly cooperative child-rearing system. Although the frequency of allomaternal care is significantly lower than it is among the Aka, Ngandu allomothers provide approximately half of the holding infants receive (Meehan 2005b). Similarly, evidence from peri-urban and rural Argentinean Toba populations demonstrate that allomothers are in charge of infants 23–50 percent of the time (Valeggia 2009).

Moreover, there is mounting evidence that care comes from a wide range of individuals. Although kin contribute more than non-kin to childcare (e.g., Ivey 2000; Ivey Henry, Morelli, and Tronick 2005; Meehan 2005a; Turke 1988), data from hunter-gatherer and other small-scale societies indicate that the social, cooperative, and sharing nature of human childcare extends beyond kin relations. Aka infants (8–12 months) interact with approximately twenty caregivers on a daily basis, ten of whom provide intensive investment. Alloparents include grandmothers, aunts, uncles, siblings, cousins, and non-kin (Meehan 2008) and this suite of caregivers are almost always nearby (see figure 9.1). Likewise, Efe children are cared for by approximately fourteen caregivers (Tronick, Morelli, and Winn 1987). Data on who holds Hadza children indicate that investment comes from a wide variety of caregivers. Hadza maternal grandmothers are responsible for only 3.7 percent of allomaternal holding. Paternal grandmothers are responsible for just over 1 percent of allomaternal holding and the remainder of holding is done by others, 12 percent of which is by non-kin (Crittenden and Marlowe 2008). Beng infants in the Ivory Coast engage with an average of 2.2 people over just a two hour and fifteen minute observation period (Gottlieb 2004). But, as the modal duration of caregiver interaction was only five minutes and as children commonly engaged with three to four individuals and occasionally as many as five or six, Gottlieb suggests that the mean likely minimizes the number of allomothers children are able to access. Finally, Ngandu infants (8–12 months) have approximately ten caregivers, represented by both kin and non-kin, who interact with them each day, half of whom intensively invest in the infant (Meehan 2009). In sum, dense social and caregiving environments seem to be the norm for human populations (Meehan 2014; Meehan and Hawks 2013).

Figure 9.1. An Aka infant, children, and caregivers. Aka infants and children are reared in dense social and caregiving networks from birth. Photo: R. Prescott.

The Role of Others in Children's Nutritional Status and Survivorship

In this section, we review the evidence regarding the nature and role of prosociality on children's physical well-being. Not surprisingly, newborn and infant physical well-being has generally been attributed to maternal health and investment patterns—maternal presence and care is the best predictor of infant survivorship (Sear and Mace 2008). Yet from the beginning, others offer high-quality investment and contribute both directly and indirectly to children's nutritional needs. In some small-scale societies, allomothers provision infants through breastfeeding (Tronick, Morelli, and Winn 1987; Hewlett and Winn 2014; Röttger-Rössler 2014). Whether the frequency of nonmaternal breastfeeding is enough to have direct nutritional effects or whether there are other associated health benefits or costs is not yet known, but this early investment speaks to the depth of care nonparental caregivers offer at the earliest, and often most critical, stage of a child's life.

As immatures age and become more capable of independent social interactions, as well as more reliant on non–breast milk foods, allomaternal provisioning becomes even more essential to physical well-being. For instance,
findings from a study among the Aka indicate that maternal care diminishes
quite rapidly over the first few years of a child's life (Meehan and Hawks 2013),
a pattern suggested to occur in many small-scale societies (Lancy 2008, chapter 8, this volume). Yet, allomaternal care, excluding the frequency of holding,
remains stable at least until the age of weaning (Meehan and Hawks 2013).
These nonmaternal caregivers are not only watching or soothing youngsters,
but provisioning, a fact that has perhaps been best illustrated by Fouts and
Brookshire (2009). They found that Aka allomothers, as a group, provision
young children more frequently than mothers. The effects of such provisioning, reviewed below, are frequently associated with improved nutritional status and survivorship.

Cross-culturally, grandmothers are standouts in their ability to provision.
They often produce resources in excess of their own needs and thus are able
to provision their grandchildren at little cost to themselves. Hadza weanlings
with access to a grandmother are nutritionally better off than those without, as
grandmothers buffer children's nutritional status and offset the loss of maternal
investment following weaning (Hawkes, O'Connell, and Blurton Jones 1997).
In the Gambia, maternal grandmothers are associated with greater infant and
child height and weight across age categories up to fifty-nine months (Sear,
Mace, and McGregor 2000). Similarly, Aka grandmothers are associated with
improved infant and child nutritional status (Meehan, Helfrecht, and Quinlan
2014). Their presence is associated with higher child weight-for-age, length/
height-for-age, and weight-for-height from nine months to ten years, with the
greatest effect during the period of mobility to weaning as infants transition
to an adult diet and experience reductions in maternal investment. That same
study also indicated that grandmothers are not the only helper, although they
are the most influential. The size of an Aka child's social network (individuals
with whom a child comes into contact with daily) also improves their weight-
for-age, suggesting that the broader network serves to buffer short-term fluc-
tuations in nutritional status across development.

The presence of nonmaternal helpers is additionally associated with
improved child survivorship rates, particularly in risky environments. Efe
infants' allomaternal network size is significantly associated with child survivorship (Ivey 2000). And once again, this pattern is not limited to foragers;

nonmaternal caregivers are associated with increased survivorship for Gambian children (Sear and Mace 2008; Sear, Mace, and McGregor 2003), the Khasi in India (Leonetti et al. 2005), the Oromo agropastoralists in Ethiopia (Gibson and Mace 2005), the Berber of Morocco (Crognier, Baali, and Hilali 2001), and the Aymara in Bolivia (Crognier, Villena, and Vargas 2002). This growing evidence suggests not only that allomothers are beneficial but that an impoverished social environment and lack of allomaternal investment may be detrimental (Meehan, Helfrecht, and Quinlan 2014).

Cooperation, however, is not unlimited and not all caregivers prove to be "helpers-at-the-nest." Beise and Voland's (2002) research on a historical German population documents a negative association between paternal grandmothers and child survivorship. They argue that an inherent tension exists between paternal grandmothers and daughters-in-law due to grandparental uncertainty and/or domestic conflicts in this community. The result of this tension is less assistance from paternal grandmothers. Additionally, and in contrast to the notable and widespread positive effects of maternal relatives around the world, Sear's (2008) research in rural Malawi found that child mortality, particularly for girls, is higher when maternal grandmothers and/ or the mother's elder sister are present. Sear argues that this association is due to resource competition among female kin. Resources are limited in this matrilineal community and, as such, grandmaternal investment is diluted. Additionally, grandmothers may unevenly distribute resources, negatively affecting girls who will create additional competition for future resources. Furthermore, adolescent girls, who are typically assumed to be important alloparents (e.g., Hrdy 1999a; Weisner and Gallimore 1977), are not universally beneficial to child well-being. Among the Ecuadorian Shuar horticulturalists, older sisters have a negative impact on younger siblings' growth and development (Hagen and Barrett 2009). Brothers, on the other hand, have a positive effect on their younger siblings' nutritional status. Hagen and Barrett argue that adolescent boys have minimal mating opportunities and thus have more time to invest in their siblings. Moreover, while nonmaternal assistance among the horticultural Pimbwe in Tanzania is associated with improved survivorship, large social networks are not universally beneficial (Hadley 2004). Pimbwe women residing in their natal communities have more kin present and have more children survive to age five. However, children of women with lower socioeconomic status (SES) benefit more from the presence of kin networks than higher SES children. For higher SES families, proximity to kin may be detrimental—kin members may reap the benefits of their association with wealthier relatives but not offer benefits in return (Hadley 2004). Finally, surprising indirect negative consequences are also associated with alloparental care. A Standard Cross-Cultural Sample study found that adult female co-residents are associated with an earlier age of weaning (Quinlan and Quinlan 2008). The association between reduced breastfeeding duration and helpers suggests that alloparental care, despite its benefits, can result in mothers returning to labor activities outside the home sooner and subsequently lead to earlier weaning.

Variation in allomaternal investment and its associated outcomes should not be surprising. The role of allomothers, like that of parents, is influenced by cultural patterns, child need, child and caregiver risk, ecology, and the presence of other willing and able helpers. For instance, paternal presence and investment show surprisingly few associations with increased child survivorship or nutritional status (see Sear and Mace 2008). Yet, human fathers should not be discounted. Among the Ache, where male contributions to the diet are essential, the presence of fathers is clearly associated with child survivorship (Hill and Hurtado 1996, 2009). And while grandmothers are often described as the "ace in the hole" (Hrdy 2005b), and by all accounts appear to be the most beneficial alloparent in cross-cultural perspective (see Voland, Chasiotis, and Schiefenhövel 2005b), social and/or ecological conditions can mute or negate their impact. The Ache, again, provide an important exception. Older Ache women do not contribute substantially to their children's household subsistence returns and do not produce a surplus such as that described among the Hadza or other sub-Saharan African hunter-gatherer grandmothers. As such, Ache grandmothers have minimal impact on the physical well-being of their grandchildren (see Hawkes, O'Connell, and Blurton Jones 1997; Hill and Hurtado 1996, 2009). Lastly, caregivers may choose not to invest if there are other willing and able investors present. Aka fathers, well-known for their intimate and attentive caregiving (see Hewlett 1991), show tremendous intra-cultural variability in investment patterns. An Aka father does relatively little caregiving when he resides in his wife's camp. In matrilocal settings, Aka mothers are surrounded by investing female relatives and it may not be necessary for a father to assist as often. However, when a family resides patrilocally, extended female kin do minimal caregiving and fathers provide the bulk of nonmaternal care (Meehan 2005a).

Despite variation in who invests, the frequency of allomaternal investment, and potential culturally or environmentally regulated negative effects by particular individuals, common themes emerge. Child physical development and well-being is enhanced when someone other than the mother invests. Additionally, we are often, albeit not always (e.g., Meehan 2005a; Meehan, Helfrecht, and Quinlan 2014), able to garner that investment from a variety of individuals. The social world in which children are reared and children's connections to their larger allomaternal network may be more important than connections to particular individuals. Capturing assistance from a wide range of individuals is a strategy that enables mothers and children to protect against the loss of the father, grandmother, or other culturally salient allomothers (Meehan, Helfrecht, and Quinlan 2014). This strategy also protects against potentially detrimental effects of specific caregivers and reduces the energetic and time burden on specific allomothers, rendering allocare relatively cheap.

In the next section we move beyond the role of others in children's physical well-being and explore the far less documented, but equally important role of allomothers, peer relationships, and the broader social networks on socioemotional well-being across children's development.

The Role of Others in Children's Socioemotional Development

Children are undoubtedly born preadapted for extensive sociality. From birth on, children display special attunement to social interactions (Tomasello 1999). Even very young children are capable of making interpersonal assessments, precocial in their ability to discern who may be helpful to them (see Hrdy, chapter 2, this volume). Intersubjectivity and joint attention, considered essential to human social interactions, emerge early, typically during the first year of life (e.g., Bakeman et al. 1990; Carpenter et al. 1998; Tomasello 1999). These capacities are directly linked to acquiring cultural norms and skills crucial to survival (Herrmann et al. 2007; Tomasello et al. 2005, 2012). Furthermore, shared understanding facilitates the extensive cooperation with both kin and non-kin that characterizes human behavior and likely serves to offset environmental risks (Hill et al. 2011).

Thus, in this section, we consider socioemotional development in light of the dense social worlds in which human immatures are reared. We focus on the development and implications of multiple attachments, as well as how peer relationships assume a greater role as children age. We review how these essential relationships serve as the foundation for later socioemotional functioning and have significant effects on life-history strategies over the course of development.

ATTACHMENT RELATIONSHIPS IN A COOPERATIVE BREEDING PERSPECTIVE

Children's attachment systems evolved to promote proximity to a caretaker as a means of enhancing infant survivorship (Bowlby 1971). Attachment is also a process where children's felt security in their relationships to caretakers develops in response to caregivers' responsiveness (Ahnert 2005; Bretherton 1985). Through repeated child-caregiver interactions, children develop internal working models (Ahnert 2005; Bowlby 1973; Bretherton 1992; Hewlett et al. 2000b; Main 1990). Responses to infant signals that are appropriate, prompt, and warm help children develop "secure" and trusting internal working models. Responses that lack these features and are inconsistent across time often result in children developing insecure attachments, which are associated with anxiety, fear, or distrust of others in their relationships. Although subject to change, these schema pattern how individuals feel about self and others (Bowlby 1973; Bretherton 1985) and have lifelong implications for social relationships (R. Thompson 2008).

Bowlby (1971, 1973), not armed with the knowledge of cross-cultural child-rearing patterns that we have today, focused almost entirely on the mother-child relationship (for review see Hrdy 2009; Meehan 2014). This emphasis on the mother–child dyad was heavily influenced by nonhuman ape studies at the time, early reports of hunter-gatherer mothering, and Western constructions of family and childcare (see Hrdy 2009). As a result, attachment theory has often failed to consider the importance of social interactions outside of the mother-child dyad (Howes and Spieker 2008; Meehan and Hawks 2013, 2014; R. Thompson 2008). His focus was not wrong—the mother-child relationship is primary—but his emphasis was overly restrictive, taken too literally, and limited our ability to understand the multiplicity of factors that contribute to child attachments and their consequences across the life course (Meehan and Hawks 2013; R. Thompson 2000).

In an evolutionary perspective, a monotropic attachment, so emphasized in developmental psychology, is a risky strategy and not likely to occur given our social upbringing (see also Crittenden and Marlow 2013). Although few in number, studies, not surprisingly, find that children form attachment relationships or closely bond with a subset of the individuals with whom they interact on a regular basis (e.g., Ainsworth 1967; Howes and Spieker 2008; Kermoian and Leiderman 1986; Lamb and Lewis 2010; Marvin et al. 1977; Sagi et al. 1995; Seymour 2004; Tronick, Morelli, and Ivey 1992; True 1994; Van IJzendoorn, Sagi, and Lambermon 1992; Van IJzendoorn and Sagi 2008). Unfortunately, the breadth and implications of multiple attachments on children's social and emotional development and life-history strategies are still underexplored.

Studies that exist, however, illustrate the importance of the social network in attachment formation. In Nigeria, Marvin and colleagues (1977) found that Hausa children form three to four attachment relationships and the primary attachment figure is not always a child's mother. Among the Aka, where children are reared in social networks of approximately twenty-five to thirty-five individuals (Hewlett 1991) and interact with approximately twenty caregivers during the day (Meehan 2009), children develop attachment relationships with an average of five to six individuals, spanning age, sex, and relationship categories. These individuals are not always members of a child's immediate family (Meehan and Hawks 2013, 2014).

Recent ethnographic literature is also ripe with examples of the importance of nonmaternal caregivers in attachment formation. In Indonesia, a wide variety of Makassar allomothers have close bodily contact with infants and these caregivers offer immediate and <u>responsive care so that crying babies</u> are "a rarity" (Röttger-Rössler 2014:146). While conducting research among the Cameroonian Nso, attachment researcher and ethnographer Hiltrud Otto had trouble identifying children's mothers because children had numerous female caregivers and were even known to stay overnight at relatives' homes or in neighboring compounds (Otto 2014), suggesting that children's relationships with allomothers are a fundamental component of their social and emotional world.

Nonmaternal attachment relationships also appear to be foundational and influential on the primary attachment relationship. Meehan and Hawks (2014) found that <u>nonmaternal attachment relationships influence maternal-child interaction styles.</u> Aka infants' experiences with allomaternal attachment figures predict their behavior toward their mothers during naturalistic mother-child reunion episodes. Others' positive affect scores (e.g., picking up, touching, soothing in response to an attachment bout) are positively, albeit marginally, associated with children directing attachment behaviors toward or physically, verbally, or visually trying to engage their mothers upon their return. On the other hand, when children have allomothers who present negative, rejecting behaviors in response to their attachment displays, children are less likely to engage their mothers during reunion episodes. Despite assumptions that children's reactions to separations should be predicted by their experiences with their mothers, maternal interaction styles do not predict infant behavior upon reunion. Thus, interpreting the effects of the mother-child attachment relationship in isolation may not uncover the "constellation of relational influences" (R. Thompson 2000:147) affecting children's attachments and socioemotional development.

The whole of a child's attachment network is also linked to socioemotional development and later functioning. Among the Gusii of Kenya, caregiving responsibilities are diffused; mothers are responsible for nutrition and care of their children while allomothers dominate social, verbal, and play activities (Kermoian and Leiderman 1986). Kermoian and Leiderman found that attachments to mothers and others serve different functions—secure attachment to mother is associated with children's physical well-being, while secure allomother-child attachments are associated with positive cognitive development, suggesting symbiotic roles for mothers and others in children's development. Additional studies undertaken in kibbutzim (Israeli communal settlements), where nonmaternal care predominates, offered an unprecedented opportunity to explore the effects of nonmaternal attachments (e.g., Sagi et al. 1994; Sagi et al. 1995; Sagi-Schwartz and Aviezer 2005; Van IJzendoorn, Sagi, and Lambermon 1992). At the time the initial studies were conducted, it was common for children in some communities, but not all, to sleep away from home. The communal nature of kibbutz living was, in part, instilled through nighttime parent-child separation (Sagi et al. 1994). Given our evolutionary pattern of co-sleeping (McKenna et al. 1993), it is not surprising that nighttime separation resulted in much lower rates of secure maternal-child attachments, yet all children were attached to their mothers. More important to this discussion, however, is that the *metapelet* (a nonmaternal caregiver) contributed to cognitive and social development. For children who spent their nights away from parents, secure attachments with parents and the metapelet were associated with improved cognitive performance and more independent behavior in kindergarten. Nonmaternal attachments contributed to cognitive and social development, at least until children commenced primary school (Van IJzendoorn, Sagi, and Lambermon 1992). Beyond kindergarten, children's socioemotional functioning was found to be best predicted by the mother-child relationship, although fathers and the *metaplot* (metapelet, pl.) continued to contribute (Sagi-Schwartz and Aviezer 2005). In sum, the role of the extended attachment network is not simply an addition or supplement to the mother–child attachment relationship but potentially an essential component in early development.

THE ROLE OF PEER RELATIONSHIPS IN THE DEVELOPMENT OF SOCIOEMOTIONAL COMPETENCY

As children move through early and middle childhood, peer relationships begin to have greater influence in their socioemotional development. Children everywhere are keenly interested in other youth and generally enter into playgroups as soon as they are physically capable (Crittenden, chapter 7, this volume; Harris 1998; Konner 2010; Tucker and Young 2005). The development of these social relationships, which later may be essential to survival, are based upon the ability to take the perspective of someone else (Hrdy, chapter 2, this volume). Thus, perhaps the most important aspect of children's peer relationships is their role in the continued maturation of intersubjectivity.

Friendships grow progressively more important for intimacy, affection, and support across development, illustrating children's growing, albeit not complete, independence from parents (or other adult caregivers) and rising dependence on peers (Austrian 2008; Cincotta 2008; Furman and Buhrmester 1992; Harris 1998; Hartup 1984; Konner 2010). During this time, children show greater internalization of social and cultural norms, and gain important feedback from their peers on adaptive behaviors (Ladd 1999). In Western populations, incompetency in peer relationships (e.g., low peer acceptance, high levels of aggressiveness) is linked to maladjustment later in life (e.g., dropping out of high school, increased criminality) (see Parker and Asher 1987). Without peer acceptance, children do not competently learn how to process social cues, which cascades into further peer rejection (Lansford et al. 2010). Additionally, lonely children—those not integrated into a social network—often have low levels of trust in others (Rotenberg et al. 2010). Rotenberg and colleagues have shown that low trust decreases social interactions and subsequently leads to reduced psychosocial functioning. Peer relationships, therefore, provide children with a positive developmental advantage (Hartup 1989).

Unfortunately, we have much less data on what happens in small-scale populations when children experience social rejection, but there is little reason to believe that it does not occasionally happen. Among the Aka, children are aware that social exclusion occurs and have expressed that spending time with friends is important to maintaining those relationships. Furthermore, rough joking and gossip—typically characterized as indirect aggression in Western societies—are not uncommon among small-scale societies and are known to occur among children (Draper 1978; Hewlett 1991; Turnbull 1978). Yet, these are considered means of maintaining social cohesion (Draper 1978; Hewlett 1991; Levy 1978; Thomas 1958; Turnbull 1965, 1978) rather than forms of peer rejection, despite serving largely similar purposes in providing feedback on behavior.

The effects of these peer relationships are durable and significant to developmental trajectories; longitudinal studies indicate that peer reputation is relatively stable over time and influential in social interactions across several years (Hartup 1992; Morison and Matsen 1991). In many societies today and throughout our evolutionary history, children can spend their entire lives interacting with the peer group formed during childhood. Their reputation, developed within their social network, has important implications for their future sharing and reproductive partners, as well as the stability of their social network. As a result, the implications of this helpful network extend beyond the period of dependency, ultimately affecting reproductive strategies, success, and physical and socioemotional health.

The Role of Others in Maternal Physical Health and Reproductive Strategies

Now we turn our attention to the role of human prosociality in adulthood, focusing on the role of others and the social network on maternal well-being, reproductive strategies, and parental investment. As noted above, human women are unique among apes in our pattern of having multiple dependent offspring simultaneously. There appear to be physical consequences of this strategy, often referred to as maternal depletion, across the life span (for exceptions to the maternal depletion hypothesis see Prentice et al. 1981; Valeggia and Ellison 2003; Winkvist et al. 1994). Stress from repeated cycles of pregnancy and lactation is negatively associated with both indirect and direct measures of maternal nutrition, including reductions in maternal body mass index (BMI) or fat stores (Adair and Popkin 1992; Barbosa et al. 1997; Khan, Chien, and Khan 1998; Little, Leslie, and Campbell 1992; Merchant, Martorell, and Haas 1990a, b; Miller, Rodríguez, and Pebley 1994; Shell-Duncan and Yung 2004; Tracer 1991) as well as specific micronutrients (Miller 2010; Papathakis et al. 2007). Additionally, stress from reproduction has been associated with increased prevalence of osteoporosis later in life (Cho et al. 2012; Jasienska 2009).

In addition to potential long-term physical consequences of the human female's reproductive strategy, women also face more immediate costs. Childcare and subsistence activities, for example, are often incompatible (e.g., Hawkes et al. 1998; Ivey 2000; Meehan 2009; Nerlove, 1974). Mothers typically manage this dilemma by reducing time allocated toward subsistence and other labor activities, rather than reducing infant care (Bove, Valeggia, and Ellison 2002; Hurtado et al. 1992; Marlowe 2003), although this is clearly not always possible. This strategy protects infant well-being, but can come at a cost to households as mothers bring in fewer resources (see Marlowe 2003). Moreover, in resource-poor environments, mothers can face more immediate nutritional deficits when caring for multiple children. Comparing the quality of diet between mothers and their children (ages four to sixteen years) among Amazonian horticulturalists in Brazil, Piperata and colleagues (2013) found that children met a higher percentage of their energy and protein needs than did their mothers. Maternal-child energetic inequities were most prominent when mothers were also supporting the energetic and nutritional needs of a new infant through lactation, suggesting that mothers allocate resources to meet their children's dietary needs over their own.

However, human cooperative breeding and prosocial behavior offer insights into how women manage these costs, both physically and in terms of their investment strategies. Piperata's (2009) study among the Ribeirinha found that mothers with nonmaternal assistance have higher energy and carbohydrate intakes postpartum compared to mothers without assistance. Although they did not delineate who helped—the presence of social support was determined by whether or not mothers were observed receiving assistance over three days of observation—it shows that women with more social support were closer to energy balance and experienced less weight loss postpartum. Aka maternal energy expenditure is also influenced by the availability of allomothers (Meehan, Quinlan, and Malcom 2013). Aka grandmothers, in particular, significantly reduced mothers' energy expenditure in work activities. Fathers and juveniles, however, increased maternal energy expenditure. Grandmothers also buffered childcare, offering almost a one-to-one substitution for maternal physical contact. Nutritional effects of this assistance on mothers were not explored, but at least some helpers buffer the maternal subsistence/childcare trade-off, allowing mothers to expend less energy, at low risk, during critical periods for child survivorship.

The role of husbands, although influencing child outcomes less than expected (Sear and Mace 2008), has been associated with improved maternal nutrition, particularly during the early postpartum period. For instance, Hadza men play a critical role in subsistence when their wives have young nurslings (Marlowe 2003). As Marlowe notes, Hadza women generally provide the most stable caloric contributions to the diet, but men contribute more daily calories when their wives are lactating, particularly in the form of honey. Among the Aka, early postpartum mothers are encouraged to consume as much honey as possible. Honey is foraged by men, suggesting that a mother's access to this prized resource is contingent upon available male kin, in particular a husband, retrieving it for her.

 In sum, evidence from small-scale societies highlights how the availability of others can affect women's nutritional status and access to rich foods essential for lactation and maintenance during what is the most energetically challenging and arguably most risky stage in the postpartum reproductive period.

The Role of Others in Maternal Emotional Health and Parental Investment

The role of the social network also goes beyond simply improving maternal physical well-being and mitigating time and energetic allocation constraints. Helpers and the broader social world in which a mother resides also influence her psychological well-being and her level of parental investment. In this section, we review the effects of others in maternal emotional health and parental investment.

Hrdy (2009) has argued that human mothers are unique among apes in that, when faced with a lack of social support, women will sometimes abandon an infant. This strategy is connected to maternal psychological health in the early postnatal period (Hagen 1999, 2002, 2003; Thornhill and Furlow 1998) and may be a mechanism that allows for the abandonment of infants unlikely to survive to adulthood (Hrdy 1999a). As infant and child survival is, in part, influenced by access to social support, a lack of allomaternal help may signal to mothers that their investment in the child is unlikely to have fitness benefits (Hrdy 1999a, 2009).

Postpartum depression may also serve as a call to garner more social support (Hagen 1999)—depression-induced decreases in investment may correlate with reduced maternal sensitivity, responsiveness, and/or attunement to infant cues (Hagen 1999, 2002, 2003; Thornhill and Furlow 1998). For infants, these maternal characteristics are associated with the development of insecure attachments, poorer cognitive performance, and, in the most extreme cases, infant death (Beck 1995; Crnic et al. 1983; Hagen 1999; Hrdy 1999a; Lyons-Ruth et al. 1990; Slykerman et al. 2005). Thus, a woman's ability to garner social support has significant ramifications for both her own physical and psychological health and for that of her children.

The availability of a supportive network (i.e., spouse, family, friends, and community) is associated with a reduction in child abuse, improved maternal health, more responsive caretaking behaviors, and higher rates of secure attachments for children (Jacobson and Frye 1991; Olds et al. 2002; Spieker and Bensley 1994). This is true even for mothers characterized as high-risk. For example, cross-culturally, first-time mothers, and young mothers in particular, are often described as less knowledgeable, emotionally immature, and having less access to resources, all of which influence their ability to adequately care for a child (García Coll and Vázquez García 1996; Hrdy 1999a). Yet there is some evidence that negative outcomes are not necessarily associated simply with a mother's biological age or parity, but rather with her developmental maturity and ability to garner social support (Kramer and Lancaster 2010). For example, primiparous Aka mothers tend to be more sensitive, not less, in their responses to their children's attachment displays than multiparous women (Meehan and Hawks 2011). First-time mothers, however, often reside in their natal communities and these women are embedded in large and supportive social networks. Findings indicate that Aka women residing in their natal communities, first-time mothers or not, are significantly more sensitive to infants' attachment displays. Social network (over age and reproductive status) may be the key factor influencing maternal sensitivity and responsiveness (Meehan and Hawks 2011).

Conclusion

Human life history is, in part, characterized by our lengthy development and dependency, which has ramifications (physical and socioemotional) for individuals as they age and move through different "stages" of childhood and adulthood. The growing body of evidence, reviewed in this chapter, clearly points to allomothers and the social network as playing an essential role in human evolution, and both continue to be vital to the development of full human potential today.

As with most forms of human cooperation, assistance is offered by a wide network of individuals, enabling mothers and children to garner help from multiple people and rendering investment relatively inexpensive. As we have reviewed, particular social and ecological conditions may result in some individuals being detrimental but, as a whole, social networks lay a pathway to successful child development and maternal reproduction and well-being. The outcomes of allomaternal assistance and peer relationships have tangible benefits in both the short- and long-term. Children embedded in supportive networks have improved nutrition and survivorship as well as positive socioemotional outcomes. In adulthood, others continue to provide benefits as evidenced by their role in buffering maternal energetics and positively influencing maternal caregiving styles.

This chapter places the evolution of childhood and its associated outcomes in the foreground, reminding us that human child development and parenting is grounded in our broader prosocial nature. We, like Sellen (chapter 10, this volume), suggest that there are essential evolutionary components to successful childhood development. We argue here that the social network is one such component. Child development and reproduction are not isolated from the social world in which children and mothers live. Mothers and allomothers during early development, peer networks for older children, and the social network for mothers comprise vital components of the "care package" (see Sellen, chapter 10, this volume) that support childhood and parenting.

Unfortunately, as argued elsewhere (Meehan 2014), most research examining the role of others in child development and child and maternal well-being still views the mother-child dyad in isolation or considers nonmaternal care as supplementary. Human cooperative breeding, prosociality, and evidence of a long evolutionary history of social groupings suggest otherwise. The social network is not supplementary to child development and human reproduction but rather serves as its foundation. This view reorients our understanding of who and what is necessary across early development and for successful human reproduction.

Acknowledgments

We offer our sincere thanks to SAR for hosting the advanced seminar and thank all the participants and contributors for their thoughts and suggestions. The impetus for this chapter came from a desire to expand upon recent review of the role of nonmaternal caregivers in child well-being (Meehan, Courtney L. [2014] Allomothers and Child Well-Being. *In* Handbook of Child Well-Being: Theories, Methods, and Policies in Global Perspective, vol. 2. Asher Ben-Arieh, Ferran Casas, Ivar Frønes, and Jill E. Korbin, eds. Pp. 1787–1816. New York: Springer). We would like to also acknowledge the National Science Foundation's support of the recent research on the Aka and Ngandu discussed throughout the chapter (NSF BCS #0955213).

CHAPTER TEN

Integrating Evolutionary Perspectives into Global Health and Implementation Science

DANIEL SELLEN

Introduction

How *should* we care for newborns, infants, and young children? How *do* parents and others care for very young children in everyday situations across time and space? How *did* human ancestors evolve to care for their young? Upon reflection, these three apparently quite separate questions, in fact, address the same knowledge gap from three different perspectives: public health, anthropology, and evolutionary biology. They can be integrated as a single, transdisciplinary question: *Is there an ancient, evolved set of salient care behaviors that together mitigate the evolved vulnerabilities of human young as they grow and develop?* This general theoretical question can be modified further to form a key question in applied, evolutionary anthropology: *Is there an evolved set of care behaviors that generally maximize human survival and capital formation in most contemporary environments?*

Such a framing of the question assumes that an evolutionary anthropological perspective can inform and guide the ongoing, global biomedical goal of equitably delivering a core care package to protect and enhance early child survival and well-being. In this chapter, I offer perspectives on the global health implications of an evolutionary approach to newborn and childcare. First, I offer thoughts on developing a general model of the salient care needs of human young based on a synthesis of the logic and evidence of evolutionary anthropology and the evidence base from epidemiology. Second, I outline a preliminary conceptual model of the behavioral components of an early care package. This model identifies a set of ancient care practices, shaped by evolutionary forces, that continue to offer large benefits to human young in contemporary settings. Third, I discuss whether and how it may be helpful to integrate evolutionary perspectives into global public health in order to set priorities in maternal, infant, and child health program design and to guide the direction of implementation research.

Ancient versus Modern Caregiving: A Heuristic Typology

The basic thesis developed in this chapter is as follows. First, contemporary biomedicine is identifying a growing array of prenatal, obstetric, perinatal, and pediatric interventions and supports that, in principle, should be universally available and delivered (Bhutta et al. 2014; table 10.1).

Second, the full suite of maternal (prenatal), newborn (perineonatal), and infant and young child (postnatal) care interventions can be broken down conceptually into multiple components and in different ways. For example, there are some behaviors (practices, interventions, etc.) long recognized as beneficial to both infants and caregivers (such as skilled birth attendance and breastfeeding). Other behaviors have been more recently recognized and tested (such as neonatal cord antiseptics, vitamin K administration, and insecticide-treated bed nets). Additionally, others are still being developed through evidence-based biomedicine (such as better recognition and management of neonatal infections), and perhaps some remain to be discovered using the scientific method. Using a different breakdown, some types of care are amenable to delivery by mothers, families, and communities without special technology or training; these contrast with types of care that are best delivered through health systems at facilities (such as clinics) or by trained, supervised, and equipped practitioners who may work in the community and visit homes (such as community health workers). Triangulating different perspectives on the categorization of early care practices helps us to see them in new ways.

Third, some practices that are scientifically recognized as beneficial bear the hallmarks of ancient caregiving adaptations (breastfeeding is a clear example). These can be construed as forming an evolved package of largely nontechnological, but powerfully efficacious, care behaviors that are mostly delivered by kin and affines. Other proven care behaviors are relatively novel and largely technological inventions that augment—sometimes significantly—the evolved care package (childhood vaccination is a clear example). Thus, it is possible to reconceptualize the full package of enhanced, state-of-the-art, early childcare appropriate for maximizing health outcomes in modern contexts as consisting of two principal components. The first is a suite of ancient, largely nontechnological practices of laypersons (i.e., a sort of evolved template). The second is a suite of evolutionarily novel, technologically mediated practices of health professionals (modern biomedicine).[1] To help achieve global health goals such as infant and child survival, it is logical that a contemporary, augmented human early care package includes *both* ancient and novel components. That means the phylogenetically deep (ancient, evolved, community-based) care behaviors are conserved and protected in contemporary populations, *and* the novel care practices (recent, technological, modern health system deliverables) are made available universally. These two suites of components are neither mutually interchangeable nor replaceable. Just as maternal and infant health outcomes cannot be maximized without the best that modern medicine has to offer, they will be compromised without the basic, evolved components as well—even when all of the technological components are delivered to the highest standard.

POTENTIAL IMPLICATIONS FOR GLOBAL CHILD HEALTH

The concept of an evolved care package offers a potentially constructive way to integrate information about human evolutionary biology into global child survival and health policy frameworks, strategies, and program delivery. Particularly useful may be the conceptual distinction between a set of evolved, relatively ancient, still valuable, and therefore core components, and a set of sociotechnological, relatively recent, also valuable, and therefore augmented components. By recognizing the specific challenges faced in providing ancient care needs that persist in today's world, and identifying additional ones entailed by modern environments, we not only have the potential to improve design and delivery of child health interventions, but also to see potential innovations. Acknowledging the significant benefits of providing both ancient and modern care components for all children could clarify decision making, equity auditing, and rights-based resource allocation in global child health policy and practice.

A reconceptualization of the gold standard for contemporary early care as one that combines ancient, adaptive, and novel, beneficial practices into a single human care package can counter some significant perceptual challenges about the value of different types of care practices. On the one hand, a full appreciation by lay caregivers, health professionals, and policy makers of the fundamental and persistent value of the evolved components of the contemporary human care package is essential to ensure that they are not displaced by novel components. An observation of key practical interest is that the ancient, largely nontechnological, but nevertheless highly protective care behaviors tend to be undermined and eroded by the conditions of modern life in many populations and, as such, are threatened by "mismatch to modernity" (to borrow a concept from evolutionary medicine; Stearns 2012). In addition, these ancient components of the augmented human care package risk becoming undervalued in discussions of global health priority setting, in part due to a current, and well-intended, focus on innovation. Although the dichotomy offered here is usually not explicitly articulated in the global health literature, an implicit distinction between nonmedicalized and medicalized care practices often works to position them in apposition. Simpler practices are framed as being beyond the health system, delivered with variable quality by laypersons, and therefore less efficacious, cost-effective, and valid. There are also well-founded concerns that they might be promoted disproportionately among the poor, while a lack of access to quality health services is ignored.

On the other hand, acknowledging the continuing value of supporting ancient caregiving behaviors in today's world is not the same as making claims that these practices alone are adequate, or are the only ones appropriate in resource-constrained settings. Any emphasis on renewing support for the ancient, adaptive components should not be seen as arguing against continued investment in the novel components, or that the lay behaviors are sufficient. On the contrary, the reasoning leads to a conclusion that all children have a right to the combined benefits of both ancient and recent best practices. Although powerful, the evolved components are not sufficient to achieve global targets for child survival and maternal and child health; in a fair world, they would be augmented for every child. Moreover, they are not necessarily cheaper because they occur outside of the health system; their successful support often requires significant investment.

Toward a General Model of the Evolution of Infant and Young Childcare

Let us develop in more detail the ideas summarized so far. As a starting point, it is useful to review the possibilities and challenges of developing a general model of the *salient* care needs of human young. I first consider the theoretical underpinnings of the idea that a package of caregiving behaviors may have evolved to meet some of the fitness-enhancing needs of our ancestral young, building upon previous models suggested by anthropologists and others (including the catarrhine care complex and hunter-gatherer childhood models reviewed by Konner, chapter 6, this volume). I then consider whether any aspect of an evolved care package is amenable to scientific investigation in today's world, suggesting that it can be identified through the examination of epidemiological evidence through an evolutionary lens. Last, I consider how such a model could be used to inform global child health policy and practice.

THE CONCEPT OF AN EVOLVED CARE PACKAGE

Evolutionary theory predicts that the *evolved needs* of infants and young children (what their salient needs are and how they emerged) should have coevolved with patterns of behavior and physiological adjustment in caregivers who titrated their investment in parenting or allocare (i.e., up- or down-regulated caregiving). It is a plausible assumption that caregivers, by definition, evolved to give adequate or better care whenever possible, given constraints and opportunities to delegate care to others. From an evolutionary perspective, the best possible care is that which maximizes returns to caregivers at reduced cost. This happens within a given range of environments that change over the life span and across generations, within evolved limitations (such as phylogenetic constraints), and through direct and indirect reproductive success of care recipients. The concept of an evolved care package is thus based on the reasonable evolutionary biological assumption that many of the key needs of infants and young children that most strongly influence their survival and functional well-being were shaped in response to the evolution of ancestral caregiving capacities and practices, and vice versa, in a coevolutionary coupling.

The hypothesis that there exists an evolved template for early childcare is based on several testable evolutionary assumptions: (1) evolutionary forces likely honed a mutual tessellation of vulnerability and care; (2) when phenotype-genotype correspondence allowed heritability, natural selection optimized and traded off evolutionary outcomes for both dependents and caregivers; and (3) when evolutionary returns to investment in caregiving were high (due to close genetic relatedness and the early developmental stage and vulnerability of the targeted young), caregiver fitness payoffs outweighed the costs. In theory, the evolved care package describes the *salient features of human caregiving* as evidenced by their association with a suite

Table 10.1. A Conventional Biomedical View of Proven Interventions to Improve Newborn Survival through Health System–Supported Care Interventions

---

A. Preconception and Antenatal

Family planning

Maternal immunization (e.g., Tetanus toxoid)

Maternal infection preventions, screening, and management (e.g., malarial prophylaxis, insecticide-treated bed nets)

Management of chronic disease (e.g., diabetes) and pregnancy-induced disorders

Maternal nutrient supplementation (e.g., balanced protein/energy, iron, folate, calcium, multiple micronutrients)

Maternal support to improve psychosocial health and manage substance abuse

B. Labor and Birth

Skilled birth attendants

Clean birth practices (home and facility, birth kits, hand washing with soap, chlorhexidine as appropriate)

Emergency obstetric care (basic and comprehensive planned or emergency Cesarean)

Management of preterm labor (steroids, antibiotics for premature rupture of membranes)

Management of post-term labor (induction)

Newborn Care (for all neonates)

Umbilical cord care (delayed clamping, cleansing with antiseptics)

Prevention of hypothermia (drying, head covering, skin-to-skin care, delayed bathing)

Breastfeeding (early initiation and exclusive)

Vitamin K administration

Newborn Care (for small and ill neonates)

Resuscitation for neonatal depression

Treatment for meconium aspiration syndrome (steroids, surfactants)

Recognition and management of neonatal infections (antibiotics for pneumonia, sepsis, meningitis)

Extra thermal care (plastic wraps, kangaroo mother care)

Phototherapy to prevent and manage hyperbilirubinemia

Note: Adapted from figure 1 and table 1 in Bhutta et al 2014; the list is selected and interventions to reduce stillbirth, preterm birth, perinatal mortality, and smallness for gestational age are not included.

of characteristics that define the evolved vulnerabilities of infancy and early childhood.

Theoretically, we should be able to identify a set of core care behaviors that likely evolved to meet many of the salient needs of most infants and children living in a range of ancestral environments. Epistemologically, the concept is amenable to empirical testing using contemporary clinical and epidemiological data. It should be possible to identify from such data what practices improve neonatal, infant, and young child survival in contemporary environments. These core behaviors can provide indirect evidence of the underlying mechanisms linking the coevolution of vulnerability and care in past environments.

What is the potential scientific and practical value of identifying what might be termed an evolved early care package? The concept of an evolved care package offers a heuristic to generate new theoretical questions and research programs in human evolutionary biology. Child-centered perspectives have a long history within anthropology (Lancy 2014, chapter 8, this volume), and there has been a recent resurgence of interest in integrating evolutionary, health, and social understandings. However, evolutionary changes in the care of ancestral young have yet to be well characterized and integrated into coherent models of the coevolution of human diet, life history, and sociality.

Identifying an evolved template for the evolutionarily salient care needs of our young also has potentially great relevance for contemporary global health. This is because it may help clarify what is an optimal, healthy, low-technology, and effective basic early care package in today's complex world. A key research question becomes: *Is there evidence that infants and young children may be adapted to a specific subset of care practices that together form an "evolved template" that scaffolds growth and development in ways that lead to fitness enhancing and generally biomedically positive outcomes?* Strong evidence of an evolved template for early childcare has the potential to guide global child health policy, strategy, and implementation. Currently, frameworks for understanding the care needs of newborns and older infants and children, though powerful (table 10.1), lack an explicit evolutionary basis for understanding.

CONCEPTUAL CHALLENGES: CORE COMPONENTS OF "CARE" AND EVOLUTIONARILY SALIENT "NEEDS"

Several conceptual challenges can be identified at various steps needed to develop a preliminary model of the evolved care package for human young. There are many questions about how we should define the concept of "care" in relation to the ancestral "needs" of infants and young children in an evolutionary context. Such putative "evolved needs" are conceptually different from needs in the sense of perceptions and conscious or unconscious desires, or an economic hierarchy (Maslow's theory), or even sociopolitical and moral value frameworks (such as rights-based approaches). Rather, they are needs in the sense of *inputs* required to mitigate evolved vulnerabilities; the aspects of phenotype that represent gaps in the functional resilience and competencies of a human newborn if she were left to interact alone with her world. Evolutionary theory predicts such vulnerabilities may persist either as a byproduct of evolutionary constraints, perhaps phylogenetic ones, or by design as economies of development or life history allocation strategies. If the latter, the apparent vulnerabilities may have features designed to mesh with particular patterns of early child caregiving. The vulnerabilities may be severe in the absence of caregivers or contexts that enable caregivers to provide salient care.

If we view an infant or young individual as a dynamic system, the vulnerabilities observed across a range of environments can be hypothesized as evolved salient needs for care. For example, we could hypothesize that putative evolved infant needs might include human milk, clean and nutritious complementary foods, play, singing, and exposure to educational television. However, only television can be excluded on logical grounds, and only human milk and complementary foods can be inferred to be salient needs on the basis of very strong epidemiological supporting evidence; nevertheless, play and singing have strong associations with modern measures of learning and social development. Inputs that cannot be shown to increase subsequent fitness indicators can be hypothesized as nonsalient. Conceptually, nonsalient inputs are not a coevolutionary response to the needs of infants. That is, they were not consistently important in shaping the evolution of infants and young in ancestral environments, and likely are not critical for survival, health, and development of contemporary young. Examples may include the age and gender identity of primary caregivers; the salient need is to have a primary caregiver, irrespective of the age, gender, or other characteristics.

The hallmark of infancy and early childhood is an acute degree of dependence on older group members, even by the human standard of high sociality and interdependence across the rest of the life course, including the senescent phase (Kaplan 1996). However, it is illogical to construe the developmental phase of any organism as a fundamentally incompetent one (Pagel and Harvey 1993; Pereira and Fairbanks 1993). Rather than simple manifestations of developmental constraints, at least some of the apparent vulnerabilities of human young may be better understood as adaptations involving evolutionary trade-offs. The idea that human young may be rather good at what they need to do, in comparison to alternative kinds of young that could not evolve (due to constraint) or did not persist across generations (due to natural selection), is a powerful and useful contribution from evolutionary biology. It helps frame questions about the possible role of natural selection in shaping the design of young as survivors within ancient envelopes of care under developmental and ecological constraint, and what we might hypothesize as adaptive incompetency.

The evolutionary perspective is that vulnerabilities are often paralleled by caregiver adaptations to meet salient needs that mitigate the vulnerabilities; they have coevolved. However, we must not assume that any apparent mismatch between care needs and care practices is simply a result of evolutionary lag (Bateson et al. 2004; Wells 2011b). Observed major mismatch between care needed and care provided could be due to evolutionary constraints or environmental novelty. Instead, we must test hypotheses about the pathways through which modern environments perturb the performance of putatively ancestral and beneficial practices (Wells 2011a). It can be challenging to avoid adaptationism in developing and testing hypotheses about the evolved vulnerabilities of human young, and about any evolved propensities of caregivers to mitigate such vulnerabilities. We should aim to tease apart any design features of infants and older young that bear the marks of adaptation from those that bear the marks of phylogenetic and developmental constraint. To do this, we can organize various data to test the general biocultural logic that predicts intimate connections between the adaptive design and constraint features of care receivers (infant and child bodies and personalities) and caregiver behaviors and bodies (physical, social, and political).

Almost all of the derived human characteristics that evolutionary anthropologists investigate may have influenced and been influenced by selection operating to shape early childcare practices (table 10.2). We already know that these traits affect human social organization, fertility, and subsistence patterns through multiple biocultural pathways. Most of these can be reduced to common pathways involving either the physio-behavioral responses of caregivers to the evolved vulnerabilities of young, or to the constraints imposed on caregivers by their response to these needs (which may be alleviated in turn by socially mediated assistance from others). However, we lack good models of how care practices might change with local context (Hurtado et al. 2006; Pelto 2008). A major challenge is to develop relatively simple explanatory frameworks that effectively identify and model the salient needs of ancestral infants that caregivers evolved to meet through naturally selected care behaviors, and to do so without losing information about flexible response to diverse and/or fluctuating local environments.

EVIDENCE: EVOLVED VULNERABILITIES AND WINDOWS OF
OPPORTUNITY FOR SALIENT CAREGIVING

We currently understand that a consequence of immature (relative to adults) somatic, immunological, and alimentary systems in human young is dependence on a mother or others for the provisioning of various immune, nutrition, and growth-modulation factors during early childhood. This is in addition to major assistance with transport, thermoregulation, and hygiene. Some of the components of this dependency, which we often implicitly construe as a "natural" package, are well studied by clinicians, psychologists, and education specialists. However, the relation of these vulnerabilities to the evolution of human caregiving remains undertheorized.

Currently, one of the best-understood examples of vulnerability among young humans is the acute vulnerability to developmental and nutritional deficits and infectious disease during the first one thousand days of life, from conception to the end of the second year postpartum (minus nine to plus twenty-four months = one thousand days). The first thousand days encompass a nexus of vulnerability that is manifest across gestation, neonatal and later infancy, and young childhood. This is the period when environmental toxins, micronutrient deficiencies, maternal psychosocial and physiological stress during gestation, hostile birthing conditions, and exposure to pathogens can have profound and lifelong effects. These include perturbed growth and development of physical and cognitive function and susceptibility to both infectious and metabolic diseases. All of these influence survival through

Table 10.2. Evolutionarily Derived Human Characteristics
that Shape Early Childcare Practices

Bipedalism
Encephalization
Extended juvenile phase
Menopause
Fat storage
Intergenerational care
Cooperative breeding
Highly selective group foraging
Diversification of feeding niches
Dispersal
Food sharing
Food processing
Cooking
Meat eating
Sex- and age-linked labor

childhood, longevity, and disease burden in adulthood, as well as socioeconomic well-being as indicated by productivity and earnings (Hoddinott
et al 2013a; Hoddinott et al 2013b; Martorell 2010; Martorell et al. 2010;
Pongcharoen et al. 2012; Stein et al. 2010; Victora et al. 2008). Among survivors,
recovery from early deficits is difficult at later ages and intergenerational
effects can be powerful (Martorell and Zongrone 2012).

The one-thousand-days insight has become a strong economic rationale
and major political impetus for a growing family of recent global health policies, strategies, and interventions, with labels such as "Scaling Up Nutrition"
(World Bank), "Alive and Thrive" (funded by the Bill and Melinda Gates
Foundation), and "Survive to Five" (Save the Children). This is because it represents a developmental window of opportunity for care by multiple stake-
holder groups within human societies: mothers, family, health systems, and
governments at all levels. Epidemiological data on the importance of this
developmental period for health is likely an indication of its importance at
earlier points in human evolution. By the logic of natural selection, the salient
needs of infants during this period of specific vulnerabilities were successfully
met by ancestral human caregivers.

We can consider the implications of the one-thousand-days insight for
understanding the developmental and life-history features of human evolutionary biology and for extending previous work on ethno-pediatrics (Konner

2005; Konner 1972; Konner 1976a; chapter 6, this volume; Small 1998; Trevathan, Smith, and McKenna 2007). Phylogenetic comparisons indicate humans reduced both birth spacing and juvenile mortality, and this has long been attributed to lineage-specific shifts in childcare (Galdikas and Wood 1990; Kaplan et al. 2000). Thinking about the first thousand days as a single, integrated phase of vulnerability helps us model the potential evolution of a package of care behaviors honed by natural selection to meet the salient needs of vulnerable infants. From an evolutionary perspective, this period of profound vulnerability represents a powerful window of opportunity for caregivers to maximize survival, growth, and "quality" (i.e., human capital formation) among young (Kaplan, Hill, and Hurtado 2011).

Indirect evidence suggests that small improvements in child survival at younger ages may have been most advantageous for ancestral caregivers, but also hardest to achieve through microevolutionary changes. Interestingly, global progress in reducing child deaths through nutritional and immunological means has been faster for older children than for younger ones (World Health Organization 2006). Reduction in the under-five mortality rate has been greater than the reduction in infant mortality rates and rates of reduction in neonatal and perinatal deaths. Progress in reducing the number of preterm births has also been proportionately slower. Since relatively higher proportions of death occur at ever younger ages, the demographic impact of these reductions is much less than it would be if more reduction was achieved for deaths at younger ages.

Assuming that improved survival, growth, and human capital formation among young are fitness-related, and that the fitness of caregivers is correlated through genetic relatedness or indirect fitness advantages, we can hypothesize that ancestral behaviors and physiological characteristics that directly mitigated any of these early life vulnerabilities would have been under strong positive natural selection. We can further hypothesize that the specific vulnerabilities identified among fetuses, infants, and children under contemporary conditions emerged in part because caregivers blunted their negative effects on young. Following this line of reasoning, this period was likely a fulcrum of coevolution of carer and caree, and thus pivotal in life-history evolution. Ancestral failure to provide salient care inputs during this phase would have been associated with catastrophic evolutionary results. This gives us an inroad into the knotty problem of defining "care" in an evolutionary sense.

The Human Early Care Package

In this section I outline a preliminary model of what might plausibly be the core components of a putative, species-typical human early care package based on current knowledge from anthropology and beyond. I use this model to draw conceptual distinctions between: (1) ancient care practices that continue to offer large benefits to human young, and often to their caregivers, across a majority of human contexts (i.e., salient or "core" components such as breastfeeding); (2) usually techno-culturally mediated and relatively recent care practices that can augment the more ancient evolved package (i.e., newly beneficial components such as vaccination); and (3) practices, new and old, that mostly have either negligible or harmful effects (i.e., nonsalient and/or apparent care practices such as swaddling, early umbilical cord clamping, and formula feeding).

HYPOTHESIZED COMPONENTS: EVOLVED VERSUS AUGMENTED

Putatively evolved components of a package of early childcare practices can be recognized when epidemiological data show a significant association between the presence or absence of a caring behavior (which can be variously defined), and comparatively advantageous outcomes for infants (and often caregivers) under a range of conditions. An evolutionary perspective, therefore, suggests that a number of widely recognized infant and young childcare and feeding practices can be divided into two major groups. The first group includes practices that likely evolved to enhance neonatal, infant, and young child survival. They are predicted to be ancient (i.e., pre-Neolithic), have the characteristics of biocultural adaptations, and are almost universally latent or expressed across all human societies. The second group includes practices that were recently invented (perhaps during the post-Neolithic, and certainly the "Anthropocene") and *further* enhance neonatal, infant, and young child survival. In theory, there may also be an additional third group of practices that do not enhance neonatal, infant, or young child survival, ancient or otherwise; they are not beneficial and may be harmful. If ancient, their persistence requires explanation.

Table 10.3 summarizes some specific best practices that are proven or suspected to improve neonatal, infant, and young child survival. The focus of this list of candidate components is care during the first one thousand days of life, with a further focus on the example of adequate care during infancy and young childhood, and specifically on infant feeding. The list could be extended to include many of the biomedical interventions listed in table 10.1 and other practices into middle and later childhood and beyond. It could add many kinds of inputs for early child development, learning, life-skills building, and social capacitation. Taken together, they offer a preliminary model for a currently optimal human early care package based on current best evidence; a contemporary gold standard.

The set of hypothesized ancient components (see table 10.3) represent candidate components of an evolved care package. Among these, some are supported by a wealth of epidemiological data and form core components of global child survival and health programs and are proven and mainstreamed (see table 10.3a, number 1). Proven care practices include breastfeeding and complementary feeding practices. Both are increasingly recognized as a low-technology key to child survival that have the greatest preventive potential of all known interventions for child health, preventing one in five deaths annually. Some likely components of this evolved minimum care package already map onto certain existing recommendations that mobilize global health efforts. For example, contemporary global recommendations for optimal infant and young child feeding practices include a package of components with well-established benefits to infant survival and function: basic hygiene, exclusive and continued breastfeeding, appropriate complementary feeding, and responsive caregiving (see table 10.3b).

Additional low-technology and likely ancient components could be added to the conventional list based on new evidence. These include doula-assisted, low-technical intervention birth (Klaus and Klaus 2010), timely cord clamping (Chaparro and Lutter 2009), kangaroo mother care (Lawn et al. 2010; Sloan et al. 2008), maternal-child co-sleeping and rooming in (DiGirolamo, Grummer-Strawn, and Fein 2008; McKenna, Ball, and Gettler 2007), and social arrangements to afford maternity leave (Nerlove 1974; Ogbuanu et al. 2011). In several cases, the intervening causal mechanisms through which these practices meet needs are well mapped and interlinked. For example, cord clamping a few minutes after mothers have delivered healthy full-term babies increases neonatal iron stores sufficient for the first six months. Additionally, body contact and warmth improves infant development, and immediate initiation of breastfeeding transfers immune factors that protect against infection and death. It is likely that new links remain to be discovered.

Table 10.3. A Preliminary Model for an Optimal Human Early Care Package

A. Hypothesized ancient components (the "evolved care package")

1) Proven, and mainstreamed:
  - basic hygiene
  - exclusive breastfeeding
  - continued breastfeeding
  - timely complementary feeding
  - use of appropriate complementary foods
  - micronutrient-rich diets for pregnant and lactating women

2) Proven, but not yet mainstreamed:
  - doula-assisted birth
  - timely cord cutting
  - skin-to-skin care
  - maternal-child co-sleeping
  - informal social support for lactation management/breast health
  - social arrangements for maternity leave
  - responsive feeding

3) Postulated, but not proven:
  - premastication
  - maintenance of moderate iron sufficiency
  - allomaternal nursing

B. Hypothesized novel components (recently invented to improve neonatal, infant, and young child survival: the "augmented care package")

4) Prenatal and perinatal:
  - prenatal nutritional supplementation and clinical care of mother
  - sterile obstetric care aimed at safe motherhood
  - a growing suite of surgical and clinical interventions at parturition
  - fortification of preterm human milk

5) Postnatal:
  - hygiene and sanitation infrastructure
  - oral rehydration solution
  - postnatal nutritional supplementation and clinical care of mother
  - vaccination
  - antihelminthics
  - antibiotics
  - integrated community management of childhood illness
  - multiple diagnostics and clinical interventions aimed at specific communicable and noncommunicable diseases

INFERENCES FROM THE MODEL

It is important that the model has a dynamic aspect; the full package of care components listed here may be optimal only in the sense that they offer the most advantageous mix of care components for human infants in the contemporary world, given the current state of knowledge, availability, and range of child-rearing environments. At some point in the past, only the ancient components existed as options, and they are hypothesized to represent an evolved template for salient childcare and the evolved components of a contemporary optimal package. Many of these components have been identified either by anthropologists (e.g., Konner's catarrhine mother-infant complex and hunter-gatherer childhood models; see chapter 6, this volume) or epidemiologists (e.g., papers in several of the recent Lancet series on child survival). In today's world, the evolved components can be augmented with a growing arsenal of other practices, at least in theory, where resource availability and governance allows (raising interesting questions about framing the package in terms of children's rights to care).

At least four crucial inferences can be drawn from this model. First, the evolved components are not sufficient to maximize health outcomes for human young. In a fair world, all children would have access to the augmented package (i.e., ancient plus recently invented). Second, the relatively recent components in the augmented part of the contemporary full package do not and, from a global health policy perspective, should not replace the evolved components; they improve survival and health most when added to the core, evolved package. Third, in marked contrast to the augmented components, the evolved components are very likely cheaper, most efficacious, and involve low or no technology. Fourth, in line with current global health knowledge, the model broadens the concept of early care to include prenatal, perinatal, and postnatal care as part of a window of opportunity for optimal influence on outcomes, and includes many social categories of caregivers beyond biological mothers.

The conceptual division between evolved and augmented components of the total early care package resonates with current tensions in global health. The arguments center around whether to invest in community-based, low-technological solutions (which are often perceived to entail overcoming major cultural and social barriers), or to invest in technological solutions that can be cheaply implemented with broad reach through health systems.

Both anthropological and clinical data converge on the "evolved" group. It is notable that these core practices are delivered to infants and young children through a combination of socially supported maternal practices and by other kin and non-kin. In all cases, epidemiological data reveal a set of simple, low-technology, and presumably ancient care practices that confer their highly significant benefits on young during the first one thousand days of life.

It is possible that this results from the longest intervention trial ever run: the natural selection of human caregivers. In theory, these practices together constitute an evolved core set that remains valuable even in contemporary environments, but to which additional valuable care practices can be added. These are the practices that may underlie the significantly lower mortality of hunter-gather children relative to the offspring of wild ape populations (Galdikas and Wood 1990; Hill and Hurtado 1996). Strikingly, although much of the fundamental scaffolding for these core care behaviors has changed, contemporary data indicate the net value of returns on these core practices in low-resource settings may exceed the value of returns on core technological solutions by a factor of two hundred or more (Bhutta et al. 2008; Horton et al. 2010).

The first one thousand days of life is also the period when more recent technological innovations can, when available, confer additional and sometimes significant benefits. Such innovations include many of the classic interventions now mainstreamed in global nutrition and public health (see table 10.3a, number 1). Most likely, these innovations address a likely mix of both ancient and modern care needs. Some of the more specific innovations may actually address specific evolved vulnerabilities that may only be widely manifest in the novel environments encountered by contemporary populations (see next section).

When we pool the evolved childcare behaviors (those that emerged as species-typical norms prior to 250,000 years ago) with the recent ones (emerging largely from medical, scientific traditions and technological changes over the last 12,000 years to the present) we arrive at something like the typologies for basic care interventions now in global use (see table 10.1). In the future, other components could be added to the core set based on new models of the evolved needs of human young—an area representing great potential for exciting research and theoretical synthesis. Several practices that are currently widespread globally, but are relatively new and may not confer net health or survival benefits, are notably absent from the hypothesized package. For example, consumption of commercial infant formula appears to offer few, if any, long-term net benefits to healthy, term infants, and the same may prove true of cow milk consumption during older childhood and beyond (Wiley 2007). An evolutionary perspective raises basic science doubts about the value of modified ungulate milks for primates.

Limitations of the Model

There are many conceptual weaknesses and potential inconsistencies in the model outlined here, but three of the most critical ones are (1) the ambiguous specificity of the ancient care package; (2) a blurred distinction between evolved and augmented components of the care package; and (3) the crucial distinction between the current construction of health as absence of disease and biological fitness in the evolutionary and genetic sense. First, the notion of a specifically defined and prescriptively interpreted evolved template for care is overly simplistic. No specific, single Environment of Evolutionary Adaptedness can have existed; only a range within which different lineages survived. As in all of biology, human caregiving likely emerged as a loosely adaptive conglomeration of sometimes-conflicting behaviors through a process of "mosaic" evolution. Second, norms of variation will complicate the expression, effects, and observed distributions of even the most powerful adaptive behaviors. Almost all human behaviors, and especially care/non-care behaviors are notable for being highly facultative, suggesting flexibility itself is part of their adaptive value. Second, many care behaviors arguably fall between the conceptual dichotomy of "ancient, evolved" versus "recent, augmented." Possible candidates include delayed cord clamping and kangaroo mother care for low-birth-weight infants, which may be ancient but have additional value in conditions of modern poverty that include very high rates of infectious disease and micronutrient deficiency ("hidden hunger"). Third, the potential nonconcordance of newborn survival and health along with an emphasis on biological fitness in the emerging field of evolutionary medicine, and the possibility of significant genetic conflicts between parents and their young, may significantly alter the logic. Although fuller scholarly discussion of these limitations is needed and will have heuristic value, it is beyond the scope of the present chapter.

GLOBAL RECOMMENDATIONS FOR CARE PRACTICES

Evidence-based global recommendations on several components of feeding and early nutrition have been developed in recent decades. Perhaps the clearest example is the "1-6-24" recommendations for breastfeeding and complementary feeding: breastfeeding initiation within one hour of birth (Bahl et al. 2005; Edmond et al. 2006), exclusive breastfeeding to six months (Bhandari et al. 2003; Duijts et al. 2010), and complementary feeding with continued breastfeeding beyond twenty-four months (Dewey 2003). Biomedical concepts of best practices and optimal standard of care have become dominant paradigms for policy and programs that now drive the assessment and audit of global child health interventions. Achieving the recommendations is a key focus of policy, programming, and investment that are becoming mainstreamed and cross-sectoral. These recommendations are based on powerful clinical and epidemiological evidence and signal much about the evolution of human biology and life history.

Despite being based on excellent public health science, however, these types of recommendations are limited in several ways. First, they are developed without reference to evolutionary or cultural models of need. The reason is a good one: direct information on clinical outcomes of randomized trials trumps indirect inferences about the relevance of past needs and behaviors to contemporary heath. Nevertheless, care needs presumably evolved within a biological range of tolerance, and even current biomedical care models can be culture-bound. Therefore, they fail to consider or recognize the usefulness of some key care practices that may not yet be incorporated into the standard model. The examples of timely cord clamping, skin-to-skin care, and co-sleeping illustrate how some potentially very powerful, evolved practices remain on the margins of clinical science (though this is changing fast). Second, these types of recommendations impose global priorities on local contexts and do not provide roadmaps on how best to support adherence in diverse settings. They do not incorporate local understanding of capacities, constraints, and trade-offs that influence daily actions and decisions of various types of caregivers. Third, practices that meet the recommendations turn out to be rare in human communities. Breastfeeding, complementary feeding, and all of the other components are proving difficult to promote and support effectively and cost-effectively, even where health systems are strengthening. This challenge is addressed in the recent rise of implementation science, which tests alternative approaches to translating the recommendations into real behaviors that improve health outcomes.

MISMATCH BETWEEN RECOMMENDATIONS AND PRACTICES

One result of the development of these recommendations is documentation of significant and widespread mismatch between actual care practices and recommended care practices. On superficial analysis, it seems impossible to reconcile this observed diversity with the concept of an evolved care package. However, this apparent paradox serves as counter-factual in support of the hypothesis that a flexible feeding strategy evolved as part of a responsive care package involving multiple caregivers. Evolutionary anthropology offers a strategy for better understanding the evolutionary basis for the observed mismatch between actual care practices and recommended care practices. It focuses on the evolutionary medical hypothesis that contemporary environments stymie the delivery of care to many human young.

In theory, there are several causes of mismatch between actual care practices and evolved needs. Many may be driven by material factors. There is indirect evidence that major pathways through which ancestrally beneficial care and feeding used to be delivered are now being eroded in many ways, including changes in food systems and work patterns. Other causes of mismatch may be driven by the decoupling of cultural models and biomedical recommendations. We know far too little about the role of social learning in the creation of cultural scripts or models for care relevant to the evolved package (Hadley, Patil, and Gulas 2010). Many experts have drawn on political economy: how caregiving is shaped by structural, sociocultural and economic conditions, gender, class, and power relations. Nevertheless, our explanatory frameworks remain weak; there is no general theory that explains observed variation and mismatch.

One evolutionary explanation is that the evolved tendency to feed other foods to breastfed infants in order to meet other allocation demands on maternal time, risk, and resources creates the potential for an unhealthy mismatch between actual and recommended infant and young child feeding practices (Sellen 2007). Taken together, epidemiological and ethnographic data suggest an evolved template of optimal infant and young child feeding as key components of a naturally selected care package for human young. Only under the significant social and material stresses of many contemporary communities is this care package eroded. A wealth of studies demonstrates that so-called clinically "suboptimal" infant feeding practices largely result from weaknesses and gaps in the social and economic support system that is necessary to enable caregivers in general, and biological mothers in particular, to provide even the minimum care needed to meet the evolved needs of newborns and older children. There are some common pathways through which breastfeeding initiation, exclusive breastfeeding, and adequate complementary feeding with continued breastfeeding are hampered among members of the caregiving envelope (Webb et al. 2009; Webb-Girard et al. 2012). While ethnographic data indicate that current evidence-based clinical recommendations for optimal feeding practices were feasible in small-scale societies (Sellen 2001), recent changes have created material and social conditions hostile to feeding recommendations.

Another specific example is vulnerability to micronutrient deficiency in the first thousand days. It is plausible to hypothesize that ancestral foragers accessing meats and premasticating nutrient-rich complementary foods experienced lower risks of deficiency disease than contemporary agrarian peoples (Pelto, Zhang, and Habicht 2010). In peasant populations today, cereal and animal milk-based gruel dominate the diet (Dewey 2013), and women's work in food production often trades off against breastfeeding. Inadequate folate, iron, iodine, vitamin A, and zinc in maternal and weaning foods can have pernicious effects (Ramakrishnan et al. 2012; Vossenaar and Solomons 2012), resulting in the most prevalent and damaging deficiencies in today's world (Ramakrishnan 2002), and a characteristic pattern of irreversible early growth stunting (Stein et al. 2010). Highly prevalent today, the major micronutrient deficiency diseases may be relatively new problems. These diseases have been engendered by recent human environments and altered social and ecological relations between population, food, and health. Fortunately, supplementation and fortification can effectively address the threat of these deficiencies for mothers or young in such communities.

Links are also being made between what were once regarded as deficiencies in human milk and other protective factors. For example, the levels of two fat-soluble vitamins of key importance in health and development, vitamin A and vitamin D, are adequate in breast milk if lactating women have high dietary intakes, or in the case of vitamin D, adequate and safe sun exposure at low latitudes. Low iron levels in human milk are actually quite safe, because evidence suggests that human infants evolved to acquire their early iron needs from placental transfer to liver stores, rather than from exclusive breastfeeding (Grajeda, Pérez-Escamilla, and Dewey 1997).

INNOVATIONS TO SUPPORT ANCIENT NEEDS

There is a pressing need to develop, pilot, and evaluate social, technological, and commercial innovations to protect, support, and enhance child health.

This must be accomplished through care that is feasible and acceptable within modern contexts, while addressing ancient needs related to evolved vulnerabilities. Globally applied concepts of basic early childcare needs can be strengthened and improved by application of theory and data from human evolutionary biology. The care package concept is especially useful for developing evidence-based responses to recent calls for innovation, and holds promise as a crucial component of ongoing efforts to reduce child illness and death. Such talk of innovation tends to focus attention on high-technology, health system–centered interventions, rather than low-technology, community-based interventions that enhance caregiver support. A focus must be retained on the species-typical needs of human young that can still be well protected through sociobehavioral pathways, even in a rapidly changing contemporary world, and in the future of unknown sociotechnical configuration.

For example, it is well understood that many recent social and economic changes work to undermine exclusive breastfeeding in most parts of the modern world. Less understood is the potential of very recent changes to protect, promote, and support exclusive breastfeeding, particularly in the domain of social media. Opportunities to apply new communication technologies to support exclusive breastfeeding, as well as to research needs are increasingly being identified and critically discussed, including cellphone-based counseling to support exclusive breastfeeding.

This care package, already significantly enhanced by powerful biomedical interventions, can be bolstered using everyday techno-social innovations, such as mobile health, to deliver much-needed interpersonal support to current and future caregivers.

Conclusion

This chapter outlined some theoretical opportunities and challenges of an evolutionary anthropological framework for understanding care needs during infancy and early childhood, and considered some potential practical implications for global child health. We have explored how an emerging evidence base concerning the evolved vulnerabilities of young children is relevant to global efforts to reduce child health disparities and the burden of disease in later life. It is argued that an evolved human early care package addresses a suite of infant and child needs that can be, within notable limits, well met by specific caregiver responses and practices. These include several ancient caregiving behaviors that should be retained as core tools for child survival and well-being in contemporary and future communities and supported both in communities and through health systems. Indeed, new tools can be found to promote and support these ancient practices that lead to meeting the evolved needs of human young. It is also argued that the evolved human early care package can, and should, be augmented by a growing and often powerfully effective suite of more technological innovations that enhance health and other outcomes for infants and children. The evolutionary rationale for retaining evolved beneficial practices is not an argument that the technological benefits of health systems are not needed and should not be fairly distributed; rather, these should be made available to all as rapidly as possible and without eroding the core practices of the evolved package.

This approach reveals how even those infants and children in resource-rich settings, with access to the whole panoply of technological innovations, may still be deprived of core components of the evolved care package (such as breastfeeding). This results in detrimental effects that are only beginning to be appreciated as new generations of children exposed to these patterns live through their life course. I argue that it is crucial to make a conceptual distinction between evolved and augmented aspects of contemporary human early care packages. By doing so, we can see the value of retaining certain salient evolved behaviors instead of replacing them with technology. Additionally, this theory highlights the usefulness of applying an equity lens to monitor access to *both* the core and augmented care practices across rich and poor environmental settings. In this way, evolutionary perspectives can help frame efforts to innovatively tackle threats to the early survival and healthy development of children, and clarify thinking about equity, bioethics, difficult decisions on policy priorities, and the appropriate allocation of scarce resources to address global child health.

Note

1. One could identify a third category of practices that are "medicalized" or codified as protocols for standard-of-care and reinforce ancient caregiving adaptations. (Timely cord clamping is a likely example.)

CHAPTER ELEVEN

Conclusion

Emerging Issues in Studies of the Evolution of Childhood

ALYSSA N. CRITTENDEN AND COURTNEY L. MEEHAN

Impetus for the Seminar and Volume

One of the primary motivations for organizing the SAR advanced seminar and bringing together the participants was to bridge the subdisciplinary divides between those scholars whose research has implications for our understanding of the evolution of human childhood. Almost ten years ago, in the first edition of *The Anthropology of Childhood*, David Lancy noted that the field of childhood studies in anthropology seemed "balkanized" (2008:ix). Lancy was referring to the whole of the anthropology of childhood, including education, archaeology, and ethnography, but his comment holds true, even when more narrowly applied. Anthropologists whose research is framed in evolutionary theory, at times, fail to integrate findings from the paleoarchaeological record or cultural approaches to studying childhood into their work, suggesting, albeit unintentionally, that childhood is uniform cross-culturally and developmental processes static throughout our evolutionary history. While valuable, cultural anthropology's focus on *childhoods* pays little attention to the universal components of development in the life-history stage of childhood and thus can lessen the impact within the broader anthropological and psychological community. Outside of anthropology, developmental psychologists' frequent emphasis on Western, educated, industrialized, rich, and democratic (WEIRD) populations (Henrich, Heine, and Norenzayan 2010a) and developmental patterns has often proved limited. These divides are not insurmountable, however, as theoretical and methodological divisions can be bridged and integration can synthesize research on childhood and serve the growing emphasis in the sciences on crossing traditional boundaries.

A second impetus for the seminar and the volume was growing interest in evolutionary-centered research on human childhood that focuses either directly or indirectly on the origins and implications of the evolution of human childhood. These works have made lasting contributions to the field (see Bogin 1999b; Hewlett and Lamb 2005; Hrdy 2009; Konner 2010; Lancy 2008; Narváez et al. 2012, 2014), yet a comprehensive work pulling multiple perspectives together into one volume was needed. Our aim was to synthesize some of the dynamic work currently being done on the developmental, ontogenetic, life-history, paleoarchaeological, cross-cultural, and applied public health perspectives on childhood.

Outcomes of SAR Advanced Seminar

The SAR advanced seminar offered a unique and collegial environment for the participants to discuss and debate emerging issues in studies of the evolution of childhood. The five-day format allowed participants to carefully explore the role that extended dependency in humans has played in ontogeny, life history evolution, childhood experience, the development of intersubjectivity, culture acquisition, and public health applications. During the first days of the seminar, conversations naturally coalesced around the aims of the seminar: (1) to define "childhood" across subdisciplines; (2) to integrate cross-species data and the paleoarchaeological record with current developmental, biological, and ethnographic approaches to studying childhood(s); (3) to evaluate how the emergence of cooperation and social cognition are linked to the evolution of human childhood; and (4) to identify the ways in which anthropological research can meaningfully contribute to the burgeoning discourse on contemporary infant and childcare practices.

The question of how different fields define "childhood" fueled a particularly lively discussion and debate throughout the week. The developmental stage of childhood is defined by dramatically different markers across cultures, disciplines, and even subdisciplines. As outlined throughout the volume, the use of the term childhood is plastic and this plasticity often results in miscommunication and misapplication of theory, policy, and law. While characteristic features of childhood manifest themselves under different cultural, political, economic, and ecological circumstances (Bluebond-Langner and Korbin 2007; Crittenden 2014b), we aimed to move toward a more unified definition of childhood. This process uncovered the fact that many, if not all, biomarkers and/or developmental markers do not map onto our current definitions of human childhood. For instance, while the eruption of the first molar is a consistent marker for nonhuman primates' movement from infancy to childhood, this may be only loosely applicable to humans (see Thompson and Nelson, chapter 4, this volume). Weaning, also consistently used as a biocultural marker of human development, displays tremendous inter- and intra-cultural variation. Even the use of the term "weaning" is frequently fraught with misunderstandings, oscillating between an event and a process. When used to refer to an event it signals the complete cessation of breastfeeding; when used to refer to a process, it references the gradual transition from a reliance on breast milk to a complete reliance on an adult diet. Children in small-scale societies begin the process of weaning early in infancy and spend much of latter infancy heavily reliant on a diet largely similar to that of adults (Meehan, Helfrecht, and Quinlan 2014), thus potentially making weaning an unreliable behavioral marker or characteristic of the transition from infancy to childhood (see Meehan, Helfrecht, and Malcom, chapter 9, this volume; Thompson and Nelson, chapter 4, this volume). Given these concerns, the seminar participants posited that "energy flow" might be a candidate criterion for the transition from infancy to childhood: when the energy flow (breastfeeding or supplemental feeding) from the mother drops below a critical threshold and significantly more begins to come from other individuals, this may mark the beginning of childhood.

The seminar also led to a fruitful discussion on how emerging cross-species research can help to identify variations and similarities in ontogenetic patterns. While human childhood is generally considered to be a novel stage not found among other primates (Bogin 1997; Bogin, Bragg, and Kuzawa, chapter 3, this volume), recent genetic and endocrinological data provide evidence that other primates experience a developmental phase that is similar, if not functionally identical, to human childhood. Adrenarche (see Bernstein, chapter 5, this volume), generally occurring at the end of the development stage typically considered childhood, is the prepubertal increase in circulating adrenal androgens (DHEA and DHEAS). While assumed to be unique among humans, and thus demarcating a human development "phase," recent advances show that nonhuman primates also experience this rise in DHEA and DHEAS. Furthermore, cross species work among extant primates highlights that the human process of growth and development evolved over millions of years (see Thompson and Nelson, chapter 4, this volume). Situating the great ape pattern in an evolutionary context allows for greater integration of the paleoanthropological data from the fossil record in informing our understanding about the evolved pattern of growth over the span of the genus *Homo*.

The importance of situating the evolution of childhood within the context of human prosociality and cooperative breeding (or biocultural reproduction) was also brought to the forefront of discussion during the seminar and emerged as a theme throughout the volume. The human child-rearing pattern of distributed care is increasingly seen as intricately interwoven with not only the biological constraints of human childhood that necessitate care and provisioning by others (see Bogin, Bragg, and Kuzawa chapter 3, this volume; Meehan, Helfrecht, and Malcom, chapter 9, this volume) but also the evolution of "emotionally modern" infants who are uniquely able to successfully solicit care from a wide range of caregivers (see Hrdy, chapter 2, this volume). Increasingly, data from small-scale societies are informing our understanding of the attachment process and we see that the mother-child dyad is not an isolated unit, but "steeped in and affected at both the physical and psychological levels by the broader social world" (see Meehan 2014; Meehan, Helfrecht, and Malcolm, chapter 9, this volume). Moreover, ethnographic data on formal and informal processes of cultural transmission (see Lancy, chapter 8, this volume) and the role of play in foraging, as well as psychosocial development among hunter-gatherer populations (see Konner, chapter 6, this volume), informed the discussion of how childhood may have evolved as part of a larger cooperative framework (see Crittenden, chapter 7, this volume).

The seminar concluded with discussion of the role and responsibility of evolutionary anthropologists in the implementation of public health policy. There is currently a mismatch between recommended and actual patterns of infant- and childcare around the world. Many of the recommended patterns have deep evolutionary roots (see Sellen, chapter 10, this volume), yet are not supported in contemporary environments. Anthropologists are uniquely positioned and have an essential role to play in highlighting the evolved needs (co-sleeping, extended and on-demand breastfeeding, and frequent, intimate physical contact) of our species. These evolved needs, associated behaviors, and positive outcomes are richly described in the ethnographic record among foraging populations, in primate life-history data, and in evolutionary medicine studies, yet our presence and ability to influence broader social policy, while improving, remains quite limited. Consequently, we discussed how to expand the dialogue and articulate the ways in which current anthropological research on the origins and implications of human childhood may support or refute the purported benefits of particular parenting practices. The integration of evolutionary theory with human biology, epidemiology, and appreciation of cross-cultural variation can inform our understanding of childhood and childcare practices and improve global maternal and child health outcomes.

With this volume, we echo Konner's assertion that "the great evolutionary geneticist Theodosius Dobzhansky famously said that nothing in biology makes sense except in the light of evolution; we can now say that nothing in childhood does either" (Konner 2010:2). One of the hallmarks of human evolution, and a turning point for early hominins, is our characteristically long, slow, and intricately dynamic stages of dependency. It is our hope that this volume, and its incorporation of multiple perspectives from various subdisciplines within anthropology, will aid in furthering our understanding of human development, life history, and the evolution of childhood.

Acknowledgments

We offer our sincere thanks to the School for Advanced Research and the Paloheimo Foundation for their support of this seminar. The SAR staff, whose generosity and hospitality was extraordinary, is offered our most heartfelt appreciation. In addition, we extend our gratitude to the contributors, who provided excellent manuscripts for discussion and engaged in five days of lively, thought-provoking, and exciting discussion and debate. Special thanks are also offered to Sarah Hrdy, who prompted us to organize this seminar several years ago at an American Anthropological Association meeting.

ADAIR, LINDA S., AND BARRY M. POPKIN

1992   Prolonged Lactation Contributes to Depletion of Maternal Energy Reserves
        in Filipino Women. Journal of Nutrition 122(8):1643–1655.

AHNERT, LIESELOTTE

2005   Parenting and Alloparenting: The Impact on Attachment in Humans. *In*
        Attachment and Bonding: A New Synthesis. Carol S. Carter, Lieselotte
        Ahnert, Klaus E. Grossmann, Sarah Blaffer Hrdy, Michael E. Lamb,
        Stephen W. Porges, and Norbert Sachster, eds. Pp. 229–244. Cambridge,
        MA: MIT Press.

AIELLO, LESLIE, AND CHRISTOPHER DEAN

1990   An Introduction to Human Evolutionary Anatomy. London: Academic
        Press.

AIELLO, LESLIE, AND CATHY KEY

2002   Energetic Consequences of Being a *Homo erectus* Female. American
        Journal of Human Biology 14(5):551–565.

AINSWORTH, MARY D. SALTER

1967   Infancy in Uganda: Infant Care and the Growth of Love. Baltimore, MD:
        Johns Hopkins University Press.

ALEXANDER, RICHARD D., AND KATHARINE M. NOONAN

1979   Concealment of Ovulation, Parental Care, and Human Social Evolution. *In*
        Evolutionary Biology and Human Social Behavior. Napoleon A. Chagnon
        and W. Irons, eds. Pp. 436–453. North Scituate, MA: Duxbury Press.

AMES, DAVID W.

1973   A Sociocultural View of Hausa Musical Activity. *In* The Traditional Artist
        in African Societies. Warren L. d'Azevedo, ed. Pp. 128–161. Bloomington:
        Indiana University Press.

ANEMONE, ROBERT L., MARK P. MOONEY, AND MICHAEL I. SIEGEL

1996   Longitudinal Study of Dental Development in Chimpanzees of Known
        Chronological Age: Implications for Understanding the Age at Death of
        Plio-Pleistocene Hominids. American Journal of Physical Anthropology
        99(1):119–133.

ANTON, SUSAN C.

2002   Cranial Growth in *Homo erectus*. *In* Human Evolution through
        Developmental Change. Nancy Minugh-Purvis and Kenneth J. McNamara,
        eds. Pp. 349–380. Baltimore, MD: Johns Hopkins University Press.

ANTON, SUSAN C., AND STEVE R. LEIGH

2003 Growth and Life History in *Homo erectus. In* Patterns of Growth and Development in the Genus *Homo.* Jennifer L. Thompson, Gail E. Krovitz, and Andrew J. Nelson, eds. Pp. 219–245. Cambridge: Cambridge University Press.

APICELLA, COREN L., AND ALYSSA N. CRITTENDEN

2015 Hunter-Gatherer Families and Parenting. *In* The Handbook of Evolutionary Psychology. David M. Buss, ed. Pp. 797–827. Hoboken, NJ: John Wiley and Sons.

ARIAS, PHILLIPPE

1962 Centuries of Childhood. New York: Vintage Books.

ARLT, WIEBKE, JOHN W. M. MARTENS, MAENGSEOK SONG, JONATHAN T. WANG, RICHARD J. AUCHUS, AND WALTER L. MILLER

2002 Molecular Evolution of Adrenarche: Structural and Functional Analysis of P450c17 from Four Primate Species. Endocrinology 143(12):4665–4672.

ARSUAGA, JUAN-LUIS, JOSÉ MARÍA BERMÚDEZ DE CASTRO, AND EUDALD CARBONELL

1997 The Sima de los Huesos Hominid Site. Journal of Human Evolution 33:219–281.

ARSUAGA, JUAN-LUIS, IGNACIO MARTÍNEZ, ANA GRACIA, AND CARLOS LORENZO

1997 The Sima de los Huesos Crania (Sierra de Atapuerca, Spain). Journal of Human Evolution 33(2–3):219–281.

ARTHUR WALLACE

2000 Intraspecific Variation in Developmental Characters: The Origin of Evolutionary Novelties. American Zoologist 40(5):811–818. Novelties.

AUNGER, ROBERT

2000 The Life History of Culture Learning in a Face-to-Face Society. Ethos 28(3):445–481.

AUSTIN, CHRISTINE, TANYA M. SMITH, ASA BRADMAN, KATIE HINDE, RENAUD JOANNES-BOYAU, DAVID BISHOP, DOMINIC J. HARE, PHILIP DOBLE, BRENDA ESKENAZI, AND MANISH ARORA

2013 Barium Distributions in Teeth Reveal Early-Life Dietary Transitions in Primates. Nature 498:216–219.

AUSTRIAN, SONIA G., ED.

2008 Developmental Theories Through the Life Cycle. New York: Columbia University Press.

AXELROD, ROBERT, AND WILLIAM D. HAMILTON

1981 The Evolution of Co-operation. Science 211(4489):390–398.

AXELSON, M., C. E. GRAHAM, AND J. SJÖVALL

1984   Identification and Quantitation of Steroids in Sulfate Fractions from
        Plasma of Pregnant Chimpanzee, Orangutan, and Rhesus Monkey.
        Endocrinology 114(2):337–344.

BAHL, RAJIV, CHRIS FROST, BETTY R. KIRKWOOD, KAREN EDMOND,
JOSE MARTINES, NITA BHANDARI, AND PAUL ARTHOR

2005   Infant Feeding Patterns and Risks of Death and Hospitalization in the First
        Half of Infancy: Multicentre Cohort Study. Bulletin of the World Health
        Organization 83(6):418–426.

BAHUCHET, SERGE

1999   Aka Pygmies. *In* The Cambridge Encyclopedia of Hunters and Gatherers.
        Robert B. Lee, and Richard Daly, eds. Pp. 190–200. Cambridge: Cambridge
        University Press.

BAILEY, ROBERT C.

1991   The Behavioral Ecology of Efe Pygmy Men in the Ituri Forest, Zaire,
        vol. 86. Ann Arbor: Museum of Anthropology, University of Michigan.

BAILLARGEON, RENÉE AND SUSAN CAREY

2012   Core Cognition and Beyond: The Acquisition of Physical and Numerical
        Knowledge. *In* Early Childhood Development and Later Outcome. Sabina
        Pauen, ed. Pp. 33–65. Cambridge: Cambridge University Press.

BAKEMAN, ROGER, LAUREN B. ADAMSON, MELVIN J. KONNER, AND
RONALD G. BARR

1990   !Kung Infancy: The Social Context of Object Exploration. Child
        Development 61(3):794–809.

BALES, KAREN, JEFFREY A. FRENCH, AND JAMES M. DIETZ

2002   Explaining Variation in Maternal Care in Cooperatively Breeding
        Mammals. Animal Behaviour 63(3):453–461.

BALIKCI, ASEN

1970   The Netsilik Eskimo. Garden City, NY: The Natural History Press.

BANDURA, ALBERT

1977   Social Learning Theory. Englewood Cliffs, NJ: Prentice-Hall.

BARBER, ELIZABETH W.

1994   Women's Work: The First 20,000 Years: Women, Cloth, and Society in
        Early Times. New York: W. W. Norton.

BARBOSA, LOURDES, NANCY F. BUTTE, SALVADOR VILLALPANDO,
WILLIAM W. WONG, AND E. O. SMITH

1997   Maternal Energy Balance and Lactation Performance of Mesoamerindians
        as a Function of Body Mass Index. American Journal of Clinical Nutrition
        66(3):575–583.

BARD, KIM A.

2005   Emotions in Chimpanzee Infants: The Value of a Comparative
        Developmental Approach to Understand the Evolutionary Bases of
        Emotion. *In* Emotional Development: Recent Research Advances.
        Jacqueline Nadel and Darwin Muir, eds. Pp. 31–60. Oxford: Oxford
        University Press.

2007   Neonatal Imitation in Chimpanzees (*Pan troglodytes*) Tested with Two
        Paradigms. Animal Cognition 10:233–242.

2012   Emotional Engagement: How Chimpanzee Minds Develop. *In* The Primate
        Mind. Frans de Waal and Pier Francesco Ferrari, eds. Pp. 224–245.
        Cambridge, MA: Harvard University Press.

BARDI, MASSIMO, ANDREW J. PETTO, AND DAVID E. LEE-PARRITZ

2001   Parental Failure in Captive Cotton-Top Tamarins (*Saguinus oedipus*).
        American Journal of Primatology 54(3):150–169.

BARLOW, KATHLEEN

2001   Working Mothers and the Work of Culture in a Papua New Guinea Society.
        Ethos 29(1):78–107.

BARR, RONALD G., MELVIN KONNER, ROGER BAKEMAN, AND LAUREN ADAMSON

1991   Crying in !Kung San Infants: A Test of the Cultural Specificity Hypothesis.
        Developmental Medicine and Child Neurology 33(7):601–610.

BARRETT, H. CLARK

2005   Adaptations to Predators and Prey. *In* Handbook of Evolutionary
        Psychology. David M. Buss, ed. Pp. 200–223. New York: Wiley.

BARRETT, H. CLARK, TANYA BROESCH, ROSE M. SCOTT, ZIJING HE,
RENÉE BAILLARGEON, DI WU, MATTHIAS BOLZ, ET AL.

2013   Early False-Belief Understanding in Traditional Non-Western Societies.
        Proceedings of the Royal Society B 280(1755):doi:10.1098/rspb.2012.2654.

BARRY, HERBERT, III, AND LEONORA M. PAXSON

1971   Infancy and Early Childhood: Cross-Cultural Codes 2. Ethnology
        10:466–508.

BATESON, PATRICK

2005   The Role of Play in the Evolution of Great Apes and Humans. *In* The Nature
        of Play: Great Apes and Humans. Anthony D. Pellegrini and
        Peter K. Smith, eds. Pp. 13–24. New York: Guilford Press.

BATESON, PATRICK, DAVID BARKER, TIMOTHY CLUTTON-BROCK, DEBAL DEB,
BRUNO D'UDINE, ROBERT A. FOLEY, PETER GLUCKMAN, ET AL.

2004   Developmental Plasticity and Human Health. Nature 430:419–421.

BAYLE, PRISCILLA, JOSE BRAGA, AMAUD MAZURIER, AND
ROBERTO MACCHIARELLI

2009a   Dental Developmental Pattern of the Neanderthal Child from Roc de
         Marsal: A High-Resolution 3D Analysis. Journal of Human Evolution 56(1):
         66–75.

2009b   Brief Communication: High-Resolution Assessment of the Dental
         Developmental Pattern and Characterization of Tooth Tissue Proportions
         in the Late Upper Paleolithic Child from La Madeleine, France. American
         Journal of Physical Anthropology 138(4):493–498.

BEATON, GEORGE H.

1992   The Raymond Pearl Memorial Lecture, 1990: Nutrition Research in Human
         Biology: Changing Perspectives and Interpretations. American Journal of
         Human Biology 4(2):159–177.

BECK, CHERYL T.

1995   The Effects of Postpartum Depression on Maternal-Infant Interaction: A
         Meta-Analysis. Nursing Research 44(2):298–304.

BEGUN, DAVID, AND ALAN WALKER

1993   The Endocast. *In* The Nariokotome *Homo erectus* Skeleton. Alan Walker
         and Richard Leakey, eds. Pp. 326–358. Cambridge, MA: Harvard University
         Press.

BEHRINGER, VEREBA, GOTTFRIED HOHMANN, JEROEN M. G. STEVENS,
ANJA WELTRING, AND TOBIAS DESCHNER

2012   Adrenarche in Bonobos (*Pan paniscus*): Evidence from Ontogenetic
         Changes in Urinary Dehydroepiandrosterone-Sulfate Levels. Journal of
         Endocrinology 214(1):55–65.

BEISE, JAN

2005   The Helping and the Helpful Grandmother: The Role of Maternal and
         Paternal Grandmothers in Child Mortality in the Seventeenth and
         Eighteenth-century Population of French Settlers in Quebec, Canada. *In*
         Grandmotherhood: The Evolutionary Significance of the Second Half of
         Female Life. Eckart Voland, Athanasios Chasiotis, and Wulf Schiefenhövel,
         eds. Pp. 215–238. New Brunswick, NJ: Rutgers University Press.

BEISE, JAN, AND ECKART VOLAND

2002   Differential Infant Mortality Viewed from an Evolutionary Biological
         Perspective. The History of the Family 7(4):515–526.

BELSKY, JAY

1997   Attachment, Mating, and Parenting: An Evolutionary Interpretation.
         Human Nature 8(4):361–381.

1999   Modern Evolutionary Theory and Patterns of Attachment. *In*
            Handbook of Attachment: Theory, Research, and Clinical Applications.
            J. S. P. R. Cassidy, ed. Pp. 141–161. New York: Guilford Press.

BELSKY, JAY, LAWRENCE STEINBERG, AND PATRICIA DRAPER
1991   Childhood Experience, Interpersonal Development, and Reproductive
            Strategy: An Evolutionary Theory of Socialization. Child Development
            62(4):647–670.

BERGELSON, ELIKA, AND DANIEL SWINGLEY
2012   At 6–9 Months, Human Infants Know the Meaning of Common Nouns.
            Proceedings of the National Academy of Sciences 109(12):3253–3258.

BERMÚDEZ DE CASTRO, JOSÉ MARÍA, J. L. ARSUAGA, E. CARBONELL, A. ROSAS,
I. MARTÍNEZ, AND M. MOSQUERA
1997   A Hominid from the Lower Pleistocene of Atapuerca, Spain: Possible
            Ancestor to Neandertals and Modern Humans. Science 276(5317):1392–1395.

BERMÚDEZ DE CASTRO, JOSÉ MARÍA, MARÍA MARTINÓN-TORRES, LEYRE PRADO,
AIDA GÓMEZ-ROBLES, JORDI ROSELL, LUCÍA LÓPEZ-POLÍN, JUAN LUÍS ARSUAGA,
AND EUDALD CARBONELL
2010   New Immature Hominin Fossil from European Lower Pleistocene Shows
            the Earliest Evidence of a Modern Human Dental Development Pattern.
            Proceedings of the National Academy of Sciences 107(26):11739–11744.

BERMÚDEZ DE CASTRO, JOSÉ MARÍA, FERNANDO V. RAMIREZ ROZZI, MARIA
MARTINÓN-TORRES, S. SARMIENTO PÉREZ, AND ANTONIO ROSAS
2003   Patterns of Dental Development in Lower and Middle Pleistocene
            Hominins from Atapuerca (Spain). *In* Patterns of Growth and
            Development in the Genus *Homo*. Jennifer L. Thompson, Gail E. Krovitz,
            and Andrew J. Nelson, eds. Pp. 246–270. Cambridge: Cambridge University
            Press.

BERMÚDEZ DE CASTRO, JOSÉ MARÍA, AND ANTONIO ROSAS
2001   Pattern of Dental Development in Hominid XVIII from the Middle
            Pleistocene Atapuerca-Sima de los Huesos Site (Spain). American Journal
            of Physical Anthropology 114(4):325–330.

BERMÚDEZ DE CASTRO, JOSÉ MARÍA, ANTONIO ROSAS, E. CARBONELL,
E. NICOLÁS, J. RODRÍGUEZ, AND J. L. ARSUAGA
1999   A Modern Human Pattern of Dental Development in Lower Pleistocene
            Hominids from Atapuerca-TD6 (Spain). Proceedings of the National
            Academy of Sciences 96(7):4210–4213.

BERNSTEIN, ROBIN M.
2005   Growth-Related Hormones in Great Apes. American Journal of Physical
            Anthropology 40:73–74.

2010   The Big and Small of It: How Body Size Evolves. Yearbook of Physical
        Anthropology 143(S51):46–62.

BERNSTEIN, ROBIN M., HEATHER DROUGHT, JANE E. PHILLIPS-CONROY, AND
CLIFFORD J. JOLLY

2013   Hormonal Correlates of Divergent Growth Trajectories in Wild Male
        Anubis (*Papio anubis*) and Hamadryas (*Papio hamadryas*) Baboons in
        the Awash River Valley, Ethiopia. International Journal of Primatology
        34(4):732–751. doi:10.1007/s10764-013-9692-x.

BERNSTEIN, ROBIN M., STEVEN R. LEIGH, SHARON M. DONOVAN, AND
MARCIA H. MONACO

2007   Hormones and Body Size Evolution in Papionin Primates. American
        Journal of Physical Anthropology 132(2):247–260.

2008   Hormonal Correlates of Ontogeny in Baboon (*Papio hamadryas anubis*)
        and Mangabeys (*Cercocebus atys*). American Journal of Physical
        Anthropology 136(2):156–168.

BERNSTEIN, ROBIN M., KRISTIN N. STERNER, AND DEREK E. WILDMAN

2012   Adrenal Androgen Production in Catarrhine Primates and the Evolution of
        Adrenarche. American Journal of Physical Anthropology 147(3):389–400.

BEYNON, A. D., AND M. C. DEAN

1988   Distinct Dental Development Pattern in Early Fossil Hominids. Nature 335:
        509–514.

1991   Hominid Dental Development. Nature 351(6323):196.

BHANDARI, NITA, RAJIV BAHL, SARMILA MAZUMDAR, JOSE MARTINES,
ROBERT E. BLACK, MAHARAJ K. BAHN, AND THE OTHER MEMBERS OF THE
INFANT FEEDING STUDY GROUP

2003   Effect of Community-Based Promotion of Exclusive Breastfeeding on
        Diarrhoeal Illness and Growth: A Cluster Randomised Controlled Trial.
        Lancet 361(9367):1418–23.

BHUTTA, ZULFIQAR A., TAHMEED AHMED, ROBERT E. BLACK, SIMON COUSENS,
KATHRYN DEWEY, ELSA GIUGLANI, BATOOL A HAIDER, ET AL.

2008   What Works? Interventions for Maternal and Child Undernutrition and
        Survival. Lancet 371(9610):417–40.

BHUTTA, ZULFIQAR A., JAI K. DAS, RAJIV BAHL, JOY E. LAWN, REHANA A. SALAM,
VINOD K. PAUL, M JEEVA SANKAR, ET AL.

2014   Can Available Interventions End Preventable Deaths in Mothers, Newborn
        Babies, and Stillbirths, and At What Cost? Lancet 384(9940):347–70.

BILSBOROUGH, ALAN, AND JENNIFER L. THOMPSON

2005   Dentition of the Le Moustier 1 Neanderthal. *In* The Neandertal Adolescent

Le Moustier 1: New Aspects, New Results. Herbert Ullrich, ed. Pp. 157–186.
Berlin: Staatliche Museen zu Berlin, Preußischer Kulturbesiz.

BIRD, DAVID, AND REBECCA BLIEGE BIRD

2005   Martu Children's Hunting Strategies in the Western Desert, Australia:
        Foraging and the Evolution of Human Life Histories. *In* Hunter-Gatherer
        Childhoods: Evolutionary, Developmental, and Cultural Perspectives.
        Barry S. Hewlett and Michael E. Lamb, eds. Pp. 129–146. New Brunswick,
        NJ: AldineTransaction.

BIRD, DOUGLAS W., AND REBECCA BLIEGE BIRD

1997   The Science of Foragers: Evaluating Variability among Hunter-Gatherers.
        Antiquity 71(272):477–480.

2000   The Ethnoarchaeology of Juvenile Foragers: Shellfishing Strategies among
        Meriam Children. Journal of Anthropological Archaeology 19(4):461–476.

2002   Children on the Reef: Slow Learning or Strategic Foraging? Human Nature
        13(2): 269–297.

2005   Martu Children's Hunting Strategies in the Western Desert, Australia. *In*
        Hunter-Gatherer Childhoods: Evolutionary, Developmental, and Cultural
        Perspectives. Barry S. Hewlett and Michael E. Lamb, eds. Pp. 129–146. New
        Brunswick, NJ: AldineTransaction.

BIRD, REBECCA BLIEGE, AND DOUGLAS W. BIRD

2002   Constraints of Knowing or Constraints of Growing? Human Nature
        13(2):239–267.

2008   Why Women Hunt: Risk and Contemporary Foraging in a Western Desert
        Aboriginal Community. Current Anthropology 49(4):655–693.

BIRD-DAVID, NURIT

1990   The Giving Environment—Another Perspective on the Economic System of
        Hunter-Gatherers. Current Anthropology 31(2):189–196.

2005   Studying Children in "Hunter-Gatherer" Societies: Reflections from
        a Nayaka Perspective. *In* Hunter-Gatherer Childhoods: Evolutionary,
        Developmental, and Cultural Perspectives. Barry S. Hewlett and Michael E.
        Lamb, eds. Pp. 92–101. New Brunswick, NJ: AldineTransaction.

2008   Feeding Nayaka Children and English Readers: A Bifocal Ethnography of
        Parental Feeding in "The Giving Environment." Anthropological Quarterly
        81(3):523–550.

BJORKLUND, DAVID F., KAYLA CAUSEY, AND VIRGINIA PERISS

2010   The Evolution and Development of Human Social Cognition. In Mind the
        Gap: Tracing the Origins of Human Universals. Peter M. Kappeler and
        Joan B. Silk, eds. Pp. 351–371. Berlin: Springer-Verlag.

BLEDSOE, CAROLINE

1992   The Cultural Transformation of Western Education in Sierra Leone. Africa 62(2):182–202.

BLEEK, DOROTHEA F.

1931   The Hadzapi or Watindega of Tanganyika Territory. Africa 4(3):273–286.

BLOCH, MAURICE E. F., GREGG E. A. SOLOMON, AND SUSAN CAREY

2001   Zafmaniry: An Understanding of What Is Passed On from Parents to Children: A Cross-Cultural Investigation. Journal of Cognition and Culture 1(1):43–68.

BLUEBOND-LANGNER, MYRA, AND JILL E. KORBIN

2007   Challenges and Opportunities in the Anthropology of Childhoods: An Introduction to "Children, Childhoods, and Childhood Studies." American Anthropologist 109(2):241–246.

BLUM, W. F., K. ALBERTSSON-WIKLAND, AND S. ROSBERG

1993   Serum Levels of Insulin-like Growth Factor I (IGF-I) and IGF Binding Protein 3 Reflect Spontaneous Growth Hormone Secretion. Journal of Clinical Endocrinology and Metabolism 76(6):1610–1616.

BLURTON JONES, NICHOLAS G.

1989   The Costs of Children and the Adaptive Scheduling of Births: Toward a Sociobiological Perspective of Demography. In The Sociobiology of Sexual and Reproductive Strategies. Anne E. Rasa, Christian Vogel, and Eckart Voland, eds. London: Chapman and Hall.

1993   The Lives of Hunter-Gatherer Children: Effects of Parental Behavior and Parental Reproductive Strategy. In Juvenile Primates: Life History, Development, and Behavior. Michael E. Pereira and Lynn A. Fairbanks, eds. Pp. 309–326. New York: Oxford University Press.

2005   Introduction to "Why Does Childhood Exist?" In Hunter-Gatherer Childhoods: Evolutionary, Developmental, and Cultural Perspectives. Barry S. Hewlett and Michael E. Lamb, eds. Pp. 105–108. New Brunswick, NJ: AldineTransaction.

2006   Contemporary Hunter-Gatherers and Human Life History Evolution. In The Evolution of Human Life History. Kristen Hawkes and Richard R. Paine, eds. Pp. 231–266. Santa Fe, NM: School of American Research Press.

BLURTON JONES, NICHOLAS G., KRISTEN HAWKES, AND PATRICIA DRAPER

1994a   Differences between Hadza and !Kung Children's Work: Original Affluence or Practical Reason? In Key Issues in Hunter-Gatherer Research. Ernest S. Burch Jr. and Linda J. Ellanna, eds. Pp. 189–215. Oxford: Berg Publishers Ltd.

1994b   Foraging Patterns of !Kung Adults and Children: Why Didn't !Kung Children Forage? Journal of Anthropological Research 50(3):217–248.

BLURTON JONES, NICHOLAS G., KRISTEN HAWKES, AND JAMES F. O'CONNELL

1989   Modeling and Measuring Costs of Children in Two Foraging Societies. *In*
        Comparative Socioecology: The Behavioral Ecology of Humans and Other
        Mammals. Special Publications of the British Ecological Society, no. 8.
        Valerie Standen, and Robert A. Foley, eds. Pp. 367–390. Oxford: Blackwell
        Scientific.

1997   Why Do Hadza Children Forage? *In* Uniting Psychology and Biology:
        Integrative Perspectives on Human Development. Nancy L. Segal, Glenn E.
        Weisfeld, and Carol Cronin, eds. Pp. 279–313. Washington, DC: American
        Psychological Association.

2005   Hadza Grandmothers as Helpers: Residence Data. *In* Grandmotherhood:
        The Evolutionary Significance of the Second Half of Female Life. Eckart
        Voland, Athanasios Chasiotis, and Wulf Schiefenhövel, eds. Pp. 160–176.
        New Brunswick, NJ: Rutgers University Press.

BLURTON JONES, NICHOLAS G., AND FRANK W. MARLOWE

2002   Selection for Delayed Maturity: Does It Take 20 Years to Learn to Hunt and
        Gather? Human Nature 13(2):199–238.

BLURTON JONES, NICHOLAS G., LAC C. SMITH, JAMES F. O'CONNELL,
KRISTEN HAWKES, AND C. L. KAMUZORA

1992   Demography of the Hadza, an Increasing and High Density Population
        of Savanna Foragers. American Journal of Physical Anthropology
        89(2):159–181.

BOAS, FRANZ

1901   The Eskimo of Baffin Land and Hudson Bay. Bulletin of the American
        Museum of Natural History 15(1):1–370.

BOCHERENS, HERVÉ, DANIEL BILLIOU, ANDRÉ MARIOTI, MICHEL TOUSSAINT,
MARYLÈNE PATOU-MATHIS, DOMINIQUE BONJEAN, AND MARCEL OTTE

2001   New Isotopic Evidence for Dietary Habits of Neandertals from Belgium.
        Journal of Human Evolution 40:497–505.

BOCK, JOHN

2002   Learning, Life History, and Productivity: Children's Lives in the Okavango
        Delta of Botswana. Human Nature 13(2):161–198.

2004   Farming, Foraging, and Children's Play in the Okavango Delta, Botswana.
        In The Nature of Play: Great Apes and Humans. Anthony D. Pellegrini and
        Peter. K. Smith, eds. Pp. 254–281. New York: Guilford Press.

BOCK, JOHN, AND SARA E. JOHNSON

2004   Subsistence Ecology and Play among the Okavango Delta Peoples of
        Botswana. Human Nature 15(1):63–82.

BOCK, JOHN, AND DANIEL W. SELLEN

2002   Childhood and the Evolution of the Human Life Course: An Introduction.
        Human Nature 13(2):153–159.

BOEHM, CHRISTOPHER

2012   Moral Origins: The Evolution of Virtue, Altruism, and Shame. New York:
        Basic Books.

BOESCH, CHRISTOPHE, AND HEDWIGE BOESCH-ACHERMANN

1990   The Chimpanzees of the Taï Forest: Behavioral Ecology and Evolution.
        Oxford: Oxford University Press.

BOESCH, CHRISTOPHE, HEDWIGE BOESCH, AND LINDA VIGILANT

2006   Cooperative Hunting in Chimpanzees: Kinship or Mutualism? *In*
        Cooperation in Primates and Humans. Peter M. Kappeler and Carel P. van
        Schaik, eds. Pp. 140–150. Berlin: Springer.

BOESCH, CHRISTOPHER, CAMILLE BOLÉ, NADIN ECKHARDT, AND
HEDWIGE BOESCH

2010   Altruism in Forest Chimpanzees: The Case of Adoption. PLoS ONE
        5(1):e8901. doi:10.1371/journal.pone.0008901.

BOGIN, BARRY

1997   Evolutionary Hypotheses for Human Childhood. Yearbook of Physical
        Anthropology 104(S25):63–89.

1999a   Evolutionary Perspective on Human Growth. Annual Review of
        Anthropology 28:109–153.

1999b   [1988] Patterns of Human Growth. 2nd edition. Cambridge: Cambridge
[1988] University Press.

2001   The Growth of Humanity. New York: Wiley-Liss.

2002   The Evolution of Human Growth. *In* Human Growth and Development.
        Nöel Cameron, ed. Pp. 295–320. San Diego, CA: Academic Press.

2003   The Human Pattern of Growth and Development in Paleontological
        Perspective. *In* Patterns of Growth and Development in the Genus *Homo*.
        Jennifer L. Thompson, Gail E. Krovitz, and Andrew J. Nelson, eds. Pp.
        15–44. Cambridge: Cambridge University Press.

2006   Modern Human Life History: The Evolution of Human Childhood and
        Fertility. *In* The Evolution of Human Life History. Kristen Hawkes and
        Richard R. Paine, eds. Pp. 197–230. Santa Fe, NM: School of American
        Research Press.

2009   Childhood, Adolescence, and Longevity: A Multilevel Model of the
        Evolution of Reserve Capacity in Human Life History. American Journal of
        Human Biology 21(4):567–577.

2010   Evolution of Human Growth. *In* Human Evolutionary Biology. Michael P. Muehlenbein, ed. Pp. 223–236. Cambridge: Cambridge University Press.

2011   Puberty and Adolescence: An Evolutionary Perspective. *In* Encyclopedia of Adolescence, vol. 1. B. Bradford Brown and Mitchell J. Prinstein, eds. Pp. 275–286. San Diego, CA: Academic Press.

2013   Childhood, Adolescence, and Longevity: A Chapter on Human Evolutionary Life History. *In* Adolescent Identity: Evolutionary, Cultural, and Development Perspectives. Bonnie L. Hewlett, ed. Pp. 23–39. New York: Routledge.

BOGIN, BARRY, JARED BRAGG, AND CHRISTOPHER KUZAWA
2014   Humans Are Not Cooperative Breeders but Practice Biocultural Reproduction. Annals of Human Biology 41(4):368–380.

BOGIN, BARRY, AND B. HOLLY SMITH
1996   Evolution of the Human Life Cycle. American Journal of Human Biology 8(6):703–716.

2012   Evolution of the Human Life Cycle. *In* Human Biology: An Evolutionary and Biocultural Perspective. 2nd edition. Sara Stinson, Barry Bogin, and Dennis O'Rourke, eds. Pp. 515–586. New York: Wiley.

BOROFSKY, ROBERT
1987   Making History: Pukapukan and Anthropological Constructions of Knowledge. Cambridge: Cambridge University Press.

BOULTON, MICHAEL J., AND PETER K. SMITH
1992   The Social Nature of Play Fighting and Play Chasing: Mechanisms and Strategies Underlying Cooperation and Compromise. *In* The Adapted Mind: Evolutionary Psychology and the Generation of Culture. Jerome H. Barkow, Leda Cosmides, and John Tooby, eds. Pp. 430–440. Oxford: Oxford University Press.

BOVE, RILEY B., CLAUDIA R. VALEGGIA, AND PETER T. ELLISON
2002   Girl Helpers and Time Allocation of Nursing Women among the Toba of Argentina. Human Nature 13(4):457–472.

BOWLBY, JOHN
1971   Attachment and Loss, vol. 1. Harmondsworth, UK: Penguin Books.
[1969]

1970   Disruption of Affectional Bonds and Its Effects on Behavior. Journal of Contemporary Psychotherapy 2(2):75–86.

1973   Attachment and Loss, vol. 2: Separation. New York: Basic Books.

1980   Attachment and Loss, vol. 3: Loss, Sadness, and Depression. New York: Random House.

BOWLES, SAMUEL

2008a   Being Human: Conflict: Altruism's Midwife. Nature 456:326.

2008b   The Coevolution of Altruism, Parochialism, and War: Rambo Meets
Mother Teresa. Lecture presented at the Santa Fe Institute, Santa Fe, NM,
September 17. http://www.youtube.com/watch?v=UYBFf9ZgkvU.

BOYD, ROBERT, AND PETER J. RICHERSON

2006   Culture and the Evolution of the Human Social Instincts. *In* Roots of
Human Socialization: Culture, Cognition, and Interaction. Nick J. Einfield
and Stephen C. Levinson, eds. Pp. 453–477. Oxford: Berg.

BRAGG, JARED M., BARRY BOGIN, AND CHRISTOPHER W. KUZAWA

2012   Rethinking Lifetime Reproductive Effort in Human Females: Does
Complementary Feeding Provide the Fuel to Extend the Human Lifespan?
American Journal of Physical Anthropology 150(S56):87.

BRETHERTON, INGE

1985   Attachment Theory: Retrospect and Prospect. Monographs of the Society
for Research in Child Development 209(1–2):3–35.

1992   The Origins of Attachment Theory: John Bowlby and Mary Ainsworth.
Developmental Psychology 28(5):759–755.

BROCH, HARALD B.

1990   Growing Up Agreeably: Bonerate Childhood Observed. Honolulu:
University of Hawaii Press.

BROMAGE, TIMOTHY G., AND M. CHRISTOPHER DEAN

1985   Re-evaluation of the Age at Death of Immature Fossil Hominids. Nature
317: 525–527.

BROWN, ANN L.

1990   Domain-Specific Principles Affect Learning and Transfer in Children.
Cognitive Science 14(1):107–133.

BROWN, P. MARGARET, FIELD W. RICKARDS, AND ANNA BORTOLI

2001   Structures Underpinning Pretend Play and Word Production in Young
Hearing Children and Children with Hearing Loss. Journal of Deaf Studies
and Deaf Education 6(1):15–31.

BRUMBACH, BARBARA H., AURELIO J. FIGUEREDO, AND BRUCE J. ELLIS

2009   Effects of Harsh and Unpredictable Environments in Adolescence on
Development of Life History Strategies. Human Nature 20(1):25–51.

BRUNER, JEROME S.

1966   On Cognitive Growth II. *In* Studies in Cognitive Growth. Jerome S.
Bruner, Rose R. Olver, and Patricia M. Greenfield, eds. Pp. 30–67. New
York: Wiley.

BRUNER, JEROME S., ALISON JOLLY, AND KATHY SYLVA, EDS.
1976   Play: Its Role in Development and Evolution. New York: Basic Books.

BUIKSTRA, JANE E., AND DOUGLAS H. UBELAKER, EDS.
1994   Standards for Data Collection from Human Skeletal Remains. Arkansas
        Archaeological Survey Research Series 44.

BULLINGER, ANKE F., EMILY WYMAN, ALICIA P. MELIS, AND MICHAEL TOMASELLO
2011   Coordination of Chimpanzees (*Pan troglodytes*) in a Stag Hunt Game.
        International Journal of Primatology 32:1296–1310.

BURGER, OSKAR, ROBERT WALKER, AND MARCUS J. HAMILTON
2010   Lifetime Reproductive Effort in Humans. Proceedings of the Royal Society
        Biological Sciences 277(1682):773–777.

BURKART, JUDITH M., ERNST FEHR, CHARLES EFFERSON, AND
CAREL P. VAN SCHAIK
2007   Other-Regarding Preferences in a Nonhuman Primate: Common
        Marmosets Provision Food Altruistically. Proceedings of the National
        Academy of Sciences 104(50):19762–19766.

BURKART, JUDITH M., AND ADOLF HESCHL
2007   Perspective Taking or Behaviour Reading? Understanding Visual
        Access in Common Marmosets (*Callithrix jacchus*). Animal Behaviour
        73(3):457–469.

BURKART, JUDITH M., SARAH B. HRDY, AND CAREL P. VAN SCHAIK
2009   Cooperative Breeding and Human Cognitive Evolution. Evolutionary
        Anthropology 18(5):175–186.

BURKART, JUDITH M., AND CAREL P. VAN SCHAIK
2010   Cognitive Consequences of Cooperative Breeding in Primates. Animal
        Cognition 13:1–19.

2012   Group Service in Macaques, Capuchins, and Marmosets: A Comparative
        Approach to Identifying Proactive Prosocial Motivations. Journal of
        Comparative Psychology. 127(2): 212–225.

BURRIDGE, KENELM O.
1957   A Tangu Game. Man 57:88–89.

BUTTE, NANCY F., WILLIAM W. WONG, JUDY M. HOPKINSON, CAROLYN J. HEINZ,
NITESH R. MEHTA, AND ELLIOT O'BRIAN SMITH
2000   Energy Requirements Derived from Total Energy Expenditure and Energy
        Deposition during the First 2 Years of Life. American Journal of Clinical
        Nutrition 72(6):1558–1569.

BYERS, JOHN A., AND CURT WALKER
1995   Refining the Motor Training Hypothesis for the Evolution of Play.
        American Naturalist 146(1):25–40.

BYRNE, RICHARD

1995   The Thinking Ape. Oxford: Oxford University Press.

2006   Parsing Behavior: A Mundane Origin for an Extraordinary Ability? *In* Roots of Human Socialization: Culture, Cognition, and Interaction. Nicholas J. Enfield and Stephen C. Levinson, eds. Pp. 478–505. Oxford: Berg.

BYRNE, RICHARD W., AND LISA G. RAPAPORT

2011   What Are We Learning from Teaching? Animal Behaviour 82(5):1207–1211.

CALLAGHAN, TARA, HENRIKE MOLL, HANNES RAKOCZY, FELIX WARNEKEN,
ULF LISZKOWSKI, TANYA BEHNE, AND MICHAEL TOMASELLO

2011   Early Social Cognition in Three Cultural Contexts. Monographs of the Society for Research in Child Development 76 (2):i–viii, 1–142.

CAMPBELL, BENJAMIN

2006   Adrenarche and the Evolution of Human Life History. American Journal of Human Biology 18(5): 569–589.

2011a   Adrenarche in Comparative Perspective. Human Nature 23(1):44–52.

2011b   Adrenarche and Middle Childhood. Human Nature 22(3):327–349.

CAMPBELL, JOHN K.

1964   Honour, Family, and Patronage: A Study of Institutions and Moral Values in a Greek Mountain Community. Oxford: Clarendon Press.

CAREY, SUSAN, AND ELIZABETH SPELKE

1996   Science and Core Knowledge. Philosophy of Science 63:515–533.

CARPENTER, MALINDA, KATHERINE NAGELL, MICHAEL TOMASELLO,
GEORGE BUTTERWORTH, AND CHRIS MOORE

1998   Social Cognition, Joint Attention, and Communicative Competence from 9 to 15 Months of Age. Monographs of the Society for Research in Child Development 63(4):1–174.

CARSTEN, JANET, ED.

2000   Cultures of Relatedness: New Approaches to the Study of Kinship. Cambridge: Cambridge University Press.

CARTER, C. SUE, LIESELOTTE AHNERT, K. E. GROSSMANN, SARAH B. HRDY,
MICHAEL E. LAMB, STEPHEN W. PORGES, AND NORBERT SACHSER, EDS.

2005   Attachment and Bonding: A New Synthesis. Dahlem Workshop Reports. Cambridge, MA: MIT Press.

CASIMIR, MICHAEL J.

2010   Growing Up in a Pastoral Society: Socialization among Pashtu Nomads. Kölner Ethnologische Beiträge. Kölon: Druck and Bindung.

CASPARI, RACHEL, AND SANG-HEE LEE

2004   Older Age Becomes Common Late in Human Evolution. Proceedings of the National Academy of Sciences 101(30):10895–10900.

CASSIDY, JUDE

2008   The Nature of the Child's Ties. *In* Handbook of Attachment. 2nd edition.
        Jude Cassidy and Phillip R. Shaver, eds. Pp. 3–22. New York: Guilford Press.

CASTRACANE, V. DANIEL, GORDON B. CUTLER JR., AND D. LYNN LORIAUX

1981   Pubertal Endocrinology of the Baboon: Adrenarche. American Journal of
        Physiology 241(4):E305–E309.

CASTRO, LAUREANO, AND MIGUEL A. TORO

2004   The Evolution of Culture: From Primate Social Learning to
        Human Culture. Proceedings of the National Academy of Sciences
        101(27):10235–10240.

CHAGNON, NAPOLEON

1979   Is Reproductive Success Equal in Egalitarian Societies? *In* Evolutionary
        Biology and Human Social Behavior: An Anthropological Perspective.
        N. Chagnon and W. Irons, eds. Pp. 374–401. North Scituate, MA: Duxbury
        Press.

1992   Yanomamö: The Fierce People. 4th edition. New York: Holt, Rinehart, and
        Winston.

CHAPARRO, CAMILA M., AND CHESSA K. LUTTER

2009   Incorporating Nutrition into Delivery Care: Delivery Care Practices That
        Affect Child Nutrition and Maternal Health. Maternal & Child Nutrition
        5(4):322–333.

CHARNOV, ERIC L.

1993   Life History Invariants: Some Explorations of Symmetry in Evolutionary
        Ecology. Oxford: Oxford University Press.

CHARNOV, ERIC L., AND DAVID BERRIGAN

1993   Why Do Female Primates Have Such Long Lifespans and So Few Babies?
        Or, Life in the Slow Lane. Evolutionary Anthropology 1(6):191–194.

CHARNOV, ERIC L., ROBIN WARNE, AND MELANIE MOSES

2007   Lifetime Reproductive Effort. American Naturalist 170(6):E129–142.

CHAVAJAY, PABLO, AND BARBARA ROGOFF

1999   Cultural Variation in Management of Attention by Children and Their
        Caregivers. Developmental Psychology 35(4):1079–1090.

CHEN, LINCOLN C., A. K. M. A. CHOWDHURY, AND SANDRA L. HUFFMAN

1981   The Use of Anthropometry for Nutritional Surveillance in Mortality
        Control Programs. American Journal of Clinical Nutrition 34(11):
        2596–2599.

CHENEY, DOROTHY, AND ROBERT SEYFARTH

2007   Baboon Metaphysics: The Evolution of a Social Mind. Chicago, IL:
        University of Chicago Press.

CHICK, GARRY

2010   Work, Play, and Learning. *In* The Anthropology of Learning in Childhood. David F. Lancy, John C. Bock, and Suzanne Gaskins, eds. Pp. 119–143. Lanham, MD: Rowman & Littlefield.

CHIPENIUK, RAYMOND

1995   Childhood Foraging as a Means of Acquiring Competent Human Cognition about Biodiversity. Environment and Behavior 27(4):490–512.

CHISHOLM, JAMES S.

1993   Death, Hope, and Sex: Life-History Theory and the Development of Reproductive Strategies. Current Anthropology 34(1):1–24.

1999   Death, Hope, and Sex: Steps to an Evolutionary Ecology of Mind and Morality. New York: Cambridge University Press.

CHO, GEUM JOON, JUNG-HO SHIN, KYONG WOOK YI, HYUN TAE PARK, TAK KIM, JUN YOUNG HUR, SUN HAENG KIM

2012   Adolescent Pregnancy Is Associated with Osteoporosis in Postmenopausal Women. Menopause 19(4):456–460.

CHOI, JUNG-KYOO, AND SAMUEL BOWLES

2007   The Coevolution of Parochial Altruism and War. Science 318(5850):636–640.

CINCOTTA, NANCY F.

2008   The Journey of Middle Childhood: Who Are "Latency"-Age Children? *In* Developmental Theories Through the Life Cycle, 2nd edition. Sonia G. Austrian, ed. Pp. 79–131. New York: Columbia University Press.

CLUM, NANCY J., MARIANNE P. FITZPATRICK, AND ELLEN S. DIERENFELD

1996   Effects of Diet on Nutritional Content of Whole Vertebrate Prey. Zoo Biology 15(5):525–537.

CLUTTON-BROCK, TIM

2002   Breeding Together: Kin Selection and Mutualism in Cooperative Vertebrates. Science 296(5565):69–72.

COCKBURN, ANDREW

2004   Mating Systems and Sexual Conflict. *In* Ecology and Evolution of Cooperative Breeding in Birds. Walter D. Koenig and Janis L. Dickson, eds. Pp. 81–101. Cambridge: Cambridge University Press.

CODDING, BRIAN F., REBECCA BLIEGE BIRD, AND DOUGLAS W. BIRD

2011   Provisioning Offspring and Others: Risk-Energy Trade-Offs and Gender Differences in Hunter-Gatherer Foraging Strategies. Proceedings of the Royal Society B 278(1717):2502–2509.

COFRAN, ZACHARY, AND J. DESILVA

2013   Early Postnatal Brain Growth in *Homo Erectus*: Incorporating Uncertainties. Abstract. American Journal of Physical Anthropology, Supplement 56:99.

CONKLIN-BRITTAIN, NANCY LOU, CHERYL D. KNOTT, AND
RICHARD W. WRANGHAM

2006   Energy Intake by Wild Chimpanzees and Orangutans: Methodological
        Considerations and a Preliminary Comparison. *In* Feeding Ecology in
        Apes and Other Primates: Ecological, Physical, and Behavioral Aspects.
        Gottfried Hohmann, Martha M. Robbins, and Christophe Boesch, eds.
        Pp. 445–471. Cambridge: Cambridge University Press.

CONLEY, ALAN J., ROBIN M. BERNSTEIN, AND ANN D. NGUYEN

2012   Adrenarche in Non-Human Primates: The Evidence for It and the Need to
        Re-define It. Journal of Endocrinology 214(2):121–131.

CONLEY ALAN J., B. C. MOELLER, ANN D. NGUYEN, S. D. STANLEY, T. M. PLANT,
AND DAVID H. ABBOTT

2011   Defining Adrenarche in the Rhesus Macaque (*Macaca mulatta*), a Non-
        Human Primate Model for Adrenal Androgen Secretion. Molecular and
        Cellular Endocrinology 336(1–2):110–116.

CONLEY, ALAN J., CHRISTINA J. PATTISON, AND IAN M. BIRD

2004   Variations in Adrenal Androgen Production among (Nonhuman)
        Primates. Seminars in Reproductive Medicine 22(4):311–326.

COPELAND, KENNETH C., JORG W. EICHBERG, C. RICHARD PARKER JR., AND
ANDZRE J. BARTKE

1985   Puberty in the Chimpanzee: Somatomedin-C and Its Relationship to
        Somatic Growth and Steroid Hormone Concentrations. Journal of Clinical
        Endocrinology and Metabolism 60(6):1154–1160.

COPELAND, KENNETH C., THOMAS J. KUEHL, AND V. DANIEL CASTRACANE

1982   Pubertal Endocrinology of the Baboon: Elevated Somatomedin C/Insulin-
        Like Growth Factor I at Puberty. Journal of Clinical Endocrinology and
        Metabolism 55(6):1198–1201.

COQUEUGNIOT, HÉLÈNE, AND JEAN-JACQUES HUBLIN

2007   Endocranial Volume and Brain Growth in Immature Neandertals.
        Periodicum Biologorum 109(4):379–385.

COQUEUGNIOT, HÉLÈNE, JEAN-JACQUES HUBLIN, F. VEILLON, F. HOUËT, AND
T. JACOB

2004   Early Brain Growth in *Homo erectus* and Implications for Cognitive
        Ability. Nature 431:299–302.

COULTER, C. L., AND V. K. M. HAN

1996   Expression of Insulin-Like Growth Factor-II and IGF-binding Protein-1
        mRNAs in Term Rhesus Monkey Placenta: Comparison with Human
        Placenta. Hormone Research 45(3–5):167–171.

CRESPI, BERNARD

2014   The Insectan Apes. Human Nature 25:6–27.

CREWS, DOUGLAS E.

2003   Human Senescence: Evolutionary and Biocultural Perspectives. Cambridge: Cambridge University Press.

2007   Senescence, Aging, and Disease. Journal of Physiological Anthropology 26(3):365–372.

CRITTENDEN, ALYSSA N.

2009   Allomaternal Care and Juvenile Foraging among the Hadza: Implications for the Evolution of Cooperative Breeding in Humans. PhD dissertation, Department of Anthropology, University of California, San Diego.

2011   The Importance of Honey Consumption in Human Evolution. Food and Foodways 19: 257–273.

2014a   Etnografía de los Hadza: su importancia para la evolución humana. *In* La Cuna de la Humanidad (Cradle of Humanity). Enrique Baquedano, ed. Pp. 209–220. Madrid: Instituto de Evolución en África (IDEA) and Museo Nacional de Antropología.

2014b   Evolutionary Studies of Childhood. Oxford Bibliographies in Childhood Studies. Heather Montgomery, ed. New York: Oxford University Press.

2016   Ethnobotany in Evolutionary Perspective: Wild Plants in Diet Composition and Daily Use among Hadza Hunter-Gatherers. *In* Wild Harvest: Plants in the Hominin and Pre-agrarian Human Worlds. Karen Hardy and Lucy Kubiak-Martens, eds. Pp. 319–339. Oxford: Oxford University Press.

CRITTENDEN, ALYSSA N., NANCY L. CONKLIN-BRITTAIN, DAVID A. ZES, MARGARET J. SCHOENINGER, AND FRANK W. MARLOWE

2013   Juvenile Foraging among the Hadza: Implications for Human Life History. Evolution and Human Behavior 34:299–304.

CRITTENDEN, ALYSSA N., AND FRANK W. MARLOWE

2008   Allomaternal Care among the Hadza of Tanzania. Human Nature 19(3):249–262.

2013   Cooperative Care among the Hadza: Situating Multiple Attachment in Evolutionary Context. *In* Attachment Reconsidered: Cultural Perspectives on a Western Theory. Naomi Quinn and Jeannette Marie Mageo, eds. Pp. 67–84. New York: Palgrave Macmillan.

CRITTENDEN, ALYSSA N., RICHARD WRANGHAM, FRANK W. MARLOWE, NANCY L. CONKLIN-BRITTAIN, AND MARGARET J. SCHOENINGER

2009   Foraging Strategies and Diet Composition of Hadza Children [abstract]. American Journal of Physical Anthropology 138(S48):112.

CRITTENDEN, ALYSSA N., AND DAVID A. ZES

2015   Food Sharing among Hadza Hunter-Gatherer Children. PLoS ONE 10(7):e0131996. doi:10.1371/journal.pone.0131996

CRITTENDEN, ALYSSA N., DAVID A. ZES, AND FRANK W. MARLOWE
2010   Juvenile Food-Sharing among the Hadza Hunter-Gatherers of Tanzania.
        American Journal of Physical Anthropology 141(Suppl. 50):87–88.

CRNIC, KEITH A., MARK T. GREENBERG, ARLENE S. RAGOZIN,
NANCY M. ROBINSON, AND ROBERT B. BASHAM
1983   Effects of Stress and Social Support on Mothers and Premature and Full-
        Term Infants. Child Development 54(1):209–217.

CROGNIER, EMILE, A. BAAIL, AND MOHAMED K. HILALI
2001   Do "Helpers-at-the-Nest" Increase Their Parents' Reproductive Success?
        American Journal of Human Biology 13:(3)365–373.

CROGNIER, EMILE, M. VILLENA, AND E. VARGAS
2002   Helping Patterns and Reproductive Success in Aymara Communities.
        American Journal of Human Biology 14(3):372–379.

CRONIN, KATHERINE A., KORI K. E. SCHROEDER, AND CHARLES T. SNOWDON
2010   Prosocial Behaviour Emerges Independent of Reciprocity in Cottontop
        Tamarins. Proceedings of the Royal Society B 277(1701):3845–3851.

CSIBRA, GERGELY, AND GYÖRGY GERGELY
2011   Natural Pedagogy as Evolutionary Adaptation. Philosophical Transactions
        of the Royal Society B 366:1149–1157.

CULOT, LAURENCE, YVAN LIEDO-FERRER, ODA HOELSCHER, FERNANDO J. J.
MUÑOZ LAZO, MARIE-CLAUDE HUYNEN, AND ECKARD W. HEYMANN
2011   Reproductive Failure, Possible Maternal Infanticide, and Cannibalism in
        Wild Moustached Tamarins, *Saguinus mystax*. Primates 52:179–186.

CUTLER, GORDON B., JR., MICHAEL GLENN, MITCHELL BUSH, GARY D. HODGEN,
CHARLES E. GRAHAM, AND D. LYNN LORIAUX
1978   Adrenarche: A Survey of Rodents, Domestic Animals, and Primates.
        Endocrinology 103(6):2112–2118.

D'ANDRADE, ROY G.
1984   Cultural Meaning Systems. *In* Culture Theory: Essays on Mind, Self, and
        Emotion. Richard A. Shweder and Robert A. LeVine, eds. Pp. 88–119.
        Cambridge: Cambridge University Press.

DARWIN, CHARLES
1877   A Biographical Sketch of an Infant. Mind: Quarterly Review of Psychology
        and Philosophy 2(7):285–294.

1974   Descent of Man and Selection in Relation to Sex. Chicago, IL: Rand/
[1874] McNally.

1998   The Expression of Emotions in Man and Animals. Oxford: Oxford
[1872] University Press.

DEAN, L. G., R. L. KENDAL, S. J. SCHAPIRO, B. THIERRY, AND K. N. LALAND
2012   Identification of the Social and Cognitive Processes Underlying Human
        Cumulative Culture. Science 335(6072):1114–1118.

DEAN, M. CHRISTOPHER
1989   The Developing Dentition and Tooth Structure in Hominoids. Folia
        Primatologica 53(1–4):160–176.

DEAN, M. CHRISTOPHER, MEAVE G. LEAKEY, DONALD REID, FRIEDEMANN
SCHRENK, GARY T. SCHWARTZ, CHRISTOPHER STRINGER, AND ALAN WALKER
2001   Growth Processes in Teeth Distinguish Modern Humans from *Homo
        erectus* and Earlier Hominins. Nature 414:628–631.

DEAN, M. CHRISTOPHER, AND B. HOLLY SMITH
2009   Growth and Development of the Nariokotome Youth, KNM-WT 15000.
        In The First Humans: Origin and Early Evolution of the Genus *Homo*.
        Frederick E. Grine, John G. Fleagle, and Richard E. Leakey, eds. Pp. 101–
        120. New York: Springer.

DEJAEGER, DOMINIQUE, PATRICK A. WILLEMS, AND NORMAN C. HEGLUND
2001   The Energy Cost of Walking in Children. Pflügers Archiv: European
        Journal of Physiology 441(4):538–543.

DEROUSSEAU, C. JEAN
1990   Life History Thinking in Perspective. *In* Primate Life History and
        Evolution. C. Jean DeRousseau ed. Pp. 1–13. New York: Wiley-Liss.

DESILVA, JEREMY M.
2011   A Shift toward Birthing Relatively Large Infants Early in Human
        Evolution. Proceedings of the National Academy of Sciences
        108(3):1022–1027.

DETTWYLER, KATHERINE A.
1995   A Time to Wean: The Hominid Blueprint for the Natural Age of Weaning
        in Modern Human Populations. *In* Breastfeeding: Biocultural Perspectives.
        Patricia Stuart-Macadam and Katherine A. Dettwyler, eds. Pp. 39–73. New
        York: Aldine de Gruyter.

DE WAAL, FRANS
2006   Morally Evolved: Primate Social Instinct, Human Morality and the Rise
        and Fall of "Veneer Theory" (Part I). *In* Primates and Philosophers: How
        Morality Evolved. Pp. 1–58. Princeton, NJ: Princeton University Press.

2012   A Bottom-Up View of Empathy. *In* The Primate Mind: Built to Connect
        with Other Minds. Frans de Waal and P. Francesco Ferrari, eds. Pp. 121–
        138. Cambridge, MA: Harvard University Press.

2013   The Bonobo and the Atheist. New York: Norton.

DE WAAL, FRANS, AND P. FRANCESCO FERRARI, EDS.

2012   The Primate Mind: Built to Connect with Other Minds. Cambridge, MA: Harvard University Press.

DEWEY, KATHRYN G.

2003   Guiding Principles for Complementary Feeding of the Breastfed Child. Washington, DC: Pan-American Health Organization.

2013   The Challenge of Meeting Nutrient Needs of Infants and Young Children during the Period of Complementary Feeding: An Evolutionary Perspective. Journal of Nutrition 143(12):2050–2054.

DHOM, G.

1973   The Prepubertal and Pubertal Growth of the Adrenal (Adrenarche). Beitrage Zur Pathologie 150:357–377.

DIGBY, LESLIE J., STEPHEN F. FERRARI, AND WENDY SALTZMAN

2007   Callitrichines: The Role of Competition in Cooperatively Breeding Species. *In* Primates in Perspective. Christina Campbell, Agustin Fuentes, Katherine C. MacKinnon, Melissa Panger, and Simon Bearder, eds. Pp. 85–105. Oxford: Oxford University Press.

DIGIROLAMO, ANN M., LAURENCE M. GRUMMER-STRAWN, AND SARA B. FEIN

2008   Effect of Maternity-Care Practices on Breastfeeding. Pediatrics 122(Suppl. 2):43–49.

DITTAMI, JOHN P.

1986   Seasonal Reproduction, Moult, and Their Endocrine Correlates in Two Tropical Ploceidae Species. Journal of Comparative Physiology B 156(5):641–647.

DOMINICI, NADIA, YURI P. IVANENKO, GERMANA CAPPELINA, ANDREA D'AVELLA, VITO MONDI, MARIKA CICCHESE, ADELE FABIANO, ET AL.

2011   Locomotor Primitives in Newborn Babies and Their Development. Science 334(6058):997–999.

DONALD, MERLIN

1991   Origins of the Modern Mind: Three Stages in the Evolution of Culture and Cognition. Cambridge, MA: Harvard University Press.

DONOVAN, S. M., AND J. ODLE

1994   Growth Factors in Milk as Mediators of Infant Development. Annual Review of Nutrition 14:147–167.

DRAPER, PATRICIA

1972   !Kung Bushman Childhood. PhD dissertation, Department of Anthropology, Harvard University.

1976   Social and Economic Constraints on Child Life among the !Kung. *In* Kalahari Hunter-Gatherers: Studies of the !Kung San and Their Neighbors.

Richard B. Lee and Irven DeVore, eds. Pp. 199–217. Cambridge, MA: Harvard University Press.

1978   The Learning Environment for Aggression and Anti-Social Behavior among the !Kung (Kalahari Desert, Botswana, Africa). *In* Learning Non-Aggression: The Experience of Non-Literate Societies. Ashley Montagu, ed. Pp. 31–53. New York: Oxford University Press.

DRAPER, PATRICIA, AND ELIZABETH CASHDAN
1988   Technological Change and Child Behavior among the !Kung. Ethnology 27(4):339–365.

DUGSTAD, SOGROD A.
2008   Early Child Caught Knapping: A Novice Early Mesolithic Flintknapper in South-West Norway. *In* Proceedings from the 2nd International Conference of the Society for the Study of Childhood in the Past. Pp. 65–74. Stavanger, Norway: University of Stavanger.

DUIJTS, LIESBETH, VINCENT W. V. JODDOE, ALBERT HOFMAN, AND
HENRIËTTE A. MOLL
2010   Prolonged and Exclusive Breastfeeding Reduces the Risk of Infectious Diseases in Infancy. Pediatrics 126(1):18–25.

EARLY, JOHN D., AND THOMAS N. HEADLAND
1998   Population Dynamics of a Philippine Rain Forest People: The San Ildefonso Agta. Gainesville: University Press of Florida.

EATON, JOSEPH W., AND ALBERT J. MAYER
1953   The Social Biology of Very High Fertility among the Hutterites: The Demography of a Unique Population. Human Biology 25(3):206–264.

EDEL, MAY M.
1996   The Chiga of Uganda, 2nd edition. New Brunswick, NJ: Transaction
[1957] Publishers.

EDMOND, KAREN M., CHARLES ZANDOH, MARIA A. QUIGLEY,
SEEBA AMENGA-ETEGO, SETH OWUSU-AGYEI, AND BETTY R. KIRKWOOD
2006   Delayed Breastfeeding Initiation Increases Risk of Neonatal Mortality. Pediatrics 117(3):380–386.

EIDEH, HASAN, BJORN JONSSON, AND ZE'EV HOCHBERG
2012   Growth of the Kalahari Desert's Bushman—The Ju/'hoansi San. Acta Paediatrica 101(5):528–532.

EINARSDOTTIR, JONINA
2004   Tired of Weeping: Mother Love, Child Death, and Poverty in Guinea-Bissau. Madison: University of Wisconsin Press.

ELIAS, CYNTHIA L. AND LAURA E. BERK
2002   Self-Regulation in Young Children: Is There a Role for Sociodramatic Play? Early Childhood Research Quarterly 17(2):216–238.

ELLIS, BRUCE J.
2004   Timing of Pubertal Maturation in Girls: An Integrated Life History
         Approach. Psychological Bulletin 130(6):920–958.

ELLISON, PETER T.
2001   On Fertile Ground: A Natural History of Human Reproduction.
         Cambridge, MA: Harvard University Press.

ELMENDORF, MARY L.
1976   Nine Mayan Women: A Village Faces Change. Cambridge, MA:
         Schenkman.

ELOWSON, A. MARGARET, CHARLES T. SNOWDON, AND CRISTINA LAZARO-PEREA
1998   "Babbling" and Social Context in Infant Monkeys: Parallels to Human
         Infants. Trends in Cognitive Science 2:31–37.

EL ZAATARI, SIREEN, FREDERICK E. GRINE, PETER S. UNGAR, AND JEAN-JACQUES
HUBLIN
2011   Ecogeographic Variation in Neandertal Dietary Habits: Evidence from
         Occlusal Molar Microwear Texture Analysis. Journal of Human Evolution
         61(4):411–424.

EMLEN, STEPHEN T.
1995   An Evolutionary Theory of the Family. Proceedings of the National
         Academy of Sciences 92(18): 8092–8099.

ENSTAM, KARIN L., LYNNE A. ISBELL, AND THOMAS W. DE MAAR
2002   Male Demography, Female Mating Behavior, and Infanticide in Wild Patas
         Monkeys (*Erythrocebus patas*). International Journal of Primatology
         23(1):85–104.

ESTIOKO-GRIFFIN, AGNES A.
1985   Women as Hunters: The Case of an Eastern Cagayan Agta Group. *In* The
         Agta of Northeastern Luzon: Recent Studies. P. Bion Griffin and Agnes
         Estioko-Griffin, eds. Cebu City, Philippines: University of San Carlos.

ESTIOKO-GRIFFIN, AGNES, AND P. BION GRIFFIN
1981   Woman the Hunter: The Agta. *In* Woman the Gatherer. Frances Dahlberg,
         ed. Pp. 121–151. New Haven, CT: Yale University Press.

EULER, HAROLD A., SABINE HOIER, AND PERCY A. ROHDE
2009   Relationship-Specific Intergenerational Family Ties: An Evolutionary
         Approach to the Structure of Cultural Transmission. *In* Cultural
         Transmission: Psychological, Developmental, Social, and Methodological
         Aspects. Ute Schönpflug, ed. Pp. 70–91. Cambridge: Cambridge University
         Press.

EULER, HAROLD A., AND BARBARA WEITZEL
1996   Discriminative Grandparental Solicitude as a Reproductive Strategy.
         Human Nature 7(1):39–59.

FAIRBANKS, LYNN A.

1990   Reciprocal Benefits of Allomothering for Female Vervet Monkeys. Animal
        Behaviour 40(3):553–562.

FAJANS, JANE

1997   They Make Themselves: Work and Play among the Baining of Papua New
        Guinea. Chicago, IL: University of Chicago Press.

FALGUÉRES, CHRISTOPHE, JEAN-JACQUES BAHAIN, YUJI YOLOYAMA,
JUAN L. ARSUAGA, JOSÉ MARÍA BERMÚDEZ DE CASTRO, EUDALD CARBONELL,
JAMES L. BISCHOFF, AND JEAN-MICHEL DOLO

1999   Earliest Humans in Europe: The Age of TD6 Gran Dolina, Atapuerca,
        Spain. Journal of Human Evolution 37(3–4):343–352.

FALK, DEAN

2004a   Prelinguistic Evolution in Early Hominins: Whence Motherese? Behavioral
        and Brain Sciences 27:491–503, 531–541.

2004b   The "Putting the Baby Down" Hypothesis: Bipedalism, Babbling, and Baby
        Slings. Behavioral and Brain Sciences 27:526–541.

FALK, DEAN, CHRISTOPHE P. E. ZOLLIKOFER, NAOKI MORIMOTO, AND
MARCIA S. PONCE DE LEÓN

2012   Metopic Suture of Taung (*Australopithecus africanus*) and Its Implications
        for Hominin Brain Evolution. Proceedings of the National Academy of
        Sciences 109(22):8467–8470.

FAULKES, CHRIS G., AND NIGEL C. BENNETT

2007   African Mole-Rats: Social and Ecological Diversity. *In* Rodent Societies:
        An Ecological and Evolutionary Perspective. Jerry. O. Wolff and Paul. W.
        Sherman, eds. Pp. 427–437. Chicago, IL: University of Chicago Press.

FEHR, ERNST, HELEN BERNHARD, AND BETTINA ROCKENBACH

2008   Egalitarianism in Young Children. Nature 454:1079–1084.

FEHR, ERNST, AND URS FISCHBACHER

2003   The Nature of Human Altruism. Nature 425:785–791.

FINE, GARY A.

1987   With the Boys: Little League Baseball and Preadolescent Culture. Chicago,
        IL: University of Chicago Press.

FISHER, RONALD A.

1930   The Genetical Theory of Natural Selection. New York: Dover Publications.

FLINN, MARK V.

2005   Culture and Developmental Plasticity. *In* Evolutionary Perspectives
        on Human Development, 2nd edition. Robert L. Burgess and Kevin
        MacDonald, eds. Pp. 73–98. Thousand Oaks, CA: Sage.

FLINN, MARK V., AND RICHARD D. ALEXANDER

2007   Runaway Social Selection in Human Evolution. *In* The Evolution of Mind:

Fundamental Questions and Controversies. S. Gangestad and J. Simpson, eds. Pp. 269–279. New York: Guilford Press.

FLINN, MARK V., AND CAROL V. WARD

2005   Ontogeny and Evolution of the Social Child. *In* Origins of the Social Mind: Evolutionary Psychology and Child Development. Bruce J. Ellis and David F. Bjorklund, eds. Pp. 19–44. New York: Guilford Press.

FORTES, MEYER

1970   Social and Psychological Aspects of Education in Taleland. *In* From Child
[1938]   to Adult: Studies in the Anthropology of Education. John Middleton, ed. Pp.14–74. Garden City, NY: Natural History Press.

FOUTS, HILLARY N.

2004   Social and Emotional Contexts of Weaning among Bofi Farmers and Foragers. Ethnology 43(1):65–81.

2008   Father Involvement with Young Children among the Aka and Bofi Foragers. Cross-Cultural Research 42(3):290–312.

FOUTS, HILLARY N., AND ROBYN A. BROOKSHIRE

2009   Who Feeds Children? A Child's-Eye-View of Caregiver Feeding Patterns among the Aka Foragers in Congo. Social Science & Medicine 69(2):285–292.

FOUTS, HILLARY N., BARRY S. HEWLETT, AND MICHAEL E. LAMB

2001   Weaning and the Nature of Early Childhood Interactions among Bofi Foragers in Central Africa. Human Nature 12(1):27–46.

2005   Parent-Offspring Weaning Conflicts among the Bofi Farmers and Foragers of Central Africa. Current Anthropology 46(1):29–50.

2012   A Biocultural Approach to Breastfeeding Interactions in Central Africa. American Anthropologist 114(1):123–136.

FOUTS, HILLARY N., AND MICHAEL E. LAMB

2005   Weaning Emotional Patterns among the Bofi Foragers of Central Africa: The Role of Maternal Availability and Sensitivity. *In* Hunter-Gatherer Childhoods: Evolutionary, Developmental, and Cultural Perspectives. Barry S. Hewlett and Michael E. Lamb, eds. Pp. 309–321. New Brunswick, NJ: AldineTransaction.

FOUTS, ROGER, WITH STEPHEN TUKEL MILLS

1997   Next of Kin: My Conversations with Chimpanzees. New York: Harper.

FOX, ROBIN

1984   Kinship and Marriage. Harmondsworth, UK: Penguin Books.

FREEMAN, DEREK

1970   Report on the Iban (Sarawak). New York: Humanities Press.

1983   Margaret Mead and Samoa: The Making and Unmaking of an Anthropological Myth. Cambridge, MA: Harvard University Press.

FRIEDL, ERIKA
1997   Children of Deh Koh: Young Life in an Iranian Village. Syracuse, NY:
            Syracuse University Press.

FRY, DOUGLAS P.
2005   Rough-and-Tumble Social Play in Humans. *In* The Nature of Play: Great
            Apes and Humans. Anthony D. Pellegrini and Peter K. Smith, eds.
            Pp. 54–85. New York: Guilford Press.

FU, GENYUE, AND KANG LEE
2007   Social Grooming in the Kindergarten: The Emergence of Flattery Behavior.
            Developmental Science 10(2):255–265.

FURMAN, WYNDOL, AND DUANE BUHRMESTER
1992   Age and Sex Differences in Perceptions of Networks of Personal
            Relationships. Child Development 63(1):103–115.

GABUNIA, LEO, ABESALOM VEKUA, DAVID LORDKIPANIDZE, CARL C. SWISHER,
REID FERRING, ANTJE JUSTUS, MEDEA NIORADZE, ET AL.
2000   Earliest Pleistocene Hominid Cranial Remains from Dmanisi, Republic of
            Georgia: Taxonomy, Geological Setting, and Age. Science 288:1019–1025.

GADGIL, MADHAV, AND WILLIAM H. BOSSERT
1970   Life Historical Consequences of Natural Selection. American Naturalist
            104(935):1–24.

GALDIKAS, BIRUTÉ M. F., AND JAMES W. WOOD
1990   Birth Spacing Patterns in Humans and Apes. American Journal of Physical
            Anthropology 83(2):185–191.

GALLIMORE, RONALD, ALAN HOWARD, AND CATHIE JORDAN
1969   Independence Training among Hawaiians: A Cross Cultural Study. *In*
            Contemporary Research in Social Psychology. Henry Clay Lindgren, ed.
            Pp. 392–397. New York: Wiley and Sons.

GARBER, PAUL
1997   One for All and Breeding for One: Cooperation and Competition as a
            Tamarin Reproductive Strategy. Evolutionary Anthropology 5(6):187–199.

GARCÍA COLL, CYNTHIA T., AND HEIDIE A. VÁZQUEZ GARCÍA
1996   Definitions of Competence During Adolescence: Lessons from Puerto
            Rican Adolescent Mothers. *In* Adolescence: Opportunities and Challenges,
            vol. 7. Dante Cicchetti and Sheree L. Toth, eds. Pp. 283–308. Rochester, NY:
            University of Rochester Press.

GASKINS, SUZANNE
2014   Pretend Play as Culturally Constructed Activity. *In* The Oxford Handbook
            of the Development of Imagination. Marjorie Tyler, ed. Pp. 224–247. New
            York: Oxford University Press.

GASKINS, SUZANNE, WENDY HAIGHT, AND DAVID F. LANCY
2007   The Cultural Construction of Play. *In* Play and Development: Evolutionary,

Sociocultural, and Functional Perspectives. Artin Göncü and Suzanne Gaskins, eds. Pp. 179–202. New York: Taylor and Francis.

GASKINS, SUZANNE, AND RUTH PARADISE
2010   Learning through Observation in Daily Life. *In* The Anthropology of Learning in Childhood. David F. Lancy, Suzanne Gaskins, and John Bock, eds. Pp. 85–117. Lanham, MD: AltaMira Press.

GETTLER, LEE T., THOMAS W. MCDADE, ALAN B. FERANIL, AND CHRISTOPHER W. KUZAWA
2011   Longitudinal Evidence that Fatherhood Decreases Testosterone in Human Males. Proceedings of the National Academy of Sciences 108(39):16194–16199.

GIBSON, MHAIRI, AND RUTH MACE
2005   Helpful Grandmothers in Rural Ethiopia: A Study of the Effect of Kin on Child Survival and Growth. Evolution and Human Behavior 26(6):469–482.

GIUDICE, MARCO DEL, AND JAY BELSKY
2011   The Development of Life-History Strategies: Toward a Multi-Stage Theory. *In* The Evolution of Personality and Individual Differences. David M. Buss and Patricia H. Hawley, eds. Pp. 154–176. Oxford: Oxford University Press.

GIVÓN, TOM
2005   Context as Other Minds: The Pragmatics of Sociality, Cognition, and Communication. Amsterdam: John Benjamins Publishing Company.

GLADWIN, THOMAS
1970   East Is a Big Bird: Navigation and Logic on Puluwat Atoll. Cambridge, MA: Harvard University Press.

GLOCKER, MELANIE L., DANIEL D. LANGLEBEN, KOSHA RUPAREL, JAMES W. LOUGHEAD, JEFFREY N. VALDEZ, MARK D. GRIFFIN, NORBERT SACHSER, AND RUBEN C. GUR
2009   Baby Schema Modulates the Brain Reward System in Nulliparous Women. Proceedings of the National Academy of Sciences 106(22):9115–9119.

GOLDMAN, LAURENCE R.
1998   Child's Play: Myth, Mimesis, and Make-Believe. Oxford: Berg.

GOLDSCHMIDT, WALTER
2006   The Bridge to Humanity: How Affect Hunger Trumps the Selfish Gene. Oxford: Oxford University Press.

GOLDSTEIN, MICHAEL H., ANDREW P. KING, AND MEREDITH J. WEST
2003   Social Interaction Shapes Babbling: Testing Parallels between Birdsong and Speech. Proceedings of the National Academy of Sciences 100(13):8030–8035.

GONCHAROVA, N. D., AND B. A. LAPIN

2000   Changes of Hormonal Function of the Adrenal and Gonadal Glands
        in Baboons of Different Age Groups. Journal of Medical Primatology
        29:26–35.

GÖNCÜ, ARTIN, AND SUZANNE GASKINS

2007   Play and Development: Evolutionary, Sociocultural, and Functional
        Perspectives. New York: Taylor and Francis.

GOODMAN, MADELEINE J., P. BION GRIFFIN, AGNES A. ESTIOKO-GRIFFIN, AND
JOHN S. GROVE

1985   The Compatibility of Hunting and Mothering among the Agta Hunter-
        Gatherers of the Philippines. Sex Roles 12(11–12):1199–1209.

GOODWIN, GRENVILLE, AND JANICE T. GOODWIN

1942   The Social Organization of the Western Apache. Chicago, IL: University of
        Chicago Press.

GOODY, ESTHER N.

1992   From Play to Work: Adults and Peers as Scaffolders of Adult Role Skills in
        Northern Ghana. Paper presented at the Annual Meeting of the American
        Anthropological Association, San Francisco, CA, December 2–6.

2006   Dynamics of the Emergence of Sociocultural Institutional Practices. *In*
        Technology, Literacy, and the Evolution of Society. David R. Olson and
        Michael Cole, eds. Pp. 241–264. Mahwah, NJ: Erlbaum.

GOODY, JACK

1977   The Domestication of the Savage Mind. Cambridge: Cambridge University
        Press.

GOPNIK, ALISON

2010   The Philosophical Baby. New York: Farrar, Straus, and Giroux.

2012   Scientific Thinking in Young Children: Theoretical Advances, Empirical
        Research, and Policy Implications. Science 337(6102):1623–1627.

GOPNIK, ALISON, ANDREW N. MELTZOFF, AND PATRICIA K. KUHL

2000   The Scientist in the Crib: What Early Learning Tells Us about the Mind.
        New York: Harper.

GORER, GEOFFREY

1967   Himalayan Village: An Account of the Lepchas of Sikkim. New York: Basic
        Books.

GOSSO, YUMI, EMMA OTTA, MARIA DE LIMA SALUM E MORAIS,
FERNANDO JOSÉ LEITE RIBEIRO, AND VERA SILVIA RAAD BUSSAB

2005   Play in Hunter-Gatherer Society. *In* The Nature of Play: Great Apes and
        Humans. Anthony D. Pellegrini and Peter K. Smith, eds. Pp. 213–254. New
        York: Guilford Press.

GOTTLIEB, ALMA

2004   The Afterlife Is Where We Come From: The Culture of Infancy in West
           Africa. Chicago, IL: University of Chicago Press.

GOULD, STEPHEN J.

1977   Ontogeny and Phylogeny. Cambridge, MA: Harvard University Press.

GRAJEDA, R., R. PÉREZ-ESCAMILLA, AND K. G. DEWEY

1997   Delayed Clamping of the Umbilical Cord Improves Hematologic Status
           of Guatemalan Infants at 2 Mo of Age. American Journal of Clinical
           Nutrition 65(2):425–431.

GRAY, PETER

2009   Play as a Foundation for Hunter-Gatherer Social Existence. American
           Journal of Play 1(4):476–522.

2013a   Free to Learn: Why Unleashing the Instinct to Play Will Make Our
           Children Happier, More Self-Reliant, and Better Prepared for Life. New
           York: Basic Books.

2013b   The Value of a Play-Filled Childhood in Development of the Hunter-
           Gatherer Individual. *In* Evolution, Early Experience, and Human
           Development: From Research to Practice and Policy. Darcia Narváez, Jaak
           Panksepp, Allan N. Schore, and Tracy R. Gleason, eds. Pp. 352–370. New
           York: Oxford University Press.

2014   The Play Theory of Hunter-Gatherer Egalitarianism. *In* Ancestral
           Landscapes in Human Evolution: Culture, Childrearing, and Social
           Well-being. Darcia Narváez, Kristin Valentino, Agustin Fuentes, James J.
           McKenna, and Peter Gray, eds. Pp. 192–215. New York: Oxford University
           Press.

GREEN, RICHARD E., JOHANNES KRAUSE, ADRIAN W. BRIGGS, TOMISLAV MARICIC,
UDO STENZEL, MARTIN KIRCHER, NICK PATTERSON, ET AL.

2010   A Draft Sequence of the Neandertal Genome. Science 328(5979):710–722.

GREGOR, THOMAS.

1988   Mehinaku: The Drama of Daily Life in a Brazilian Indian Village. Chicago,
           IL: University of Chicago Press.

GRIFFIN, P. BION, AND AGNES ESTIOKO-GRIFFIN.

1985   The Agta of Northeastern Luzon. Cebu City, Philippines: University of San
           Carlos.

GRIFFIN, P. BION, AND MARCUS B. GRIFFIN

1992   Fathers and Childcare among the Cagayan Agta. *In* Father-Child Relations:
           Cultural and Biosocial Contexts. Barry S. Hewlett, ed. Pp. 297–320. New
           Brunswick, NJ: AldineTransaction.

GRILNER, STEN

2011   Human Locomotor Circuits Conform. Science 334(6058):912–913.

GRINDAL, BRUCE T.

1972   Growing Up in Two Worlds: Education and Transition among the Sisala of Northern Ghana. New York: Holt, Rinehart, and Winston.

GROOS, KARL

1901   The Play of Man. Elizabeth L. Baldwin, trans. New York: D. Appleton and Company.

GUATELLI-STEINBERG, DEBBIE

2009   Recent Studies of Dental Development in Neandertals: Implications for Neandertal Life Histories. Evolutionary Anthropology 18(1):9–20.

GUATELLI-STEINBERG, DEBBIE, DONALD J. REID, AND THOMAS A. BISHOP

2007   Did the Lateral Enamel of Neandertal Anterior Teeth Grow Differently from That of Modern Humans? Journal of Human Evolution 52(1):72–84.

GUATELLI-STEINBERG, DEBBIE, DONALD J. REID, THOMAS A. BISHOP, AND CLARK S. LARSEN

2005   Anterior Tooth Growth Periods in Neandertals Were Comparable to Those of Modern Humans. Proceedings of the National Academy of Sciences 102(40):14197–14202.

GUNZ, PHILLIP, SIMON NEUBAUER, BRUNO MAUREILLE, AND JEAN-JACQUES HUBLIN

2011   Virtual Reconstruction of Le Moustier 2 Newborn Skull: Implications for Neandertal Ontogeny. Paleo 22:155–172.

GURVEN, MICHAEL, AND HILLARD KAPLAN

2006   Determinants of Time Allocation across the Lifespan. Human Nature 17(1):1–49.

GURVEN, MICHAEL, HILLARD KAPLAN, AND MAGUIN GUTIERREZ

2006   How Long Does It Take to Become a Proficient Hunter? Implications for the Evolution of Extended Development and Long Life Span. Journal of Human Evolution 51(5):454–470.

GURVEN, MICHAEL, AND ROBERT WALKER

2006   Energetic Demand of Multiple Dependents and the Evolution of Slow Human Growth. Proceedings of the Royal Society B 273(1588):835–841.

HADLEY, CHRIS

2004   The Costs and Benefits of Kin: Kin Networks and Children's Health among the Pibwe of Tanzania. Human Nature 15(4):377–395.

HADLEY, CRAIG, CRYSTAL L. PATIL, AND CAROLYN GULAS

2010   Social Learning and Infant and Young Child Feeding Practices. Current Anthropology 51(4):551–560.

HAGEN, EDWARD

1999   The Functions of Postpartum Depression. Evolution and Human Behavior 20(5):325–359.

2002   Depression as Bargaining: The Case Postpartum. Evolution and Human
          Behavior 23(5):323–336.

2003   The Bargaining Model of Depression. *In* Genetic and Cultural Evolution of
          Cooperation. Peter Hammerstein, ed. Pp. 95–123. Cambridge, MA:
          MIT Press.

HAGEN, EDWARD, AND H. CLARK BARRETT
2009   Cooperative Breeding and Adolescent Siblings. Current Anthropology
          50(5):727–737.

HAMANN, KATHARINA, FELIX WARNEKEN, AND MICHAEL TOMASELLO
2011   Collaboration Encourages Equal Sharing in Children but Not in
          Chimpanzees. Nature 476:328–331.

HAMES, RAYMOND, AND PATRICIA DRAPER
2004   Women's Work, Child Care, and Helpers-at-the-Nest in a Hunter-Gatherer
          Society. Human Nature 15(4):319–341.

HAMILTON, ANNETTE
1981   Nature and Nurture: Aboriginal Child-Rearing in North-Central Arnhem
          Land. Canberra: Australian Institute of Aboriginal Studies.

HAMILTON, MARCUS J., OSKAR BURGER, JOHN P. DELONG, ROBERT S. WALKER,
MELANIE E. MOSES, AND JAMES H. BROWN
2009   Population Stability, Cooperation, and the Invasibility of the
          Human Species. Proceedings of the National Academy of Sciences
          106(30):12255–12260.

HAMILTON, WILLIAM D.
1964   Genetical Evolution of Social Behaviour: Parts 1 and 2. Journal of
          Theoretical Biology 7(1):1–52.

1966   The Moulding of Senescence by Natural Selection. Journal of Theoretical
          Biology 12(1):12–45.

HAMLIN, J. KILEY, KAREN WYNN, AND PAUL BLOOM
2007   Social Evaluation by Preverbal Infants. Nature 450:557–559.

2010   Three-Month-Olds Show a Negativity Bias in Their Social Evaluations.
          Developmental Science 13(6):923–929.

HAMLIN, J. KILEY, KAREN WYNN, PAUL BLOOM, AND NEHA MAHAJAN
2011   How Infants and Toddlers React to Antisocial Others. Proceedings of the
          National Academy of Sciences 108(50):19931–19936.

HARE, BRIAN
2012   How Does a More Cooperative Ape Evolve? Plenary Lecture at the Annual
          Meeting of the Human Behavior and Evolution Society, Albuquerque,
          June 15.

HARE, BRIAN, AND S. KWETUENDA

2010   Bonobos Voluntarily Share Their Own Food with Others. Current Biology
        20(5):8230–8231.

HARE, BRIAN, ALICIA P. MELIS, VANESSA WOODS, SARA HASTINGS, AND
RICHARD WRANGHAM

2007   Tolerance Allows Bonobos to Outperform Chimpanzees in a
        Cooperative Task. Current Biology 17(7):619–623.

HARRIS, JUDITH R.

1998   The Nurture Assumption: Why Children Turn Out the Way They Do.
        London: Bloomsbury.

HARTUP, WILLARD W.

1984   The Peer Context in Middle Childhood. *In* Development During Middle
        Childhood: The Years from Six to Twelve. W. Andrew Collins, ed.
        Pp. 240–282. Washington, DC: National Academy Press.

1989   Social Relationships and Their Developmental Significance. American
        Psychologist 44(2):12–126.

1992   Peer Relations in Early and Middle Childhood. *In* Handbook of Social
        Development: A Lifespan Perspective. Vincent B. Van Hasselt and Michel
        Hersen, eds. Pp. 257–281. New York: Plenum Press.

HAUSER, MARC D., M. KEITH CHEN, FRANCES CHEN, AND EMMELINE CHUANG

2003   Give unto Others: Genetically Unrelated Cotton-Top Tamarin Monkeys
        Preferentially Give Food to Those Who Altruistically Give Food Back.
        Proceedings of the Royal Society B 270(1531):2363–2370.

HAWKES, KRISTEN

2003   Grandmothers and the Evolution of Human Longevity. American Journal
        of Human Biology 15(3):380–400.

2006a   Life History Theory and Human Evolution: A Chronicle of Ideas and
        Findings. *In* The Evolution of Human Life History. Kristen Hawkes and
        Richard R. Paine, eds. Pp. 45–93. Santa Fe, NM: School of American
        Research Press.

2006b   Slow Life Histories and Human Evolution. *In* The Evolution of Human Life
        History. Kristen Hawkes and Richard R. Paine, eds. Pp. 95–126. Santa Fe,
        NM: School of American Research Press.

HAWKES, KRISTEN, JAMES F. O'CONNELL, AND NICHOLAS G. BLURTON JONES

1989   Hardworking Hadza Grandmothers. *In* Comparative Socioecology: The
        Behavioral Ecology of Humans and Other Mammals. V. Standen and
        R. A. Foley, eds. Pp. 341–366. London: Basil Blackwell.

1997   Hadza Women's Time Allocation, Offspring Provisioning, and the
            Evolution of Long Postmenopausal Life Spans. Current Anthropology
            38(4):551–577.

HAWKES, KRISTEN, JAMES F. O'CONNELL, NICHOLAS G. BLURTON JONES,
HELEN ALVAREZ, AND ERIC L. CHARNOV
1998   Grandmothering, Menopause, and the Evolution of Human Life Histories.
            Proceedings of the National Academy of Sciences 95(3):1336–1339.

HAWKES, KRISTEN, AND RICHARD PAINE, EDS.
2006   The Evolution of Human Life History. Santa Fe, NM: School of American
            Research Press.

HAWKS, JOHN, KEITH HUNLEY, SANG-HEE LEE, AND MILFORD WOLPOFF
2000   Population Bottlenecks and Pleistocene Evolution. Molecular Biology and
            Evolution 17(1):2–22.

HAYASHI, MISATO, AND TETSURO MATSUZAWA
2003   Cognitive Development in Object Manipulation by Infant Chimpanzees.
            Animal Cognition 6:225–233.

HEADLAND, THOMAS N.
1989   Population Decline in a Philippine Negrito Hunter-Gatherer Society.
            American Journal of Human Biology 1(1):59–72.

HENRICH JOSEPH, AND FRANCISCO GIL-WHITE
2001   The Evolution of Prestige: Freely Conferred Deference as a Mechanism for
            Enhancing the Benefits of Cultural Transmission. Evolution and Human
            Behavior 22(3):65–96.

HENRICH, JOSEPH, STEVEN J. HEINE, AND ARA NORENZAYAN
2010   Most People Are Not WEIRD. Nature 466(7302):29–29.

2010   The Weirdest People in the World? Behavioral and Brain Sciences
            33(2–3):61–81.

HENRY, AMANDA G., ALISON S. BROOKS, AND DOLORES R. PIPERNO
2011   Microfossils in Calculus Demonstrate Consumption of Plants and Cooked
            Foods in Neanderthal Diets (Shanidar III, Iraq; Spy I and II, Belgium).
            Proceedings of the National Academy of Sciences 108(2):486–491.

HENRY, PAULA I., GILDA A. MORELLI, AND EDWARD Z. TRONICK
2005   Child Caretakers Among Efe Foragers of the Ituri Forest. *In* Hunter-
            Gatherer Childhoods: Evolutionary, Developmental, and Cultural
            Perspectives. Barry S. Hewlett and Michael E. Lamb, eds. Pp.191–213. New
            Brunswick, NJ: Transaction Publishers.

HERNANDEZ, THEODORE
1941   Children among the Drysdale River Tribes. Oceania 12(2):122–133.

HERRMANN, ESTHER, JOSEPH CALL, MARÍA VICTORIA HERNÀNDEZ-LLOREDA,
BRIAN KARE, AND MICHAEL TOMASELLO

2007   Humans Have Evolved Specialized Skills of Social Cognition: The Cultural
        Intelligence Hypothesis. Science 317(5843):1360–1366.

HEWLETT, BARRY S.

1988   Sexual Selection and Paternal Investment among Aka Pygmies. *In*
        Human Reproductive Behavior: A Darwinian Perspective. Laura Betzig,
        Monique Borgerhoff Mulder, and Paul Turke, eds. Pp. 263–276. Cambridge:
        Cambridge University Press.

1991a   Demography and Childcare in Preindustrial Societies. Journal of
        Anthropological Research 47(1):1–37.

1991b   Intimate Fathers: The Nature and Context of Aka Pygmy Paternal Infant
        Care. Ann Arbor: University of Michigan Press.

HEWLETT, BARRY S., AND ADAM H. BOYETTE

2013   Commentary: Play in Hunter-Gatherers. *In* Evolution, Early Experience
        and Human Development: From Research to Practice and Policy. Darcia
        Narváez, Jaak Panksepp, Allan N. Schore, and Tracy R. Gleason, eds.
        Pp. 388–396. New York: Oxford University Press.

HEWLETT, BARRY S., AND LUIGI L. CAVALLI-SFORZA

1986   Cultural Transmission among Aka Pygmies. American Anthropologist
        88(4):922–934.

HEWLETT, BARRY S., HILLARY N. FOUTS, ADAM H. BOYETTE, AND
BONNIE L. HEWLETT

2011   Social Learning among Congo Basin Hunter-Gatherers. Philosophical
        Transactions of the Royal Society B 366(1567):1168–1178.

HEWLETT, BARRY S., AND MICHAEL E. LAMB, EDS.

2005   Hunter-Gatherer Childhoods: Evolutionary, Developmental, and Cultural
        Perspectives. New Brunswick, NJ: AldineTransaction.

HEWLETT, BARRY S., MICHAEL E. LAMB, BIRGIT LEYENDECKER, AND
AXEL SCHÖLMERICH

2000   Internal Working Models, Trust, and Sharing among Foragers. Current
        Anthropology 41(2):287–297.

2000   Parental Investment Strategies among Aka Foragers, Ngandu Farmers, and
        Euro-American Urban-Industrialists. *In* Adaptation and Human Behavior:
        An Anthropological Perspective. Lee Cronk, Napoleon Chagnon, and
        William Irons, eds. Pp. 155–178. New York: Aldine de Gruyter.

HEWLETT, BARRY S., MICHAEL E. LAMB, DONALD SHANNON,
BIRGIT LEYENDECKER, AND AXEL SCHÖLMERICH

1998   Culture and Early Infancy among Central African Foragers and Farmers.
        Developmental Psychology 34(4):653–661.

HEWLETT, BARRY, AND STEVEN WINN

2014   Allomaternal Nursing in Humans. Current Anthropology 55(2): 200–229.

HEWLETT, BONNIE L.

2005   Vulnerable Lives: The Experience of Death and Loss among the Aka and
          Ngandu Adolescents of the Central African Republic. *In* Hunter-Gatherer
          Childhoods: Evolutionary, Developmental, and Cultural Perspectives.
          Barry S. Hewlett and Michael E. Lamb, eds. Pp. 322–342. New Brunswick,
          NJ: AldineTransaction.

2013   Listen, Here Is a Story: Ethnographic Life Narratives from Aka and
          Ngandu Women of the Congo Basin. New York: Oxford University Press.

HILGER, SISTER M. INEZ

1957   Araucanian Child Life and Cultural Background. Smithsonian
          Miscellaneous Collections, vol. 133. Washington, DC: Smithsonian
          Institution.

HILL, KIM, MICHAEL BARTON, AND A. MAGDALENA HURTADO

2009   The Emergence of Human Uniqueness: Characters Underlying Behavioral
          Modernity. Evolutionary Anthropology 18:187–200.

HILL, KIM R., AND A. MAGDALENA HURTADO

1996   Aché Life History: The Ecology and Demography of a Foraging People.
          Hawthorne, NY: Aldine de Gruyter.

1999   The Aché of Paraguay. *In* The Cambridge Encyclopedia of Hunters and
          Gatherers. Richard B. Lee and Richard Daly, eds. Pp. 92–96. Cambridge:
          Cambridge University Press.

2009   Cooperative Breeding in South American Hunter-Gatherers. Proceedings
          of the Royal Society B 276(1674):3863–3870.

HILL, KIM R., ROBERT S. WALKER, MIRAN BOŽIČEVIĆ, JAMES EDER,
THOMAS HEADLAND, BARRY HEWLETT, A. MAGDALENA HURTADO,
FRANK MARLOWE, POLLY WIESSNER, AND BRIAN WOOD

2011   Co-Residence Patterns in Hunter-Gatherer Societies Show Unique Human
          Social Structure. Science 331(6022):1286–1289.

HIRASAWA, AYAKO

2005   Infant Care among the Sedentarized Baka Hunter-Gatherers in
          Southeastern Cameroon. *In* Hunter-Gatherer Childhoods: Evolutionary,
          Developmental, and Cultural Perspectives. Barry S. Hewlett and Michael E.
          Lamb, eds. Pp. 365–384. New Brunswick, NJ: AldineTransaction.

HIRSHFIELD, MICHAEL F., AND DONALD W. TINKLE

1975   Natural Selection and the Evolution of Reproductive Effort. Proceedings of
          the National Academy of Sciences 72(6):2227–2231.

HOBSON, PETER

2004   The Cradle of Thought: Exploring the Origins of Thinking. Oxford: Oxford University Press.

HOCHBERG, ZE'EV

2008   Juvenility in the Context of Life History Theory. Archives of Disease in Childhood 93(6):534–539.

2012   Evo-Devo of Child Growth: Treatise on Child Growth and Human Evolution. Hoboken, NJ: Wiley and Sons.

HOCHBERG, ZE'EV, AND KERSTIN ALBERTSSON-WIKLAND

2008   Evo-Devo of Infantile and Childhood Growth. Pediatric Research 64(1):2–7.

HODDINOTT, JOHN, HAROLD ALDERMAN, JERE R. BEHRMAN, LAWRENCE HADDAD, AND SUSAN HORTON

2013a   The Economic Rationale for Investing in Stunting Reduction. Maternal and Child Nutrition 9 (Suppl. 2):69–82

HODDINOTT, JOHN, JERE R. BEHRMAN, JOHN A. MALUCCIO, PAUL MELGAR, AGNES R. QUISUMBING, MANUEL RAMIREZ-ZEA, ARYEH D. STEIN, KATHRYN M. YOUNT, AND REYNALDO MARTORELL

2013b   Adult Consequences of Growth Failure in Early Childhood. American Journal of Clinical Nutrition 98(5):1170–1178.

HOGBIN, H. IAN

1970   A New Guinea Childhood: From Weaning Till the Eighth Year in Wogeo, *In* From Child to Adult. John Middleton, ed. Pp. 134–162. Garden City, NY: Natural History Press.

HOPPER, LYDIA M., SARAH MARSHALL-PESCINI, AND ANDREW WHITEN

2012   Social Learning and Culture in Child and Chimpanzee. *In* The Primate Mind: Built to Connect with Other Minds. Frans B. M. De Waal and Pier F. Ferrari, eds. Pp. 99–118. Cambridge, MA: Harvard University Press.

HORNER, VICTORIA, AND ANDREW WHITEN

2005   Causal Knowledge and Imitation/Emulation Switching in Chimpanzees (*Pan troglodytes*) and Children. Animal Cognition 8:164–181.

HORTON, SUSAN, MEERA SHEKAR, CHRISTINE MCDONALD, AJAY MAHAL, AND JANA KRYSTENE BROOKS

2010   Scaling Up Nutrition: What Will It Cost? Washington, DC: World Bank.

HOUSE, BAILEY R., JOSEPH HENRICH, SARAH F. BROSNAN, AND JOAN B. SILK

2012   The Ontogeny of Human Prosociality: Behavioral Experiments with Children Aged 3 to 8. Evolution and Human Behavior 33: 291–308.

HOWELL, NANCY

2010   Life Histories of the Dobe !Kung: Food, Fatness, and Well-Being Over the Life Span. Berkeley: University of California Press.

HOWELL, SIGNE

1988   From Child to Human: Chewong Concepts of Self. *In* Acquiring Culture:
           Cross Cultural Studies in Child Development. Gustav Jahoda and Ioan M.
           Lewis, eds. Pp. 147–168. London: Croom Helm.

HOWES, CAROLLEE, AND SUSAN SPIEKER

2008   Attachment Relationships in the Context of Multiple Caregivers. *In*
           Handbook of Attachment: Theory, Research, and Clinical Applications.
           2nd edition. Jude Cassidy and Phillip R. Shaver, eds. Pp. 317–332. New York:
           Guilford Press.

HRDY, SARAH B.

1976   Care and Exploitation of Nonhuman Primate Infants by Conspecifics
           Other than the Mother. Advances in the Study of Behavior 6:101–158.

1997   Fitness Tradeoffs in the History and Evolution of Delegated Mothering
           with Special Reference to Wet-Nursing, Abandonment, and Infanticide.
           In Human Nature: A Critical Reader. Laura Betzig, ed. Pp. 402–422. New
           York: Oxford University Press.

1999a   Mother Nature: A History of Mothers, Infants, and Natural Selection. New
           York: Pantheon, Random House.

1999b   Mother Nature: Maternal Instincts and How They Shape the Human
           Species. New York: Ballantine.

2005a   Comes the Child Before Man: How Cooperative Breeding and Prolonged
           Post-Weaning Dependence Shaped Human Potential. *In* Hunter-Gatherer
           Childhoods: Evolutionary, Developmental, and Cultural Perspectives.
           Barry S. Hewlett and Michael E. Lamb, eds. Pp. 65–91. New Brunswick, NJ:
           AldineTransaction.

2005b   Evolutionary Context of Human Development: The Cooperative Breeding
           Model. *In* Attachment and Bonding: A New Synthesis. Carol Sue Carter,
           Lieselotte Ahnert, K. E. Grossmann, Sarah B. Hrdy, Michael E. Lamb,
           Stephen W. Porges, and Norbert Sachser, eds. Pp. 9–32. Cambridge, MA:
           MIT Press.

2009   Mothers and Others: The Evolutionary Origins of Mutual Understanding.
           Cambridge, MA: Belknap Press of Harvard University Press.

2010   Estimating the Prevalence of Shared Care and Cooperative Breeding in the
           Order Primates: An Appendix to Mothers and Others. http://www.citrona.
           com/vitae.html.

2012   Comes the Child Before Man: Development Plus Social Selection in the
           Emergence of "Emotionally Modern" Humans. Paper presented at School
           for Advanced Research Seminar: Multiple Perspectives on the Evolution of
           Childhood. Santa Fe, November 4–8.

HUBLIN, JEAN-JACQUES

2009   The Origin of Neandertals. Proceedings of the National Academy of
        Sciences 106(38):16022–16027.

HUIZINGA, JOHAN

1955   *Homo ludens*: A Study of the Play Element in Culture. London: Roy
        Publishers.

HUNN, EUGENE S.

2002   Evidence for the Precocious Acquisition of Plant Knowledge by Zapotec
        Children. *In* Ethnobiology and Biocultural Diversity: Proceedings of the
        Seventh International Congress of Ethnobiology. John R. Stepp, Felice S.
        Wyndham, and Rebecca K. Zarger, eds. Pp. 604–613. Athens: University Of
        Georgia Press.

HURTADO, A. MAGDALENA, KIM HILL, INES HURTADO, AND HILLARD KAPLAN

1992   Trade-Offs between Female Food Acquisition and Child Care among Hiwi
        and Ache Foragers. Human Nature 3(3):185–216.

HURTADO, A. MAGDALENA, CAROL A. LAMBOURNE, KIM R. HILL, AND
KAREN KESSLER

2006   The Public Health Implications of Maternal Care Trade-Offs. Human
        Nature 17(2):129–154.

INGOLD, TIM

2001   From the Transmission of Representations to the Education of Attention.
        In The Debated Mind: Evolutionary Psychology versus Ethnography.
        Harvey Whitehouse, ed. Pp. 113–153. Oxford: Berg.

INSTITUTE OF MEDICINE OF THE NATIONAL ACADEMIES

2002   Dietary Reference Intakes for Energy, Carbohydrate, Fiber, Fat, Fatty
        Acids, Cholesterol, Protein, and Amino Acids. Washington, DC: National
        Academies Press.

ISAACS, SUSAN

1929   *Review of* The Language and Thought of the Child; Judgment and
        Reasoning in the Child; and The Child's Conception of the World.
        Pedagogical Seminary and Journal of Genetic Psychology 36(4):597–609.

ISLER, KARIN, AND CAREL P. VAN SCHAIK

2012   Allomaternal Care, Life History, and Brain Size Evolution in Mammals.
        Journal of Human Evolution 63(1):52–63.

ISTOMIN, KIRILL V., AND MARK J. DWYER

2009   Finding the Way: A Critical Discussion of Anthropological Theories
        of Human Spatial Orientation with Reference to Reindeer Herders
        of Northeastern Europe and Western Siberia. Current Anthropology
        50(1):29–49.

IVERSON, JANA M.

2010   Developing Language in a Developing Body: The Relationship between Motor Development and Language Development. Journal of Child Language 37(2):229–261.

IVEY, PAULA K.

2000   Cooperative Reproduction in Ituri Forest Hunter-Gatherers: Who Cares for Efe Infants? Current Anthropology 41(5):856–866.

IVEY HENRY, PAULA, GILDA A. MORELLI, AND EDWARD Z. TRONICK

2005   Child Caretakers among Efe Foragers of the Ituri Forest. *In* Hunter-Gatherer Childhoods: Evolutionary, Developmental, and Cultural Perspectives. Barry S. Hewlett and Michael E. Lamb, eds. Pp. 191–213. New Brunswick, NJ: AldineTransaction.

JACOB, FRANÇOIS

1977   Evolution and Tinkering. Science 196(4295):1161–1166.

JACOBSON, SANDRA W., AND KAREN F. FRYE

1991   Effect of Maternal Social Support on Attachment: Experimental Evidence. Child Development 62(3):572–582.

JAEGGI, ADRIAN V., JUDITH M. BURKART, AND CAREL P. VAN SCHAIK

2010   On the Psychology of Cooperation in Humans and Other Primates: Combining the Natural History and Experimental Evidence of Prosociality. Philosophical Transactions of the Royal Society B 365(1553):2723–2735.

JAEGGI, ADRIAN V., MARIA VAN NOORDWIJK, AND CAREL P. VAN SCHAIK

2008   Begging for Information: Mother-Offspring Food Sharing among Wild Bornean Orangutans. American Journal of Primatology 70(6):533–541.

JAEGGI, ADRIAN V., AND CAREL P. VAN SCHAIK

2011   The Evolution of Food Sharing in Primates. Behavioral Ecology and Sociobiology 65:2125–2140.

JANSON, CHARLES H., AND CAREL P. VAN SCHAIK

1993   Ecological Risk Aversion in Juvenile Primates: Slow and Steady Wins the Race. *In* Juvenile Primates: Life History, Development, and Behavior. Michael E. Pereira and Lynn A. Fairbanks, eds. Pp. 57–74. Chicago, IL: University of Chicago Press.

JASIENSKA, GRAZYNA

2009   Reproduction and Lifespan: Trade-offs, Overall Energy Budgets, Intergenerational Costs, and Costs Neglected by Research. American Journal of Human Biology 21(4):524–532.

JELLIFFE, DERRICK B., JAMES WOODBURN, F. J. BENNETT, AND
E. F. PATRICE JELLIFFE

1962   The Children of the Hadza Hunters. The Journal of Pediatrics 60(6):907–913.

JENNESS, DIAMOND

1922   The Life of the Copper Eskimos: Report of the Canadian Arctic Expedition, 1913–18, vol. 12(A). Ottawa: Canadian Government Publications.

JETZ, WALTER, AND DUSTIN R. RUBENSTEIN

2011   Environmental Uncertainty and the Global Biogeography of Cooperative Breeding in Birds. Current Biology 21(5):72–78.

JOHANSON, DONALD C., AND BLAKE EDGAR

1996   From Lucy to Language. New York: Nevraumont Publishing Company.

JUNG, MIN-JUNG, AND HILLARY N. FOUTS

2011   Multiple Caregivers' Touch Interactions with Young Children among the Bofi Foragers in Central Africa. International Journal of Psychology 46(1):24–32.

KAARE, BWIRE, AND JAMES WOODBURN

1999   The Hadza of Tanzania. *In* The Cambridge Encyclopedia of Hunters and Gatherers. Richard B. Lee and Richard Daly, eds. Pp. 200. Cambridge: Cambridge University Press.

KACHEL, A. FRIEDERIKE, LUKE S. PREMO, AND JEAN-JACQUES HUBLIN

2011   Modeling the Effects of Weaning Age on Length of Female Reproductive Period: Implications for the Evolution of Human Life History. American Journal of Human Biology 23(4):479–487.

KAMEI, NOBUTAKA

2005   Play among Baka Children in Cameroon. *In* Hunter-Gatherer Childhoods: Evolutionary, Developmental, and Cultural Perspectives. Barry S. Hewlett and Michael E. Lamb, eds. Pp. 343–362. New Brunswick, NJ: AldineTransaction.

KANNGIESSER, PATRICIA, AND FELIX WARNEKEN

2012   Young Children Consider Merit When Sharing Resources with Others. PLoS ONE 7(8):e43979. doi:10.1371/journal.pone.0043979.

KANO, TAKAYOSHI

1992   The Last Ape: Pygmy Chimpanzee Behavior and Ecology. Stanford, CA: Stanford University Press.

KAPLAN, HILLARD S.

1994   Evolutionary and Wealth Flows Theories of Fertility: Empirical Tests and New Models. Population and Development Review 20(4):753–791.

1996   A Theory of Fertility and Parental Investment in Traditional and Modern Human Societies. American Journal of Physical Anthropology 101(23):91–135.

KAPLAN, HILLARD, AND HEATHER DOVE

1987   Infant Development among the Ache of Eastern Paraguay. Developmental Psychology 23(2):190–198.

KAPLAN, HILLARD, KIM HILL, AND A. MAGDALENA HURTADO

2011   The Embodied Capital Theory of Human Evolution. In Reproductive
        Ecology and Human Evolution. Peter T. Ellison, ed. Pp. 293–317. New
        Brunswick: Transaction Publishers.

KAPLAN, HILLARD S., KIM HILL, JANE B. LANCASTER, AND
A. MAGDALENA HURTADO

2000   A Theory of Human Life History Evolution: Diet, Intelligence, and
        Longevity. Evolutionary Anthropologist 9(4):156–185.

KAPLAN, HILLARD S., JANE B. LANCASTER, AND ARTHUR J. ROBSON

2003   Embodied Capital and the Evolutionary Economics of the Human
        Lifespan. Population and Development Review, Supplement 29:152–182.

KAPLAN, HILLARD S., AND ARTHUR J. ROBSON

2002   The Emergence of Humans: The Coevolution of Intelligence and Longevity
        with Intergenerational Transfers. Proceedings of the National Academy of
        Sciences 99(15):10221–10226.

KAPLAN, S. L., M. M. GRUMBACH, AND T. K. SHEPARD

1972   The Ontogenesis of Human Fetal Hormones: I. Growth Hormone and
        Insulin. Journal of Clinical Investigation 51(12):3080–3090.

KAPPELMAN, JOHN

1996   The Evolution of Body Mass and Relative Brain Size in Fossil Hominids.
        Journal of Human Evolution 30(3):243–276.

KARLBERG, JOHAN

1989   A Biologically-Oriented Mathematical Model (ICP) for Human Growth.
        Acta Paediatrica Scandinavica 78(Suppl. 350):70–94.

KARLBERG, JOHAN, AND KERSTIN ALBERTSSON-WIKLAND

1988   Infancy Growth Pattern Related to Growth Hormone Deficiency. Acta
        Paediatrica Scandinavica 77(3):385–391.

KARLBERG, JOHAN, I. ENGSTRÖM, P. KARLBERG, AND J. G. FRYER

1987   Analysis of Linear Growth Using a Mathematical Model I. From Birth to
        Three Years. Acta Paediatrica 76(3):478–488.

KATZ, CINDI

1986   Children and the Environment: Work, Play and Learning in Rural Sudan.
        Children's Environment Quarterly 3(4):43–51.

KATZ, MARY MAXWELL, AND MELVIN J. KONNER

1981   The Role of the Father: An Anthropological Perspective. In The Role of the
        Father in Child Development. 2nd edition. Michael E. Lamb, ed.
        Pp. 155–186. New York: Wiley.

KATZ, RICHARD

1981   Education Is Transformation: Becoming a Healer among the !Kung and the
        Fijians. Harvard Education Review 51(1):57–78.

KEESING, ROGER M.

1975   Kin Groups and Social Structure. New York: Holt, Rinehart, and Winston.

KEITH, ARTHUR

1895   The Growth of Brain in Men and Monkeys, with a Short Criticism of the Usual Method of Stating Brain-Ratios. Journal of Anatomy and Physiology 29(Pt 2):282–303.

KELLER, HEIDI

2007   Cultures of Infancy. Mahwah, NJ: Lawrence Erlbaum Associates.

KELLY, ROBERT L.

1995   The Foraging Spectrum: Diversity in Hunter-Gatherer Lifeways. Washington, DC: Smithsonian Institution Press.

KENT, SUSAN, ED.

1996   Cultural Diversity among Twentieth Century Foragers: An African Perspective. Cambridge: Cambridge University Press.

KERMOIAN, ROSANNE, AND P. HERBERT LEIDERMAN

1986   Infant Attachment to Mother and Child Caretaker in an East African Community. International Journal of Behavioral Development 9(4):455–469.

KETTERSON, ELLEN D., AND VAL NOLAN JR.

1992   Hormones and Life Histories: An Integrative Approach. American Naturalist 140:S33–S62.

KHAN, KHALID S., PATRICK F. W. CHIEN, AND NEELOFUR B. KHAN

1998   Nutritional Stress of Reproduction: A Cohort Study Over Two Consecutive Pregnancies. Acta Obstetricia et Gynecologica Scandinavica 77(4):395–401.

KIDD, CELESTE, STEPHEN T. PIANTADOSI, AND RICHARD N. ASLIN

2012   The Goldilocks Effect: Human Infants Allocate Attention to Visual Sequences That Are Neither Too Simple nor Too Complex. PLoS ONE 7(5): e36399. doi:10.1371/journal.pone.0036399.

KIM, PETER S., JAMES E. COXWORTH, AND KRISTEN HAWKES

2012   Increased Longevity Evolves from Grandmothering. Proceedings of the Royal Society B 279(1749):4880–4804. doi:10.1098/rspb.2012.1751.

KING, BARBARA J.

1994   The Information Continuum: Evolution of Social Information Transfer in Monkeys, Apes, and Hominids. Santa Fe, NM: School of American Research Press.

KIRKWOOD, THOMAS B. L.

1987   Immortality of the Germ-Line versus Disposability of the Soma. *In* Evolution of Longevity in Animals: A Comparative Approach. Avril D. Woodhead and Keith H. Thompson, eds. Pp. 209–218. New York: Plenum Publishing Corporation.

KLAUS, MARSHALL, AND PHYLLIS KLAUS

2010   Academy of Breastfeeding Medicine Founder's Lecture 2009: Maternity
            Care Re-evaluated. Breastfeeding Medicine 5(1):3–8.

KLEIN, ROBERT E., ROBERT E. LASKY, CHARLES YARBROUGH, J. P. HABICHT, AND
MARTHA JULIA SELLERS

1977   Relationship of Infant/Caretaker Interaction, Social Class, and Nutritional
            Status to Developmental Test Performance among Guatemalan Infants.
            In Culture and Infancy: Variations in the Human Experience. P. Herbert
            Leiderman, Steven R. Tulkin, and Anne Rosenfeld, eds. Pp. 218–227. New
            York: Academic Press.

KLINE, MICHELLE A., ROBERT BOYD, AND JOSEPH HENRICH

2013   Teaching and the Life History of Cultural Transmission in Fijian Villages.
            Human Nature 24: 351–374.

KLINNERT, MARY D., JOSEPH J. CAMPOS, JAMES F. SORCE, ROBERT N. EMDE, AND
MARYLIN SVEJDA

1983   Emotions as Behavior Regulators: Social Referencing in Infancy. *In*
            Emotion: Theory, Research, and Experience. Robert Plutchik and Henry
            Kellerman, eds. Pp. 57–86. New York: Academic Press.

KNIGHT, CHRISTOPHER

2016   Chomsky's Tower: Language and Revolution. New Haven, CT: Yale Univer-
            sity Press.

KNOCH, DARIA, ALVARO PASCUAL-LEONE, KASPAR MEYER, VALERIE TREYER, AND
ERNST FEHR

2006   Diminishing Reciprocal Fairness by Disrupting the Right Prefrontal
            Cortex. Science 314(5800):829–832.

KNOTT, CHERYL D.

2001   Female Reproductive Ecology of the Apes: Implications for Human
            Evolution. *In* Reproductive Ecology and Human Evolution. Peter Ellison,
            ed. Pp. 429–463. New York: Aldine de Gruyter.

KOENIG, ANDREAS, AND CAROLLA BORRIES

2012   Hominoid Dispersal Patterns and Human Evolution. Evolutionary
            Anthropology 21(3):108–112.

KOENIG, WALTER D., AND JANIS L. DICKINSON

2004   Introduction. *In* Ecology and Evolution of Cooperative Breeding in Birds.
            Walter D. Koenig and Janis L. Dickinson, eds. Cambridge: Cambridge
            University Press.

KONNER, MELVIN J.

1972   Aspects of the Developmental Ethology of a Foraging People. *In*
            Ethological Studies of Child Behavior. Nicholas G. Blurton Jones, ed.
            Pp. 285–304. Cambridge: Cambridge University Press.

1975   Relations among Infants and Juveniles in Comparative Perspective. *In* Friendship and Peer Relations. Michael Lewis and Leonard A. Rosenblum, eds. Pp. 99–129. New York: Wiley and Sons.

1976a   Maternal Care, Infant Behavior, and Development among the !Kung. *In* Kalahari Hunter-Gatherers. Richard B. Lee and Irven DeVore, eds. Pp. 218–245. Cambridge, MA: Harvard University Press.

1976b   Relations among Infants and Juveniles in Comparative Perspective. *In* Friendship and Peer Relations. M. Lewis and L. A. Rosenblum, eds. Pp. 99–129. New York: Wiley and Sons.

1977   Infancy among the Kalahari Desert San. *In* Culture and Infancy. P. Herbert Leiderman, Steven R. Tulkin, and Anne Rosenfeld, eds. Pp. 287–328. New York: Academic Press.

1981   Evolution of Human Behavior Development. *In* Handbook of Cross-Cultural Human Development. R. H. Munroe, R. L. Munroe, and B. B. Whiting, eds. Pp. 3–51. New York: Garland STPM Press.

2005   Hunter-Gatherer Infancy and Childhood: The !Kung and Others. *In* Hunter-Gatherer Childhoods: Evolutionary, Developmental, and Cultural Perspectives. Barry S. Hewlett and Michael E. Lamb, eds. Pp. 19–64. New Brunswick, NJ: AldineTransaction.

2010   The Evolution of Childhood: Relationships, Emotion, Mind. Cambridge, MA: The Belknap Press of Harvard University Press.

KONNER, MELVIN J., AND CHARLES M. SUPER
1987   Sudden Infant Death Syndrome: An Anthropological Hypothesis. *In* The Role of Culture in Developmental Disorder. Charles M. Super, ed. Pp. 95–108. New York: Academic Press.

KONNER, MELVIN J., AND CAROL WORTHMAN
1980   Nursing Frequency, Gonadal Function, and Birth Spacing among !Kung Hunter-Gatherers. Science 207(4432):788–791.

KRAMER, KAREN L.
2002   Variation in Juvenile Dependence. Human Nature 13(2):299–325.

2005a   Children's Help and the Pace of Reproduction: Cooperative Breeding in Humans. Evolutionary Anthropology 14(6):224–237.

2005b   Maya Children: Helpers at the Farm. Cambridge, MA: Harvard University Press.

2010   Cooperative Breeding and Its Significance to the Demographic Success of Humans. Annual Review of Anthropology 39:417–436.

2011   The Evolution of Human Parental Care and Recruitment of Juvenile Help. Trends in Ecology & Evolution 26(10):533–40.

KRAMER, KAREN L., AND PETER T. ELLISON

2010   Pooled Energy Budgets: Resituating Human Energy-Allocation Trade-Offs. Evolutionary Anthropology: Issues, News, and Reviews 19(4):136–147.

KRAMER, KAREN L. AND RUSSELL D. GREAVES

2011   Juvenile Subsistence Effort, Activity Levels, and Growth Patterns. Human Nature, 22(3), 303–326.

KRAMER, KAREN L., AND JANE B. LANCASTER

2010   Teen Motherhood in Cross-Cultural Perspective. Annals of Human Biology 37(5):613-628.

KRAMER, KAREN L, AND ANDREW F. RUSSELL

2014   Kin-Selected Cooperation without Lifetime Monogamy: Human Insights and Animal Implications. Trends in Ecology and Evolution 29(11):600–606. doi:10.1016/j.tree.2014.09.001.

KRAMER, PATRICIA A.

1998   The Costs of Human Locomotion: Maternal Investment in Child Transport. American Journal of Physical Anthropology 107(1):71–85.

KRAUSE, RICHARD A.

1985   The Clay Sleeps: An Ethnoarchaeological Study of Three African Potters. Birmingham: University of Alabama Press.

KRINGELBACH, MORTEN L., ANNUKKA LEHTONEN, SARAH SQUIRE, ALLISEN G. HARVEY, MICHELLE G. CRASKE, IAN E. HOLLIDAY, ALEXANDER L. GREEN, ET AL.

2008   A Specific and Rapid Neural Signature for Parental Instinct. PLoS ONE 3(2):e1664. doi:10.1371/journal.pone.0001664.

KROEBER, ALFRED LOUIS

1948   Anthropology: Race, Language, Culture, Psychology, Prehistory. New York: Harcourt, Brace, and Company.

KRUGER, ANN CALE

2010   Communion and Culture. *In* Mimesis and Science. Scott Garrels, ed. Pp. 111–127. East Lansing: Michigan State University Press.

KRUGER, ANN CALE, AND MELVIN KONNER

2010   Who Responds to Crying? Maternal and Allocare among the !Kung. Human Nature 21(3):309–329.

KRUGER, ANN CALE, AND MICHAEL TOMASELLO

1996   Cultural Learning and Learning Culture. *In* Handbook of Education and Human Development: New Models of Learning, Teaching, and Schooling. David Olson and Nancy Torrance, eds. Pp. 369–387. Oxford: Basil Blackwell.

KUHN, STEVEN L., AND MARY C. STINER

2006   What's a Mother to Do? The Division of Labor among Neandertals and Modern Humans in Eurasia. Current Anthropology 47(6):953–980.

KUYKENDALL, KEVIN L., AND GLENN C. CONROY

1996   Permanent Tooth Calcification in Chimpanzees (*Pan troglodytes*):
        Patterns and Polymorphisms. American Journal of Physical Anthropology
        99(1):159–174.

KUZAWA, CHRISTOPHER

1998   Adipose Tissue in Human Infancy and Childhood: An Evolutionary
        Perspective. Yearbook of Physical Anthropology 41:177–209.

KUZAWA, CHRISTOPHER W., AND JARED M. BRAGG

2012   Plasticity in Human Life History Strategy: Implications for Contemporary
        Human Variation and the Evolution of Genus *Homo*. Current
        Anthropology 53(S6):S369–S382.

KUZAWA, CHRISTOPHER W., HARRY T. CHUGANI, LAWRENCE I. GROSSMAN,
LEONARD LIPOVICH, OTTO MUZIK, PATRICK R. HOF, DEREK E. WILDMAN,
CHET C. SHERWOOD, WILLIAM R. LEONARD, AND NICHOLAS LANGE

2014   Metabolic Costs and Evolutionary Implications of Human Brain
        Development. Proceedings of the National Academy of Sciences
        111(36):13010–13015.

LABRIE, FERNAND, ALAIN BÉLANGER, VAN LUU-THE, CLAUDE LABRIE,
JACQUES SIMARD, LEONELLO CUSAN, JOSE-LUIS GOMEZ, AND BERNARD CANDAS

1998   DHEA and the Intracrine Formation of Androgens and Estrogens in
        Peripheral Target Tissues: Its Role During Aging. Steroids 63(5–6):322–328.

LACK, DAVID

1947   The Significance of Clutch-Size. Ibis 89(2):302–352.

LADD, G.

1999   Peer Relationships and Social Competence during Early and Middle
        Childhood. Annual Review of Psychology 50:333–359.

LAFRENIERE, PETER

2005   Human Emotions as Multipurpose Adaptations: An Evolutionary
        Perspective on the Development of Fear. *In* Evolutionary Perspectives
        on Human Development, 2nd edition. Robert L. Burgess and Kevin
        MacDonald, eds. Pp. 189–205. Thousand Oaks, CA: Sage.

LAGUNA, FREDERICA DE

1965   Childhood among the Yakutat Tlingit: In Context and Meaning. *In*
        Cultural Anthropology. Melford E. Spiro, ed. Pp. 3–23. New York: Free
        Press.

LAHDENPERÄ, MIRKKA, VIRPI LUMMAA, SAMULI HELLE, MARC TREMBLAY, AND
ANDREW F. RUSSELL

2004   Fitness Benefits of Prolonged Post-Reproductive Life Span in Women.
        Nature 428:178–181.

LAMB, MICHAEL E., AND CHARLIE LEWIS

2010   The Development and Significance of Father-Child Relationships in

Two-Parent Families. In The Role of the Father in Child Development. 5th edition. Pp. 94–104. Michael E. Lamb, ed. Hoboken, NJ: Wiley and Sons.

LANCASTER, JANE B., AND CHET S. LANCASTER

1983a   Parental Investment: The Hominid Adaptation. *In* How Humans Adapt. Donald J. Ortner, ed. Pp. 33–65. Washington, DC: Smithsonian Institution Press.

1983b   The Watershed: Change in Parental-Investment and Family-Formation Strategies in the Course of Human Evolution. *In* Parenting across the Life Span: Biosocial Dimensions. Jane B. Lancaster, Jeanne Altmann, Alice Rossi, and Lonnie R. Sherrod, eds. Pp. 187–205. New York: Aldine de Gruyter.

LANCY, DAVID F.

1980a   Play in Species Adaptation. Bernard J. Siegel, ed. Annual Review of Anthropology 9:471–495.

1980b   Becoming a Blacksmith in Gbarngasuakwelle. Anthropology and Education Quarterly 11(4):266–274.

1984   Play in Anthropological Perspective. *In* Play in Animals and Humans. Peter K. Smith, ed. Pp. 295–304. London: Basil Blackwell.

1996   Playing on the Mother Ground: Cultural Routines for Children's Development. New York: Guilford Press.

2010   Learning "From Nobody": The Limited Role of Teaching in Folk Models of Children's Development. Childhood in the Past 3(1):79–106.

2012a   The Chore Curriculum. *In* African Children at Work: Working and Learning in Growing Up for Life. Gerd Spittler and Michael Bourdillion, eds. Pp. 23–57. Berlin: Lit Verlag.

2012b   Apprenticeship: A Survey and Analysis of the Ethnographic Record. Society for the Anthropology of Work Review 33:113–126.

2014   The Anthropology of Childhood: Cherubs, Chattel, Changelings. 2nd
[2008]   edition. Cambridge: Cambridge University Press.

LANCY, DAVID F. AND M. ANNETTE GROVE

2010   Learning Guided by Others. *In* The Anthropology of Learning in Childhood. David F. Lancy, Suzanne Gaskins, and John Bock, eds. Pp. 145–179. Lanham, MD: AltaMira Press.

2011a   "Getting Noticed": Middle Childhood in Cross-Cultural Perspective. Human Nature 22(3):281–302.

2011b   Marbles and Machiavelli: The Role of Game Play in Children's Social Development. American Journal of Play 3(4):489–499.

LANGEN, TOM A.

2000   Prolonged Offspring Dependence and Cooperative Breeding in Birds.
        Behavioral Ecology 11(4):367–377.

LANGEN, TOM, AND SANDRA VEHRENCAMP

1999   How White-Throated Magpie Jay Helpers Contribute during Breeding.
        Auk 116(1):131–140.

LANGER, PETER

2008   Phases of Maternal Investment in Eutherian Mammals. Zoology (Jena)
        111(2):148–162.

LANGERGRABER, KEVIN E., KAY PRÜFER, CAROLYN ROWNEY,

CHRISTOPHE BOESCH, CATHERINE CROCKFORD, KATIE FAWCETT, EIJI INOUE,

ET AL.

2012   Generation Times in Wild Chimpanzees and Gorillas Suggest Earlier
        Divergence Times in Great Ape and Human Evolution. Proceedings of the
        National Academy of Sciences 109(39):15716–15721.

LANSFORD, JENNIFER E., PATRICK S. MALONE, KENNETH A. DODGE,

GREGORY S. PETTIT, AND JOHN E. BATES

2010   Developmental Cascades of Peer Rejection, Social Information Processing
        Biases, and Aggression During Middle Childhood. Development and
        Psychopathology 22(3):593–602.

LANZA, NORBERTO A., KEVIN M. BURKE, AND CLAUDIA VALEGGIA

2008   Fertility Patterns in the Toba, an Argentine Indigenous Population in
        Transition. Society, Biology, and Human Affairs 73(1–2):26–34.

LAPPAN, SUSAN

2009   The Effects of Lactation and Infant Care on Adult Energy Budgets in Wild
        Siamangs (*Symphalangus syndactylus*). American Journal of Physical
        Anthropology 140(2):290–301.

LARKE, AMIEE, AND DOUGLAS E. CREWS

2006   Parental Investment, Late Reproduction, and Increased Reserve Capacity
        are Associated with Longevity in Humans. Journal of Physiological
        Anthropology 25(1):119–131.

LAVE, JEAN, AND ETIENNE WENGER

1991   Situated Learning: Legitimate Peripheral Participation. Cambridge:
        Cambridge University Press.

LAVELLI, MANUELA, AND ALAN FOGEL

2002   Developmental Changes in Mother-Infant Face-to-Face Communication,
        Birth to 3 Months. Developmental Psychology 38(2):288–305.

LAWN, JOY E., JUDITH MWANSA-KAMBAFWILE, BERNARDO L. HORTA,
FERNANDO C. BARROW, AND SIMON COUSENS

2010   "Kangaroo Mother Care" to Prevent Neonatal Deaths Due to Preterm Birth
         Complications. International Journal of Epidemiology 39(Suppl. 1):144–154.

LEAVENS, DAVID A., WILLIAM D. HOPKINS, AND KIM A. BARD

1996   Indexical and Referential Pointing in Chimpanzees (*Pan troglodytes*).
         Journal of Comparative Psychology 110(4):346–353.

LEAVITT, STEPHEN C.

1989   Cargo, Christ, and Nostalgia for the Dead: Themes of Intimacy and
         Abandonment in Bumbita Arapesh Social Experience. PhD dissertation,
         Department of Anthropology, University of California, San Diego.

LEE, PHYLLIS C.

1996   The Meanings of Weaning: Growth, Lactation, and Life History.
         Evolutionary Anthropology 5(3):87–98.

LEE, RICHARD B.

1979   The !Kung San: Men, Women, and Work in a Foraging Society. Cambridge:
         Cambridge University Press.

LEE, RICHARD B, AND RICHARD DALY, EDS.

1999   The Cambridge Encyclopedia of Hunters and Gatherers. Cambridge:
         Cambridge University Press.

LEGER, JULIANE, J. F. OURY, MICHÈLE NOEL, S. BARON, K. BENALI, P. BLOT, AND
PAUL CZERNICHOW

1996   Growth Factors and Intrauterine Growth Retardation. I. Serum Growth
         Hormone, Insulin-Like Growth Factor (IGF)-I, IGF-II, and IGF Binding
         Protein Levels in Normal Growth and Growth-Retarded Human Fetuses
         During the Second Half of Gestation. Pediatric Research 40:94–100.

LEIGH, STEVEN R.

1992   Patterns of Variation in the Ontogeny of Primate Body Size Dimorphism.
         Journal of Human Evolution 23(1):27–50.

1996   Evolution of Human Growth Spurts. American Journal of Physical
         Anthropology 101(4):455–474.

2001   The Evolution of Human Growth. Evolutionary Anthropology
         10(6):223–236.

2004   Brain Growth, Life History, and Cognition in Primate and Human
         Evolution. American Journal of Primatology 62(3):139–164.

2006   Brain Ontogeny and Life History in *Homo erectus*. Journal of Human
         Evolution 50(1):104–108.

LEIGH, STEVEN R., AND BRIAN T. SHEA

1996   Ontogeny of Body Size Variation in African Apes. American Journal of
         Physical Anthropology 99(1):43–65.

LEIMGRUBER, KRISTIN, A. SHAW, L. SANTOS, AND K. OLSON

2012   Young Children Are More Generous When Others Are Aware of Their
        Actions. PLOS 7(10):e48292. doi:10.1371/journal.pone.0048292.

LEÓN, LOURDES DE

2012   Socializing Attention: Directive Sequences, Participation, and Affect in a
        Mayan Family at Work. Unpublished manuscript, CIESAS, Mexico D.F.,
        Mexico.

LEONARD, WILLIAM R., AND MARCIA L. ROBERTSON

1994   Evolutionary Perspectives on Human Nutrition: The Influence of Brain and
        Body Size on Diet and Metabolism. American Journal of Human Biology
        6(1):77–88.

1997   Comparative Primate Energetics and Hominid Evolution. American
        Journal of Physical Anthropology 102(2):265–281.

LEONARD, WILLIAM R., MARCIA L. ROBERTSON, J. JOSH SNODGRASS, AND
CHRIS W. KUZAWA

2003   Metabolic Correlates of Hominid Brain Evolution. Comparative
        Biochemistry and Physiology, Part A 136(1):5–15.

LEONETTI, DONNA L., DILIP C. NATH, NATABAR S. HEMAM, AND DAWN B. NEILL

2005   Kinship Organization and the Impact of Grandmothers on Reproductive
        Success among the Matrilineal Khasi and Patrilineal Bengali of Northeast
        India. *In* Grandmotherhood: The Evolutionary Significance of the Second
        Half of Female Life. Eckart Voland, Athanasios Chasiotis, and Wulf
        Schiefenhövel, eds. Pp. 195–214. New Brunswick, NJ: Rutgers University
        Press.

LEPOWSKY, MARIA

1987   Food Taboos and Child Survival: A Case Study from the Coral Sea.
        In Child Survival: Anthropological Perspectives on the Treatment
        and Maltreatment of Children. Nancy Scheper-Hughes, ed. Pp. 71–92.
        Dordrecht, Netherlands: D. Reidel Publishing Company.

LEVINE, ROBERT A.

2009   Historical and Cultural Perspectives. *In* The Child: An Encyclopedic
        Companion. Richard A. Schweder, ed. Pp. 139–143. Chicago, IL: University
        of Chicago Press.

LEVINE, ROBERT A, PATRICE M MILLER, AND MARY MAXWELL WEST, EDS.

1988   Parental Behavior in Diverse Societies. San Francisco, CA: Jossey-Bass.

LEVY, ROBERT I.

1978   Tahitian Gentleness and Redundant Controls. *In* Learning Non-aggression:
        The Experience of Non-literate Societies. Ashley Montagu, ed. Pp. 222–235.
        New York: Oxford University Press.

LIGON, J. DAVID

1999   The Evolution of Avian Breeding Systems. Oxford: Oxford University
          Press.

LIGON, J. DAVID, AND D. BRENT BURT

2004   Evolutionary Origins. *In* Ecology and Evolution of Cooperative Breeding
          Birds. Walter D. Koening and Janis L. Dickinson, eds. Pp. 5–34. New York:
          Cambridge University Press.

LITTLE, CHRISTOPHER A. J. L.

2011   How Asabano Children Learn; Or, Formal Schooling amongst Informal
          Learners. Oceania 81(2):146–166.

LITTLE, MICHAEL A., PAUL W. LESLIE, AND KENNETH L. CAMPBELL

1992   Energy Reserves and Parity of Nomadic and Settled Turkana Women.
          American Journal of Human Biology 4(6):729–738.

LIU, F., D. R. POWELL, D. M. STYNE, AND R. L. HINTZ

1991   Insulin-Like Growth Factors (IGF) and IGF-Binding Proteins in the
          Developing Rhesus Monkey. Journal of Clinical Endocrinology and
          Metabolism 72(4):905–911.

LIU, YOUXUE, F. JALIL, AND JOHAN KARLBERG

1998   Growth Stunting in Early Life in Relation to the Onset of the Childhood
          Component of Growth. Journal of Pediatric Endocrinology and
          Metabolism 11(2):247–260.

LIU, YOUXUE, KERSTIN ALBERTSSON-WIKLAND, AND JOHAN KARLBERG

2000   Long-Term Consequences of Early Linear Growth Retardation (Stunting)
          in Swedish Children. Pediatric Research 47:475–480.

LIVERSIDGE, HELEN

2003   Variation in Modern Human Dental Development. *In* Patterns of Growth
          and Development in the Genus *Homo*. Jennifer L. Thompson, Gail E.
          Krovitz, and Andrew J. Nelson, eds. Pp. 73–113. Cambridge: Cambridge
          University Press.

LOCKE, J., AND B. BOGIN

2006   Language and Life History: A New Perspective on the Development and
          Evolution of Language. Behavioral and Brain Sciences 29(3):259–325.

LOCKWOOD, CHARLES A., AND JOHN G. FLEAGLE

1999   The Recognition and Evaluation of Homoplasy in Primate and Human
          Evolution. American Journal of Physical Anthropology 110(Suppl.
          29):189–232.

LORDKIPANIDZE, DAVID, TEA JASHASHVILI, ABESALOM VEKUA,
MARCIA S. PONCE DE LEÓN, CHRISTOPH P. E. ZOLLIKOFER, G. PHILIP RIGHTMIRE,
HERMAN PONTZER, ET AL.

2007   Postcranial Evidence from Early *Homo* from Dmanisi, Georgia. Nature
          449:305–310.

LOW, L. C. K., S. Y. M. TAM, E. Y. W. KWAN, A. M. C. TSANG, AND JOHAN KARLBERG
2001   Onset of Significant GH Dependence of Serum IGF-I and IGF Binding
        Protein 3 Concentrations in Early Life. Pediatric Research 50(6):737–742.

LUBY, JOAN L., DEANNA M. BARCH, ANDY BELDEN, MICHAEL S. GAFFREY,
REBECCA TILIMAN, CASEY BABB, TOMOYUKI NISHINO, HIDEO SUZUKI, AND
KELLY N. BOTTERON
2012   Maternal Support in Early Childhood Predicts Larger Hippocampal
        Volumes at School Age. Proceedings of the National Academy of Sciences
        109(8):2854–2859.

LUKAS, DIETER, AND TIM CLUTTON-BROCK
2012   Cooperative Breeding and Monogamy in Mammalian Societies.
        Proceedings of the Royal Society B 279(1736):2151–2156.

LYONS, BRUCE, AND ROBERT MONTGOMERIE
2012   Sexual Selection Is a Form of Social Selection. Philosophical Transactions
        of the Royal Society B 367(1600):2266–2273.

LYONS-RUTH, KARLEN, DAVID B. CONNELL, HENRY U. GREUNEBAUM, AND
SHEILA BOTEIN
1990   Infants at Social Risk: Maternal Depression and Family Support Services
        as Mediators of Infant Development and Security of Attachment. Child
        Development 61(1):85–98.

MACCHIARELLI, ROBERTO, LUCA BONDIOLI, ANDRÉ DEBÉHATH, ARNAUD
MAZURIER, JEAN-FRANÇOIS TOURNEPICHE, WENDY BIRCH, AND
M. CHRISTOPHER DEAN
2006   How Neandertal Molar Teeth Grew. Nature 444:748–751.

MACDONALD, KATHERINE
2007   Cross-Cultural Comparison of Learning in Human Hunting: Implications
        for Life History Evolution. Human Nature 18(4):386–402.

MACDONALD, KEVIN, AND SCOTT L. HERSHBERGER
2005   Theoretical Issues in the Study of Evolution and Development. *In*
        Evolutionary Perspectives on Human Development, 2nd edition. Robert L.
        Burgess and Kevin MacDonald, eds. Pp. 21–72. Thousand Oaks, CA: Sage.

MACE, RUTH
2000   Evolutionary Ecology of Human Life History. Animal Behaviour 59(1):1–10.

MACE, RUTH, AND REBECCA SEAR
2005   Are Humans Cooperative Breeders? *In* Grandmotherhood: The
        Evolutionary Significance of the Second Half of Female Life. Eckart
        Voland, Athanasios Chasiotis and Wulf Schiefenhövel, eds. Pp. 143–159.
        New Brunswick, NJ: Rutgers University Press.

MACKINNON, KATHERINE C.
2007   Social Beginnings. *In* Primates in Perspective. Christina Campbell,

Agustin Fuentes, Katherine C. MacKinnon, Melissa Panger, and Simon K. Bearder, eds. Pp. 571–591. Oxford: Oxford University Press.

MAESTRIPIERI, DARIO, AND KELLY A. CARROLL

2000   Causes and Consequences of Infant Abuse and Neglect in Monkeys. Aggression and Violent Behavior 5(3):245–254.

MAGILL, CLAYTON, GAIL M. ASHLEY, AND KATHERINE FREEMAN

2013   Ecosystem Variability and Early Human Habitats in Eastern Africa. Proceedings of the National Academy of Sciences 110(4):1167–1174.

MAGVANJAV, OYUNBILEG, EDUARDO A. UNDURRAGE, DAN T. A. EISENBERG, WU ZENG, TSOGZOLMAA DORJGOCHOO, WILLIAM R. LEONARD, AND RICARDO A. GODOY

2013   Sibling Composition and Children's Anthropometric Indicators of Nutritional Status: Evidence from Native Amazonians in Bolivia. Annals of Human Biology 40(1):23–34.

MAIN, MARY

1990   Cross-Cultural Studies of Attachment Organization: Recent Studies, Changing Methodologies, and the Concept of Conditional Strategies. Human Development 33(1):48–61.

MANN, A., M. LAMPL, AND J. M. MONGE

1996   The Evolution of Childhood: Dental Evidence for the Appearance of Human Maturation Patterns. American Journal of Physical Anthropology, Supplement 21:156.

MAREAN, CURTIS W., MIRYAM BAR-MATTHEWS, JOCELYN BERNATCHEZ, ERICH FISHER, PAUL GOLDBERG, ANDY I. R. HERRIES, ZENOBIA JACOBS, ANTONIETA JERARDINO, PANAGIOTIS KARKANAS, TOM MINICHILLO, PETER J. NILSSEN, ERIN THOMPSON, IAN WATTS, AND HOPE M. WILLIAMS

2007   Early Human Use of Marine Resources and Pigment in South Africa during the Middle Pleistocene. Nature 449(7164):905–908.

MARLOWE, FRANK W.

1999   Male Care and Mating Effort among Hadza Foragers. Behavioral Biology and Sociobiology 46(1):57–64.

2000   Paternal Investment and the Human Mating System. Behavioral Processes 51(1–3):45–61.

2001   Male Contribution to the Diet and Female Reproductive Success among Foragers. Current Anthropology 42(5):755–760.

2003   A Critical Period for Provisioning by Hadza Men: Implications for Pair Bonding. Evolution and Human Behavior 24(3):217–229.

2005a   Hunter-Gatherers and Human Evolution. Evolutionary Anthropology: Issues, News, and Reviews 14(2):54–67.

2005b   Who Tends Hadza Children? *In* Hunter-Gatherer Childhoods: Evolutionary, Developmental, and Cultural Perspectives. Barry S. Hewlett and Michael E. Lamb, eds. Pp. 177–190. New Brunswick, NJ: AldineTransaction.

2010   The Hadza: Hunter-Gatherers of Tanzania. Berkeley: University of California Press.

MARSHALL, LORNA J.

1960   !Kung Bushman Bands. Africa 30(4):325–355.

1976   The !Kung of Nyae. Cambridge, MA: Harvard University Press.

MARTIN, ROBERT D.

1983   Human Brain Evolution in an Ecological Context. Fifty-Second James Arthur Lecture. New York: American Museum of Natural History.

MARTÍN-GONZÁLEZ, JESÚS, ANA A. MATEOS, IDOIA GOIKOETXEA, WILLIAM R. LEONARD, AND JESÚS RODRÍGUEZ

2012   Differences between Neandertal and Modern Human Infant and Child Growth Models. Journal of Human Evolution 63(1):140–149.

MARTINI, MARY

1994   Peer Interactions in Polynesia: A View from the Marquesas. *In* Children's Play in Diverse Cultures. Jaipaul L. Roopnarine, James E. Jonson, and Frank H. Hooper, eds. Pp. 73–103. Albany: State University of New York Press.

MARTINI, MARY, AND JOHN KIRKPATRICK

1992   Parenting in Polynesia: A View from the Marquesas. *In* Parent-Child Socialization in Diverse Cultures. Jaipaul L. Roopnarine and D. Bruce Carterm, eds. Pp. 199–222. Norwood, NJ: Ablex.

MARTORELL, REYNALDO

1999   The Nature of Child Malnutrition and Its Long-Term Implications. Food and Nutrition Bulletin 20(3):288–292.

2010   Physical Growth and Development of the Malnourished Child: Contributions from 50 Years of Research at INCAP. Food and Nutrition Bulletin 31(1):68–82.

MARTORELL, REYNALDO, AND AMANDA ZONGRONE

2012   Intergenerational Influences on Child Growth and Undernutrition. Paediatric and Perinatal Epidemiology 26(Suppl. 1):302–314

MARTORELL, REYNALDO, PAUL MELGAR, JOHN A. MALUCCIO, ARYEH D. STEIN, AND JUAN A. RIVERA

2010   The Nutrition Intervention Improved Adult Human Capital and Economic Productivity. Journal of Nutrition 140(2):411–414. doi:10.3945/jn.109.114504.

MARVIN, ROBERT S., T. L. VAN DEVENDER, M. I. IWANAGA, S. LEVINE, AND
R. A. LEVINE

1977   Infant-Caregiver Attachment among the Hausa of Nigeria. *In* Ecological
          Factors in Human Development. Harry McGurk, ed. Pp. 247–260. New
          York: North-Holland Publishing Company.

MASTORAKOS, GEORGE, AND IOANNIS ILIAS

2003   Maternal and Fetal Hypothalamic-Pituitary-Adrenal Axes during
          Pregnancy and Postpartum. Annals of New York Academy of Sciences
          997(1):136–149.

MATSUZAWA, TETSURO

2007   Comparative Cognitive Development. Developmental Science 10(1):97–103.

2012   What Is Uniquely Human? A View from Comparative Cognitive
          Development in Humans and Chimpanzees. *In* The Primate Mind: Built to
          Connect with Other Minds. Frans de Waal and P. Francesco Ferrari, eds.
          Pp. 289–305. Cambridge, MA: Harvard University Press.

MATSUZAWA, TETSURO, MASAKI TOMONAGA, AND MASAYUKI TANAGA, EDS.

2006   Cognitive Development in Chimpanzees. Tokyo: Springer.

MAYNARD, ASHLEY E.

2002   Cultural Teaching: The Development of Teaching Skills in Maya Sibling
          Interactions. Child Development 73(3):969–982.

MAYNARD, ASHLEY E., AND KATHERINE E. TOVOTE

2010   Learning from Other Children. *In* The Anthropology of Learning in
          Childhood. David F. Lancy, Suzanne Gaskins, and John Bock, eds.
          Pp. 181–205. Lanham, MD: AltaMira Press.

MAYR, ERNST

1963   Animal Species and Evolution. Cambridge, MA: Harvard University Press.

MCDADE, THOMAS W.

2003   Life History Theory and the Immune System: Steps toward a Human
          Ecological Immunology. Yearbook of Physical Anthropology 46:100–125.

MCELREATH, RICHARD, AND PONTUS STRIMLING

2008   When Natural Selection Favors Imitation of Parents. Current
          Anthropology 49(2):307–316.

MCHENRY, HENRY M.

1991   Femoral Lengths and Stature in Plio-Pleistocene Hominids. American
          Journal of Physical Anthropology 85(2):148–158.

MCKENNA, JAMES J., HELEN L. BALL, AND LEE T. GETTLER

2007   Mother-Infant Cosleeping, Breastfeeding and Sudden Infant Death
          Syndrome: What Biological Anthropology Has Discovered about Normal
          Infant Sleep and Pediatric Sleep Medicine. American Journal of Physical
          Anthropology 134(Suppl. 45):133–161.

MCKENNA, JAMES J., EVELYN B. THOMAN, THOMAS F. ANDERS, ABRAHAM SADEH, VICKI L. SCHECTMAN, AND STEVEN F. GLOTZBACH

1993 Infant-Parent Co-Sleeping in an Evolutionary Perspective: Implications for Understanding Infant Sleep Development and the Sudden Infant Death Syndrome. Sleep 16(3):263–282.

MEAD, MARGARET

1928 Samoan Children at Work and Play. Natural History 28:626–636.

MEEHAN, COURTNEY L.

2005a The Effects of Residential Locality on Parental and Alloparental Investment among the Aka Foragers of the Central African Republic. Human Nature 16(1):58–80.

2005b Multiple Caregiving and Its Effect on Maternal Behavior among the Aka Foragers and Ngandu Farmers of Central Africa. PhD dissertation, Department of Anthropology, Washington State University.

2008 Allomaternal Investment and Relational Uncertainty among Ngandu Farmers of the Central African Republic. Human Nature 19(2):211–226.

2009 Maternal Time Allocation in Two Cooperative Childrearing Societies. Human Nature 20(4):375–393.

2014 Allomothers and Child Well-Being. *In* Handbook of Child Well-Being: Theories, Methods, and Policies in Global Perspective, vol. 2. Asher Ben-Arieh, Ferran Casas, Ivar Frønes, and Jill E. Korbin, eds. Pp. 1787–1816. New York: Springer.

MEEHAN, COURTNEY L., AND SEAN HAWKS

2011 Cooperation and Attachment in Early Childhood. Paper presented at the Annual Meeting of the American Anthropological Association, Montreal, Canada, November 16–20, 2011.

2013 Cooperative Breeding and Attachment among the Aka Foragers. *In* Attachment Reconsidered: Cultural Perspectives on a Western Theory. Naomi Quinn and Jeannette Mageo, eds. Pp. 85–114. New York: Palgrave.

2014 Maternal and Allomaternal Responsiveness: The Significance of Cooperative Caregiving in Attachment Theory. *In* Different Faces of Attachment: Cultural Variations of a Universal Human Need. Hiltrud Otto and Heidi Keller, eds. Pp. 113–140. Cambridge: Cambridge University Press.

MEEHAN, COURTNEY L., COURTNEY HELFRECHT, AND ROBERT QUINLAN

2014 Cooperative Breeding and Aka Children's Nutritional Status: Is Flexibility Key? American Journal of Physical Anthropology 153(4):513–525.

MEEHAN, COURTNEY L., ROBERT QUINLAN, AND COURTNEY D. MALCOM

2013 Cooperative Breeding and Maternal Energy Expenditure among Aka Foragers. American Journal of Human Biology: The Official Journal of the Human Biology Council 25(1):42–57.

MEEHAN, COURTNEY L., AND JENNIFER W. ROULETTE

2013   Early Supplementary Feeding among Central African Foragers and
           Farmers: A Biocultural Approach. Social Science and Medicine 96:112–120.

MELIS, ALICIA P., BRIAN HARE, AND MICHAEL TOMASELLO

2006   Chimpanzees Recruit the Best Collaborators. Science 311(5765):1297–1300.

MELLARS, PAUL

1996   The Neanderthal Legacy. Princeton, NJ: Princeton University Press.

MELLARS, PAUL, AND JENNIFER C. FRENCH

2011   Tenfold Population Increase in Western Europe at the Neandertal-to-
           Modern Human Transition. Science 333(6042):623–627.

MENZEL, CHARLES R.

1999   Unprompted Recall and Reporting of Hidden Objects by a Chimpanzee
           (*Pan troglodytes*) after Extended Delays. Journal of Comparative
           Psychology 113(4):426–434.

MERCHANT, KATHLEEN, REYNALDO MARTORELL, AND JERE HAAS

1990a   Maternal and Fetal Responses to the Stresses of Lactation Concurrent
           with Pregnancy and of Short Recuperative Intervals. American Journal of
           Clinical Nutrition 52(2):280–288.

1990b   Consequences for Maternal Nutrition of Reproductive Stress across
           Consecutive Pregnancies. American Journal of Clinical Nutrition
           52(4):616–620.

MIGLIANO, ANDREA B., LUCIO VINICIUS, AND MARTA M. LAHR

2007   Life History Trade-Offs Explain the Evolution of Human Pygmies.
           Proceedings of the National Academy of Sciences 104(51):20216–20219.

MILLER, DANIEL J., TETYANA DUKA, CHERYL D. STIMPSON, STEVEN J. SCHAPIRO,
WALLACE B. BAZE, MARK J. MCARTHUR, ARCHIBALD J. FOBBS, ET AL.

2012   Prolonged Myelination in Human Neocortical Evolution. Proceedings of
           the National Academy of Sciences 109(41):16480–16485.

MILLER, ELIZABETH M.

2010   Maternal Hemoglobin Depletion in a Settled Northern Kenyan Pastoral
           Population. American Journal of Human Biology 22(6):768–764.

MILLER, JANE E., GERMAN RODRÍGUEZ, AND ANNE R. PEBLEY

1994   Lactation, Seasonality, and Mother's Postpartum Weight Change in
           Bangladesh: An Analysis of Maternal Depletion. American Journal of
           Human Biology 6(4):511–524.

MIQUELOTE, AUDREI F., DENISE C. C. SANTOS, PRISCILA M. CAÇOLA,
MARIA IMACULADA DE L. MONTEBELO, AND CARL GABBARD

2012   Effect of the Home Environment on Motor and Cognitive Behavior of
           Infants. Infant Behavior and Development 35(3):329–334.

MITANI, JOHN

2006   Reciprocal Exchanges in Chimpanzees and Other Primates. *In* Cooperation in Primates and Humans. Peter M. Kappeler and Carel P. van Schaik, eds. Pp. 107–119. Berlin: Springer.

MOGGI-CECCHI, JACOPO

2001   Human Evolution: Questions of Growth. Nature 414:595–596.

MONTAGU, M. F. ASHLEY

1955   Time, Morphology, and Neoteny in the Evolution of Man. American Anthropologist 57(1):13–27.

MONTESSORI, MARIA, AND ANNE E. GEORGE

1964   The Montessori Method. New York: Frederick A. Stokes Company.

MONTGOMERY, HEATHER

2008   An Introduction to Childhood: Anthropological Perspectives on Children's Lives. New York: Wiley-Blackwell.

MORELLI, GILDA A., AND EDWARD Z. TRONICK

1992   Efe Fathers: One among Many? A Comparison of Forager Children's Involvement with Fathers and Other Males. Social Development 1(1):36–54.

MORI, SHIRO, HIROKI NAKAMOTO, HIROSHI MIZUOCHI, SACHI IKUDOME, AND CARL GABBARD

2013   Influence of Affordances in the Home Environment on Motor Development of Young Children in Japan. Child Development Research, vol. 2013, Article ID 898406, 5 pages. doi:10.1155/2013/898406.

MORISON, PATRICIA, AND ANN S. MATSEN

1991   Peer Reputation in Middle Childhood as a Predictor of Adaptation in Adolescence: A Seven-Year Follow-Up. Child Development 62:991–1007.

MORRISSEY, ANNE-MARIE, AND P. MARGARET BROWN

2009   Mother and Toddler Activity in the Zone of Proximal Development for Pretend Play as a Predictor of Higher Child IQ. Gifted Child Quarterly 53(2):106–120.

MULLER, GERD B., AND GÜNTER P. WAGNER

1991   Novelty in Evolution: Restructuring the Concept. Annual Review of Ecology and Systematics 22:229–256.

MURDOCK, GEORGE P.

1981   Atlas of World Cultures. Pittsburgh, PA: University of Pittsburgh Press.

MURPHY, LORNA, LYNETTE SIEVERT, KHURSHIDA BEGUM, TANIYA SHARMEEN, ELAINE PULEO, OSUL CHOWDHURY, SHANTHI MUTTUKRISHNA, AND GILLIAN BENTLEY

2013   Life Course Effects on Age at Menopause among Bangladeshi Sedentees and Migrants to the UK. American Journal of Human Biology 25(1):83–93.

MUSIL, ALOIS

1928   The Manners and Customs of the Rwala Bedouin. New York: American
        Geographical Society.

MYOWA, MASAKO

1996   Imitation of Facial Gestures by an Infant Chimpanzee. Primates
        37(2):207–213.

MYOWA-YAMAKOSHI, MASAKO, MASAKI TOMONAGA, MASAYUKI TANAKA, AND
TETSURO MATSUZAWA

2004   Imitation in Neonatal Chimpanzees (*Pan troglodytes*). Developmental
        Science 7(4):437–442.

NAKAMURA, YASUHIRO, HUI XIAO GANG, TAKASHI SUZUKI, HIRONOBU SASANO,
AND WILLIAM E. RAINEY

2009   Adrenal Changes Associated with Adrenarche. Reviews in Endocrine and
        Metabolic Disorders 10(1):19–26.

NAKANO, YOSHIHIKO, AND TASUKU KIMURA

1992   Development of Bipedal Walking in *Macaca fuscata* and *Pan Troglodytes*.
        In Topics in Primatology, vol. 3. S. Matano, R. H. Tuttle, H. Ishida, and
        M. Goodman, eds. Pp. 177–190. Tokyo: University of Tokyo Press.

NARVÁEZ, DARCIA, JAAK PANKSEPP, ALLAN N. SCHORE, AND TRACY R. GLEASON

2012   Evolution, Early Experience, and Human Development: From Research to
        Practice and Policy. Oxford: Oxford University Press, 2012.

NARVÁEZ, DARCIA, KRISTIN VALENTINO, AGUSTIN FUENTES, JAMES J. MCKENNA,
AND PETER GRAY

2014   Ancestral Landscapes in Human Evolution: Culture, Childrearing, and
        Social Wellbeing. Oxford: Oxford University Press.

NAVARRETE, ANA F., CAREL P. VAN SCHAIK, AND KARIN ISLER

2011   Energetics and the Evolution of Human Brain Size. Nature 480:91–92.

NELSON, ANDREW J., AND JENNIFER L. THOMPSON

1999   Growth and Development in Neandertals and Other Fossil Hominids:
        Implications for Hominid Phylogeny and the Evolution of Hominid
        Ontogeny. *In* Human Growth in the Past: Studies from Bones and Teeth.
        Robert D. Hoppa and Charles M. FitzGerald, eds. Pp. 88–110. Cambridge:
        Cambridge University Press.

2002   Neanderthal Adolescent Postcranial Growth. *In* Human Evolution through
        Developmental Change. Nancy Minugh-Purvis and Kenneth McNamara,
        eds. Pp. 442–463. Baltimore, MD: Johns Hopkins University Press.

2005   Le Moustier 1 and the Interpretation of Stages in Neandertal Growth and
        Development. *In* The Neandertal Adolescent Le Moustier 1: New Aspects,
        New Results. Herbert Ullrich, ed. Pp. 328–338. Berlin: Staatliche Museen zu
        Berlin, Preußischer Kulturbesiz.

NERLOVE, SARA B.

1974   Women's Workload and Infant Feeding Practices: A Relationship with
        Demographic Implications. Ethnology 13(2):207–214.

NERLOVE, SARA B., JOHN M. ROBERTS, ROBERT E. KLEIN, CHARLES YARBROUGH,
AND JEAN-PIERRE HABICHT

1974   Natural Indicators of Cognitive Development: An Observational Study of
        Rural Guatemalan Children. Ethos 2(3):265–295.

NESSE, RANDOLPH M.

2007   Runaway Social Selection for Displays of Partner Value and Altruism.
        Biological Theory 2(2):143–155.

2010   Social Selection and the Origins of Culture. *In* Evolution, Culture, and the
        Human Mind. Mark Schaller, Ara Norenzayan, Steven J. Heine, Toshio
        Yamagishi, and Tatsuya Kameda, eds. Pp. 137–150. Philadelphia, PA:
        Lawrence Erlbaum Associates.

NEUWELT-TRUNTZER, SANDRA

1981   Ecological Influences on the Physical, Behavioral, and Cognitive
        Development of Pygmy Children. PhD dissertation, Department of
        Behavioral Sciences, University of Chicago.

NEWSON, LESLEY, AND PETER J. RICHERSON

2013   The Evolution of Flexible Parenting. *In* Evolution's Empress: Darwinian
        Perspectives on the Nature of Women. Maryanne L. Fisher, Justin R.
        Garcia, and Rosemarie Sokol Chang, eds. Pp. 151–167. Oxford: Oxford
        University Press.

NGUYEN, ANN D., AND ALAN J. CONLEY

2008   Adrenal Androgens in Humans and Nonhuman Primates: Production,
        Zonation, and Regulation. Endocrine Development 13:33–54.

NONACS, PETER

2011   Monogamy and High Relatedness Do Not Preferentially Favor the
        Evolution of Cooperation. BMC Evolutionary Biology 11:58.

NORENZAYAN, ARA, AND SCOTT ATRAN

2004   Cognitive and Emotional Processes in the Cultural Transmission of
        Natural and Nonnatural Beliefs. *In* The Psychological Foundations of
        Culture. Mark Schaller and Christian S. Crandall, eds. Pp. 149–169.
        Mahwah, NJ: Lawrence Erlbaum.

NOWAK, RONALD M., AND JOHN L. PARADISO

1999   Walker's Mammals of the World, vols. 1 and 2. 6th edition. Baltimore, MD:
        Johns Hopkins University Press.

OCHOA, SUZANNE ELISE

1995   Relationships between Social environment and Growth Processes in

Rhesus Monkeys (*Macaca mulatta*). PhD dissertation, Graduate School of
Arts and Science, New York University.

OCHS, ELINOR, AND CAROLINA IZQUIERDO
2009   Responsibility in Childhood: Three Developmental Trajectories. Ethos
        37(4):391–413.

O'CONNELL, JAMES F., KRISTEN HAWKES, AND NICHOLAS G. BLURTON JONES
1999   Grandmothering and the Evolution of *Homo erectus*. Journal of Human
        Evolution 36(5):461–485.

O'CONNELL, JAMES F., KRISTEN HAWKES, KAREN D. LUPO, AND NICHOLAS G.
BLURTON JONES
2002   Male Strategies and Plio-Pleistocene Archaeology. Journal of Human
        Evolution 43(6):461–485.

ODDEN, HAROLD, AND PHILLIPE ROCHAT
2004   Observational Learning and Enculturation. Educational and Child
        Psychology 21:39–50.

OGBUANU, CHINELO, SAUNDRA GLOVER, JANICE PROBOST, JIHONG LIU, AND
JAMES HUSSEY
2011   The Effect of Maternity Leave Length and Time of Return to Work on
        Breastfeeding. Pediatrics 127(6):1414–1427.

OHMAGARI, KAYO, AND FIKRET BERKES
1997   Transmission of Indigenous Knowledge and Bush Skills among the
        Western James Bay Cree Women of Subarctic Canada. Human Ecology
        25(2):197–222.

OKAMOTO-BARTH, SANAE, CHRIS MOORE, JOCHEN BARTH, FRANCYS SUBIAUL,
AND DANIEL J. POVINELLI
2011   Carryover Effect of Joint Attention to Repeated Events in Chimpanzees
        and Young Children. Developmental Science 14(2):440–452.

OKAMOTO-BARTH, SANAE, MASAYUKI TANAKA, NOBUYUKI KAWAI, AND
MASAKI TOMONAGA
2007   Looking Compensates for the Distance Between Mother and Infant
        Chimpanzee. Developmental Science 10(2):172–182.

OLDS, DAVID L., CHARLES R. HENDERSON JR., ROBERT CHAMBERLIN, AND
ROBERT TATELBAUM
2002   Preventing Child Abuse and Neglect: A Randomized Controlled Trial.
        Pediatrics 110:486–496.

OLDS, DAVID L., LOLA SADLER, AND HARRIET KITZMAN
2007   Programs for Parents of Infants and Toddlers: Recent Evidence from
        Randomized Trials. Journal of Child Psychology and Psychiatry
        48(3–4):355–391.

ORENTREICH, NORMAN, JOEL L. BRIND, RONALD L. RIZER, AND JOSEPH H.
VOGELMAN
1984   Age Changes and Sex Differences in Serum Dehydroepiandrosterone
        Sulfate Concentrations throughout Adulthood. Journal of Clinical
        Endocrinology and Metabolism 59(3):551–555.

OTTENBERG, SIMON
1968   Double Descent in an African Society: The Afikpo Village-Group. Seattle,
        WA: University of Washington Press.

OTTO, HILTRUD
2014   Don't Show your Emotions! Emotional Regulation and Attachment in the
        Cameroonian Nso. *In* Different Faces of Attachment: Cultural Variations
        of a Universal Human Need. Hiltrud Otto and Heidi Keller, eds.
        Pp. 215–230. Cambridge: Cambridge University Press.

PAGEL, MARK D., AND PAUL H. HARVEY
1993   Evolution of the Juvenile Period in Mammals. In Juvenile Primates: Life
        History, Development, and Behavior. Michael E. Pereira and Lynn A.
        Fairbanks, eds. Pp. 28–37. New York: Oxford University Press.

PAINE, RICHARD R., AND JESPER L. BOLDSEN
2006   Paleodemographic Data and Why Understanding Holocene Demography
        Is Essential to Understanding Human Life History Evolution in the
        Pleistocene. *In* The Evolution of Human Life History. Kristen Hawkes and
        Richard R. Paine, eds. Pp. 307–330. Santa Fe, NM: School of American
        Research Press.

PALMERT, MARK R., DOUGLAS L. HAYDEN, M. JOAN MANSFIELD, JOHN F. CRIGLER,
WILLIAM F. CROWLEY, DONALD W. CHANDLER, AND PAUL A. BOEPPLE
2001   The Longitudinal Study of Adrenal Maturation during Gonadal
        Suppression: Evidence That Adrenarche Is a Gradual Process. Journal of
        Clinical Endocrinology and Metabolism 86(9):4536–4542.

PAPATHAKIS, PEGGY C., NIGEL C. ROLLINS, CAROLINE J. CHANTRY,
MICHAEL L. BENNISH, AND KENNETH H. BROWN
2007   Micronutrient Status during Lactation in HIV-Infected and HIV-
        Uninfected South African Women during the First 6 Months after
        Delivery. American Journal of Clinical Nutrition 85(1):182–192.

PARADISE, RUTH, AND BARBARA ROGOFF
2009   Side by Side: Learning by Observing and Pitching In. Ethos 37(1):102–138.

PARKER, JEFFREY G., AND STEVEN R. ASHER
1987   Peer Relations and Later Personal Adjustment: Are Low-Accepted Children
        at Risk? Psychological Bulletin 102(3):357–389.

PARKER, ROZSIKA
1995   Mother Love/Mother Hate: The Power of Maternal Ambivalence. New
        York: Basic Books.

PATTISON, J. CHRISTINA, WENDY SALTZMAN, DAVID H. ABBOTT, BRYNN K.
HOGAN, ANN D. NGUYEN, BETTINA HUSEN, ALMUTH EINSPANIER, ALAN J.
CONLEY, AND IAN M. BIRD

2007   Gender and Gonadal Status Differences in Zona Reticularis Expression
        in Marmoset Monkey Adrenals: Cytochrome B5 Localization with
        Respect to Cytochrome P450 17, 20-lyase Activity. Molecular and Cellular
        Endocrinology 265–266:93–101.

PEACOCK, NADINE R.

1991   Rethinking the Sexual Division of Labor: Reproduction and Women's
        Work among the Efe. *In* Gender at the Crossroads of Knowledge: Feminist
        Anthropology in the Postmodern Era. Micaela di Leonardo, ed. Pp. 339–
        360. Berkeley: University of California Press.

PELISSIER, CATHERINE

1991   The Anthropology of Teaching and Learning. Annual Review of
        Anthropology 20:75–95.

PELLEGRINI, ANTHONY D., AND ADAM F. A. PELLEGRINI

2013   Play, Plasticity, and Ontogeny in Childhood. *In* Evolution, Early
        Experience, and Human Development: From Research to Practice and
        Policy. Darcia Narváez, Jaak Panksepp, Allan N. Schore, and Tracy R.
        Gleason, eds. Pp. 339–351. New York: Oxford University Press.

PELLEGRINI, ANTHONY D., AND PETER K. SMITH

1998   Physical Activity Play: The Nature and Function of a Neglected Aspect of
        Play. Child Development 69(3):577–598.

PELLEGRINI, ANTHONY D., DANIELLE DUPUIS, AND PETER K. SMITH

2007   Play in Evolution and Development. Developmental Review 27(2):261–276.

PELTO, GRETEL

2008   Taking Care of Children: Applying Anthropology in Maternal and Child
        Nutrition and Health. Human Organization 67(3):237–243.

PELTO, GRETEL H., YUANYUAN ZHANG, AND JEAN-PIERRE HABICHT

2010   Premastication: The Second Arm of Infant and Young Child Feeding for
        Health and Survival? Maternal & Child Nutrition 6(1):4–18.

PEREIRA, MICHAEL E., AND JEANNE ALTMANN

1985   Development of Social Behavior in Free-Living Nonhuman Primates. *In*
        Nonhuman Primate Models for Growth and Development. E. S. Watts, ed.
        Pp. 217–309. New York: Alan R Liss.

PEREIRA, MICHAEL E., AND LYNN A. FAIRBANKS

1993   What Are Juvenile Primates All About? In Juvenile Primates: Life History,
        Development, and Behavior. Michael E. Pereira and Lynn A. Fairbanks,
        eds. Pp. 3–12. New York: Oxford University Press.

PERNER, JOSEF, TED RUFFMAN, AND SUSAN R. LEEKAM

1994   Theory of Mind Is Contagious: You Catch It from Your Sibs. Child Development 5:1228–1235.

PETERS, JOHN F.

1998   Life among the Yanomami: The Story of Change among the Xilixana on the Mucajai River in Brazil. Orchard Park, NY: Broadview.

PETERSON, JEAN T.

1978   The Ecology of Social Boundaries: Agta Foragers of the Philippines. Urbana: University of Illinois Press.

PHILIPS, SUSAN

1972   Participant Structures and Communicative Competence: Warm Springs Children in Community and Classroom. *In* Functions of Language in the Classroom. Courtney Cazden, Vera P. John, and Dell Hymes, eds. Pp. 370–394. New York: Teachers College Press.

PIAGET, JEAN

1954   The Construction of Reality in the Child. New York: Basic Books.

1962   Play, Dreams, and Imitation in Childhood. New York: Norton.

PIEL, L. HALLIDAY

2012   Food Rationing and Children's Self-Reliance in Japan, 1942–1952. Journal of the History Childhood and Youth 5:393–418.

PIGEOT, NICOLE

1990   Technical and Social Actors: Flintknapping Specialists at Magdalenian Etiolles. Archaeological Review 9:126–41.

PIGLIUCCI, MASSIMO

2008   What, If Anything, Is an Evolutionary Novelty? Philosophy of Science 75(5):887–898.

PIPERATA, BARBARA A.

2009   Variation in Maternal Strategies during Lactation: The Role of the Biosocial Context. American Journal of Human Biology 21(6):817–827.

PIPERATA, BARBARA A., KAMMI K. SCHMEER, CRAIG HADLEY, AND GENEVIEVE RITCHIE-EWING

2013   Dietary Inequalities of Mother-Child Pairs in the Rural Amazon: Evidence of Maternal-Child Buffering? Social Science and Medicine 96:183–191.

POLAK, BARBARA

2003   Little Peasants: On the Importance of Reliability in Child Labour. *In* Le Travail en Afrique Noire: Représentations et Pratiques à l'Époque Contemporaine. Hélène d'Almeida-Topor, Monique Lakroum, and Gerd Spittler, eds. Pp. 125–136. Paris: Karthala.

2011   Die Könige der Feldarbeit. PhD dissertation, Kulturwissenschaftlichen Fakultät der Universität Bayreuth.

POMPONIO, ALICE

1992   Seagulls Don't Fly into the Bush. Belmont, CA: Wadsworth.

PONCE DE LEÓN, MARCIA S., LUBOV GOLOVANOVA, VLADIMIR DORONICHEV,
GALINA ROMANOVA, TAKERU AKAZAWA, OSAMU KONDO, JAJIME ISHIDA, AND
CHRISTOPH P. E. ZOLLIKOFER

2008   Neanderthal Brain Size at Birth Provides Insights into the Evolution of
        Human Life History. Proceedings of the National Academy of Sciences
        105(37):13764–13768.

PONGCHAROEN, TIPPAWAN, USHA RAMAKRISHNAN, ANN M. DIGIROLAMO,
PATTANEE WINICHAGOON, RAFAEL FLORES, JINTANA SINGKHORNARD, AND
REYNALDO MARTORELL

2012   Influence of Prenatal and Postnatal Growth on Intellectual Functioning
        in School-Aged Children. Archives of Pediatrics & Adolescent Medicine
        166(5):411–416.

PORTMANN, A.

1962   Cerebralisation und Ontognese. Medizinicche Grundlagenforschung
        4:1–62.

POSTMAN, NEIL

1982   The Disappearance of Childhood. New York: Delacorte Press.

POTTS, RICHARD

1996   Humanity's Descent: The Consequences of Ecological Instability. New
        York: Avon Books.

PRANGE, HENRY D., JOHN F. ANDERSON, AND HERMANN RAHN

1979   Scaling of Skeletal Mass to Body Mass in Birds and Mammals. American
        Naturalist 113(1):103–122.

PRENTICE, ANDREW M., CAROLINE J. SPAAIJ, GAIL R. GOLDBERG, SALLY D.
POPPITT, JOOP M. VAN RAAIJ, MICHAEL TOTTON, DEBBIE SWANN, AND ALISON E.
BLACK

1996   Energy Requirements of Pregnant and Lactating Women. European
        Journal of Clinical Nutrition 50(Suppl. 1):S82–111.

PRENTICE, ANDREW M., ROGER G. WHITEHEAD, SUSAN B. ROBERTS, AND
ALISON A. PAUL

1981   Long-Term Energy Balance in Child-Bearing Gambian Women. American
        Journal of Clinical Nutrition 34(12):2790–2799.

PURI, RAJINDRA K.

2005   Deadly Dances in the Bornean Rainforest: Hunting Knowledge of the
        Punan Benalui. Leiden, Netherlands: KITLV Press.

PUSEY, ANNE E., JENNIFER M. WILLIAMS, AND JANE GOODALL

1997   The Influence of Dominance Rank on the Reproductive Success of
        Chimpanzees. Science 277(5327):828–831.

QUINLAN, ROBERT, AND MARSHA QUINLAN

2008   Human Lactation, Pair-Bonds, and Alloparents. Human Nature
        19(1):87–102.

RAINEY, WILLIAM E., B. R. CARR, Z. N. WANG, AND C. R. PARKER JR.

2001   Gene Profiling of Human Fetal and Adult Adrenals. Journal of
        Endocrinology 171(2):209–215.

RAINEY, WILLIAM E., AND YASUHIRO NAKAMURA

2008   Regulation of the Adrenal Androgen Biosynthesis. Journal of Steroid
        Biochemistry and Molecular Biology 108(3–5):281–286.

RAMAKRISHNAN, USHA

2002   Prevalence of Micronutrient Malnutrition Worldwide. Nutrition Reviews
        60(Suppl. 5):S46–S52.

RAMAKRISHNAN, USHA, ALYSSA LOWE, SHEILA VIR, SHUBA KUMAR,
RANI MOHANRAJ, ANURAAG CHATURVEDI, ELIZABETH A. NOZNESKY,
REYNALDO MARTORELL, AND JOHN B. MASON

2012   Public Health Interventions, Barriers, and Opportunities for Improving
        Maternal Nutrition in India. Food Nutrition Bulletin 33(Suppl. 1):71–92.

RAMIREZ ROZZI, FERNANDO V., AND JOSÉ M. BERMÚDEZ DE CASTRO

2004   Surprisingly Rapid Growth in Neanderthals. Nature 428:936–939.

RAMSAY, HEATHER L., DENNIS S. WEAVER, AND HORST SEIDLER

2005   Bone Histology in the Le Moustier Neandertal Child. *In* The Neandertal
        Adolescent Le Moustier 1: New Aspects, New Results. Herbert Ullrich, ed.
        Pp. 282–292. Berlin: Staatliche Museen zu Berlin, Preußischer Kulturbesiz.

RAND, DAVID G., JOSHUA D. GREENE, AND MARTIN A. NOWAK

2012   Spontaneous Giving and Calculated Greed. Nature 489:427–430.

RAPAPORT, LISA G.

2011   Progressive Parenting Behavior in Wild Golden Lion Tamarins. Behavioral
        Ecology 2(4):745–754.

RAPAPORT, LISA G., AND GILLIAN R. BROWN

2008   Social Influences on Foraging Behavior in Young Primates: Learning
        What, Where, and How to Eat. Evolutionary Anthropology 17(4):189–201.

RAPAPORT, LISA G., AND CARLOS R. RUIZ-MIRANDA

2002   Tutoring in Wild Golden Lion Tamarins. International Journal of
        Primatology 23(5):1063–1070.

RAUM, OTTO F.

1940   Chaga Childhood. Oxford: Oxford University Press.

REBELSKY, FRIEDA, AND CHERYL HANKS

1971   Fathers' Verbal Interaction with Infants in the First Three Months of Life.
        Child Development 42(1):63–68.

REDDY, VASUDEVI

2003   On Being the Object of Attention: Implications for Self-Other
         Consciousness. Trends in Cognitive Sciences 7(9):397–402.

REICHES, MEREDITH W., PETER T. ELLISON, SUSAN F. LIPSON,
KATHERINE C. SHARROCK, ELIZA GARDINER, AND LAURA G. DUNCAN

2009   Pooled Energy Budget and Human Life History. American Journal of
         Human Biology 2(4): 421–429.

REID, DONALD J., DEBBIE GUATELLI-STEINBERG, AND PAMELA WALTON

2008   Variation in Modern Human Premolar Enamel Formation Times:
         Implications for Neandertals. Journal of Human Evolution 54(2):225–235.

REMER, THOMAS, AND FRIEDRICH MANZ

2001   The Midgrowth Spurt in Healthy Children Is Not Caused by Adrenarche.
         Journal of Clinical Endocrinology and Metabolism 86(9):4183–4816.

RENFREW, COLIN

1998   Mind and Matter: Cognitive Archaeology and External Storage. *In*
         Cognition and Material Culture: The Archaeology of Symbolic Storage.
         Colin Renfrew and Chris Scarre, eds. Pp. 1–6. Oxford: Oxbow Books.

REPACHOLI, B. M., AND A. GOPNIK

1997   Early Reasoning about Desire: Evidence from 14- and 18-Month-Olds.
         Developmental Psychology 33(1):12–21.

REYES-GARCIA, VICTORIA, JAMES BROESCH, AND TAPS BOLIVIAN STUDY TEAM

2013   The Transmission of Ethnobotanical Knowledge and Skills among Tsimanè
         in the Bolivian Amazon. *In* Understanding Cultural Transmission in
         Anthropology. Roy Ellen, Stephen J. Lycett, and Sarah E. Johns, eds.
         Pp. 181–212. New York: Berghahn.

RHEINGOLD, HARRIET

1982   Little Children's Participation in the Work of Adults: A Nascent Prosocial
         Behavior. Child Development 53(1):114–125.

RICHERSON, PETER J., AND ROBERT BOYD

1992   Cultural Inheritance and Evolutionary Ecology. *In* Evolutionary Ecology
         and Human Behavior. Eric A. Smith and Bruce Winterhalder, eds.
         Pp. 61–92. New York: Aldine de Gruyter.

RICKLEFS, ROBERT E.

2000   Lack, Skutch, and Moreau: The Early Development of Life-History
         Thinking. Condor 102(1):3–8.

RIESMAN, PAUL

1992   First Find Yourself a Good Mother. New Brunswick, NJ: Rutgers University
         Press.

RILLING, JAMES K., DAVID A. GUTMAN, THORSTEN R. ZEH, GIUSEPPI PAGNONI,
GREGORY S. BERNS, AND CLINTON D. KILTS

2002   A Neural Basis for Social Cooperation. Neuron 35(2):395–405.

RINDSTEDT, CAMILLA, AND KARIN ARONSSON

2003   ¿Quieres Bañar? Sibling Caretaking, Play, and Perspective-Taking in an
        Andean Community. Paper presented at the 33rd Annual Meeting of the
        Jean Piaget Society, Chicago, June 5.

RIVAL, LAURA M.

2002   Trekking through History: The Hauorani of Amazonian Ecuador. New
        York: Columbia University Press.

ROBBINS, ANDREW M., TARA STOINSKI, KATIE FAWCETT, AND
MARTHA M. ROBBINS

2011   Lifetime Reproductive Success of Female Mountain Gorillas. American
        Journal of Physical Anthropology 146(4):582–593.

ROBERTS, JOHN M., MALCOLM J. ARTH, AND ROBERT R. BUSH

1959   Games in Culture. American Anthropologist 61(4):597–605.

ROBERTS, JOHN M., AND BRIAN SUTTON-SMITH

1962   Child Training and Game Involvement. Ethnology 1(2):166–185.

ROBSON, SHANNEN L., CAREL P. VAN SCHAIK, AND KRISTEN HAWKES

2006   The Derived Features of Human Life History. *In* The Evolution of Human
        Life History. Kristen Hawkes and Richard R. Paine, eds. Pp. 17–44. Santa
        Fe, NM: School of American Research Press.

ROBSON, SHANNEN L., AND BERNARD WOOD

2008   Hominin Life History: Reconstruction and Evolution. Journal of Anatomy
        212(4):394–425.

ROFFMAN, ITAI, SUE SAVAGE-RUMBAUGH, ELIZABETH RUBERT-PUGH,
AVRAHAM RONEN, AND EVIATAR NEVO

2012   Stone Tool Production and Utilization by Bonobo Chimpanzees
        (*Pan paniscus*). Proceedings of the National Academy of Sciences
        109(36):14500–14503.

ROGOFF, BARBARA

1981   Adults and Peers as Agents of Socialization: A Highland Guatemalan
        Profile. Ethos 9:18–36.

ROGOFF, BARBARA, MARTHA J. SELLERS, SERGIO PIRROTTA, NATHAN FOX, AND
SHELDON H. WHITE

1975   Age of Assignment of Roles and Responsibilities to Children. Human
        Development 18(5):353–369.

ROHNER, RONALD P., AND MANJUSRI CHAKI-SIRCAR

1988   Women and Children in a Bengali Village. Hanover, NH: University Press
        of New England.

ROSENBERG, KAREN. R.

1992   The Evolution of Modern Human Childbirth. Yearbook of Physical
        Anthropology 35:89–124.

ROSENFELD, RON G., AND BARBARA C. NICODEMUS

2003   The Transition from Adolescence to Adult Life: Physiology of the "Transition" Phase and Its Evolutionary Basis. Hormone Research 60(Suppl. 1):74–77.

ROSS, CAROLINE

1998   Primate Life Histories. Evolutionary Anthropology 6(2):54–63.

ROTENBERG, KEN J., NICK ADDIS, LUCY R. BETTS, AMANDA CORRIGAN, CLAIRE FOX, ZOE HOBSON, SARAH RENNISON, MARK TRUEMAN, AND MICHAEL J. BOULTON

2010   The Relation between Trust Beliefs and Loneliness during Early Childhood, Middle Childhood, and Adulthood. Personality and Social Psychology Bulletin 36(8):1086–1100.

RÖTTGER-RÖSSLER, BIRGITT

2014   Bonding and Belonging beyond WEIRD Worlds: Rethinking Attachment Theory on the Basis of Cross-Cultural Anthropological Data. *In* Different Faces of Attachment: Cultural Variations of a Universal Human Need. Hiltrud Otto and Heidi Keller, eds. Pp. 141–168. Cambridge: Cambridge University Press.

ROWELL, THELMA E.

1975   Growing Up in a Monkey Group. Ethos 3(2):113–128.

RUBENSTEIN, DUSTIN R., AND IRBY J. LOVETTE

2007   Temporal Environmental Variability Drives the Evolution of Cooperative Breeding in Birds. Current Biology 17(16):1414–1419.

RUDDLE, KENNETH, AND RAY CHESTERFIELD

1977   Education for Traditional Food Procurement in the Orinoco Delta. Los Angeles: University of California Press.

RUFF, CHRISTOPHER

2009   Relative Limb Strength and Locomotion in *Homo habilis*. American Journal of Physical Anthropology 138(1):90–100.

RUFF, CHRISTOPHER B., ERIK TRINKAUS, AND TRENTON W. HOLLIDAY

1997   Body Mass and Encephalization in Pleistocene *Homo*. Nature 387:173–176.

RUFF, CHRISTOPHER B., ERIK TRINKAUS, ALAN WALKER, AND CLARK S. LARSEN

1993   Postcranial Robusticity in *Homo*. I: Temporal Trends and Mechanical Interpretation. American Journal of Physical Anthropology 91(1):21–53.

RUFF, CHRISTOPHER B., ALAN WALKER, AND ERIK TRINKAUS

1994   Postcranial Robusticity in *Homo*. III: Ontogeny. American Journal of Physical Anthropology 93(1):35–54.

RUFFMAN, T. J., J. PERNER, M. NAITO, L. PARKIN, AND W. CLEMENTS

1998   Older (But Not Younger) Siblings Facilitate False Belief Understanding. Developmental Psychology 34(1):164–74.

SACHER, GEORGE A.

1959   Relation of Lifespan to Brain Weight and Body Weight in Mammals. *In*
        Ciba Foundation Colloquia on Ageing, vol. 5: The Lifespan of Animals.
        G. E. W. Wolstenholme and M. O'Connor, eds. Pp. 115–133. London:
        Churchill Press.

1975   Maturation and Longevity in Relation to Cranial Capacity in Hominid
        Evolution. *In* Primate Functional Morphology and Evolution. Russell H.
        Tuttle, ed. Pp. 417–441. The Hague, Netherlands: Mouton.

SAENGER, P., AND J. DIMARTINO-NARDI

2001   Premature Adrenarche. Journal of Endocrinological Investigation
        24(9):724–733.

SAFFRAN, JENNY R., RICHARD N. ASLIN, AND ELISSA L. NEWPORT

1996   Statistical Learning by 8-Month-Old Infants. Science 274(5294):1926–1928.

SAGI, ABRAHAM, MARINUS H. VAN IJZENDOORN, ORA AVIEZER, FRANK DONNELL,
NINA KOREN-KARIE, TIRTSA JOELS, AND YAEL HARL

1995   Attachments in a Multiple-Caregiver and Multiple-Infant Environment:
        The Case of the Israeli Kibbutzim. Monographs of the Society for Research
        in Child Development 60(2–3):71–91.

SAGI, ABRAHAM, MARINUS H. VAN IJZENDOORN, ORA AVIEZER, FRANK DONNELL,
AND OFRA MAYSELESS

1994   Sleeping Out of Home in a Kibbutz Communal Arrangement: It Makes
        a Difference for Infant-Mother Attachment. Child Development
        65(4):992–1004.

SAGI-SCHWARTZ, AVI, AND ORA AVIEZER

2005   Correlates of Attachment to Multiple Caregivers in Kibbutz Children from
        Birth to Emerging Adulthood: The Haifa Longitudinal Study. *In* Attachment
        from Infancy to Adulthood. Klaus E. Grossmann, Karin Grossmann, and
        Everett Waters, eds. Pp. 165–197. New York: Guilford Press.

SAKAI, TOMOKO, DAICHI HIRAI, AKICHIKA MIKAMI, JURI SUZUKI,
YUZURU HAMADA, MASAKI TOMONAGA, MASAYUKI TANAKA, ET AL.

2010   Prolonged Maturation of Prefrontal White Matter in Chimpanzees.
        Available from Nature Precedings, http://precedings.nature.com/
        documents/4411/version/1/html

SAKAI, TOMOKO, AKICHIKA MIKAMI, MASAKI TOMONAGA, MIE MATSUI,
JURI SUZUKI, YUZURU HAMADA, MASAUYIK TANAKA, ET AL.

2011   Differential Prefrontal White Matter Development in Chimpanzees and
        Humans. Current Biology 21(16):1–6.

SANKARARAMAN, SRIRAM, MALLICK SWAPAN, MICHAEL DANNERMANN,
KAY PRÜFER, JANET KELSO, SVANTE PÄÄBO, NICK PATTERSON, AND DAVID REICH

2014   The Genomic Landscape of Neanderthal Ancestry in Present-Day Humans.
        Nature 507:354–358.

SAPOLSKY, ROBERT M., AND E. MARTIN SPENCER

1997   Insulin-Like Growth Factor I Is Suppressed in Socially Subordinate Male
        Baboons. American Journal of Physiology 273(4):R1346–R1351.

SAPOLSKY, ROBERT M., JOSEPH H. VOGELMAN, NORMAN ORENTREICH, AND
JEANNE ALTMANN

1993   Senescent Decline in Serum Dehydroepiandrosterone Sulfate
        Concentrations in a Population of Wild Baboons. Journals of Gerontology
        48(5):B196–B200.

SBRZESNY, HEIDE

1976   Die Spiele der !Ko-Buschleute: Unter Besonderer Berücksichtigung ihrer
        Sozialisierenden und Gruppenbindenden Funktionen. Munich: Piper
        Verlag.

SCALLY, AYLWYN, JULIEN Y. DUTHEIL, LADEANA W. HILLIER,
GREGORY E. JORDAN, IAN GOODHEAD, JAVIER HERRERO, ASGER HOBOLTH, ET AL.

2012   Insights into Hominid Evolution from the Gorilla Genome Sequence.
        Nature 483:169–175.

SCELZA, BROOKE A.

2009   The Grandmaternal Niche: Critical Caretaking among Martu Aborigines.
        American Journal of Human Biology 21(4):448–454.

2010   Fathers' Presence Speeds the Social and Reproductive Careers of Sons.
        Current Anthropology 51(2):295–303.

2011   Female Mobility and Postmarital Kin Access in a Patrilocal Society.
        Human Nature 22(4):377–393.

SCHINO, GABRIELE, AND FILIPPO AURELI

2009   Reciprocal Altruism in Primates: Partner Choice, Cognition, and
        Emotions. Advances in the Study of Behavior 39:45–69.

SCHLEGEL, ALICE

1973   The Adolescent Socialization of the Hopi Girl. Ethnology 12(4):449–462.

SCHLEGEL, ALICE, AND HERBERT BARRY III, EDS.

1991   Adolescence: An Anthropological Inquiry. New York: Free Press.

SCHNEIDER, DAVID M.

1984   A Critique of the Study of Kinship. Ann Arbor: University of Michigan
        Press.

SCHOETENSACK, OTTO

1908   Der Unterkiefer des Homo heidelbergensis aus den Sanden von Mauer bei
        Heidelberg. Leipzig, Germany: Wilhelm Engelmann.

SCHÖNPFLUG, UTE

2009   Epilogue: Toward a Model of Cultural Transmission. *In* Cultural
        Transmission: Psychological, Developmental, Social, and Methodological

Aspects. Ute Schönpflug, ed. Pp. 460–477. Cambridge: Cambridge University Press.

SCHÖNPFLUG, UTE, AND LUDWIG BILZ

2009   The Transmission Process; Mechanisms and Contexts. *In* Cultural Transmission: Psychological, Developmental, Social, and Methodological Aspects. Ute Schönpflug, ed. Pp. 212–239. Cambridge: Cambridge University Press.

SCHREIER, AMY L., AND LARISSA SWEDELL

2012   Ecology and Sociality in a Multilevel Society: Ecological Determinants of Spatial Cohesion in Hamadryas Baboons. American Journal of Physical Anthropology 148(4):580–588.

SCHULTZ, ADOLPH H.

1960   Age Changes in Primates and Their Modification in Man. *In* Human Growth. J. M. Tanner, ed. Pp. 1–20. Oxford: Pergamon Press.

SCHWARTZMAN, HELEN B.

1978   Transformations: The Anthropology of Children's Play. New York: Plenum.

SEAR, REBECCA

2008   Kin and Child Survival in Rural Malawai: Are Matrilineal Kin Always Beneficial in a Matrilineal Society? Human Nature 19(3):277–293.

SEAR, REBECCA, AND RUTH MACE

2008   Who Keeps Children Alive? A Review of the Effects of Kin on Child Survival. Evolution and Human Behavior 29(1):1–18.

SEAR, REBECCA, RUTH MACE, AND IAN A. MCGREGOR

2000   Maternal Grandmothers Improve Nutritional Status and Survival of Children in Rural Gambia. Proceedings of the Royal Society B 267(1453):1641–1647.

2003   The Effects of Kin on Female Fertility in Rural Gambia. Evolution and Human Behavior 24(1):25–42.

SEAR, REBECCA, FIONA STEELE, IAN A. MCGREGOR, AND RUTH MACE

2002   The Effects of Kin on Child Mortality in Rural Gambia. Demography 39(1):43–63.

SELLEN, DANIEL W.

2001   Comparison of Infant Feeding Patterns Reported for Nonindustrial Populations with Current Recommendations. Journal of Nutrition 131(10):2707–27015.

2006   Lactation, Complementary Feeding, and Human Life History. *In* The Evolution of Human Life History. Kristen Hawkes and Richard Paine, eds. Pp. 155–196. Santa Fe, NM: School of American Research Press.

2007   Evolution of Infant and Young Child Feeding: Implications for Contemporary Public Health. Annual Review of Nutrition 27:123–148.

SELLEN, DANIEL W., AND DIANA B. SMAY

2001   Relationship between Subsistence and Age at Weaning in "Preindustrial"
        Societies. Human Nature 12(1):47–87.

SEYFARTH, ROBERT M., AND DOROTHY L. CHENEY

2012   The Evolutionary Origins of Friendship. Annual Review Psychology
        63:153–177.

SEYMOUR, SUSAN

2004   Multiple Caretaking of Infants and Young Children: An Area in Critical
        Need of a Feminist Psychological Anthropology. Ethos 32(4):538–556.

SHELL-DUNCAN, BETTINA, AND STACIE A. YUNG

2004   The Maternal Depletion Transition in Northern Kenya: The Effects of
        Settlement, Development, and Disparity. Social Science and Medicine
        58(12):2485–2498.

SHELTON, JO-ANN

1998   As the Romans Did: A Sourcebook in Roman Social History. New York:
        Oxford University Press.

SHENNAN, STEPHEN J., AND JAMES STEELE

1999   Cultural Learning in Hominids: A Behavioural Ecological Approach. *In*
        Mammalian Social Learning: Comparative and Ecological Perspectives.
        Hilary O. Box and Kathleen R. Box, eds. Pp. 367–388. Cambridge:
        Cambridge University Press.

SHORT, ROGER V.

1976   The Evolution of Human Reproduction. Proceedings of the Royal Society,
        Series B 195(1118):3–24.

SHOSTAK, MARJORIE

1981   Nisa: The Life and Words of a !Kung Woman. Cambridge, MA: Harvard
        University Press.

SHUBIN, NEIL H.

2002   Origin of Evolutionary Novelty: Examples from Limbs. Journal of
        Morphology 252(1):15–28.

SIEGEL, DANIEL J.

2012   The Developing Mind. 2nd edition. New York: Guilford Press.

SILK, JOAN B.

1978   Patterns of Food-Sharing among Mothers and Infant Chimpanzees at
        Gombe National Park, Tanzania. Folia Primatologica 29(2):129–141.

SILK, JOAN B., SARAH BROSNAN, JENNIFER VONK, JOSEPH HENRICH,
DANIEL J. POVINELLI, AMANDA S. RICHARDSON, SUSAN P. LAMBETH,
JENNY MASCARO, AND STEVEN J. SCHAPIRO

2005   Chimpanzees Are Indifferent to the Well-Being of Unrelated Group
        Members. Nature 437(7063):1357–1359.

SILVA, KATIE G., MARICELA CORREA-CHAVÉZ, AND BARBARA ROGOFF
2011   Mexican-Heritage Children's Attention and Learning from Interactions
        Directed at Others. Child Development 81: 898–912.

SIMPSON, SCOTT W., KATHERINE F. RUSSELL AND C. OWEN LOVEJOY
1996   Comparison of Diaphyseal Growth between the Libben Population and
        the Hamann-Todd Chimpanzees Sample. American Journal of Physical
        Anthropology 99(1):67–78.

SINERVO, BARRY, AND ERIK SVENSSON
1998   Mechanistic and Selective Causes of Life History Trade-Offs and Plasticity.
        Oikos 83:432–442.

SKINNER, MATTHEW M., AND BERNARD WOOD
2006   The Evolution of Modern Human Life History: A Paleontological
        Perspective. *In* The Evolution of Human Life History. Kristen Hawkes and
        Richard R. Paine, eds. Pp. 331–364. Santa Fe, NM: School of American
        Research Press.

SLOAN, NANCY L., SALAHUDDIN AHMED, SATINDRA N. MITRA,
NUZHAT CHOUDHURY, MUSHTAQUE CHOWDHURY, UBAIDER ROB, AND
BEVERLY WINIKOFF
2008   Community-Based Kangaroo Mother Care to Prevent Neonatal and
        Infant Mortality: A Randomized, Controlled Cluster Trial. Pediatrics
        121(5):1047–1059.

SLYKERMAN, R. F., J. M. D. THOMPSON, J. E. PRYOR, D. M. O. BECROFT,
E. ROBINSON, P. M. CLARK. C. J. WILD, AND E. A. MITCHELL
2005   Maternal Stress, Social Support, and Preschool Children's Intelligence.
        Early Human Development 81(10):815–821.

SMAIL, PETER J., CHARLES FAIMAN, WILLIAM C. HOBSON, GENE B. FULLER, AND
JEREMY S. WINTER
1982   Further Studies on Adrenarche in Nonhuman Primates. Endocrinology
        111(3):844–848.

SMALL, MEREDITH F.
1998   Evolution of Infant Feeding. *In* Our Babies, Ourselves: How Biology and
        Culture Shape the Way We Parent. Pp. 1–42. New York: Random House.

SMITH, B. HOLLY
1986   Dental Development in *Australopithecus* and Early *Homo*. Nature
        323:327–330.

1989   Dental Development as a Measure of Life History in Primates. Evolution
        43(3):373–392.

1991   Dental Development and the Evolution of Life History in Hominidae.
        American Journal of Physical Anthropology 86(2):157–174.

1992   Life History and the Evolution of Human Maturation. Evolutionary
        Anthropology 1(4):134–142.

1993   The Physiological Age of KNM-WT 15000. *In* The Nariokotome *Homo
        erectus* Skeleton. Alan Walker and Richard Leakey, eds. Pp. 195–220.
        Cambridge, MA: Harvard University Press.

SMITH, B. HOLLY, TRACY L. CRUMMETT, AND KARI L. BRANDT
1994   Ages of Eruption of Primate Teeth: A Compendium for Aging Individuals
        and Comparing Life Histories. Yearbook of Physical Anthropology
        37(Suppl. 19):177–231.

SMITH, B. HOLLY, AND ROBERT L. TOMPKINS
1995   Toward a Life History of the Hominidae. Annual Review of Anthropology,
        24, 257–279.

SMITH, BENJAMIN
2010   Of Marbles and (Little) Men: Bad Luck and Masculine Identification in
        Aymara Boyhood. Journal of Linguistic Anthropology 20(1):225–239.

SMITH, CHRISTOPHER C., AND STEPHEN D. FRETWELL
1974   The Optimal Balance between Size and Number of Offspring. American
        Naturalist 108(962):499–506.

SMITH, PETER K.
1982   Does Play Matter? Functional and Evolutionary Aspects of Animal and
        Human Play. Behavioral and Brain Sciences 5(1):139–155.

2005   Play: Types and Functions in Human Development. *In* Origins of the Social
        Mind: Evolutionary Psychology and Child Development. Bruce J. Ellis and
        David F. Bjorklund, eds. Pp. 271–291. New York: Guilford Press.

SMITH, TANYA M., WITH K. HARVATI, A. J. OLEJNICZAK, D. J. REID, J. J. HUBLIN,
AND E. PANAGOPOULOU
2009   Brief Communication: Dental Development and Enamel Thickness in the
        Lakonis Neanderthal Molar. American Journal of Physical Anthropology
        138(1):112–118.

SMITH, TANYA M., AND ZERESENAY ALEMSEGED
2013   Reconstructing Hominin Life History. Nature Education Knowledge 4(4):2.

SMITH, TANYA M., ZARIN MACHANDA, ANDREW B. BERNARD, RONAN M.
DONOVAN, AMANDA M. PAPAKYRIKOS, MARTIN N. MULLER, AND RICHARD
WRANGHAM
2013   First Molar Eruption, Weaning, and Life History in Living Wild
        Chimpanzees. Proceedings of the National Academy of Sciences 110 (8):
        2787–2791

SMITH, TANYA M., DONALD J. REID, ANTHONY J. OLEJICZAK, SHARA BAILEY,
MICA GLANTZ, BENCE VIOLA, AND JEAN-JACQUES HUBLIN
2011   Dental Development and Age at Death of a Middle Paleolithic Juvenile

Hominin from Obi-Rakhmat Grotto, Uzbekistan. *In* Continuity and Discontinuity in the Peopling of Europe. Silvani Condemi and Gerd-Christian Weniger, eds. Pp. 155–163. New York: Springer.

SMITH, TANYA M., PAUL TAFFOREAU, DONALD J. REID, RAINER GRÜN, STEPHEN EGGINS, MOHAMED BOUTAKIOUT, AND JEAN-JACQUES HUBLIN
2007   Earliest Evidence of Modern Human Life History in North African Early *Homo sapiens*. Proceedings of the National Academy of Sciences 104(15):6128–6133.

SMITH, TANYA M., PAUL TAFFOREAU, DONALD J. REID, JOANE POUECH, VINCENT LAZZARIB, JOHN P. ZERMENOA, DEBBIE GUATELLI-STEINBERG, ET AL.
2010   Dental Evidence for Ontogenetic Differences between Modern Humans and Neanderthals. Proceedings of the National Academy of Sciences 107(49):20923–20928.

SMITH, TANYA M., MICHEL TOUSSAINT, DONALD J. REID, ANTHONY J. OLEJNICZAK, AND JEAN-JACQUES HUBLIN
2007   Rapid Dental Development in a Middle Paleolithic Belgian Neanderthal. Proceedings of the National Academy of Sciences 104(51):20220–20225.

SNARE, DAVID
2012   Juvenile Gorillas in Africa Observed Disarming Snare Traps: It's a First. GrindTV (blog). http://www.grindtv.com/random/juvenile-gorillas-in-africa-observed-disarming-snare-traps-it-s-a-first/.

SOLOMON, N. G., AND J. A. FRENCH
1997   Cooperative Breeding in Mammals. Cambridge: Cambridge University Press.

SORENSEN, MARK V., AND WILLIAM R. LEONARD
2001   Neandertal Energetics and Foraging Efficiency. Journal of Human Evolution 40(6):483–495.

SPELKE, ELIZABETH
1990   Principles of Object Perception. Cognitive Science 14(1):29–56.

SPETH, JOHN D.
2010   The Paleoanthropology and Archaeology of Big-Game Hunting: Protein, Fat, or Politics. New York: Springer.

SPIEKER, SUSAN J., AND LILLIAN BENSLEY
1994   The Roles of Living Arrangements and Grandmother Social Support in Adolescent Mothering and Infant Attachment. Developmental Psychology 30(1):102–111.

SROUFE, L. ALAN, ELIZABETH A. CARLSON, ALISSA K. LEVY, AND BYRON EGELAND
1991   Implications of Attachment Theory for Developmental Psychopathology. Development and Psychopathology 11(1):1–13.

SROUFE, L. ALAN, AND EVERETT WATERS

1977   Attachment as an Organizational Construct. Child Development
          48(4):1184–1199.

STACEY, PETER B., AND WALTER D. KOENIG

1990   Introduction. *In* Cooperative Breeding in Birds. Peter B. Stacey and Walter D.
          Koenig, eds. Pp. ix–xviii. Cambridge: Cambridge University Press.

STEARNS, STEPHEN C.

1992   The Evolution of Life Histories. London: Oxford University Press.

2012   Evolutionary Medicine: Its Scope, Interest, and Potential. Proceedings of
          the Royal Society B 279(1746):4305–4321.

STEARNS, STEPHEN C., AND JACOB C. KOELLA

1986   The Evolution of Phenotypic Plasticity in Life-History Traits: Predictions of
          Reaction Norms for Age and Size at Maturity. Evolution 40(5):893–913.

STEIN, ARYEH, MENG WANG, REYNALDO MARTORELL, SHANE A. NORRIS,
LINDA S. ADAIR, ISABELITA BAS, HARSHPAL SINGH SACHDEV, ET AL.

2010   Growth Patterns in Early Childhood and Final Attained Stature: Data from
          Five Birth Cohorts from Low- and Middle-Income Countries. American
          Journal of Human Biology 22(3):353–359.

STERN, JUDITH M., MELVIN KONNER, TALIA H. HERMAN, AND SEYMOUR REICHLIN

1986   Nursing Behavior, Prolactin, and Postpartum Amenorrhoea during
          Prolonged Lactation in American and !Kung Mothers. Clinical
          Endocrinology 25(3):247–258.

STRASSMANN, BEVERLY

2000   Polygyny, Family Structure, and Child Mortality: A Prospective Study
          among the Dogon of Mali. *In* Adaptation and Human Behavior: An
          Anthropological Perspective. Lee Cronk, Napoleon Chagnon, and William
          Irons, eds. Pp. 49–67. New York: Aldine de Gruyter.

STRASSMANN, BEVERLY I., AND WENDY M. GARRARD

2011   Alternatives to the Grandmother Hypothesis: A Meta-analysis of the
          Association between Grandparental and Grandchild Survival in Patrilineal
          Populations. Human Nature 22(1–2):201–222.

STRATHERN, MARILYN

1988   Social Relations and the Idea of Externality. *In* Cognition and Material
          Culture: The Archaeology of Symbolic Storage. Colin Renfrew and Chris
          Scarre, eds. Pp. 135–147. Oxford: Oxbow Books.

STRIER, KAREN B.

2007   Primate Behavioral Ecology. San Francisco, CA: Allyn and Bacon.

STYNE, D. M.

1991   Serum Insulin-Like Growth Factor I Concentrations in the Developing
          Rhesus Monkey. Journal of Medical Primatology 20(7):338–344.

SUGIYAMA, LAWRENCE S., AND RICHARD CHACON

2005 Juvenile Responses to Household Ecology among the Yora of Peruvian Amazonia. *In* Hunter-Gatherer Childhoods: Evolutionary, Developmental, and Cultural Perspectives. Barry S. Hewlett and Michael E. Lamb, eds. Pp. 237–261. New Brunswick, NJ: AldineTransaction.

TAGUE, ROBERT G.

2012 Small Anatomical Variant Has Profound Implications for Evolution of Human Birth and Brain Development. Proceedings of the National Academy of Sciences 109(22):8360–8361.

TAMIR, DIANA L., AND JASON P. MITCHELL

2012 Disclosing Information about the Self Is Intrinsically Rewarding. Proceedings of the National Academy of Sciences 109(21):8038–8043.

TANNER, JAMES M.

1990 Foetus into Man: Physical Growth from Conception to Maturity. Cambridge, MA: Harvard University Press.

TANNER, JAMES M., M. E. WILSON, AND C. G. RUDMAN

1990 Pubertal Growth Spurt in the Female Rhesus Monkey: Relation to Menarche and Skeletal Maturation. American Journal of Human Biology 2(2):101–106.

TARDIEU, CHRISTINE

1998 Short Adolescence in Early Hominids: Infantile and Adolescent Growth of the Human Femur. American Journal of Physical Anthropology 107:163–178.

TEHRANI, JAMSHID J., AND MARK COLLARD

2009 On the Relationship between Interindividual Cultural Transmission and Population-Level Cultural Diversity: A Case Study of Weaving in Iranian Tribal Populations. Evolution and Human Behavior 30(4):286–300.

TENNIE, CLAUDIO, JOSEP CALL, AND MICHAEL TOMASELLO

2009 Ratcheting up the Ratchet: On the Evolution of Cumulative Culture. Philosophical Transactions of the Royal Society B 364(1528):2405–2415.

THOMAS, ELIZABETH M.

1958 The Harmless People. New York: Vintage Books.

THOMPSON, JENNIFER L.

1998 Neanderthal Growth and Development. *In* The Cambridge Encyclopedia of Human Growth and Development. Stanley J. Ulijaszek, Francis E. Johnston, and Michael A. Preece, eds. Pp. 106–107. Cambridge: Cambridge University Press.

2005 Le Moustier 1 and Its Place among the Neandertals. *In* The Neandertal Adolescent Le Moustier 1: New Aspects, New Results. Herbert Ullrich, ed. Pp. 311–320. Berlin: Staatliche Museen zu Berlin, Preußischer Kulturbesiz.

THOMPSON, JENNIFER L., AND ALAN BILSBOROUGH

1997   The Current State of the Le Moustier 1 Skull. Acta Praehistorica et
           Archaeologica 29:17–38.

2005   The Skull of Le Moustier 1. *In* The Neandertal Adolescent Le Moustier 1:
           New Aspects, New Results. Herbert Ullrich, ed. Pp. 79–94. Berlin:
           Staatliche Museen zu Berlin, Preußischer Kulturbesiz.

THOMPSON, JENNIFER L., GAIL E. KROVITZ, AND ANDREW J. NELSON, EDS.

2003   Patterns of Growth and Development in the Genus *Homo*. Cambridge:
           Cambridge University Press.

THOMPSON, JENNIFER L., AND ANDREW J. NELSON

2000   The Place of Neandertals in the Evolution of Hominid Patterns of Growth
           and Development. Journal of Human Evolution 38(4):475–495.

2001   Relative Postcranial and Cranial Growth in Neandertals and Modern
           Humans. American Journal of Physical Anthropology 114(Suppl. 32):149.

2005a   Estimated Age at Death and Sex of Le Moustier 1. *In* The Neandertal
           Adolescent Le Moustier 1: New Aspects, New Results. Herbert Ullrich, ed.
           Pp. 208–224. Berlin: Staatliche Museen zu Berlin, Preußischer Kulturbesiz.

2005b   The Postcranial Skeleton of Le Moustier 1. *In* The Neandertal Adolescent
           Le Moustier 1: New Aspects, New Results. Herbert Ullrich, ed. Pp. 265–281.
           Berlin: Staatliche Museen zu Berlin, Preußischer Kulturbesiz.

2011   Middle Childhood and Modern Human Origins. Human Nature
           22(3):249–280.

THOMPSON, JENNIFER L., ANDREW J. NELSON, AND B. ILLERHAUS

2003   A Study of the Le Moustier 1 Neandertal: Summary of Results. *In* Le
           Moustier und Combe Capelle. A. Hoffmann, ed. Pp. 65–73. Berlin:
           Staatliche Museen zu Berlin, Preußischer Kulturbesiz.

THOMPSON, ROSS A.

2000   The Legacy of Early Attachments. Child Development 71(1):145–152.

2008   Early Attachment and Later Development: Familiar Questions, New
           Answers. *In* Handbook of Attachment: Theory, Research, and Clinical
           Applications. Jude Cassidy and Phillip R. Shaver, eds. Pp. 348–365. New
           York: Guildford Press.

THORNHILL, RANDY, AND BRYANT FURLOW

1998   Stress and Human Reproductive Behavior: Attractiveness, Women's Sexual
           Development, Postpartum Depression, and Baby's Cry. Advances in the
           Study of Behavior 27(1998):319–369.

THORNTON, ALEX, AND KATHERINE MCAULIFFE

2006   Teaching in Wild Meerkats. Science 313(5784):227–229.

THORNTON, ALEX, AND NICHOLA J. RAIHANI

2008   The Evolution of Teaching. Animal Behavior 75(6):1823–1836.

TIRADO HERRERA, EMERITA R., CHRISTOPH KNOGGE, AND ECKHARD W. HEYMANN

2000   Infanticide in a Group of Wild Saddle-Back Tamarins, *Saguinus fuscicollis.* American Journal of Primatology 50(2):153–157.

TOMASELLO, MICHAEL

1999   The Cultural Origins of Human Cognition. Cambridge, MA: Harvard University Press.

TOMASELLO, MICHAEL, AND MALINDA CARPENTER

2007   Shared Intentionality. Developmental Science 10(1):121–125.

TOMASELLO, MICHAEL, MALINDA CARPENTER, JOSEP CALL, TANYA BEHNE, AND HENRIKE MOLL

2005   Understanding and Sharing Intentions: The Origins of Cultural Cognition. Behavioral and Brain Sciences 28:675–735.

TOMASELLO, MICHAEL, ANN C. KRUGER, AND HILARY H. RATNER

1993   Cultural Learning. Behavioral and Brain Sciences 16(3):495–552.

TOMASELLO, MICHAEL, ALICIA P. MELIS, CLAUDIO TENNIE, EMILY WYMAN, AND ESTHER HERRMANN

2012   Two Key Steps in the Evolution of Human Cooperation: The Interdependence Hypothesis. Current Anthropology 53:673–692.

TOMONAGA, MASAKI

2006   Triadic Relations and Emergence of Mind in Nonhuman Primates. Japanese Journal of Animal Psychology 56(1):67–78.

TOMONAGA, MASAKI, MASAYUKI TANAKA, TETSURO MATSUZAWA, MASAKO MYOWA-YAMAKOSHI, DAISUKE KOSUGI, YUU MIZUNO, SANAE OKAMOTO, MASAMI K. YAMAGUCHI, AND KIM A. BARD

2004   Development of Social Cognition in Infant Chimpanzees (*Pan troglodytes*): Facial Recognition, Smiling, Gaze, and the Lack of Triadic Interactions. Japanese Psychological Research 46(3):227–235.

TONKINSON, ROBERT

1991   The Mardu Aborigines: Living the Dream in Australia's Desert. 2nd edition. New York: Holt, Rinehart, and Winston.

TRACER, DAVID P.

1991   Fertility-Related Changes in Maternal Body Composition among the Au of Papua New Guinea. American Journal of Physical Anthropology 85(4):393–405.

TREVARTHEN, COLWYN

2005   "Stepping Away From the Mirror—Pride and Shame in Adventures of Companionship"—Reflections on the Emotional Needs of Infant Intersubjectivity. *In* Attachment and Bonding: A New Synthesis. C. Sue Carter, Liselotte Ahnert, K. E. Grossmann, Sarah B. Hrdy, Michael E. Lamb, Steven W. Porges, and Neil Sachser, eds. Pp. 55–84. Cambridge, MA: MIT Press.

TREVATHAN, WENDA R., E. O. SMITH, AND JAMES MCKENNA, EDS.
2007   Evolutionary Medicine and Health: New Perspectives. Oxford: Oxford University Press.

TRINKAUS, ERIK
1983   The Shanidar Neanderthals. New York: Academic Press.

1995   Neanderthal Mortality Patterns. Journal of Archeological Science 22(1):121–142.

1997   Appendicular Robusticity and the Paleobiology of Modern Human Emergence. Proceedings of the National Academy of Sciences 94(24):13367–13373.

TRIVERS, ROBERT L.
1972   Parental Investment and Sexual Selection. *In* Sexual Selection and the Descent of Man. Bernard Campbell, ed. Pp. 136–179. Chicago, IL: Aldine Publishing Company.

TRONICK, EDWARD Z., GILDA A. MORELLI, AND PAULA K. IVEY
1992   The Efe Forager Infant and Toddler's Pattern of Social Relationships: Multiple and Simultaneous. Developmental Psychology 28(4):568–577.

TRONICK, EDWARD Z., GILDA A. MORELLI, AND STEVE WINN
1987   Multiple Caretaking of Efe (Pygmy) Infants. American Anthropologist 89(1):96–106.

1989   The Caretaker-Child Strategic Model: Efe and Aka Child Rearing as Exemplars of the Multiple Factors Affecting Child Rearing—A Reply to Hewlett. American Anthropologist 91(1):192–194.

TRUE, MARY MCMAHAN
1994   Mother-Infant Attachment and Communication among the Dogon of Mali. PhD dissertation, Department of Psychology, University of California, Berkeley.

TUCKER, BRAM, AND ALYSON G. YOUNG
2005   Growing Up Mikea: Children's Time Allocation and Tuber Foraging in Southwestern Madagascar. *In* Hunter-Gatherer Childhoods: Evolutionary, Developmental, and Cultural Perspectives. Barry S. Hewlett and Michael E. Lamb, eds. Pp. 147–171. New Brunswick, NJ: AldineTransaction.

TULKIN, STEVEN R.
1973   Social Class Differences in Attachment Behaviors of Ten-Month-Old Infants. Child Development 44(1):171–174.

TULKIN, STEVEN R., AND JEROME KAGAN

1972   Mother-Child Interaction in the First Year of Life. Child Development
        43:31–41.

TULKIN, STEVEN R., AND MELVIN KONNER

1973   Alternative Conceptions of Intellectual Functioning. Human Development.
        16(1–2):33–52.

TURKE, PAUL

1988   Helpers-at-the-Nest: Childcare Networks on Ifaluk. *In* Human
        Reproductive Behavior: A Darwinian Perspective. Laura Betzig, Monique
        Borgerhoff Mulder, and Paul Turke, eds. Pp. 173–188. Cambridge:
        Cambridge University Press.

TURNBULL, COLIN M.

1962   The Forest People. New York: Simon and Schuster.

1965   The Mbuti Pygmies: An Ethnographic Survey. New York: American
        Museum of Natural History.

1978   The Politics of Non-Aggression (Zaire). *In* Learning Non-Aggression: The
        Experience of Non-Literate Societies. Ashley Montagu, ed. Pp. 161–221.
        New York: Oxford University Press.

TURNER, SARAH E., LINDA M. FEDIGAN, H. DAMON MATTHEWS, AND
MASAYUKI NAKAMICHI

2012   Disability, Compensatory Behavior, and Innovation in Free-Ranging
        Adult Female Japanese Macaques (*Macaca fuscata*). American Journal of
        Primatology 74(9):788–803.

TURNEY-HIGH, HARRY H.

1978   Arrowheads and Atlatl Darts: How the Stones Got the Shaft. American
        Antiquity 43(3):461–472.

ULLRICH, HERBERT

1955   Paläolithische Menschenreste aus der Sowjet-union: Das Moustierian-
        kind von Starselje (Krim). Zeischrift für Morphologie und Anthropologie
        47:91–98.

US DEPARTMENT OF AGRICULTURE, AGRICULTURAL RESEARCH SERVICE USDA

2008   National Nutrient Database for Standard Reference. Release 21. Nutrient
        Data Laboratory home page, accessed November 3, 2013, https://www.ars.
        usda.gov/Services/docs.htm?docid=8964.

VALEGGIA, CLAUDIA R.

2009   Flexible Caretakers: Responses of Toba Families in Transition. *In*
        Substitute Parents: Biological and Social Perspectives on Alloparenting in
        Human Societies. Studies in Biosocial Science Series, vol. 3. Gillian Bentley
        and Ruth Mace, eds. Pp. 100–115. New York: Berghahn Press.

VALEGGIA, CLAUDIA R., AND PETER T. ELLISON

2001   Lactation, Energetics, and Postpartum Fecundity. *In* Reproductive Ecology
          and Human Evolution. Peter T. Ellison, ed. Pp. 85–105. New York: Aldine
          de Gruyter.

2003   Impact of Breastfeeding on Anthropometric Changes in a Population of
          Toba Women. American Journal of Human Biology 15(5):717–724.

2004   Lactational Amenorrhoea in Well-Nourished Toba Women of Formosa,
          Argentina. Journal of Biosocial Science 36(5):573–595.

2009   Interactions between Metabolic and Reproductive Functions in the
          Resumption of Postpartum Fecundity. American Journal of Human
          Biology 21(4):559–566.

VAN IJZENDOORN, MARINUS H., KIM A. BARD,
MARIAN I. BAKERMANS-KRANENBURG, AND KRISZTINA IVAN

2009   Enhancement of Attachment and Cognitive Development of Young
          Nursery-Reared Chimpanzees in Responsive versus Standard Care.
          Developmental Psychobiology 51(2):173–185.

VAN IJZENDOORN, MARINUS H., AND ABRAHAM SAGI

2008   Cross-Cultural Patterns of Attachment: Universal and Contextual
          Dimensions. *In* Handbook of Attachment: Theory, Research, and Clinical
          Applications. Jude Cassidy and Phillip R. Shaver, eds. Pp. 880–905. New
          York: Guilford Press.

VAN IJZENDOORN, MARINUS H., ABRAHAM SAGI, AND MIRJAM LAMBERMON

1992   The Multiple Caretaker Paradox: Data from Holland and Israel. *In* Beyond
          the Parent: The Role of Other Adults in Children's Lives. Robert C. Pianta,
          ed. Pp. 5–24. New Directions for Child and Adolescent Development 57.
          San Francisco, CA: Jossey-Bass.

VAN SCHAIK, CAREL P., NANCY BARRICKMAN, MEREDITH L. BASTIAN,
ELISSA B. KRAKAUER, AND MARIA A. VAN NOORDWIJK

2006   Primate Life Histories and the Role of Brains. *In* The Evolution of Human
          Life History. Kristen Hawkes and Richard R. Paine, eds. Pp. 127–154. Santa
          Fe, NM: School of American Research Press.

VEKUA, ABESALOM, DAVID LORDKIPANIDZE, G. PHILIP RIGHTMIRE,
JORDI AGUSTI, REID FERRING, GIVI MAISURADZE, ALEXANDER
MOUSKHELISHVILI, ET AL.

2002   A New Skull of Early *Homo* from Dmanisi, Georgia. Science
          297(5578):85–89.

VELDHUIS, JOHANNES D.

1996   Gender Differences in Secretory Activity of the Human Somatotropic
          (Growth Hormone) Axis. European Journal of Endocrinology 134:287–295.

VERMONDEN, DANIEL

2009　　Reproduction and Development of Expertise within Communities of Practice: A Case Study of Fishing Activities in South Butonin. Studies in Environmental Anthropology and Ethnobiology. Serena Heckler, ed. Pp. 205–229. New York: Berghahn Books.

VICTORA, CESAR V., LINDA ADAIR, CAROLINE FALL, PEDRO C. HALLAL, REYNALDO MARTORELL, LINDA RICHTER, AND HARSHPAL SINGH SACHDEV

2008　　Maternal and Child Undernutrition: Consequences for Adult Health and Human Capital. Lancet 371(9609):340–357.

VOLAND, ECKART, AND JAN BIESE

2005　　The Husband's Mother Is a Devil in the House. *In* Grandmotherhood: The Evolutionary Significance of the Second Half of Female Life. Eckart Voland, Athanasios Chasiotis, and Wulf Schiefenhövel, eds. Pp. 230–255. New Brunswick, NJ: Rutgers University Press.

VOLAND, ECKART, ATHANASIOS CHASIOTIS, AND WULF SCHIEFENHÖVEL

2005　　Grandmotherhood: A Short Overview of Three Fields of Research on the Evolutionary Significance of Postgenerative Female Life. *In* Grandmotherhood: The Evolutionary Significance of the Second Half of Female Life. Eckart Voland, Athanasios Chasiotis, and Wulf Schiefenhövel, eds. Pp. 1–17. New Brunswick, NJ: Rutgers University Press.

VOLAND, ECKART, ATHANASIOS CHASIOTIS, AND WULF SCHIEFENHÖVEL, EDS.

2005　　Grandmotherhood: The Evolutionary Significance of the Second Half of Female Life. New Brunswick, NJ: Rutgers University Press.

VOSSENAAR, MARIEKE, AND NOEL W. SOLOMONS

2012　　The Concept of "Critical Nutrient Density" in Complementary Feeding: The Demands on the "Family Foods" for the Nutrient Adequacy of Young Guatemalan Children with Continued Breastfeeding. American Journal of Clinical Nutrition 95(4):859–866.

VYGOTSKY, LEV S.

1978　　Mind in Society: The Development of Higher Psychological Processes. Cambridge, MA: Harvard University Press.

WALKER, ALAN, AND RICHARD LEAKEY

1993　　The Nariokotome *Homo erectus* Skeleton. Cambridge, MA: Harvard University Press.

WALKER, ROBERT S., MICHAEL GURVEN, OSKAR BURGER, AND MARCUS J. HAMILTON

2008　　The Trade-Off between Number and Size of Offspring in Humans and Other Primates. Proceedings of the Royal Society B 275(1636):827–833.

WALKER, ROBERT, MICHAEL GURVEN, KIM HILL, ANDREA MIGLIANO, NAPOLEON
CHAGNON, ROBERTA DE SOUZA, GRADIMIR DJUROVIC, ET AL.
2006   Growth Rates and Life Histories in Twenty-Two Small-Scale Societies.
        American Journal of Human Biology 18(3):95–311.

WARNEKEN, FELIX, BRIAN HARE, ALICIA P. MELIS, DANIEL HANUS, AND
MICHAEL TOMASELLO
2007   Spontaneous Altruism by Chimpanzees and Young Children. PLoS Biology
        5(7):e184. doi.1371/journal.pbio.0050184.

WARNEKEN, FELIX, AND MICHAEL TOMASELLO
2006   Altruistic Helping in Human Infants and Young Chimpanzees. Science
        311(5765):1301–1303.

WATSON, JOHN
1928   Psychological Care of Infant and Child. New York: W. W. Norton.

WATSON-GEGEO, KAREN A., AND DAVID W. GEGEO
1989   The Role of Sibling Interaction in Child Socialization. *In* Sibling
        Interaction across Cultures. Patricia G. Zukow, ed. Pp. 54–76. New York:
        Springer-Verlag.

WATTS, DAVID, AND JOHN C. MITANI
2000   Hunting Behavior of Chimpanzees at Ngogo, Kibale National Park,
        Uganda. International Journal of Primatology 23(1):1–28.

WATTS, ELIZABETH S.
1985   Adolescent Growth and Development of Monkeys, Apes, and Humans.
        In Nonhuman Primate Models for Human Growth and Development.
        Elizabeth S. Watts, ed. Pp. 41–65. New York: Alan R. Liss.

1986   The Evolution of the Human Growth Curve. *In* Human Growth, vol. 1.
        Frank Faulkner and J. M. Tanner, eds. 2nd edition. Pp. 153–156. New York:
        Plenum Press.

WEBB, AIMEE L., DANIEL W. SELLEN, USHA RAMAKRISHNAN, AND
REYNALDO MARTORELL
2009   Maternal Years of Schooling but Not Academic Skills Is Independently
        Associated with Infant Feeding Practices in a Cohort of Rural Guatemalan
        Women. Journal of Human Lactation 25(3):297–306.

WEBB-GIRARD, AIMEE, ANNE CHEROBON, SAMWELL MBUGUA,
ELIZABETH KAMAU-MBUTHIA, ALLISON AMIN, AND DANIEL W. SELLEN
2012   Food Insecurity Is Associated with Attitudes toward Exclusive
        Breastfeeding among Women in Urban Kenya. Maternal and Child
        Nutrition 8(2):199–214.

WEINERT, HANS
1925   Der Schädel des eiszeitlichen Menschen von Le Moustier in neuer
        Zusammensetzung. Berlin: Springer.

WEISFELD, GLENN E.

1999 Evolutionary Principles of Human Adolescence. New York: Basic Books.

WEISFELD, GLENN E., AND HAROLD E. LINKEY

1985 Dominance Displays as Indicators of a Social Success Motive. *In* Power, Dominance, and Nonverbal Behavior. Steve L. Ellyson and John F. Dovidio, eds. Pp. 109–128. New York: Springer-Verlag.

WEISNER, THOMAS S.

1989 Cultural and Universal Aspects of Social Support for Children: Evidence from the Abaluyia of Kenya. *In* Children's Social Networks and Social Supports. Deborah Belle, ed. Pp. 70–90. New York: John Wiley.

1996a The 5 to 7 Transition as an Ecocultural Project. *In* The Five to Seven Year Shift: The Age of Reason and Responsibility. Arnold J. Sameroff and Marshall M. Haith, eds, Pp. 295–236. Chicago, IL: University of Chicago Press.

1996b Why Ethnography Should Be the Most Important Method in the Study of Human Development. *In* Ethnography and Human Development: Context and Meaning in Social Inquiry. Richard Jessor, Anne Colby, and Richard W. Shweder, eds. Pp. 305–324. Chicago, IL: University of Chicago Press.

WEISNER, THOMAS S., AND RONALD GALLIMORE

1977 My Brother's Keeper: Child and Sibling Caretaking. Current Anthropology 18(2):169–190.

WELLMAN, HENRY M., DAVID CROSS, AND JULANNE WATSON

2001 Meta-Analysis of Theory-of-Mind Development: The Truth about False Belief. Child Development 72(3):655–684.

WELLMAN, HENRY M., SARAH LOPEZ-DURAN, JENNIFER LA BOUNTY, AND BETSY HAMILTON

2008 Infant Attention to Intentional Action Predicts Preschool Theory of Mind. Developmental Psychology 44(2):618–623.

WELLS, JONATHAN C. K.

2011a An Evolutionary Perspective on the Trans-generational Basis of Obesity. Annals of Human Biology 38(4):400–409.

2011b The Thrifty Phenotype: An Adaptation in Growth or Metabolism? American Journal of Human Biology 23(1):65–75.

2012 Ecological Volatility and Human Evolution: Perspective on Life History and Reproductive Strategy. Evolutionary Anthropology 21:277–288.

WENGER, MARTHA

1989 Work, Play, and Social Relationships among Children in a Giriama Community. *In* Children's Social Networks and Social Supports. Deborah Belle, ed. Pp. 91–115. New York: John Wiley.

WEST, MARY MAXWELL, AND MELVIN J. KONNER

1976   The Role of the Father: An Anthropological Perspective. *In* The Role of the Father in Child Development. Michael E. Lamb, ed. Pp: 185–217. New York: John Wiley.

WEST-EBERHARD, MARY JANE

1979   Sexual Selection, Social Competition, and Evolution. Proceedings of the American Philosophical Society 123(4):222–234.

1983   Sexual Selection, Social Competition, and Speciation. Quarterly Review of Biology 58(2):155–183.

2003   Developmental Plasticity and Evolution. Oxford: Oxford University Press.

2010   Social Selection: Darwinian Competition, Social Display, and the Origins of Cooperation. Paper presented at the CARTA Symposium on Social Selection, San Diego, CA, November 11.

WHITE, ROBERT W.

1959   Motivation Reconsidered: The Concept of Competence. Psychological Review 66(5):297–333.

WHITE, SHELDON H.

1996   The Child's Entry into the "Age of Reason." *In* The Five to Seven Year Shift: The Age of Reason and Responsibility. Arnold J. Sameroff and Marshall M. Haith, eds. Pp. 17–30. Chicago, IL: University of Chicago Press.

WHITEN, ANDREW, AND CAREL P. VAN SCHAIK

2007   The Evolution of Animal "Cultures" and Social Intelligence. Philosophical Transactions of the Royal Society B 362 (1480):603–620.

WHITING, BEATRICE B., AND JOHN W. M. WHITING

1975   Children of Six Cultures: A Psychocultural Analysis. Cambridge, MA: Harvard University Press.

WHITING, JOHN W. M.

1941   Becoming a Kwoma: Teaching and Learning in a New Guinea Tribe. New Haven, CT: Yale University Press.

WHITTEMORE, ROBERT D.

1989   Child Caregiving and Socialization to the Mandinka Way: Toward an Ethnography of Childhood. PhD dissertation, Department of Anthropology, University of California, Los Angeles.

WIESSNER, POLLY

1977   Hxaro: A Regional System of Reciprocity for Reducing Risk among the !Kung San. PhD dissertation, Department of Anthropology, University of Michigan.

2002a   Taking the Risk out of Risky Transactions: A Forager's Dilemma. *In* Risky Transactions: Trust, Kinship, and Ethnicity. Frank K. Salter, ed. Pp. 21–43. New York: Berghahn Books.

2002b   Hunting, Healing, and *Hxaro* Exchange: A Long-Term Perspective on !Kung (Ju/'hoansi) Large-Game Hunting. Evolution and Human Behavior 23(6):407–436.

WILBERT, JOHANNES

1976   To Become a Maker of Canoes: An Essay in Warao Enculturation. *In* Enculturation in Latin America. Johannes Wilbert, ed. Pp. 303–358. Los Angeles, CA: UCLA Latin American Center Publications.

WILEY, ANDREA S.

2007   Transforming Milk in a Global Economy. American Anthropologist 109(4):666–667.

WILLERSLEV, RANE

2007   Soul Hunters: Hunting, Animism, and Personhood among the Siberian Yukaghirs. Berkeley, CA: University of California Press.

WILLIAMS, GEORGE C.

1966   Adaptation and Natural Selection. Princeton, NJ: Princeton University Press.

WILLIAMS, THOMAS R.

1969   A Borneo Childhood: Enculturation in Dusun Society. New York: Holt, Reinhart, and Winston.

WINKVIST, ANNA, FEHMIDA JALIL, JEAN-PIERRE HABICHT, AND KATHLEEN M. RASMUSSEN

1994   Maternal Energy Depletion Is Buffered among Malnourished Women in Punjab, Pakistan. Journal of Nutrition 124:2376–2385.

WINN, STEVE, EDWARD Z. TRONICK, AND GILDA A. MORELLI, EDS.

1989   The Infant and the Group: A Look at Efe Caretaking Practices in Zaire. Westport, CT: Ablex Publishing.

WINZELER, ROBERT L.

2004   The Architecture of Life and Death in Borneo. Honolulu: University of Hawaii Press.

WOOD, BERNARD, AND MARK COLLARD

1999   The Human Genus. Science 284:65–71.

WOODBURN, JAMES

1968a   An Introduction to Hazda Ecology. *In* Man the Hunter. Richard B. Lee and Irven DeVore, eds. Pp. 49–55. Chicago, IL: AldineTransaction.

1968b   Stability and Flexibility in Hadza Residential Groupings. *In* Man the Hunter. Richard B. Lee and Irven DeVore, eds. Pp. 103–110. Chicago, IL: AldineTransaction.

1970   Hunters and Gatherers: The Material Culture of the Nomadic Hadza. London: British Museum.

WRANGHAM, R., AND RACHEL CARMODY

2010   Human Adaptation to the Control of Fire. Evolutionary Anthropology
         19(5):187–199.

WRANGHAM, R., AND DALE PETERSON

1996   Demonic Males: Apes and the Origins of Human Violence. New York:
         Houghton Mifflin.

YAMAMOTO, SHINYA, TATYANA HUMLE, AND MASAYUKI TANAKA

2009   Chimpanzees Help Each Other Upon Request. PLoS ONE 4(10):e7416.
         doi:10.1371/journal.pone.0007416.

2012   Chimpanzees' Flexible Targeted Helping Based on an Understanding of
         Conspecifics' Goals. Proceedings of the National Academy of Sciences
         109(9):3588–3592.

YANOVSKI, JACK A., KARA N. SOVIK, TUC T. NGUYEN, AND NANCY G. SEBRING

2000   Insulin-Like Growth Factors and Bone Mineral Density in African
         American and White Girls. Journal of Pediatrics 137(6):826–832.

YEUNG, MELINDA Y, AND JOHN P. SMYTH

2003   Nutritionally Regulated Hormonal Factors in Prolonged Postnatal Growth
         Retardation and Its Associated Adverse Neurodevelopmental Outcome in
         Extreme Prematurity. Biology of the Neonate 84(1):1–23.

ZARGER, REBECCA K., AND JOHN R. STEPP

2004   Persistence of Botanical Knowledge among Tzeltal Maya Children.
         Current Anthropology 45(3):413–418.

ZELLER, ANTHONY C.

1987   A Role for Children in Hominid Evolution. Man 22(3):528–557.

ZEMPLENI-RABAIN, JACQUELINE

1973   Food and Strategy Involved in Learning Fraternal Exchange among Wolof
         Children. In French Perspective in African Studies. Pierre Alexandre, ed.
         Pp. 220–233. London: Oxford University Press for the International African
         Institute.

ZERA, ANTHONY J., AND LAWRENCE G. HARSHMAN

2001   The Physiology of Life History Trade-Offs in Animals. Annual Review of
         Ecology and Systematics 32:95–126.

ZOLLIKOFER, CHRISTOPH P. E., AND MARCIA S. PONCE DE LEÓN

2010   The Evolution of Hominin Ontogenies. Seminars in Cell and
         Developmental Biology 21(4):441–452.

ZUCKERMAN, MICHAEL

2009   Ariès, Philippe. In The Child: An Encyclopedic Companion. Richard A.
         Schweder, ed. Pp. 60–61. Chicago, IL: University of Chicago Press.

ZUCKERMAN-LEVIN, N., AND Z. HOCHBERG

2007   Delayed Infancy-Childhood Spurt (DICS) in SGA Children with No Catch Up Growth. Hormone Research 68(Suppl. 1):167.

ZVEREV, Y., AND J. CHISI

2004   Anthropometric Indices in Rural Malawians Aged 45–75 Years. Annals of Human Biology 31(1):29–37.

Participants in the School for Advanced Research advanced seminar "Multiple Perspectives on the Evolution of Childhood" co-chaired by Alyssa N. Crittenden and Courtney L. Meehan, November 4–8, 2012. Standing, from left: Daniel Sellen, Barry Bogin, Jennifer L. Thompson, Sarah B. Hrdy, Sanae Okamoto-Barth, Melvin Konner, and Robin M. Bernstein. Sitting, from left: Alyssa N. Crittenden, Courtney L. Meehan, and David F. Lancy. Photograph by Jason S. Ordaz.

ROBIN M. BERNSTEIN
Department of Anthropology, University of Colorado, Boulder

BARRY BOGIN
School of Sport, Exercise, and Health Sciences, Loughborough University

JARED BRAGG
Department of Anthropology, Northwestern University

ALYSSA N. CRITTENDEN
Department of Anthropology, University of Nevada, Las Vegas

COURTNEY HELFRECHT
Department of Anthropology, Washington State University

SARAH B. HRDY
Department of Anthropology, University of California, Davis, A. D. White
    Professor-at-Large, Cornell University

MELVIN KONNER
Department of Anthropology, Emory University

CHRISTOPHER KUZAWA
Department of Anthropology, Northwestern University

DAVID F. LANCY
Department of Sociology, Social Work, and Anthropology, Utah State University

COURTNEY D. MALCOM
Department of Anthropology, Washington State University

COURTNEY L. MEEHAN
Department of Anthropology, Washington State University

ANDREW J. NELSON
Department of Anthropology, University of Western Ontario

DANIEL SELLEN
Department of Anthropology, University of Toronto

JENNIFER L. THOMPSON
Independent Scholar

epiphyseal fusion, 85
errand running, 138, 186, 187, 188
estradiol, 54, 114
estrogen, 111–112
evolution: of care, general model for, 224–232; EEA in, 23, 123, 147, 149, 152, 238; of food sharing and shared care, 19–22; of humans characteristics needing care, 229–230, *231*
evolutionarily derived human characteristics, care shaped by, 229–230, *231*
evolved: care behaviors, 221–225, 224, 227, 228, 234, *235*, 240, 243; needs, 225, 228, 237, 240, 243, 248; vulnerabilities, 221, 225, 227, 228–229, 230–232, 237, 242
extended dependency, 199, 200–201

face recognition, 12, 30, 175
facultative adaptation, 6, 61, 124, 149, 151, 152–153, 238
Falk, Dean, 36
false beliefs, 195n5
family formation, 1–2, 23, 57–58
family life: fitting in and, 183–187, 194; for Pleistocene hominins, 19–22
fantasy/social play, 162–163, *164*, 167
farming, 151–152, 188–192
fathers: Ache, 209; Agta, 140; Aka, 135–136, 148, 209; American, 128; Bofi, 141; in cooperative breeding, 24–25; Efe, 133; in HGC model, 153; !Kung, 128–129; Martu, 142; maternal nutrition and, 217; stepfathers as, 130; survivorship and, 209
fatness, of human infants, 26–27
female life span, 22, 29
fertility rates, 66–67, 133–134, 140, 143–144, 147
fetal hormone regulation, 109
fetal zone (FZ), 114, 115, 116
fictive kinship, 56, 63–64
filing, of teeth, 136
first one thousand days of life, 230–232, 233–234, 237, 241

first-time mothers, 218
Fisher, Ronald A., 67
fitting in, 183–187, 194
Flinn, Mark, 175
food sharing, 12; brain size linked to, 170; evolution of, 19–22; among Hadza children, 168; other-regarding linked to, 42–44
foraging: as embodied capital, 131, 149–150, 156–157, 161, 170; as play, 151, 155, 168–169; sexual division of, 158. *See also* Hunter-Gatherer Childhood model; hunter-gatherers
formula, 109, 237–238
Fortes, Meyer, 179
fossil record, 49, 55; of childhood, 76, 85–95; juvenile stage in, 84; skeletal and dental markers in, 77
foster care, 63
freedom, of Hadza, 170
functionalist models of play, 163
FZ. *See* fetal zone

Gambia, the, 208
gamesmanship, 179–181
gender bias, in learning, 185
genetic relatedness, 59. *See also* kinship
GH. *See* growth hormone
Givón, Tom, 14
global child health recommendations, 223–224, 227, 238–239
globularization phase, 92
"Goldilocks Effect," 174–175
Goldschmidt, Walter, 61–62
Goody, Esther, 178
gorillas, 11, 116–118, *117*, 247
Gottlieb, Alma, 205
Gould, Stephen, 103
grammar, 14
grandmother hypothesis, 98
grandmothers: allomaternal involvement of, 136, 139, 205, 209, 216–217; provisioning by, 25, 130–131, 137–138, 207–209, 216–217